Modern Relationships

Modern Relationships

Romance, Friendship, and Family in the 21st Century

Edited by
MAHZAD HOJJAT
AND
ANNE MOYER

OXFORD
UNIVERSITY PRESS

Oxford University Press is a department of the University of Oxford. It furthers the University's objective of excellence in research, scholarship, and education by publishing worldwide. Oxford is a registered trade mark of Oxford University Press in the UK and certain other countries.

Published in the United States of America by Oxford University Press
198 Madison Avenue, New York, NY 10016, United States of America.

© Oxford University Press 2024

All rights reserved. No part of this publication may be reproduced, stored in a retrieval system, or transmitted, in any form or by any means, without the prior permission in writing of Oxford University Press, or as expressly permitted by law, by license, or under terms agreed with the appropriate reproduction rights organization. Inquiries concerning reproduction outside the scope of the above should be sent to the Rights Department, Oxford University Press, at the address above.

You must not circulate this work in any other form
and you must impose this same condition on any acquirer.

Library of Congress Cataloging-in-Publication Data
Names: Hojjat, Mahzad, editor. | Moyer, Anne (Anne Elizabeth), editor.
Title: Modern relationships : romance, friendship, and family
in the 21st century / Edited by Mahzad Hojjat and Anne Moyer.
Description: New York, NY : Oxford University Press, [2024] |
Includes bibliographical references and index.
Identifiers: LCCN 2023038583 (print) | LCCN 2023038584 (ebook) |
ISBN 9780197655504 (hardback) | ISBN 9780197655528 (epub) | ISBN 9780197655535
Subjects: LCSH: Interpersonal relations. |
Friendship—Psychological aspects. | Intimacy (Psychology)
Classification: LCC HM1106 .M64 2024 (print) |
LCC HM1106 (ebook) | DDC 302—dc23/eng/20230901
LC record available at https://lccn.loc.gov/2023038583
LC ebook record available at https://lccn.loc.gov/2023038584

DOI: 10.1093/oso/9780197655504.001.0001

Printed by Integrated Books International, United States of America

To my husband Mike, for his unwavering love and support, and to my children Marcus and Lily, who inspire me every day to study love and friendship. —M. H.

For Marc, the love of my life; Blair, my best friend; Mom, Dad, and Jennifer, my family. —A. M.

Contents

Foreword	xi
Elaine Hatfield and Richard L. Rapson	
List of Contributors	xix
Introduction: Modern Relationships of the 21st Century	xxiii
Mahzad Hojjat and Anne Moyer	

PART I: DATING IN THE 21ST CENTURY

1. Ideal Partner Characteristics in the 21st Century: What Are We Looking for?   3
   Claudia C. Brumbaugh and Jaclyn K. Doherty

2. Online or in Person: How Do We Find Our Ideal Partner?   21
   Kathryn Coduto

3. Cohabitation Versus Marriage: Understanding Young Adults' Preference for Cohabitation   38
   Sharon Sassler

4. Being Single in the 21st Century: Reasons and Consequences   55
   Elyakim Kislev

PART II: MARRIAGE IN THE 21ST CENTURY

5. Modern Marital Satisfaction: Are We Expecting Too Much?   73
   Daniel Perlman and Rowland S. Miller

6. Equity and Gender Roles in Marriage: Are We Finally Equal?   90
   Grace M. Wetzel and Diana T. Sanchez

7. What Is a Marriage? The Rise of More Diverse Unions   106
   Rhonda N. Balzarini, Karen L. Blair, and Marissa Walter

8. Marriage and Ethnicity Around the World: Marrying Someone From a Different Race, Religion, or Nationality — 124
Stanley O. Gaines, Jr.

9. Conscious Uncoupling: Divorce in the 21st Century — 141
Abdullah S. Salehuddin, Tamara D. Afifi, and Jade Salmon

PART III: GENDER AND SEXUALITY IN THE 21ST CENTURY

10. Sexuality in the 21st Century: A Feminist and Queer Theoretical Perspective on Sex and Sexuality in Emerging Adulthood — 161
Jasna Jovanovic and Jean Calterone Williams

11. Who Do We Love? Shifts in Attitudes About Gender Identity, Sexual Orientation, and Same-Sex Close Relationships — 178
Karen L. Blair, Erin L. Courtice, and Rhea Ashley Hoskin

PART IV: FRIENDSHIP IN THE 21ST CENTURY

12. Modern Friendships: Mixing Multiple Media and Affordances When Communicating With Friends — 199
Kelly Sweeney, Daniel A. Lee, and Andrew C. High

13. The New and Significant Role of Friendship in the 21st Century — 217
Emily T. Beauparlant, Mahzad Hojjat, Nicole Melancon, and Laura V. Machia

14. Friendships in the Time of COVID-19 — 232
Mahzad Hojjat, Anne Moyer, Sydney Brake, Brady D. Nelson, Lauren L. Richmond, Jessica L. Schleider, and Bonita London

15. Diverse Friendships: Formation, Maintenance, and Benefits — 251
J. Nicole Shelton, Kate M. Turetsky, Yeji Park, and Lindsey Eikenburg

PART V: FAMILIES IN THE 21ST CENTURY

16. Adoption and Relationships in the 21st Century — 273
Ellen E. Pinderhughes, Seungmi M. Lee, and Madeline C. Smith

17. Communication and Resilience in Stepfamilies:
    Talking Close Relationships With Parents, Siblings, and
    Family Members Into Being   291
    Dawn O. Braithwaite and Bailey M. Oliver-Blackburn

18. Technology-Assisted Parenthood and Modern
    Families in the 21st Century   308
    Sofia Gameiro

PART VI: CURRENT TRENDS IN HEALTH AND CLOSE RELATIONSHIPS IN THE 21ST CENTURY

19. Relationships and Health   327
    Anne Moyer, K. Olivia Mock, and Rose Martillotti

20. Close Relationships and Mental Health   343
    Charlotte R. Esplin, S. Gabe Hatch, and Scott R. Braithwaite

Conclusion   361
   Arthur Aron

Index   371

Foreword

Elaine Hatfield and Richard L. Rapson

When it comes to the study of love and relationships, the changes over the course of my lifetime have been nothing short of astounding. From being a taboo topic of scientific inquiry, the latest research has permeated nearly all of the academic disciplines. And its findings, not always accurately reported, have flooded the popular culture and social media.

In the spring of 1975, my lifelong collaborator and friend, Ellen Berscheid, and I embarked on a program to learn more about the nature of passionate love and sexual desire. The National Science Foundation (NSF) awarded us a tiny grant, allowing us to investigate the importance of social justice and equity in romantic exchanges. Our early results, not always accurately reported, were promising. We found considerable evidence that in love relationships, equity mattered. Specifically, we had concluded that:

1. The more socially desirable people are (the more attractive, personable, famous, rich, or considerate they are), the more socially desirable they will expect a mate to be.
2. Dating couples are more likely to fall in love if they perceive their relationships to be equitable.
3. Couples are likely to end up with someone fairly close to themselves in social desirability. They are also likely to be matched on the basis of self-esteem, looks, intelligence, education, and mental and physical health (or disability).
4. Couples who perceive their relationships to be equitable are more likely to get sexually involved.
5. Equitable relationships are comfortable relationships.
6. Equitable relationships are stable relationships.

When Wisconsin's U.S. Senator William Proxmire discovered what we were up to, he "awarded" us the very first and infamous "Golden Fleece

Award," claiming we were "fleecing" taxpayers with our "unneeded" and "frivolous" scientific research. The senator had launched his well-publicized campaign against a bevy of love and sex researchers by firing off the first in a series of seriocomic and sarcastic press releases:

> I object to this not only because no one—not even the National Science Foundation—can argue that falling in love is a science; not only because I'm sure that even if they spend $84 million or $84 billion they wouldn't get an answer that anyone would believe. *I'm also against it because I don't want the answer.*
>
> I believe that 200 million other Americans want to leave some things in life a mystery, and right on top of the things we don't want to know is why a man falls in love with a woman and vice versa . . .
>
> So National Science Foundation—get out of the love racket. Leave that to Elizabeth Barrett Browning and Irving Berlin. Here if anywhere Alexander Pope was right when he observed, "If ignorance is bliss, tis folly to be wise." (cited in Hatfield, 2006).

In terms that will sound all too familiar to today's International Association for Relationship Research (IARR) members, the senator urged the U.S. Senate to seize control over the NSF's and National Institute of Mental Health's (NIMH's) scientific granting and peer review process.

In subsequent weeks, Senator Proxmire and his political allies issued a whirlwind of press releases. Alas for love and sex researchers, he and his scriptwriters possessed a diabolical and withering sense of humor. Today's right-wing critics and "know-nothings" tend to be a bit more humorless, sanctimonious, sinister, and more effective (I fear) than was Proxmire.

A few hours after Senator Proxmire's original and dismaying sneak attack, the following mocking letter appeared in the "Letters to the Editor" in *The Washington Post*:

> President Pierce-Martin Condemns NSF Grant
> To Study Sex Life of Polish Frogs
> Today Peter Croft Pierce-Martin, President of the Acme Wire and Spring Corporation in Dallas, Texas, and his seventy-two employees sent the President and the National Science Foundation an open letter. "We at Acme Wire and Spring object to our hard-earned tax dollars being squandered on studies of the sex lives of Polish frogs, why kids fall off tricycles, and such."

President Pierce-Martin pointed out that last year the Acme Corporation and its employees paid $2.82 million in taxes. He then went on to list NSF and NIMH grants, totaling exactly that amount. Among the projects listed were:
- $375,000 for a Pentagon study of the Frisbee
- $84,000 for a scientific study of love
- $70,000 to study the smell of perspiration given off by Australian aborigines
- $5,000 to the author of the one one-word poem—"Light"
- $20,000 to study the blood groups of Polish Zlotnika pigs
- $5,000 for an analysis of violin varnish

Since this clever "Letter to the Editor" appeared only a few hours after the senator's original press release, I couldn't help but wonder just how spontaneous President Pierce-Martin's cri de cœur was. How did Acme suck up all those figures in an hour and a half? Still, I and all my colleagues had to admit the letter had wit.

A few days after President Pierce-Martin's letter hit the wire services, NSF proffered its earnest rejoinder. The *Washington Post* buried it on one of the inside pages. The NSF rebuttal informed readers—who probably didn't care in the first place—that the $375,000 "Frisbee" study was actually a Pentagon project designed to develop a new aircraft-launched naval flare, the $2,000 study of "why children fall off of tricycles" was a Federal FDA project to test the safety of children's toys, and the $80,000 "down the toilet" program was actually part of the NASA space program. A compelling rebuttal, but, of course, nothing can kill a good joke.

Proxmire's attacks generated so much public attention that before his siege ended, 13 scientists exploring the mysteries of love and sex had been attacked for their "scientific boondoggles" and "con games"—including such luminaries as Ellen, Robert Baron, and Zick Rubin.

To our surprise, considering that dangerous political climate, many distinguished citizens came to our support. Senator Barry Goldwater, three University of Chicago Nobel Prize winners, and the editor of *Science* wrote laudatory letters to the *New York Times*, the *Capital Times*, and *Science* magazine praising our research. So did columnist James Reston. In his piece in the *New York Times*, Reston wryly agreed that love will always be a mystery.

But if the sociologists and psychologists can get even a suggestion of the answer to our pattern of romantic love, marriage, disillusions, divorce—and the children left behind—it would be the best investment of federal money since Jefferson made the Louisiana Purchase.

The University of Wisconsin Madison Faculty Senate met, debated the senator's charges, and voted to condemn the Senator's "unjust and misleading attacks" by a vote of 84 to 1.

Not all our early relationship research, however, garnered the public's unwavering support.

A friend, Dr. Roland W. Radloff (program director of the Social Psychology Program, of the National Science Foundation) suggested I refrain from submitting any grants to NSF for a while. "Let it blow over," he advised. Research on this topic had become too hot to handle. I agreed. (And indeed, since then all my research has been privately funded.)

My mother's Roman Catholic bishop got into the act. Right Reverend Richard S. Emrich issued a message to the Detroit parishes denouncing the NSF for supporting scientists' attempts to unravel the "most sacred mysteries of love and life." He went on:

> Who granted these "scientists" the ability to see into men's minds and hearts? Were our findings going to eliminate pride, selfishness, jealously, suffering, and war?
>
> Jesus Christ has taught us all that we need to know about love and life.... His Word waits there, in *The Holy Bible*, for us. He has been waiting for us for almost 2,000 years. It is *His* commands we must follow, not the childish "advice" of some arrogant, secular scientist, who presumes to know more than Our Lord.

A Chicago tabloid—*The Chicago Daily News*—ran a contest. "Who is right—Proxmire or Hatfield?" A massive number of readers (and even a few friends) wrote in to say I was "naive" to think love and sex could be studied scientifically. I lost the contest: Proxmire 87.5%, me 12.5%.

This silliness went on for many years. The news stories began to swirl around like some kind of toxic cosmic dust. When Senator Proxmire would return to Madison on Saturdays to attend Badgers' football games, he would take that opportunity to appear on some local TV show in order to denounce (sigh!) love research. I would be asked to reply.

On Monday, one of Senator Proxmire's comic writers would issue a devastating press release (inaccurate but beguiling) about the inanities of our love and sex research. By Tuesday morning, I'd be reeling from its aftershock. On

Wednesday, the fallout would be settling in near Tokyo. Stories began to appear in the *Asahi Shimbun*, *Mainichi Shimbun*, and *Yomiuri Shimbun*. A few weeks later, *The Bangladeshi Standard*'s Geiger counters would be clicking out the news.

Each time an editor in Japan, Bangladesh, or Mozambique translated the story, a name would get misspelled here, a word altered there, and the next thing you know, the Wisconsin *State Journal* would have picked up these new Pythonesque news stories. The facts would be crazily altered and fictionalized. By now, Dr. Hatfield, the mad doctor of love, would be caught slipping women dime bags of marijuana, asking students to confess their darkest secrets while both were doing God-knows-what in their bedrooms. The *Journal* would assume that somehow they'd missed a heck of a story. Then once more the dust would start swirling around the earth, entering newer and higher orbits of madness with each new news cycle.

I got to know the postman very well indeed during this period as he dragged in mail by the bagful. I saved the best of those letters, and recently, when I decided to write a comic novel about *Rosie*, a young sexuality researcher who gets in trouble for *her* research, I had those Proxmire newscasts, enraged attacks, and weird letters to draw on. Rosie's adventures are pure fantasy—except for those amazing letters I actually received. I could not construct missives more stunning. Crazy persons' letters, with blood-curdling threats. Spiky letters, painstakingly, tremblingly constructed. Letters written in Day-Glo colors. Words marching in an orderly way across the top of the page, down the sides, and along the bottom. Then they began to sprawl in upon themselves, growing smaller and smaller as they whirled around the page. At the vortex, the microscopic calligraphy ended in a sinister inkblot. Letters filled with pain and suffering. Many people wanted to know how they could scam some of the U.S. government's research "loot" for themselves. When they discovered they would have to dash off a grant application—and actually get that proposal reviewed—they were irate.

Scientists were not without their own Jon Stewarts, and their own biting humor, of course. Art Buchwald (the Molly Ivens of his day) and a host of lesser known commentators caricatured Senator Proxmire's "paroxyms," and "love spats" with relationship researchers. Researchers such as Ronald Hutchinson began to sue Senator Proxmire for his distortions—and won!

How did I cope? Not very well, I'm afraid. I am a shy person, not on the lookout for conflict; I just like to pursue my intellectual interests. So *L'Affaire Proxmire* was actually painful to me. When I remember those days, I do so mostly with embarrassment, despite the eventual positive and rewarding outcome.

Thank God for longevity! I have hung around long enough to see things change wildly for the better. When Ellen Berscheid and I wrote *Interpersonal Attraction* (in 1969), we were able to ferret out precious little research on passionate love and sexual desire. It was pathetic. We had to speculate about the nature of love with little or no data (and shockingly little experience of our own) to guide us.

What a change has occurred in 50+ years! There are historical periods when scientific and technological advances allow scientists to take giant strides forward. This is certainly one of those times. Despite the anti-science fervor of the xenophobic nationalists, supporting right-wing authoritarians opposing vaccines, and endorsing magical thinking over science, we still live in a time of amazing scientific ferment, including lots of love research.

Today, scholars from a variety of academic disciplines—social psychologists, anthropologists, historians, microbiologists, evolutionary psychologists, neuroscientists, literary scholars, and more—are addressing the same relationship issues with which we struggled. They are employing an impressive array of new techniques, ranging from primatologists who are studying primates in the wild and in captivity and neuroscientists, pouring over functional magnetic resonance images (fMRIs), all the way to historians, who are now studying history from the "bottom up" rather than the "top down." They are examining less the lives of kings and queens and more those of the majority of our deceased sisters and brothers, utilizing demographic data (marriage, birth, death, and divorce records), architectural and archaeological remains, medical manuals, church edicts, law cases, song lyrics, and whatever diaries and letters they can find. And when they do that, matters of love, divorce, and personal relationships loom very large indeed.

Recently, my husband and historian, Richard L. Rapson, and I summarized this impressive research in the book *What's Next in Love and Sex: Psychological and Cultural Perspectives* (Hatfield et al., 2020).

In the very near future, I suspect that social psychologists, among many others, will be well on the way to answering some of the questions that have plagued humans for centuries. These inquiries will undoubtedly continue to raise hackles in some quarters of society, but the quest for knowledge and understanding cannot be stilled indefinitely.

And that noble search clearly continues in the book before you. In *Modern Relationships*, Mahzad Hojjat and Anne Moyer have assembled a superb group of essays and research articles that serve as a testament to that search. These send off a very clear signal of the richness and brilliance and variety in the study of love and of relationship science. They are global in scope and multidisciplinary in technique, and even Senator Proxmire would be impressed with what has been discovered.

References

Cacioppo, S. (in press). Wired for love: A neuroscientist's journey through romance, loss, and the essence of human connection.

Hatfield, E. (Spring, 2006). Proxmire and the Golden Fleece Awards. *Relationship Research News, 4*(Spring), 5–9.

Hatfield, E., Rapson, R. L. & Purvis, J. (2020). *What's next in love and sex: Psychological and cultural perspectives.* Oxford University Press.

List of Contributors

Tamara D. Afifi
Department of Communication, University of California, Santa Barbara

Arthur Aron
Institute of Personality and Social Research, University of California, Berkeley, and Department of Psychology, Stony Brook University

Rhonda N. Balzarini
Department of Psychology, Texas State University, The Kinsey Institute

Emily T. Beauparlant
Department of Psychology, Syracuse University

Karen L. Blair
Department of Psychology, Trent University

Dawn O. Braithwaite
Department of Communication Studies, University of Nebraska-Lincoln

Scott R. Braithwaite
Department of Psychology, Brigham Young University

Sydney Brake
Department of Psychology, University of Massachusetts Dartmouth

Claudia C. Brumbaugh
Psychology Department, Queens College and Graduate Center; City University of New York

Kathryn Coduto
Department of Mass Communication, Advertising and Public Relations, Boston University

Erin L. Courtice
Faculty of Social Sciences, School of Psychology, University of Ottawa

Jaclyn K. Doherty
Psychology Department, Graduate Center; City University of New York

Lindsey Eikenburg
ZS, Global Management Consulting Firm

Charlotte R. Esplin
Department of Psychology, Brigham Young University

LIST OF CONTRIBUTORS

Stanley O. Gaines, Jr.
College of Health, Medicine and Life Sciences, Centre for Culture and Evolution, Brunel University

Sofia Gameiro
School of Psychology, Cardiff University

S. Gabe Hatch
Utah Valley University

Elaine Hatfield
Department of Psychology, University of Hawaii

Andrew C. High
Department of Communication Arts and Sciences, The Pennsylvania State University

Mahzad Hojjat
Department of Psychology, University of Massachusetts Dartmouth

Rhea Ashley Hoskin
Departments of Sociology & Legal Studies and Sexuality, Marriage & Family Studies, University of Waterloo & St. Jerome's University

Jasna Jovanovic
Psychology & Child Development Department, California Polytechnic State University, San Luis Obispo

Elyakim Kislev
School of Public Policy and Governance, The Hebrew University of Jerusalem

Daniel A. Lee
Department of Communication Arts and Sciences, The Pennsylvania State University

Seungmi M. Lee
Eliot Pearson Department of Child Study and Human Development, Tufts University

Bonita London
Department of Psychology, Stony Brook University

Laura V. Machia
Department of Psychology, Syracuse University

Rose Martillotti
Department of Psychology, Stony Brook University

Nicole Melancon
Department of Psychology, University of Massachusetts Dartmouth

Rowland S. Miller
Department of Psychology and Philosophy, Sam Houston State University

K. Olivia Mock
Department of Psychology, Stony Brook University

Anne Moyer
Department of Psychology, Stony Brook University

Brady D. Nelson
Department of Psychology, Stony Brook University

Bailey M. Oliver-Blackburn
Applied Communication Department, University of Arkansas at Little Rock

Yeji Park
Department of Psychology, Princeton University

Daniel Perlman
Department of Psychology, University of Winnipeg

Ellen E. Pinderhughes
Eliot Pearson Department of Child Study and Human Development, Tufts University

Richard L. Rapson
Department of History, University of Hawaii

Lauren L. Richmond
Department of Psychology, Stony Brook University

Abdullah S. Salehuddin
Department of Communication, University of California, Santa Barbara

Jade Salmon
Department of Communication, University of California, Santa Barbara

Diana T. Sanchez
Department of Psychology, Rutgers University

Sharon Sassler
Department of Sociology, The Jeb E. Brooks School of Public Policy, Cornell University

Jessica L. Schleider
Department of Psychology, Stony Brook University

J. Nicole Shelton
Department of Psychology, Princeton University

Madeline C. Smith
Eliot Pearson Department of Child Study and Human Development, Tufts University

Kelly Sweeney
Department of Communication Arts and Sciences, The Pennsylvania State University

Kate M. Turetsky
Department of Psychology, Barnard College, Columbia University

Marissa Walter
Department of Psychology, Acadia University

Grace M. Wetzel
Department of Psychology, Rutgers University

Jean Calterone Williams
Political Science Department, California Polytechnic State University, San Luis Obispo

Introduction

Modern Relationships of the 21st Century

Mahzad Hojjat and Anne Moyer

The landscape of our close interpersonal relationships looks significantly different in the 21st century. Cultural, political, and legal changes have to some degree formed this landscape. For example, many adults choose to remain single, or get married much later in life, in their late 30s or even 40s. Online dating and cohabitation prior to or even instead of marriage have become more readily accepted and the norm rather than an exception. The nature and significance of our intimate relationships have significantly changed as well. Our friendships, on display on social media, have gained special importance in our lives. Issues surrounding gender identity and equity, as well as sexual orientation, have also loomed large in the last few decades. With the help of technology, more couples, including same-sex couples, are now able to become parents. From same-sex to open and polyamorous marriages, our society has witnessed important changes in how we define and perceive some of our most important close relationships. The dissolution and reformation of partnerships and families are also important to understand in an age when divorce and stepfamilies are common. The formation of families through adoption, whether domestic or international, raises questions of identity and successful parenting. Relationships across cultural, racial, religious, and national lines are also more relevant than ever in today's pluralistic societies. Finally, what types of relationships and phenomena are considered worthy of scholarly and scientific attention, and the lenses with which to study them, have also evolved.

This volume compiles the latest research and theory on close relationships of the 21st century from multidisciplinary and international perspectives with the intent of taking stock of this shifting terrain. We were fortunate to have an outstanding group of scholars from across the United States and the world (Canada, the United Kingdom, and Israel) who agreed to be part of this book project. Our contributors include 52 scholars from 30 universities and academic centers, representing seven different areas of study (psychology, sociology, communication, human development and family studies, political science, public policy, and history). This volume may be used as a primary or secondary source, in advanced undergraduate and graduate courses, and serve as a resource for researchers who study relationships in any field of study.

Finally, we would like to thank Abby Gross, Katie Pratt, and especially Nadina Persaud at Oxford University Press for their invaluable support and assistance during the entire publication process. We hope this book provides the knowledge and direction that our readers seek to better understand how our relationships have evolved in the 21st century and contributes to the advancement of relationship science.

PART I
DATING IN THE 21ST CENTURY

PART 1
DATING IN THE 21ST CENTURY

1
Ideal Partner Characteristics in the 21st Century
What Are We Looking for?

Claudia C. Brumbaugh and Jaclyn K. Doherty

Romantic attraction typically determines whether we develop a relationship with another person and is often the first step in forming a long-term committed relationship. Some romantically attractive features endure because of their adaptive functionality, whereas others are more malleable according to the historical time point and societal norms. In the 1970s, researchers began to consider the general features of similarity, familiarity, and proximity that led to attraction. In the following decade, evolutionary psychologists made in-depth cross-cultural examinations of specific features people look for, with a focus on sex differences. The most classic sex difference findings of women's concern over status and men's focus on physical appearance were to become well-established, replicated patterns (e.g., Li et al., 2011; Shackelford et al., 2005). Importantly for this chapter, these sex differences continue to hold universally into the 21st century (Walter et al., 2020). However, even some of these evolutionarily grounded preferences show flexibility according to societal shifts such as women's gains in earning power. In this chapter, we discuss recent changes surrounding dating life that may affect interpersonal attraction, discuss historical shifts in attraction preferences before and after the year 2000, and review the attraction literature, specifically examining what people are attracted to, beginning in the transition to the 21st century. The existing attraction literature centers on heterosexual relationships, making heterosexual preferences a focus in this chapter, but we also explore romantic preferences among other sexual orientations.

Gender Norms in Romance

Gender norms in heterosexual relationships shape the ways that men and women express their desires and navigate romantic contexts. Traditionally, men are expected to be assertive—initiating romantic interactions and orchestrating dates. Meanwhile, women are to be passive—their role is to be physically attractive and maintain conversation. In this dynamic, men tend to have more power in relationships. As society has become increasingly egalitarian in the 21st century, with women assuming positions of power and attaining higher salaries, women also may be becoming more active in the romantic domain.

In 2011, Eaton and Rose conducted a review of the dating research published in *Sex Roles* from 1975 to 2010, exploring romantic norm shifts over time. Although the researchers found examples of people acting against the traditional "female passivity and male agency" standards, dominant traditional scripts were not overcome through this time period. In the 2000s, women continued to be heavily sexualized in male-targeted media, and people still largely expected men to initiate romantic relationships and organize dates. While it has become more common for women to invest resources into romantic relationships (e.g., helping to pay for dates), most romantic dynamic expectations remained consistent entering the 21st century (Eaton & Rose, 2011).

Another decade has passed since Eaton and Rose's review—enough time for gender norms to change, but there is little evidence for subsequent shifts. In 2017, interviews with urban adolescents from around the world revealed that young people still hold traditional expectations in romantic contexts (De Meyer et al., 2017). While few reported having direct romantic experience, interviewees generally reported that it was the man's place to be "active and dominant" and the woman's place to be "innocent with less (romantic) agency." Such beliefs likely reflect societal norms that are transmitted generationally. Another study similarly found that college students on the currently popular dating app Tinder continued to follow conventional gender norms (Berkowitz et al., 2021). Especially given dating apps' emphasis on physical attraction, people may fall back on traditional ideas about what makes a preferable mate when making quick "swipe" decisions about who to pursue.

Despite the overall consistency in traditional gender norms, there is some evidence of increased egalitarianism in romantic relationships. For example, Bumble is a popular dating app released in 2014 that gives women more control, allowing only female users to make the first contact with matches. Thus, women now have more options to be active participants in relationship initiation. Egalitarianism is also reflected in women's shifting preference for family-oriented men, which likely parallels women's increasing involvement in the workplace and need for partners who are more involved in communal family life (Meeussen et al., 2019).

Roles in the domestic sphere and in the workplace have become more flexible (Livingston & Parker, 2019), and there are fewer expectations that men make the greater share of earnings and women do all of the housework. Women's employment, especially mothers', has increased dramatically in the last 50 years (U.S. Bureau of Labor Statistics, 2021). During that period, men slightly increased their participation in household labor (Bianchi et al., 2000). In sum, there are hints of potential trajectories in romantic relationships as women gain more social and financial power, but gender norms remain surprisingly steadfast.

Shifts in Partner Preferences in the 21st Century

Reflecting on changes in partner preferences over the past 20–30 years, the literature suggests that while some preferences shifted, others remain consistent. When comparing overall trends, two driving factors tend to emerge: evolved preferences and societal preferences. Certain mate preferences, such as perceptions of physical attractiveness, were shaped by evolution over the course of human history, and these preferences are unlikely to change across generations (Walter et al., 2020). However, societal expectations shift more quickly than evolution, such that mate preferences shaped by social norms change more visibly over time.

Bech-Sørensen and Pollet (2016) replicated a study from the 1990s (Sprecher et al., 1994) to assess whether prior sex differences held in the 21st century. In 2016, marrying an older mate with high earning potential was more important to women than men. Men continued to care more than women about physical appearance and were more likely to marry a younger mate with lower earning potential—these preferences remained consistent between 1994 and 2016. Although these sex differences held, there were some notable changes. First, unlike in the 1990s when women were less likely than men to be romantically attracted to someone of a different race, there were no longer sex differences in willingness to marry or date a partner of a different ethnicity in 2016. This finding aligns with increasing rates of interethnic marriage (see Chapter 8, this volume) and is reflected in other intergroup contexts. For example, the frequency of interfaith and religious/secular marriage increased nearly 20% between 1960 and 2015 (Murphy, 2015). Second, in 2016 women were more inclined than men to marry someone who was previously married, which was not the case in the 1990s. This shift may reflect marriage's declining social importance and increased divorce rates in recent generations (see Chapters 3, 4, and 13 in this volume).

Another study sheds light on preference shifts; Boxer et al. (2015) explored changes in partner preferences over time between 1985, 1996, and 2008. Compared with 1996, women in 2008 cared less about pleasing dispositions, emotional stability/maturity, similar educational background, intelligence, and sexual chastity. However, compared with 1985, women in 2008 cared more about having similar political backgrounds. Compared with 1985, men in 2008 cared more about their partner having good financial prospects and being dependable and intelligent. Relative to 1996, men in 2008 cared less about potential partners having pleasing dispositions, similar educational backgrounds, and chastity. Thus, these three features became less important to both sexes, demonstrating aligning preference shifts between the genders.

Overall, preferences for physical appearance, age, and resources remain relatively consistent over time. This aligns with evolutionary expectations, as these features convey fitness for reproduction and supporting families. Preferences like these are unlikely to change quickly since they are deeply embedded in our biology. However, more socially driven factors like personality, intergroup processes, and education preferences change more rapidly between generations, or even decades. Next, we transition from preference shifts since 2000 to features that people currently prefer. The following sections are based on the attraction literature *since* 2000.

The Appeal of "Negative" Characteristics

People may not always be attracted to what is expected. Features that most would consider negative are sometimes attractive too. For instance, the classic appeal of the "bad boy" is a well-known caricature, and, indeed, women prefer men who exhibit daredevil-like behavior (Kelly & Dunbar, 2001). These preferences for traits in men are likely rooted in sexual selection processes, given that features like recklessness are *negatively* correlated with personal survival. Furthermore, men are more likely than women to engage in daring behavior, which again suggests that sexual selection may influence men's risk-taking behavior in spite of the inherent dangers of recklessness. Heroic acts, which are more often performed by men and are more attractive to women (Margana et al., 2019), often involves risk-taking as well. Risk-taking may correspond to both direct benefits (the ability to gain resources) and indirect benefits (the possession of good genes). Thus, the attractiveness of some bad boy traits is probably long-standing and fairly stable over time, as these features are rooted in our evolutionary heritage. Although an evolutionary argument for the adaptiveness of risky traits in men has been made, it is not only women who are drawn to bad behavior. Men prefer risk-takers in shorter-term contexts as well (Bassett & Moss, 2004). In another domain, the dark triad trait of narcissism also currently appears to be attractive, as indicated by narcissism's positive correlation with number of sex partners and self-perceived mate value (Borráz-León & Rantala, 2021; Jonason et al., 2009), and by women's judgments as well (Marcinkowska et al., 2015).

Positive Features

Attraction to positive features in others is not surprising in any context, and certainly not when it comes to finding a romantic partner with whom one might spend their life. The appeal of such positive traits would not be expected to shift substantially over historical time periods. Characteristics such as altruism, humor, kindness, attachment security, and intelligence are appealing because they make interactions smoother and more successful and sometimes have additional adaptive benefits.

Altruism is one such adaptive trait in potential mates. Altruistic acts in burgeoning relationships may draw in partners, as these behaviors are indicative of how a mate will behave down the road. When considering a long-term mate, choosing an individual who is kind and selfless, both as a partner and future parent, is an adaptive mate choice (Margana et al., 2019). Women care more about altruism and cooperativeness in long-term mates than do men (Bhogal et al., 2019). However, because both men and women play a part in relationship functioning and in raising children, altruism should be attractive to both sexes. As a mating strategy, there is some evidence that men deliberately use altruistic acts to attract women. For example, men are more likely to provide assistance to younger women than to older women

(Kawamura & Kusumi, 2017). A similar quality, heroism, is considered by some to be an extreme version of altruism that often comes with heightened risks (Margana et al., 2019). Again, men are more willing to take chances in mating situations, which suggests that risk-taking is used by men as an intentional mating strategy (Greitemeyer et al., 2013).

Humor is another feature that is generally attractive. After all, humor is inherently happy! It also conveys that a person is fun-loving, playful, and has a youthful spirit (Chick et al., 2012). Humor may imply other positive traits as well, like having an overall positive disposition and being someone who will create less conflict. In terms of sex differences, men may be funnier than women (Greengross & Miller, 2011), but these findings are mixed (Hofmann et al., 2020). Some propose a dynamic where women like humorous men, and men like women who think *they* themselves are particularly funny (Bressler et al., 2006). However, other work finds that both sexes highly prefer humor (McGee & Shevlin 2009).

Humor also has links to creative thinking, which may be especially attractive to women (Nettle & Clegg, 2006). Humor corresponds to verbal creativity (Kaufman et al., 2008) and intelligence (Greengross & Miller, 2011), which both men and women prefer, possibly because intellect is an indicator of fitness. Intelligence relates to one's ability to succeed and gain resources (Kuncel et al., 2004) and is attractive in both short- and long-term contexts (Prokosch et al., 2009).

Similarity was identified long ago as a key feature of romantic attraction (Berscheid & Hatfield, 1969) and similarity effects still hold true today. Similarity remains attractive regardless of historical time point partially because it signals safety. Potential mates are less threatening if they are more like you. Similarity provides a sense of familiarity and often makes interactions flow more easily. The appeal of similarity can also stem from people's self-love and implicit egotism. People tend to like others who resemble themselves, because these features provide self-validation and a means of sustaining self-worth (Jones et al., 2004). These effects are based both in basic psychological needs and in classical conditioning principles where individuals positively associate others with themselves. Indeed, the more favorably people feel about themselves, the more they want partners to be similar to them (Brown & Brown, 2015). Likewise, people who have higher self-perceived value are more discriminating in mate preferences, as people who have higher mate value can be more selective (Buss & Shackelford, 2008; Buston & Emlen, 2003). These types of effects are tied to positive assortative mating, where similarity between partners sometimes follows from an active desire to find a similar mate. Indeed, active assortative mating is known to create couples with similar attitudes about patriotism, politics, and religion (Watson et al., 2014).

Finally, something needs to be said of physical beauty as a powerful determinant of initial attraction for both sexes. Speed dating paradigms are ideal for identifying the influence of physical appearance in initial meetings when little else is known aside from the way that the potential partner looks. One speed dating study that included over 12,000 subjects (Kurzban & Weeden, 2005) found that men who were taller and more physically attractive were more popular. In the same study, women's physical appearance (especially lower BMI) was most important to men's attraction.

What Is Attractive? Not Everyone Agrees

Not everyone will concur on what is *most* attractive in a romantic partner. And that is a good thing! If we all agreed, it would be nearly impossible to find a mate who pleased us, as all of the people who possessed that one feature would likely already be paired with others who possess that singular feature (assortative mating at work). People vary in what they prefer; some of this variation is due to who *they* are and can result in similarity effects between partners. Attraction and mate choice can also be affected by environmental variables that switch on some preferences and switch off others. Much of the variation described here pertains to women's preferences, as they are the choosier sex. Women also have *broader* preferences; compared with men who have a high degree of consensus about what is attractive (primarily physical appearance), women have a wider range in the features they seek in mates (Wood & Brumbaugh, 2009). In this section, we discuss some key between- and within-sex differences in what people are attracted to in romantic mates.

Health

One of the more important determinants of attraction is health. Health can sometimes be a local quality, as health varies between geographical regions. For instance, DeBruine et al. (2010) found that women universally preferred masculinity according to local health indicators. As mortality and communicable disease rates increased, women's desire for masculine traits in partners increased cross-culturally. Because masculine traits correspond to men's health and their ability to produce healthy offspring (Gangestad & Scheyd, 2005), masculine traits become more essential in less healthy areas of the world. This situational pressure can also explain variations in women's preferences for masculinity. Masculine men report a lower desire for long-term relationships (Boothroyd et al., 2007), which aligns with impressions of masculine men—that they're adulterous and uninvested in relationships and parenting, as well as dishonest, uncooperative, and aggressive (Kruger, 2006). However, if local environmental health conditions steer people's preferences toward these seemingly undesirable masculine traits, this can partly explain why overall research findings on women's preference for masculinity is inconsistent.

Life history theory (MacArthur & Wilson, 1967) is an idea that also pertains to health and local conditions. People with faster strategies usually originate from harsher environments where survival is more tenuous. Fast strategies correspond to shorter-term mating preferences and less investment in offspring. Fast (versus slow) strategies also correspond to attraction preferences. Specifically, men with faster life history strategies prefer signs of fertility and good genes (i.e., physical attractiveness) over women's caregiving potential (Lu et al., 2017). Thus, men with fast life strategies are focused on partner traits having to do with mating rather than parenting. Similarly, people with short- versus long-term approaches to relationships place differing weight on physical appearance, regardless of sex (Vigil et al., 2006). In sum, when the desire is a short-term relationship, attraction becomes more centered on physical appearance and health.

Health as reflected by reproductive status also factors into mate preferences. For instance, women with a lower waist-to-hip ratio—an indicator of better reproductive potential—have higher demands in mates and are more selective about men's resource potential (Pawlowski & Jasienska, 2008). If reproductive value corresponds to mate value, then women with more of it can afford to be more discerning in their mate choices. Similarly, women have higher standards when they are fertile (Beaulieu & Havens, 2015). Preferences for masculine traits (features signaling high genetic quality) are highest during ovulation when women can conceive (Gangestad et al., 2015). Preferences also shift with childbirth—at one year postpartum, women preferred more feminine looking men (Escasea-Dorne et al., 2017). These findings highlight shifts from women's mating efforts (when masculinity is preferred) to their parenting efforts (when femininity is preferred).

During late pregnancy (Limoncin et al., 2015) and after the birth of a child, more feminine traits in men are attractive to women because they facilitate pair bonding and caregiving at a time when children and family coherence become central concerns.

Age

With a close relation to health, age also affects mate preferences. What people are attracted to in their 20s does not map perfectly to what they prefer in later years. People may grow "older and wiser" with age and also have different priorities at different phases of life. To some degree, these shifts in desires and concerns over the life span correspond to what people care most about in mates at different ages.

In general, the trend is that people become what might be described as "less shallow" in their mate preferences as they age. The emphasis shifts to a mate's communal features, such as sensitivity, agreeableness, and emotional stability. With age, people also have an increased desire for creativity and domesticity in a partner (Schwarz & Hassebrauck, 2012). Meanwhile, the importance of physical attractiveness in mates lessens (Bleske-Rechek et al., 2009). Importantly, this trend has been found cross-culturally, which signals an adaptive shift, probably grounded in needs to have a stable relationship with a mate who will be a good caregiver for both oneself in old age and one's offspring (Brumbaugh & Wood, 2013). These attraction preferences are especially true for women, who simultaneously shift away from desiring more sexy physical characteristics, such as being seductive and trendy, as they get older (Bleske-Rechek et al., 2009; Brumbaugh & Wood, 2013). Finally, while women are attracted to somewhat older men across their life span, men are typically more attracted to younger women, especially women in their mid-20s, irrespective of their own age (Antfolk et al., 2015). Thus, with age, men prefer increasingly younger women, unlike women who continue to prefer men closer in age to themselves.

Financial Resources

Variations in women's preferences may rest on their ability to earn and control resources. Women are often faced with the choice of gaining resources versus gaining good genes from men (Gangestad & Simpson, 2000). When women lack financial independence, they are more obligated out of necessity to choose resources. Physical attractiveness in men is thus considered "a luxury" that women are often forced to trade for status (Waynforth, 2001). However, we previously described one of the notable changes to societal functioning that impacts relational life—that of women's greater earning power and financial independence. As societies become more equal between the sexes, global differences between men's and women's mate preferences should narrow (Eagly & Wood, 1999). Indeed, Zentner and Mitura (2012) found that sex differences in partner preferences decrease as gender equality increases.

Gaps in income between American women and men have decreased such that women no longer need to rely heavily on men for resources (Moore & Cassidy, 2007). These effects are seen at a global level, but also at an individual level. Theoretically, women's preferences should vary according to their own personal financial status. In other words, when women are higher status, they should find resources in a mate less important. However, some have found the opposite where women's income is *positively* related to their preference for resources in a man (Anderson & Klofstad, 2012). In contrast, most find a pattern of decreasing sex differences when women have more economic power. For instance, Moore and Cassidy (2007) examined effects of women's preferences in nonindustrial societies and found that women who had more equality in terms of household power valued physical attractiveness more than status in mates. Others have also found women's financial status and control over resources corresponds to their preference for physically attractive men (Koyama et al., 2004). Meanwhile, higher intelligence in women negatively correlates with women's desire for financially secure men (Stanik & Ellsworth, 2010), suggesting that smarter women are more capable of earning money so that they do not need to worry about men's resource provision.

While women with a good salary can worry less about finding a man who is a provider, they need to worry more about finding a man who will be good father. In other words, if a woman has a career, she has less time at home to care for children, so finding a more domestic mate who will contribute to childcare increases in importance. Indeed, in contemporary societies where women have good economic situations, attraction to "good-father features" such as kindness and domesticity increases (Lu et al., 2015).

Beyond Traditional Relationships

Although research on romantic relationship preferences has primarily been conducted among straight people seeking monogamous relationships—and our review thus far has focused on these relationships—there is a growing body of work investigating preferences among those outside of this category. Most of these studies investigate gay men's preferences. Work finds that unlike straight men, who prioritize physical attractiveness when choosing mates, gay men are equally concerned with both physical attractiveness and socioeconomic traits (Bartos & Rusu, 2010). Gay men also preferred taller partners, but this effect was moderated by personal height (taller men preferred shorter partners, and shorter men preferred taller partners). Additionally, gay men who favored a dominant sex role preferred shorter partners, while those who favored a submissive sex role preferred taller partners (Valentova et al., 2014). Further, gay men more strongly preferred male bodies with more "developed upper body builds" than straight men (Swami & Tovée, 2008).

However, other studies report contradicting evidence, suggesting that further work is needed. For example, while one study found that gay men preferred partners who were older (Bartos & Rusu, 2010), another found a preference for younger men (Conway et al., 2015). However, Conway et al. (2015) found that gay men were more flexible with age preferences than straight people—straight men consistently preferred younger women and straight women consistently preferred older men, but gay men were more accepting of a greater range of ages.

While studies have begun to establish general mate preferences in the gay male community, the preferences of gay men may be more flexible than assumed. For instance, Flave-Novak and Coleman (2019) demonstrated "pluralistic ignorance" about attractiveness in the gay community. Although gay men believed that their peers were most attracted to thin and muscular men, there was much more variability in what gay men actually found attractive. The authors concluded that people in the gay male community believe (inaccurately) that other gay men are quite rigid in their desires when in reality they are open to a range of body types. One factor involved in this discrepancy may be the type of relationship sought; for example, gay men more strongly prefer "muscular and lean figures" for short- than for long-term relationships (Varangis et al., 2012).

A handful of studies have addressed partner preferences among lesbian and bisexual women. Overall, BMI seems to be a leading contributor to physical attractiveness of female bodies, both among straight people and lesbian women (Hitsch et al., 2005; Swami & Tovée, 2008). One study found that lesbian and bisexual women preferred women with lower waist-to-hip ratio (i.e., more typically "feminine" physiques), heavy figures, and large breasts (Cohen & Tannenbaum, 2001). Another study corroborated these results, finding that, relative to straight women, lesbians preferred female bodies with higher BMIs (Swami & Tovée, 2006), suggesting their rejection of societal expectations for thinness (Cohen & Tannenbaum, 2001). Beyond physical attractiveness, other work found that lesbian women were less interested in long-term relationships than gay men, but both were more interested in long-term relationships when same-sex relationships are more normalized (Potârcă et al., 2015). Lesbian women also prefer younger partners, but like with gay men, this preference is much less strict for lesbians than straight women (Conway et al., 2015).

Future Directions

There have been recent significant changes in relationship types and environmental pressures that may affect attraction. With rising rates of open relationship styles, some work has begun to explore characteristics of non-monogamous relationships (see Chapter 7, this volume). Another major change in our social lives corresponds to the COVID-19 pandemic, which began in early 2020. We believe that ideas from evolutionary psychology best fit here. Specifically, a dangerous, pathogen-filled environment is thought to switch on and off certain preferences, leading people to sacrifice other desirable features for good genes to optimize offspring fitness in a threatening environment. According to research on the effects of pathogen prevalence on attraction to features signaling health (e.g., Cantu & Simpson, 2013; Lee & Zietsch, 2011), we presume that the COVID-19 pandemic is actively creating environmental pressures and currently affecting mate preferences. Today and in the near future, both men and women should theoretically value physical appearance more than they did before the pandemic, as it is an important signal of health.

In this chapter we described what characteristics are currently attractive in mates, the conditions under which features are attractive, and what has shifted since the turn of the 21st century. We conclude that, because many attractive features are likely evolutionarily based, romantic attraction remains quite stable over time. As they did in our ancestral past, these features may still serve to alert us to valuable qualities in mates.

References

Anderson, R. C., & Klofstad, C. A. (2012). For love or money? The influence of personal resources and environmental resource pressures on human mate preferences. *Ethology, 118*(9), 841–849. https://doi.org/10.1111/j.1439-0310.2012.02077.x

Antfolk, J., Salo, B., Alanko, K., Bergen, E., Corander, J., Sandnabba, N. K., & Santtila, P. (2015). Women's and men's sexual preferences and activities with respect to the partner's age: Evidence for female choice. *Evolution and Human Behavior, 36*(1), 73–79. https://doi.org/10.1016/j.evolhumbehav.2014.09.003

Bartos, S. E., & Rusu, A. S. (2010). Do Romanian heterosexual men differ from the homosexual men in expressing their mate preferences? A preliminary evolutionary psychological investigation of the online personal advertisements. *Journal of Cognitive and Behavioral Psychotherapies, 10*(2), 199–210.

Bassett, J. F., & Moss, B. (2004). Men and women prefer risk takers as romantic and nonromantic partners. *Current Research in Social Psychology, 9*(10), 135–144. https://doi.org/10.1177/0146167215577366

Beaulieu, D. A., & Havens, K. (2015). Fertile women are more demanding: Ovulatory increases in minimum mate preference criteria across a wide range of characteristics and relationship contexts. *Personality and Individual Differences, 72*, 200–207. https://doi.org/10.1016/j.paid.2014.09.018

Bech-Sørensen, J., & Pollet, T. V. (2016). Sex differences in mate oreferences: A replication study, 20 years later. *Evolutionary Psychological Science, 2*(3), 171–176. https://doi.org/10.1007/s40806-016-0048-6

Berkowitz, D., Tinkler, J., Peck, A., & Coto, L. (2021). Tinder: A game with gendered rules and consequences. *Social Currents, 8*(5), 491–509. https://doi.org/10.1177/2329496521 1019486

Berscheid, E., & Hatfield, E. (1969). *Interpersonal attraction* (Vol. 69, pp. 113–114). Addison-Wesley.

Bhogal, M. S., Farrelly, D., & Galbraith, N. (2019). The role of prosocial behaviors in mate choice: A critical review of the literature. *Current Psychology, 38*(4), 1062–1075. https://doi.org/10.1007/s12144-019-00308-8

Bianchi, S. M., Milkie, M. A., Sayer, L. C., & Robinson, J. P. (2000). Is anyone doing the housework? Trends in the gender division of household labor. *Social Forces, 79*(1), 191–228. https://doi.org/10.1093/sf/79.1.191

Bleske-Rechek, A., VandenHeuvel, B., & Vander Wyst, M. (2009). Age variation in mating strategies and mate preferences: Beliefs versus reality. *Evolutionary Psychology, 7*(2), 179–205. https://doi.org/10.1177/147470490900700204

Boothroyd, L. G., Jones, B. C., Burt, D. M., & Perrett, D. I. (2007). Partner characteristics associated with masculinity, health and maturity in male faces. *Personality and Individual Differences, 43*(5), 1161–1173. https://doi.org/10.1016/j.paid.2007.03.008

Borráz-León, J. I., & Rantala, M. J. (2021). Does the Dark Triad predict self-perceived attractiveness, mate value, and number of sexual partners both in men and women? *Personality and Individual Differences, 168*, Article 110341. https://doi.org/10.1016/j.paid.2020.110341

Boxer, C. F., Noonan, M. C., & Whelan, C. B. (2015). Measuring mate preferences: A replication and extension. *Journal of Family Issues, 36*(2), 163–187. https://doi.org/10.1177/0192513x13490404

Bressler, E. R., Martin, R. A., & Balshine, S. (2006). Production and appreciation of humor as sexually selected traits. *Evolution and Human Behavior, 27*(2), 121–130. https://doi.org/10.1016/j.evolhumbehav.2005.09.001

Brown, M. A., & Brown, J. D. (2015). Self-enhancement biases, self-esteem, and ideal mate preferences. *Personality and Individual Differences, 74*, 61–65. https://doi.org/10.1016/j.paid.2014.09.039

Brumbaugh, C. C., & Wood, D. (2013). Mate preferences across life and across the world. *Social Psychological and Personality Science, 4*(1), 100–107. https://doi.org/10.1177/1948550612442396

Buss, D. M., & Shackelford, T. K. (2008). Attractive women want it all: Good genes, economic investment, parenting proclivities, and emotional commitment. *Evolutionary Psychology, 6*(1), 134–146. https://doi.org/10.1177/147470490800600116

Buston, P. M., & Emlen, S. T. (2003). Cognitive processes underlying human mate choice: The relationship between self-perception and mate preference in Western society. *Proceedings of the National Academy of Sciences, 100*(15), 8805–8810. https://doi.org/10.1073/pnas.1533220100

Cantu, S., & Simson, J. (2013). *When are women especially attracted to attractive men?: Human mate preferences in a pathogen prevalent ecology* (Doctoral dissertation, University of Minnesota). University Digital Conservancy. https://hdl.handle.net/11299/162437

Chick, G., Yarnal, C., & Purrington, A. (2012). Play and mate preference: Testing the signal theory of adult playfulness. *American Journal of Play, 4*(4), 407–440. https://doi.org/10.1080/00224499.2022.2077289

Cohen, A. B., & Tannenbaum, I. J. (2001). Lesbian and bisexual women's judgments of the attractiveness of different body types. *Journal of Sex Research, 38*(3), 226–232. https://doi.org/10.1080/00224490109552091

Conway, J. R., Noë, N., Stulp, G., & Pollet, T. V. (2015). Finding your soulmate: Homosexual and heterosexual age preferences in online dating. *Personal Relationships, 22*(4), 666–678. https://doi.org/10.1111/pere.12102

DeBruine, L. M., Jones, B. C., Crawford, J. R., Welling, L. L., & Little, A. C. (2010). The health of a nation predicts their mate preferences: Cross-cultural variation in women's preferences for masculinized male faces. *Proceedings of the Royal Society B: Biological Sciences, 277*(1692), 2405–2410. https://doi.org/10.1098/rspb.2009.2184

De Meyer, S., Kågesten, A., Mmari, K., McEachran, J., Chilet-Rosell, E., Kabiru, C. W., Maina, B., Jerves, E. M., Currie, C., & Michielsen, K. (2017). "Boys should have the courage to ask a girl out": Gender norms in early adolescent romantic relationships. *Journal of Adolescent Health, 61*(4), S42–S47. https://doi.org/10.1016/j.jadohealth.2017.03.007

Eagly, A. H., & Wood, W. (1999). The origins of sex differences in human behavior: Evolved dispositions versus social roles. *American Psychologist, 54*(6), 408–423. https://doi.org/10.1037/0003-066x.54.6.408

Eaton, A. A., & Rose, S. (2011). Has dating become more egalitarian? A 35 year review using sex roles. *Sex Roles*, *64*(11), 843–862. https://doi.org/10.1007/s11199-011-9957-9

Escasa-Dorne, M. J., Manlove, H., & Gray, P. B. (2017). Women express a preference for feminized male faces after giving birth. *Adaptive Human Behavior and Physiology*, *3*(1), 30–42. https://doi.org/10.1007/s40750-016-0048-6

Flave-Novak, D. E., & Coleman, J. M. (2019). Pluralistic ignorance of physical attractiveness in the gay male community. *Journal of Homosexuality*, *66*(14), 2002–2020. https://doi.org/10.1080/00918369.2018.1522811

Gangestad, S. W., & Haselton, M. G. (2015). Human estrus: Implications for relationship science. *Current Opinion in Psychology*, *1*, 45–51. https://doi.org/10.1016/j.copsyc.2014.12.007

Gangestad, S. W., & Scheyd, G. J. (2005). The evolution of human physical attractiveness. *Annual Review of Anthropology*, *34*, 523–548. https://doi.org/10.1146/annurev.anthro.33.070203.143733

Gangestad, S. W., & Simpson, J. A. (2000). The evolution of human mating: Trade-offs and strategic pluralism. *Behavioral and Brain Sciences*, *23*(4), 573–587. https://doi.org/10.1017/S0140525X0000337X

Greengross, G., & Miller, G. (2011). Humor ability reveals intelligence, predicts mating success, and is higher in males. *Intelligence*, *39*(4), 188–192. https://doi.org/10.1016/j.intell.2011.03.006

Greitemeyer, T., Kastenmüller, A., & Fischer, P. (2013). Romantic motives and risk-taking: An evolutionary approach. *Journal of Risk Research*, *16*(1), 19–38. https://doi.org/10.1080/13669877.2012.713388

Hitsch, G. J., Hortaçsu, A., & Ariely, D. (2005, January). What makes you click: An empirical analysis of online dating. In Society for Economic Dynamics, *2005 Meeting Papers* (Vol. 207, pp. 1–51). Society for Economic Dynamics. https://doi.org/10.1007/s11129-010-9088-6

Hofmann, J., Platt, T., Lau, C., & Torres-Marín, J. (2020). Gender differences in humor-related traits, humor appreciation, production, comprehension, (neural) responses, use, and correlates: A systematic review. *Current Psychology*. Advance online publication. https://doi.org/10.1007/s12144-020-00724-1

Jonason, P. K., Li, N. P., Webster, G. W., & Schmitt, D. P. (2009). The Dark Triad: Facilitating short-term mating in men. *European Journal of Personality*, *23*, 5–18. https://doi.org/10.1002/per.698

Jones, J. T., Pelham, B. W., Carvallo, M., & Mirenberg, M. C. (2004). How do I love thee? Let me count the Js: Implicit egotism and interpersonal attraction. *Journal of Personality and Social Psychology*, *87*(5), 665. https://doi.org/10.1037/0022-3514.87.5.665

Kaufman, S. B., Kozbelt, A., & Bromley, M. L. (2008). The role of creativity and humor in human mate selection. In G. Geher & G. Miller (Eds.), *Mating intelligence: Sex, relationships, and the mind's reproductive system* (pp. 227–262). Lawrence Erlbaum Associates Publishers.

Kawamura, Y., & Kusumi, T. (2017). Selfishness is attributed to men who help young women: Signaling function of male altruism. *Letters on Evolutionary Behavioral Science*, *8*(2), 45–48. https://doi.org/10.5178/lebs.2017.64

Kelly, S., & Dunbar, R. I. (2001). Who dares, wins. *Human Nature*, *12*(2), 89–105. https://doi.org/10.1007/s12110-001-1018-6

Koyama, N. F., McGain, A., & Hill, R. A. (2004). Self-reported mate preferences and "feminist" attitudes regarding marital relations. *Evolution and Human Behavior, 25*(5), 327–335. https://doi.org/10.1016/j.evolhumbehav.2004.06.004

Kruger, D. J. (2006). Male facial masculinity influences attributions of personality and reproductive strategy. *Personal Relationships, 13*(4), 451–463. https://doi.org/10.1111/j.1475-6811.2006.00129.x

Kuncel, N. R., Hezlett, S. A., & Ones, D. S. (2004). Academic performance, career potential, creativity, and job performance: Can one construct predict them all? *Journal of Personality and Social Psychology, 86*(1), 148–161. https://doi.org/10.1037/0022-3514.86.1.148

Kurzban, R., & Weeden, J. (2005). HurryDate: Mate preferences in action. *Evolution and Human Behavior, 26*(3), 227–244. https://doi.org/10.1016/j.evolhumbehav.2004.08.012

Lee, A. J., & Zietsch, B. P. (2011). Experimental evidence that women's mate preferences are directly influenced by cues of pathogen prevalence and resource scarcity. *Biology Letters, 7*(6), 892–895. https://doi.org/10.1098/rsbl.2011.0454

Li, N. P., Valentine, K. A., & Patel, L. (2011). Mate preferences in the US and Singapore: A cross-cultural test of the mate preference priority model. *Personality and Individual Differences, 50*(2), 291–294. https://doi.org/10.1016/j.paid.2010.10.005

Limoncin, E., Ciocca, G., Gravina, G. L., Carosa, E., Mollaioli, D., Cellerino, A., . . . & Jannini, E. A. (2015). Pregnant women's preferences for men's faces differ significantly from nonpregnant women. *The Journal of Sexual Medicine, 12*(5), 1142–1151. https://doi.org/10.1111/jsm.12849

Livingston, G., & Parker, K. (2019). Facts about American dads. *Pew Research Center.* https://www.pewresearch.org/fact-tank/2019/06/12/fathers-day-facts

Lu, H. J., Wong, K. C., & Chang, L. (2017). The association between life history strategy and mate preference in men. *Personality and Individual Differences, 116,* 157–163. https://doi.org/10.1016/j.paid.2017.04.047

Lu, H. J., Zhu, X. Q., & Chang, L. (2015). Good genes, good providers, and good fathers: Economic development involved in how women select a mate. *Evolutionary Behavioral Sciences, 9,* 215–228. https://doi.org/10.1037/ebs0000048

MacArthur, R. H. & Wilson, E. O. (1967). *The theory of island biogeography.* Princeton University Press.

Marcinkowska, U. M., Helle, S., & Lyons, M. T. (2015). Dark traits: Sometimes hot, and sometimes not? Female preferences for Dark Triad faces depend on sociosexuality and contraceptive use. *Personality and Individual Differences, 86,* 369–373. https://doi.org/10.1016/j.paid.2015.06.030

Margana, L., Bhogal, M. S., Bartlett, J. E., & Farrelly, D. (2019). The roles of altruism, heroism, and physical attractiveness in female mate choice. *Personality and Individual Differences, 137,* 126–130. https://doi.org/10.1016/j.paid.2018.08.018

McGee, E., & Shevlin, M. (2009). Effect of humor on interpersonal attraction and mate selection. *The Journal of Psychology, 143*(1), 67–77. https://doi.org/10.3200/jrlp.143.1.67-77

Meeussen, L., Van Laar, C., & Verbruggen, M. (2019). Looking for a family man? Norms for men are toppling in heterosexual relationships. *Sex Roles, 80*(7), 429–442. https://doi.org/10.1007/s11199-018-0946-0

Moore, F. R., & Cassidy, C. (2007). Female status predicts female mate preferences across nonindustrial societies. *Cross-Cultural Research, 41*(1), 66–74. https://doi.org/10.1177/1069397106294860

Murphy, C. (2015). Interfaith marriage is common in U.S., particularly among the recently wed. Pew Research Center. https://www.pewresearch.org/fact-tank/2015/06/02/interfaith-marriage/

Nettle, D., & Clegg, H. (2006). Schizotypy, creativity and mating success in humans. *Proceedings of the Royal Society B: Biological Sciences, 273*(1586), 611–615. https://doi.org/10.1098/rspb.2005.3349

Pawlowski, B., & Jasienska, G. (2008). Women's body morphology and preferences for sexual partners' characteristics. *Evolution and Human Behavior, 29*(1), 19–25. https://doi.org/10.1016/j.evolhumbehav.2007.07.003

Potârcă, G., Mills, M., & Neberich, W. (2015). Relationship preferences among gay and lesbian online daters: Individual and contextual influences. *Journal of Marriage and Family, 77*(2), 523–541. https://doi.org/10.1111/jomf.12217

Prokosch, M. D., Coss, R. G., Scheib, J. E., & Blozis, S. A. (2009). Intelligence and mate choice: Intelligent men are always appealing. *Evolution and Human Behavior, 30*(1), 11–20. https://doi.org/10.1016/j.evolhumbehav.2008.07.004

Schwarz, S., & Hassebrauck, M. (2012). Sex and age differences in mate-selection preferences. *Human Nature, 23*(4), 447–466. https://doi.org/10.1007/s12110-012-9152-x

Shackelford, T. K., Schmitt, D. P., & Buss, D. M. (2005). Universal dimensions of human mate preferences. *Personality and Individual Differences, 39*(2), 447–458. https://doi.org/10.1016/j.paid.2005.01.023

Sprecher, S., Sullivan, Q., & Hatfield, E. (1994). Mate selection preferences: Gender differences examined in a national sample. *Journal of Personality and Social Psychology, 66*(6), 1074–1080. https://doi.org/10.1037/0022-3514.66.6.1074

Stanik, C. E., & Ellsworth, P. C. (2010). Who cares about marrying a rich man? Intelligence and variation in women's mate preferences. *Human Nature, 21*(2), 203–217. https://doi.org/10.1007/s12110-010-9089-x

Swami, V., & Tovée, M. J. (2006). The influence of body mass index on the physical attractiveness preferences of feminist and nonfeminist heterosexual women and lesbians. *Psychology of Women Quarterly, 30*(3), 252–257. https://doi.org/10.1111/j.1471-6402.2006.00293.x

Swami, V., & Tovée, M. J. (2008). The muscular male: A comparison of the physical attractiveness preferences of gay and heterosexual men. *International Journal of Men's Health, 7*(1), 59–71. https://doi.org/10.3149/jmh.0701.59

U.S. Bureau of Labor Statistics. (2021). *Women in the labor force*. https://www.bls.gov/opub/reports/womens-databook/2020/home.htm

Valentova, J. V., Stulp, G., Třebický, V., & Havlíček, J. (2014). Preferred and actual relative height among homosexual male partners vary with preferred dominance and sex role. *PLoS ONE, 9*(1), Article e86534. https://doi.org/10.1371/journal.pone.0086534

Varangis, E., Lanzieri, N., Hildebrandt, T., & Feldman, M. (2012). Gay male attraction toward muscular men: Does mating context matter? *Body Image, 9*(2), 270–278. https://doi.org/10.1016/j.bodyim.2012.01.003

Vigil, J. M., Geary, D. C., & Byrd-Craven, J. (2006). Trade-offs in low-income women's mate preferences. *Human Nature, 17*(3), 319–336. https://doi.org/10.1007/s12110-006-1012-0

Walter, K. V., Conroy-Beam, D., Buss, D. M., Asao, K., Sorokowska, A., Sorokowski, P., ... & Zupančič, M. (2020). Sex differences in mate preferences across 45 countries: A large-scale replication. *Psychological Science, 31*(4), 408–423. https://doi.org/10.1177/0956797620904154

Watson, D., Beer, A., & McDade-Montez, E. (2014). The role of active assortment in spousal similarity. *Journal of Personality, 82*(2), 116–129. https://doi.org/10.1111/jopy.12039

Waynforth, D. (2001). Mate choice trade-offs and women's preference for physically attractive men. *Human Nature, 12*(3), 207–219. https://doi.org/10.1007/s12110-001-1007-9

Wood, D., & Brumbaugh, C. C. (2009). Using revealed mate preferences to evaluate market force and differential preference explanations for mate selection. *Journal of Personality and Social Psychology, 96*(6), 1226–1244. https://doi.org/10.1037/a0015300

Zentner, M., & Mitura, K. (2012). Stepping out of the caveman's shadow: Nations' gender gap predicts degree of sex differentiation in mate preferences. *Psychological Science, 23*(10), 1176–1185. https://doi.org/10.1177/0956797612441004

2

Online or in Person

How Do We Find Our Ideal Partner?

Kathryn Coduto

Initiating, developing, managing, and, in some cases, ending romantic relationships are all processes that are fundamental to being human. Humans exist because we achieve intimacy with each other, both physically and mentally. As we continue to seek and develop romantic relationships, our options for connection have continued to grow. Whereas formal courtship, involving parents and structured interactions, was the norm in a distant past, we can now connect with potential mates through online dating services, many of which are housed on our smartphones. Someone can match with a potential partner while commuting to work, waiting for an appointment, cooking a meal, and just about any other activity you can imagine.

This chapter explores the many ways individuals can connect with one another and the processes they navigate as they develop romantic relationships. We consider how aspects of mate finding have shifted with the emergence of computer-mediated communication, especially when we consider the role that attraction and potential partner visibility play in this process. We also explore how individuals shift from meeting online to meeting in person, a process that often involves numerous steps and considerations, especially related to one's safety. An important aspect of understanding these numerous processes is considering the technology used itself. We therefore interrogate the affordances of online mating options from the point of view of those who use them. We also consider the numerous challenges that finding love online still provides.

Mate Finding and Attraction: Offline Behaviors and Online Considerations

Although much work in online dating focuses on the processes that occur once individuals have swiped, matched, or sent a first message to a potential partner, it is important to consider how people first decide who to engage with in these platforms. Individuals have to identify prospective partners before they can ever send a message, much less develop a relationship. A large body of research has investigated how individuals find mates without the help of the Internet; much of this work takes on an evolutionary perspective, whereby individuals seek mates with a focus on reproduction (e.g., Buss, 1989; Buss & Schmitt, 1993). Buss (1989) argued that individuals seek specific rewards or have specific needs met by their partners. More specifically, his work has suggested that women need a mate who can help with the provision of important resources, whereas men look for mates capable of producing the healthiest offspring (Buss, 1989). Together, these ensure the survival not just of individuals and family units but also of the species as a whole.

Aspects of an individual's appearance tend to be more important for men evaluating women, as aspects of a woman's physical appearance can indicate the potential health of her children (Buss, 1989; Schmitt, 2008). For women, attraction is more likely (in this perspective) to be based on a man's resources that would be available to her in raising a child. The evolutionary perspective also suggests that individuals may shift between a variety of mating strategies depending on what they are looking for; there are those who seek short-term mates and long-term mates (Buss & Schmitt, 1993), and attraction may vary based on these requirements (see Schmitt, 2008, for a full discussion).

Yet the evolutionary perspective provides only one view of attraction in developing romantic relationships offline. The early identification of a potential partner has also been investigated through a *courtship* lens (Cunningham & Barbee, 2008), where the first step in courtship is attracting attention. Cunningham and Barbee (2008) suggest that there are numerous ways to attract attention to oneself as a person searches for a partner. Of importance in this process is the expression of nonverbal cues, such as smiling and confidence demonstrated through one's posture (Cunningham & Barbee, 2008). Other cues that may attract attention include grooming oneself (such as having one's hair done); the display of personal possessions and/or indicators of wealth; and the appearance of sexual maturity (Cunningham & Barbee,

2008). Many of these features that individuals use to determine attraction to a potential partner can also be assessed in online settings.

Who Is in the Dating Pool? The Market Metaphor in Online Dating

When an individual decides to join an online dating site or application, they become part of and are searching through a pool of potential mates. The perception of the range of dating options available to people is often explored as a *marketplace* for online dating. The idea of market conditions as applied to dating predates dating applications (Adelman & Ahuvia, 1991), but the key words of the metaphor remain apt for considering who is in the pool of potential partners.

Adelman and Ahuvia (1991) described three processes that individuals may engage in when they enter into this marketplace. The first part of the process is referred to as *searching*: The search for a mate includes identifying individuals who might be potential partners and gathering more information about them. Once individuals have identified potential partners, they then have to engage in *matching* with them. At this stage, a person will consider the information they have on their potential partners and evaluate it. It is here where someone will decide which relationships are worth pursuing and which might be better left unexplored. The next step, *interacting*, is the process of initiating the relationship. Prospective partners will be contacted in some way, and the relationship may escalate from there.

Fiore and Donath (2004) point out that online dating options therefore provide a wider pool than traditional, face-to-face dating options might—in other words, a wider market with more potential goods to select from. Not only do these online tools (in their example, online personals advertising) allow for a wider choice of potential partners, but also more information on those partners. The market metaphor was also explored by Heino et al. (2010). Their findings revealed that individuals made evaluation decisions of potential matches based on the ability to filter within websites: Certain characteristics, such as age, could be used as a tool to include or exclude people from even being seen. Thus, considering Adelman and Ahuvia's (1991) searching, individuals in the Heino et al. (2010) study could filter their searches before ever seeing any potential partner. Heino and colleagues (2010) further found that people thought of online dating as a numbers game; there are so many people in the pool, participants reasoned, that you would eventually *have* to have success and go on some kind of date. The marketplace has a large inventory from which online daters can choose and find potential mates.

A major difference between traditional dating and online dating platforms (particularly desktop-based) compared with mobile dating applications is the integration of *gamified* features. Gamification in a dating app typically includes a "swipe" feature, where individuals can swipe left to say "no" to a potential partner and right to indicate interest (Tziallas, 2015). When both individuals swipe right, they are then matched to one another and are able to have a conversation. The swipe feature specifically and gamification broadly can further impact how individuals perceive the dating pool and their options. Some individuals may swipe on everyone, wishing only to see those that are already interested in them; others may carefully peruse and consider each match before swiping right or left. Aspects of attraction can help us to understand why some people swipe the way they do.

Mate Finding Online: Profiles and Attraction

As stated, individuals have to find a potential mate before they can ever send a message or go on a date. Much of the research into mate finding focuses on the role of *attraction* between individuals. Eastwick and Finkel (2008, p. 219) explain attraction as "fundamentally a social process whereby two individuals simultaneously perceive and are perceived by one another." Cunningham and Barbee (2008, p. 101) elaborate, considering the importance of one's physical appearance in this process: "One of the primary nonverbal stimuli that capture the attention of others is physical appearance." Thus, individuals have to perceive one another and often evaluate each other on physical qualities before furthering any potential relationship.

When someone chooses to use online dating, they are able to gather an incredible amount of information about another person before ever matching with or messaging that person (e.g., Ranzini, et al., 2022). All online dating options, whether websites or mobile dating applications (apps), offer the ability to upload photos of oneself. Research has found that the inclusion of a photo is important to gaining interest from prospective matches (e.g., Carpenter & McEwan, 2016). The same judgments that might be used for evaluation in in-person meetings can translate to online impressions via one's photos (Ward, 2017). We can map many of Cunningham and Barbee's (2008) characteristics of attraction onto the profiles that individuals create in dating apps, especially when we consider the photos that they upload. These photos may include cues about one's grooming, status and wealth, and confidence—further suggesting that many of the cues that individuals look for in-person are equally applicable online.

However, there are additional cues that individuals may look for, especially in one's online dating profile. Recent research found that individuals in a mock dating app tended to prefer mates with White (or White-sounding, compared with Dutch-sounding) names (Ranzini et al., 2022). Further, those people who were highly educated (relative to the sample) looked for university names in others' profiles (Ranzini et al., 2022). Cues that might not be immediately apparent in person (such as where one went to college or the degree that they have attained) are readily provided in online dating settings. This even extends to cues including age, astrological sign, and beliefs (including both political and religious). Numerous apps provide users with the ability to display this information as embedded in one's profile, and all are cues that may be evaluated as one determines who is or is not attractive.

Relationship Escalation: From Searching and Matching to Interacting

Once a person has completed the steps of searching for potential partners and matching with those partners, they then enter into Adelman and Ahuvia's (1991) third step, interacting with them. Online daters may interact with hopes of talking for a while through the interface, communicating through social media channels, or meeting in person (McEwan, 2021; Ramirez & Zhang, 2007). The *modality switching perspective* can help us to understand what happens as individuals shift from conversing online to meeting in person (Ramirez & Zhang, 2007; Ramirez et al., 2015).

When two people have matched with each other or otherwise decided to interact, they usually start by engaging within the platform where they have matched. A couple who meets on Tinder will be able to use the app's interface to send direct messages; the same applies to those who match in Grindr, Bumble, Hinge, OkCupid, eHarmony, and so on. All online dating options are created with internal messaging readily available. These apps started with text-based options as the primary way to send communication; however, as of 2022, many of these now also allow individuals to send photos and videos in the course of a conversation.

Yet most people do not start online dating with intentions of only staying online (though some do and/or might end up having online-only relationships; Ramirez et al., 2015). Thus, individuals must determine at what point they are ready to have an in-person meeting or date. The modality switching perspective considers when individuals might meet in person with the greatest success. *Modality switching* means that individuals shift from one modality (a dating application or online dating site) to another modality (a face-to-face meeting).

In an experiment testing the timing of a switch from online conversation to in-person meeting, Ramirez et al. (2015) had individuals chat online for either two weeks, six weeks, or online only. Those in the online-only condition sent text-only messages; no video or audio was exchanged, nor did they ever meet in person. They then measured differences in aspects of the relationships including how much the partners liked each other and how happy they were with their partner upon meeting in person. Individuals at the two-week mark were generally positive about their match; at six weeks, the researchers noticed a drop in liking. They reasoned that, with six weeks of online-only contact prior to meeting in person, individuals had started to create a version of the person in their heads that the real-life person couldn't match. The people who were happiest of all? Those who stayed online only, who couldn't have their expectations of their partner violated by an in-person meeting. Everything they thought about them could stay true.

This leads us to consider some of the major concerns that individuals face when navigating a modality shift. Many people start to craft an image of their partner in their head when they meet online first; then, when they do eventually meet up, those images do not match with what they have imagined (Ramirez & Zhang, 2007). This is often considered in terms of *expectancy violations theory* (Burgoon, 1993), whereby individuals start to imagine how a partner will be and then feel differently when the partner acts in unexpected ways. In the modality switching literature, as discussed, these violations often occur when a person expects a partner to act one way and they inevitably act differently upon meeting.

Modality Weaving: Integrating Multiple Channels in Relational Escalation

An update to the modality switching perspective may offer online daters additional help in managing expectations and in determining when to meet in person. Instead of simply switching from a dating application or online dating site to an in-person meeting, individuals may include other channels in their early discussion. Thus, *modality weaving* considers the use of multiple channels in the online dating process (McEwan, 2021). It is rare that someone meets a person in a dating app and immediately meets them in person. Instead, individuals typically add additional channels to communicate, building up to an in-person meeting (Coduto & Fox, 2018). These additional channels include social media channels (such as Snapchat, Instagram, and Facebook), texting (including via SMS messaging or direct messaging via third-party apps), and video chats (including FaceTime and Skype).

Online daters report a number of reasons for modality weaving. Modality weaving in some situations allows a person to see another person for who they really are. For instance, someone who puts in their dating profile that they are an avid hiker likely posts photos from their hikes on social media like Instagram. An interested potential partner could see those photos on their Instagram and know that they are indeed an avid hiker and are not lying about this hobby (Coduto & Fox, 2018). In this way, modality weaving can act as a *verification tool* for daters who are trying to ensure that aspects of a profile, especially those they find appealing, are true.

Another key component of modality weaving is ensuring one's safety before an in-person meeting. Many online daters report that adding someone on social media channels allows them to see that they are a real person, and not someone with a fake profile. The creation of fake profiles is known as *catfishing* (Mosley et al., 2020). When a person catfishes another, they are creating an entirely fake profile, usually using someone else's images and information. Often, catfishing relationships do not move offline, as the catfisher does not wish to be caught; however, it can be dangerous when these relationships do move into the real world. Thus, individuals seek others on social media to not only verify who they are but to ensure safety upon planning for an in-person meeting (Coduto & Fox, 2018).

Online daters can also use modality weaving as a way to conduct *secret tests* with their potential partners (Baxter & Wilmot, 1984). Secret tests were originally studied in the context of ongoing relationships, as partners often information seek about the state of their relationships even once they are in them. However, secret tests can also be used in online dating to gauge a potential partner's interest in early stages of a relationship (Coduto & Fox, 2018). Secret tests might include following a potential partner on another platform to see if they follow back; watching their publicly available content, such as an Instagram story, to see if they engage or notice; or posting provocative content on platforms to see if they will engage.

Modality weaving represents an opportunity for online daters to learn more about one another as the relationship escalates; it can also provide a tool for verification of another and safety as one considers or plans an in-person meeting with a potential partner. While we have considered the stages of relationship formation when one is online, it is also important to consider the motivations for using these tools and engaging with people in this way.

Motivations for Online and Mobile Dating

Individuals have to have reasons for using online dating platforms in the first place, especially when in-person dating options (such as speed dating; Eastwick and Finkel, 2008) are still available as well. Considerable research has explored the motivations individuals have for using online dating. *Uses and gratifications theory* explicates the reasons why people choose certain media over others (Katz et al., 1973). When we consider the reasons why people choose certain media (and therefore, certain media channels) over others, we can also consider the *affordances* of those channels that encourage or support certain types of use. Taken together, certain uses and affordances of media channels can help to better understand the motivations for their use.

An *affordance* of an object is the relation an object has to the actor upon it (Fox & McEwan, 2017). The way one person uses a given object could vary drastically compared with how another uses it (Fox & McEwan, 2017). The same object can have widely different uses from person to person. The motivations individuals have for using certain channels can vary in a similar way. One individual might use social media as an information-seeking tool during breaking news; another person might use social media to relax or to avoid chores.

Research repeatedly shows that one of the top reasons that individuals use online dating is (perhaps unsurprisingly) for finding love (Kallis, 2020; LeFebvre, 2018; Sumter et al., 2017). Dating websites and apps have relational reasons at the forefront of their marketing and design; many people who download these apps or sign up on these websites do so knowing that the entire purpose of the platform is to connect them romantically with others (Sumter et al., 2017). Because people can see the wide dating pool available to them and evaluate those whom they wish to connect with, especially while considering their relational goals, dating apps are most often used for seeking a romantic relationship.

Seeking a long-term romantic relationship is a common reason for using dating apps and sites, yet other reasons also exist. Within popular culture, dating apps have been assumed to be designed and used for casual sex (Sales, 2015). Research bears this out as well. Casual sex, or *hookups*, are indeed another top reason individuals cite for using dating apps (LeFebvre, 2018; Sevi et al., 2018). Individuals who are interested in hookups may be looking for a one-night stand, where they have sexual intercourse with another person one time and never see them again; they may also be looking for someone to regularly have sex with but never elevate the relationship beyond the act of sex (Sevi et al., 2018). In some situations, such as during lockdowns due to the COVID-19 pandemic, individuals sought casual hookups that stayed online only; individuals matched with and sexted with others without ever meeting in-person (Vendemia & Coduto, 2022). *Sexting* involves sending sexually explicit messages to another person via mediated channels, including dating apps and sites (Vendemia & Coduto, 2022).

Dating sites and apps are used for casual sex in part because of their affordances. A key aspect of these online options is their *locatability* or *geotargeted locations* (Blackwell et al., 2015). A dating app user can restrict their location to see only those close to them physically; this enables easy access to hookup partners. Further, the gamification aspect allows users to match with those who have similar interests, such as hooking up compared with a long-term relationship (Tziallas, 2015; Vendemia & Coduto, 2022). Individuals interested in longer-term romantic relationships may cast a wider net in their search for love, with the belief that a meaningful relationship takes time (Coduto & Fox, 2018). Thus, the affordance of locatability may be less immediately important to those looking for love compared with hookups.

While love and sex are the top reasons for using dating apps and sites, other motivations exist. Some individuals use these platforms in the search for friendship (Kallis, 2020; Sumter et al., 2017). This may be especially true when a person moves to a new city and is trying to make connections beyond their professional or familial network (Vendemia & Coduto, 2022). The affordance of locatability can aid individuals in this quest. *Network association*, the ability to see people in others' social networks, can also be useful in this motivation (Fox & McEwan, 2017). Network association is commonly seen through friends of friends on social networking sites. If you are friends with someone on Facebook, their other friends can see your friendship. You become a *potential* part of those friends' network; they could add you on Facebook or otherwise reach out to you. Some dating apps and sites will show you friends that you have in common with a potential match (if you connect your Facebook account, for instance). This can help in the facilitation of introductions—and it can also assist in verification of another individual, as discussed previously.

One other common motivation individuals cite for using dating apps and sites is for *entertainment* or to *pass the time* (Kallis, 2020; Sumter et al., 2017). Many people download dating apps with no real intention to meet someone, at least not right away. Instead, these individuals may use the platforms available to them to pass the time, swiping to see who is out there but unsure if they will ever act on the knowledge. Many individuals will try to find friends who are using the platforms or make games out of swiping with friends (Coduto & Fox, 2018). All of the affordances previously discussed—*gamification*, *locatability*, and *network association*—can be at work when individuals engage in this way.

Affordances for Messaging

There are other affordances worth considering when thinking about how individuals use dating apps and sites. While the previously mentioned affordances can be especially helpful as individuals determine what they are looking for when using an app or site, other affordances are useful once individuals decide to message another person. Two key affordances for messaging are *editability* and *asynchrony* (Fox & McEwan, 2017).

Dating sites and apps, as mentioned, support messaging within the platform. These platforms afford *editability*, which means that an individual can edit a message before sending it (Fox & McEwan, 2017). The first person to send a message has to think about what the opening line will be—what will be the first thing they say to this new potential partner (similar to in-person opening lines; Cunningham & Barbee, 2008). Editability means that a person can type a message as a draft, backspace to edit out any words, and rewrite the opening line, all before sending it to the prospective new partner. Editability can also apply to someone's profile. Once a person writes their online dating profile, they can go back and change it later, whether by adding new photos or new information.

Along with editability, which requires time on the part of the writer, is *asynchrony* (Fox & McEwan, 2017). *Asynchrony* refers to how quickly a person does or does not respond to another. Some individuals expect to receive messages from their new matches right away, which would be more synchronous messaging; others expect delays between messages, which would be asynchronous messaging (Coduto & Fox, 2018). Dating sites and apps afford asynchrony; no one engaging in these apps *has* to message another person right away. They have time to edit their messages; they can also manipulate time so as not to seem too eager in the early stages of the relationship. There is a careful balance, though, as partners who wait too long for a response or an initial message may lose interest in the relationship (or its potential) before messages are ever sent.

An Ideal Partner? Investigating the Hyperpersonal Model and Online Dating

There are steps to the online dating process: searching, matching, and interacting. Individuals have to be attracted to one another and must evaluate a number of profiles before reaching out to someone. People who use online dating have a number of motivations for why they use these platforms, ranging from seeking serious relationships to casual sex. Many aspects of the platforms can support them in their search for these desires.

But we haven't yet answered the question of how one finds an *ideal* partner in an online setting—if they can. Individuals have been able to use computers to meet one another since the technology's earliest inceptions; though online dating did not become a true option until the early 1990s (Adelman & Ahuvia, 1991; Whitty, 2008), people using computers could access online forums to communicate with others both near and far. These text-based forms of computer-mediated communication (CMC) led to the development of *social information processing theory* (SIPT; Walther, 1994). This theory suggests that, despite the limitations of the online context (such as the lack of nonverbal cues like eye contact or head nodding), individuals can still develop relationships online. SIPT argues that these processes may be slower as a result of the limited cues, but it is still possible to find love (among other types of relationships, such as friendships) online.

As studies of SIPT progressed, the authors started noticing that, in some cases, people were having *better* relationships online compared with similar groups who were meeting in person, face to face. Perhaps, they reasoned, SIPT was only one part of the story for individuals who met online. In some situations, people could have better relationships that were online first or online only. This insight led to the development of the *hyperpersonal model* (Walther, 1996).

The hyperpersonal model posits that individuals who meet online first can come to idealize each other through aspects of the sender, receiver, and channel (Walther, 1996). Specifically, a sender can engage in *selective self-presentation*, presenting themselves in such a way as to be highly desirable to a receiver (Walther, 2007). In online dating, a person's profile allows for this kind of self-presentation (Ward, 2017). A person can choose their best photos featuring their most attractive qualities. The profile can also include a biography with whatever information the writer chooses; this may include hints at wealth (similar to what we see in traditional mating; Schmitt, 2008) or educational attainment (Ranzini & Rosenbaum, 2020). Thus, a receiver (a potential partner) can evaluate a sender (the profile the person made) and make inferences about them without ever meeting them.

The hyperpersonal model further argues that receivers interpret these cues in highly positive ways, leading to *idealization* (Coduto et al., 2022; Walther, 1996). Idealization occurs when a receiver starts to experience overly positive illusions about the sender. Although this may start because of the contents of a profile, a sender can also take advantage of editability and asynchrony to craft especially enticing or endearing messages that further support the selectively presented image of themselves. Aspects of the chosen channel can further perpetuate these feelings, as the channel may support the sending and receiving of photos or videos; voice messages; and links to other social media platforms. Taken together, a receiver may feel they have found an ideal partner through these online interactions—yet these interactions are fundamentally cognitions about another person, not based on the real-life meetings one could have.

Thus, though the hyperpersonal model posits that individuals who meet online can have overly positive interactions, these interactions may fall apart when individuals meet in-person—as proposed in the modality switching literature (Ramirez et al., 2015; Sharabi & Caughlin, 2017). As previously discussed, individuals who met online and spent six weeks chatting before meeting were disappointed when they met in person (Ramirez et al., 2015). This is likely because they were experiencing hyperpersonal effects—they had started to idealize one another when online, and upon meeting, those idealized expectations couldn't be met.

SIPT and the hyperpersonal model are encouraging for individuals who date online. The theories together suggest that relationships can start and flourish online. However, they also come with precautions: A partner who appears perfect online may not be ideal upon meeting in real life. Online dating, like any form of dating, has its limitations.

Concerns About Online Dating

Though online dating has become a common practice among adults of all ages and is no longer considered a "new" technology, there are still numerous concerns that individuals have about utilizing the technology in their search for a variety of relationships. It is worth considering some of those concerns here.

When individuals engage in online dating, there is uncertainty permeating the experience (Gibbs, et al., 2011). In the most extreme cases, online daters may be concerned about being catfished or lied to by potential partners. Lies could range from being misleading about one's appearance to falsifying one's marital or work status (Gibbs et al., 2011). Thus, many people who use online dating platforms use information-seeking strategies to reduce their uncertainty about their potential partner. This might include Googling them, asking friends (or friends of friends) about the person, and verifying they work and live where they say they do (Gibbs et al., 2011).

Online dating also often leads to people favoring similar others, typically along racial lines (Ranzini & Rosenbaum, 2020; Ranzini et al., 2022). Although dating sites and apps can show a larger dating pool than people might have otherwise had access to, people still tend to gravitate toward those who look like them, have similar educational experiences as them, and come from similar financial backgrounds. Thus, an ongoing concern about online dating is that it ends up further compounding racial difference and not supporting the search for a wider variety of partners.

Dating sites and, perhaps most especially, apps can lead to compulsive use of the technology (Coduto et al., 2020). Individuals may be so determined to find a relationship that they constantly login to a site or app, check it, and evaluate potential partners—engaging almost mindlessly. Research has shown that this compulsive use can displace other important activities, including performing at work or school (Coduto et al., 2020). This is particularly true for individuals who suffer from social anxiety, as they may turn to the Internet as a safer space for making connections compared with in-person activities (Coduto et al., 2020). Online daters need to be mindful of the consequences of overuse of the technology, especially when they consider what their goals are.

A major limitation of research into dating sites and apps, and therefore our understanding of these processes, is that much of this work focuses on a gender binary. The work in evolutionary psychology as discussed subscribes to gender essentialism—the belief that individuals are inherently male/masculine or female/feminine (i.e., Skewes, et al., 2018). This leaves little room for understanding the role of transgender and nonbinary individuals in the existing literature, much less in the practice of online dating. A growing body of research has investigated gay men's experiences with apps such as Grindr (Blackwell et al., 2015), but there is still much to learn concerning how those with marginalized identities use online dating and what their outcomes are.

A similar consideration about the online dating literature is a lack of understanding of the field's options broadly. Many studies, including those cited here, tend to focus on specific platforms. Work on dating apps often focuses exclusively on Tinder, in part because it was the first major dating app to gain popularity (though Grindr, made specifically for gay men, came before; Blackwell et al., 2015). Although Tinder is popular and has many users, numerous other apps are available, including Hinge, Bumble, Coffee Meets Bagel, Her, The League, and more. Many of these target specific audiences and may tie more explicitly to certain motivations compared with others. It will be important for future research to broaden the scope of work to understand the different ways these technologies are used and to what end.

Conclusion

Individuals who choose to online date engage in a process of searching, matching, and interacting as they determine which potential partners from their dating pool could be a good match for them. As they engage in the process, they consider the attractiveness of their potential partner, perhaps coming to idealize them as they plan for in-person meetings. Yet individuals may not just be motivated by the search for a romantic relationship; people choose to online date for numerous reasons, including finding casual sex and friendships. There is still a considerable amount of work left to be done in online dating, a field that is only going to grow as the technology shifts from new to established in everyday use.

References

Adelman, M. B., & Ahuvia, A. C. (1991). Mediated channels for mate seeking: A solution to involuntary singlehood? *Critical Studies in Media Communication, 8*(3), 273–289. https://doi.org/10.1080/15295039109366798

Baxter, L. A., & Wilmot, W. W. (1984). Secret tests: Social strategies for acquiring information about the state of the relationship. *Human Communication Research, 11*(2), 171–201. https://doi.org/10.1111/j.1468-2958.1984.tb00044.x

Blackwell, C., Birnholtz, J., & Abbott, C. (2015). Seeing and being seen: Co-situation and impression formation using Grindr, a location-aware gay dating app. *New Media and Society, 17*, 1117–1136. https://doi.org/10.1177/1461444814521595

Burgoon, J. K. (1993). Interpersonal expectations, expectancy violations, and emotional communication. *Journal of Language and Social Psychology, 12*(1-2), 30–48. https://doi.org/10.1177/0261927X93121003

Buss, D. M. (1989). Sex differences in human mate preferences: Evolutionary hypotheses tested in 37 cultures. *Behavioral and Brain Sciences, 12*(1), 1–49. https://doi.org/10.1017/S0140525X00023992

Buss, D. M., & Schmitt, D. P. (1993). Sexual strategies theory: An evolutionary perspective on human mating. *Psychological Review, 100*(2), 204–232. https://doi.org/10.1037/0033-295X.100.2.204

Coduto, K. D., & Fox, J. (2018, November). *Relationship escalation from dating apps to IRL: Affordances, modality switching, and paradoxical beliefs* [Paper presentation]. Annual meeting of the National Communication Association, Salt Lake City, UT, United States.

Coduto, K. D., Lee-Won, R. J., & Baek, Y. M. (2020). Swiping for trouble: Problematic dating application use among psychosocially distraught individuals and the paths to negative outcomes. *Journal of Social and Personal Relationships, 37*(1), 212–232. https://doi.org/10.1177/0265407519861153

Coduto, K. D., Vendemia, M. A., Viverette, S., & Williams, E. (2022). Exploring sexual, romantic, and platonic features and functions of the imagined interactions framework. *Imagination, Cognition and Personality, 42*(1), 24–41. https://doi.org/10.1177/02762366221089279

Cunningham, M. R., & Barbee, A. P. (2008). Prelude to a kiss: Nonverbal flirting, opening gambits, and other communication dynamics in the initiation of romantic relationships. In S. Sprecher, A. Wenzel, & J. Harvey (Eds.), *Handbook of relationship initiation* (pp. 97–120). Psychology Press.

Eastwick, P. W., & Finkel, E. J. (2008). Speed-dating: A powerful and flexible paradigm for studying romantic relationship initiation. In S. Sprecher et al. (Eds.), *Handbook of relationship initiation* (pp. 217–234).

Fiore, A. T., & Donath, J. S. (2004, April 24–29). *Online personals: An overview* [Paper presentation]. Association for Computing Machinery, Conference on Computer-Human Interaction, Vienna, Austria.

Fox, J., & McEwan, B. (2017). Distinguishing technologies for social interaction: The perceived social affordances of communication channels scale. *Communication Monographs, 84*(3), 298–318. https://doi.org/10.1080/03637751.2017.1332418

Gibbs, J. L., Ellison, N. B., & Lai, C.-H. (2011). First comes love, then comes Google: An investigation of uncertainty reduction strategies and self-disclosure in online dating. *Communication Research, 38* (1), 70–100. https://doi.org/10.1177/0093650210377091

Heino, R. D., Ellison, N. B., & Gibbs, J. L. (2010). Relationshopping: Investigating the market metaphor of online dating. *Journal of Social and Personal Relationships, 27*(4), 427–447. https://doi.org/10.1177/0265407510361614

Kallis, R. B. (2020). Understanding the motivations for using Tinder. *Qualitative Research Reports in Communication, 21*(1), 66–73. https://doi.org/10.1080/17459435.2020.1744697

Katz, E., Blumler, J. G., & Gurevitch, M. (1973). Uses and gratifications research. *The Public Opinion Quarterly, 37*(4), 509–523. https://www.jstor.org/stable/2747854

LeFebvre, L. E. (2018). Swiping me off my feet: Explicating relationship initiation on Tinder. *Journal of Social and Personal Relationships, 35*(9), 1205–1229. https://doi.org/10.1177/0265407517706419

McEwan, B. (2021). Modality switching to modality weaving: Updating theoretical perspectives for expanding media affordances. *Annals of the International Communication Association, 45*(1), 1–19. https://doi.org/10.1080/23808985.2021.1880958

Mosley, M. A., Lancaster, M., Parker, M. L., & Campbell, K. (2020). Adult attachment and online dating deception: A theory modernized. *Sexual and Relationship Therapy, 35*(2), 227–243. https://doi.org/10.1080/14681994.2020.1714577

Ramirez, A., Sumner, E. M., Fleuriet, C., & Cole, M. (2015). When online dating partners meet offline: The effect of modality switching on relational communication between online daters. *Journal of Computer-Mediated Communication, 20*(1), 99–114. https://doi.org/10.1111/jcc4.12101

Ramirez, A., & Zhang, S. (2007). When online meets offline: The effect of modality switching on relational communication. *Communication Monographs, 74*(3), 287–310. https://doi.org/10.1080/03637750701543493

Ranzini, G., & Rosenbaum, J. E. (2020). It's a match (?): Tinder usage and attitudes toward interracial dating. *Communication Research Reports, 37*(1–2), 44–54. https://doi.org/10.1080/08824096.2020.1748001

Ranzini, G., Rosenbaum, J. E., & Tybur, J. M. (2022). Assortative (online) dating: Insights into partner choice from an experimental dating app. *Computers in Human Behavior, 127*, Article 10739. https://doi.org/10.1016/j.chb.2021.107039

Sales, N. J. (2015, August 6). Tinder and the dawn of the "dating apocalypse." *Vanity Fair.* https://www.vanityfair.com/culture/2015/08/tinder-hook-up-culture-end-of-dating

Schmitt, D. P. (2008). An evolutionary perspective on mate choice and relationship initiation. In S. Sprecher, A. Wenzel, & J. Harvey (Eds.), *Handbook of relationship initiation* (pp. 55–74). Psychology Press.

Sevi, B., Aral, T., & Eskenazi, T. (2018). Exploring the hook-up app: Low sexual disgust and high sociosexuality predict motivation to use Tinder for casual sex. *Personality and Individual Differences, 133*, 17–20. https://doi.org/10.1016/j.paid.2017.04.053

Sharabi, L. L., & Caughlin, J. P. (2017). What predicts first date success? A longitudinal study of modality switching in online dating. *Personal Relationships, 24*(2), 370–391. https://doi.org/10.1111/pere.12188

Skewes, L., Fine, C., & Haslam, N. (2018). Beyond Mars and Venus: The role of gender essentialism in support for gender inequality and backlash. *PLoS ONE, 13*(7), Article e020092. https://doi.org/10.1371/journal.pone.0200921

Sumter, S. R., Vandenbosch, L., & Ligtenberg, L. (2017). Love me Tinder: Untangling emerging adults' motivations for using the dating application Tinder. *Telematics and Informatics, 34*, 67–78. https://doi.org/10.1016/j.tele.2016.04.009

Tziallas E. (2015). Gamified eroticism: Gay male "social networking" applications and self-pornography. *Sexuality and Culture, 19*, 759–775. https://doi.org/10.1007/s12119-015-9288-z

Vendemia, M. A., & Coduto, K. D. (2022). Online daters' sexually explicit media consumption and imagined interactions. *Computers in Human Behavior, 126*, Article 106981. 106981.https://doi.org/10.1016/j.chb.2021.106981

Walther, J. B. (1994). Anticipated ongoing interaction versus channel effects on relational communication in computer-mediated interaction. *Human Communication Research, 20*(4), 473–501. https://psycnet.apa.org/doi/10.1111/j.1468-2958.1994.tb00332.x

Walther, J. B. (1996). Computer-mediated communication: Impersonal, interpersonal, and hyperpersonal interaction. *Communication Research, 23*(3), 3–43. https://doi.org/10.1177/009365096023001001

Walther, J. B. (2007). Selective self-presentation in computer-mediated communication: Hyperpersonal dimensions of technology, language, and cognition. *Computers in Human Behavior, 23*(5), 2538–2557. https://doi.org/10.1016/j.chb.2006.05.002

Ward J. (2017). What are you doing on Tinder? Impression management on a matchmaking mobile app. *Information, Communication and Society, 11*, 1644–1659. https://doi.org/10.1080/1369118X.2016.1252412

Whitty, M. T. (2008). Revealing the "real" me, searching for the "actual" you: Presentations of self on an internet dating site. *Computers in Human Behavior, 24*(4), 1707–1723. https://psycnet.apa.org/doi/10.1016/j.chb.2007.07.002

3

Cohabitation Versus Marriage

Understanding Young Adults' Preference for Cohabitation

Sharon Sassler

For many young Americans, marriage has become ever more volitional. Only about half of American adults are currently married, although larger proportions have ever been wed (Sassler & Lichter, 2020). As recently as the 1970s, marriage was nearly universal; about 90% of American adults ever married (Raley et al., 2015). By the closing decades of the 20th century the primacy of marriage had weakened. Demographers now estimate that among young adults coming of age today, substantial proportions of Americans—upward of a quarter, with a large gap between Whites and Blacks—will never marry (Bloome & Ang, 2020). While there is some evidence that divorce rates have stabilized, many marriages end in divorce, and remarriage rates have also declined (Smock & Schwartz, 2020; Sweeney & Raley, 2020). Attitudes toward marriage have become far more jaundiced. In fact, a sizable share of American adults believe that the institution of marriage is becoming obsolete (Pew, 2010). Many young people assert that marriage doesn't change much—that the marriage certificate is "just a piece of paper" (Miller et al., 2011).

Yet contemporary adults remain interested in forming intimate partnerships. Cohabitation—living with a partner in a romantic and sexual relationship without being married—has replaced marriage as the first intimate coresidential union for the majority of American young adults in the 21st century. If current patterns continue, most American young adults will cohabit with a partner prior to marrying them. Many young adults express the belief that living with a partner will help them "divorce proof" their marriages (Manning et al., 2007; Miller et al., 2011). But while cohabitation has become normative for American adults in the 21st century, the majority of cohabitations formed in the 21st century do not progress into marriages.

Cohabitation's role has changed over time. Whereas it once served as a precursor or stepping stone to marriage, it currently initially is utilized more as an alternative to dating (Sassler & Miller, 2023).

Support for cohabitation has increased among many groups, including teenagers (Manning et al., 2007). Yet most young adults still express a desire to get married, although often in the distant future (Manning et al., 2019). Marriage remains the dominant ideal for most, a "capstone" of reaching adulthood (Cherlin, 2004), even as the primacy of marriage is increasingly challenged (Sassler & Miller, 2023). The following sections explore the role that cohabitation has come to play in the union formation patterns of contemporary young Americans. Like many family forms, cohabitation is not a static arrangement. We conclude by contemplating whether the research shows that young people prefer cohabitation over marriage, or whether existing structural factors shape the prevalence of cohabitation. For brevity's sake, this review focuses on marriage and cohabitation among heterosexual-identifying young adults in the United States. The meaning of cohabitation differs in substantive ways in other countries (see Sassler & Lichter, 2020).

Young Adults' Retreat From Marriage

Over the past five decades, young adults' family behaviors have changed in important ways. For many young people it has become increasingly difficult to attain the prerequisites often deemed necessary for marriage: completing schooling, having a stable job, paying down debts, and buying a home (Gibson-Davis et al., 2018; Smock et al., 2005). As meeting the economic bar to marriage has risen, so has the age at marriage. In 2021, the estimated median age at first marriage, the age at which half of adults are wed, reached 30.4 for men and 28.6 for women (U.S. Census Bureau, 2021). As a result, the share of American adults under the age of 35 who are married has declined precipitously. In 2018, only 29% of Americans between the ages of 18 and 34 were married (U.S. Census Bureau, 2018).

This retreat from marriage matters because in our society marriage is a privileged institution. Marriage provides numerous benefits not attainable to those who are cohabiting (Cherlin, 2004). It is therefore concerning that there are stark racial and ethnic disparities in the shares who are married. In 2020, only 33% and 27% of White men and women aged 15 and older were never married, compared with 46% and 38% of Hispanic men and women, and 51% and 48% of Black men and women (U.S. Census Bureau, 2021; see also Bloome & Ange, 2020; Raley et al., 2015). Such disparities contribute to high levels of inequality in the United States, even though historical legacies of racist policies have prevented Blacks and Hispanics from experiencing the returns to marriage that Whites have (Addo & Lichter, 2013).

Those holding positive views of marriage in young adulthood are more likely to wed (Carlson, 2015; Sassler & Schoen, 1999). But the shares who express the belief that they will not marry have become larger. Nationally representative surveys of never-married adults finds that a desire to remain unmarried remains rare; only 13% of never-married adults surveyed by the Pew Research Center in 2014 reported that they did not want to get married (Wang & Parker, 2014). But demographers project that the proportion who will remain never married will increase (Bloome & Ang, 2020). That is reflected in millennials' beliefs about their likelihood of getting married. Over a fifth (21%) of youth (aged 13–19) surveyed in the mid-1990s felt that they had almost no chance or only some chance of being married by age 25 (which was women's median age at marriage at the time they were interviewed). Non-Hispanic Black adolescents were far more likely to hold negative views of their marriage prospects than were non-Hispanic Whites, Asians, or Hispanics (Zhang & Sassler, 2022). Although it was not possible to ascertain whether such views reflected a lack of desire for marriage or the belief that marriage was unattainable, an even larger proportion of those respondents remained unmarried in 2018, when they were in their mid-30s to early 40s. Those who as adolescents did not anticipate being married were significantly less likely to be wed in adulthood.

In essence, there has been large-scale marital delay among those coming of age in the 21st century. First marriages are taking place at older ages, as young adults view economic stability as a necessary prerequisite for marriage, and attainment of markers of "a good fortune" more difficult to attain (Gibson-Davis et al., 2018; Sassler & Goldscheider, 2004; Smock et al., 2005). Although marriage remains a cultural ideal for most young Americans, a substantial proportion have begun to question the necessity of marriage for their own well-being or doubt whether they can ever attain what is deemed necessary to become a desired commodity in the marriage market. It is not surprising, then, that a "marriage-like" alternative—cohabitation—has increased both in prevalence and acceptance over the past few decades. Is this, then, simply an acknowledgment that marriage is increasingly unattainable for many young Americans? Or is the increasing proportion of young

Americans who live with partners outside of the legal strictures of marriage evidence that the institution of marriage has been fatally weakened? Is cohabitation now preferred over marriage, or is it simply an acceptable, if less desired, compromise? To assess these alternatives requires a review of how living together has changed over the past few decades, and where it appears to be heading as we move into the second quarter of the 21st century.

Cohabitation in the 21st Century

Cohabitation has, ostensibly, filled the marriage void. The average age at which adults form their first coresidential union has not changed much over the past few decades (Manning et al., 2014). Growing shares of young adults endorse the logic of living with a partner (Allred, 2019; Manning et al., 2019), although a substantial minority remain hesitant about cohabitation.

Monitoring the Future, also known as the National High School Senior Survey, has been asking teenagers nationwide about their views of cohabitation since 1976 (National Institute on Drug Abuse, 2022). Students are asked the extent to which they agree or disagree with the statement "It is usually a good idea for a couple to live together before getting married in order to find out whether they really get along." In 1976–1977 about a third (33%) of female high school seniors agreed that living together was a good idea. But approval of cohabitation increased significantly throughout the 1980s and into the 1990s. By the late 1990s, 59.1% of female high school seniors thought cohabitation before getting married was a good idea. An even larger shares of male high school seniors, just over two-thirds, agreed with living with a partner prior to marriage. Teenagers' acceptance of cohabitation as a way to assess compatibility increased even more in the 21st century, particularly among women, although gender differences remain. As of 2017, three out of four male high school seniors approved of premarital cohabitation as a means of assessing compatibility for marriage, compared with 69% of female high school seniors (Allred, 2019).

But support for cohabitation is not universal among all young Americans. Racial and ethnic minorities are less supportive of cohabitation than non-Hispanic Whites, perhaps due to their greater religiosity. In fact, while cohabitation has increased in prevalence among all racial and ethnic groups in the United States, the shares cohabiting have grown more among Whites and Latinx young adults than among Blacks (Manning et al., 2014). Black young adults also take longer to enter into cohabiting unions than their Hispanic or White counterparts (Addo, 2012; Sassler et al., 2018). Cohabitation among minority young adults may also be driven by conception and a focus on shared childrearing rather than as a precursor to marriage (Hummer & Hamilton, 2010; Reed 2006), though early cohabitation may also precipitate conception, as unintended pregnancy rates are particularly high among younger cohabiting women (Sassler & Miller, 2014). Yet even religious young adults view cohabitation as a way to reach economic goals prior to marriage (Harris, 2021). Full-throated endorsement of cohabitation is not necessary; many cohabiters feel like they lack other options (Harris, 2021; Sassler & Miller, 2017).

Attitudes toward cohabitation have changed more than expectations for marriage. But while cohabitation has become far more acceptable, marriage remains the ultimate goal for most, even if it is an ideal or "capstone" (Cherlin, 2004; Sassler & Miller, 2023). One recent study focusing on single (unmarried and not cohabiting) female respondents aged 18–24 found that while the overwhelming majority (93.5%) expected to marry, only 54.7% expected to cohabit prior to marriage. The authors concluded that "expectations to marry surpass expectations to cohabit" (Manning et al., 2019, p. 335). Even though many young people expect to live with their partners prior to marriage, a sizable share do *not* plan on cohabiting before the wedding. Furthermore, despite the rising prevalence of cohabitation, it remains incompletely institutionalized in the courtship process (Cherlin, 2004; Sassler & Miller, 2023), and, as we discuss below, does not inevitably lead to marriage. It has therefore not (yet) become a clear stage of the courtship process with well-established norms regarding its timing, progression, or rituals of acknowledgment (e.g., anniversaries).

Increasing Prevalence of Cohabitation, Declining Transitions Into Marriage

Cohabitation has become more prevalent as a living arrangement over the past five decades. The number of different-sex cohabiting couples increased from 1.6 million in 1970 to 8.5 million in 2018 (U.S. Census Bureau, 2018). Most of this growth was driven by changes in the living arrangements of young adults (those under age 35), who account for the majority of cohabiters (Stepler, 2017). In recent years, roughly three-fourths of all young adults in their early 30s have ever cohabited. Among women ages 25–29, for example, 73% had ever lived with a partner (Smock & Schwartz, 2020), a considerably larger share than those who had ever married. Although smaller proportions of emerging adults, those aged 18–24, have ever lived with a partner, more are currently cohabiting than married. Cohabitation has supplanted marriage as the first intimate coresidential union.

Although cohabitation has become relatively normative, there remain important differences by education level in the proportions who have ever cohabited. The highly educated, those who have a college degree or more, are less likely to have ever cohabited than those with less than a college degree, though these disparities have narrowed in the 21st century (Manning, 2020; Sassler & Miller, 2017; Smock & Schwartz, 2020). The likelihood that even the most educationally advantaged will live with a partner as their first coresidential intimate union has increased, as acceptance of cohabitation has diffused broadly across the population at large. Yet the college educated remain substantially less likely to have ever cohabited, as Figure 3.1 highlights. Researchers exploring cohabitation in the closing decades of the 20th century asked if the highly educated had been trendsetters in living with a partner outside of marriage and concluded that college graduates had

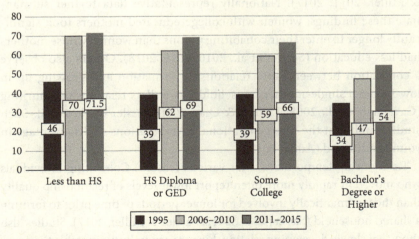

Figure 3.1 Percentage of Women Aged 22–44 Whose First Union was a Cohabitation, by Educational Attainment.

Source: National Health Statistics reports, No. 64 (2013) for 1995, 2006–2010; author estimates for 2011–2015 from the National Survey of Family Growth data. Note that the unit of analysis is women aged 22 and older, to enable them to complete a college degree (though some may complete their schooling beyond age 22). Copen, Daniels, & Mosher, 2013.

been the imitators, rather than the innovators, in rising levels of cohabitation (Bumpass et al., 1991). They remain laggards even in the 21st century.

In addition to being more likely to cohabit, the less educated enter cohabiting unions at younger ages than do college graduates. By age 25, almost two-thirds of women who had obtained a high school diploma (or GED) but no more schooling (64%) had ever cohabited, compared with only 36% of women who had obtained a college degree (Copen et al., 2013). Whether the pursuit of a college degree deters cohabitation, or those who enter cohabiting unions while pursuing advanced education then become less likely to complete their degree, is a causal question. Cohabitation at young ages can affect subsequent well-being, if it prematurely forecloses the pursuit of human capital, as early marriage did in previous generations, and exposes young adults to additional risks such as unintended pregnancy or intimate partner violence.

Both qualitative and quantitative research also reveal that the tempo of entering into cohabiting unions differs by social class. Qualitative research that explored the relationship progression of cohabiters in various cities has found that those with less education often move in with a partner within a few months, whereas the college educated generally have dated for about a year before moving in together (Sassler, 2004; Sassler & Miller, 2011, 2017). Nationally representative data further substantiate these findings; women with college-educated mothers took significantly longer to enter their cohabiting unions than women whose mothers had less education (Sassler et al., 2010, 2016, 2018). Others also observe a correlation between rapid relationship formation and growing up in low-income, single-mother households, as well as relationship churning (Cavanagh et al., 2008; Lichter & Qian 2008; Sassler et al., 2016). Such studies highlight the intergenerational reverberations of disadvantage in young adulthood (Addo, 2012).

Relationship tempo matters for various reasons. Cohabiting individuals who moved in rapidly more often report lower levels of relationship quality than those romantically involved for longer periods of time prior to forming a shared household (Sassler et al., 2012; Sassler & Miller, 2017). Studies also show that slowly developing relationships are generally more stable than rapidly formed ones. Changes in commitment driven by relationship intensification take time, whereas event-driven relationships, such as those precipitated by a need for housing or job loss, progress due to attributes well known to be challenging for relationship stability (Cate & Lloyd, 1988; Surra et al., 1988).

Just as rapid transitions into marriage during World War II resulted in a subsequent jump in divorce following the war (Coontz, 2006), rapidly formed cohabiting unions may also founder and disrupt. Documenting relationship churning, however, is challenging given the omission of data collection on the dissolution of cohabiting unions and, in recent years, of marriages (Kennedy & Ruggles, 2014).

Serial cohabitation—living with multiple cohabiting partners—has also increased as more individuals cohabit (Eickmeyer & Manning, 2018; Lichter et al., 2010; Lichter & Qian, 2008). By the early years of the 21st century, a quarter of cohabiters had lived with more than one partner (Lichter et al., 2010), and by 2010 over a third of cohabiters had coresided with two (or more) partners (Vespa, 2014). Serial cohabiters are disproportionately drawn from less advantaged populations—those with low levels of educational attainment, teen parents, or those from resource-poor families (Eickmeyer & Manning, 2018; Lichter et al., 2010; Vespa, 2014). They are also more likely to be parents than those who have only lived with one partner (Lichter et al., 2010; Parker, et al., 2020). Furthermore, serial cohabitation contributes to the general racial gap in cohabitation, as it is more prevalent among non-Hispanic White women than among Black or Hispanic women (Eickmeyer & Manning, 2018).

Finally, as cohabitation has become more prevalent, the outcomes associated with shared living have changed. At the population level, cohabitation has become a precursor to marriage; most marital unions are preceded by living together. But at the individual level, the share of cohabiting unions that results in marriage has declined (Kennedy & Bumpass, 2008; Lichter et al., 2006; Manning, 2020). Whereas the majority (about 60%) of those who formed a cohabiting union in the late 1980s went on to marry their first partner, in each subsequent decade this proportion has declined. Guzzo (2014) found that those forming cohabiting unions in the 1990s were less likely to marry that partner than those who cohabited in the 1980s, but they were more likely to marry their partners than those who began cohabiting in the new millennium. In the early 21st century, researchers found that only 40.3% of women aged 15–44 who were in their first cohabiting union married their partner within three years of moving in together (Copen et al., 2013). More recent estimates suggest that this transition rate has dropped even more; among women forming their first cohabiting union between 2006 and 2013, only 22% married their first partner within five years (Lamidi et al., 2019).

The Changing Meaning of Cohabitation

Changes in the prevalence, attitudes toward, and outcomes of cohabitation are evident. Looked at as a whole, these shifts suggest that the *process* of relationship progression, and the role that cohabitation serves in that sequence, has changed over time. There are notable social class differences in how relationships unfold and progress. The demographic evidence also suggests heterogeneity in how racial and ethnic minorities experience relationship advancement. Over the past few decades, an ever-growing body of literature has examined how cohabitation "fits" in the constellation of family forms (Casper & Sayer, 2002; Parker, 2021; Rindfuss & VandenHeuvel, 1990; Sassler & Miller, 2023). Much of the early quantitative research on cohabitation conceptualized living together as a *precursor to marriage.* That might be because the majority of cohabiters studied in the 1980s and early 1990s expressed intentions to marry and did so (Bumpass et al., 1991). Casper and Sayer (2002) reported that nearly half of cohabiters reported definite plans to marry their partners, high levels of satisfaction with their cohabiting relationship, and commitment to their current partner—which they viewed as clear indications that these unions were precursors to marriage. They differentiated these couples from those who utilized cohabitation as a *trial for marriage*, who hoped to marry someone someday but were unsure that their current partner was "the one"—about 15% of cohabiters in their sample. The belief that living together is a good way to "try out" a relationship to determine its marriage worthiness has only strengthened over time (Manning et al., 2007; Miller et al., 2011). Yet recent studies suggest that fewer cohabiters initially begin their cohabiting unions as an explicit precursor to marriage (Parker, 2021). Those who do are disproportionately drawn from religious or more advantaged groups (Harris, 2021; Parker, 2021). Cohabiters who described their relationships as *alternatives to marriage* were rare among the cohabiters in the Casper and Sayer (2002) study, accounting for about 1 in 10 cohabiters; more recent studies indicate that they continue to be rare into the 21st century (Sassler & Miller, 2017).

In fact, scholars have long argued that most cohabiters view shared living, at least initially, as a form of intensive dating. Rindfuss and VandenHeuvel (1990), in one of the earliest nationally representative studies of cohabiters, argued that cohabiters were far more like singles than marrieds in terms of their near-term childbearing intentions, school enrollment, home ownership rates, and financial dependence upon parents. Casper and Sayer

(2002) suggested that about 30% of the cohabiters in their sample were "coresidential daters"; recent studies suggest that this group is the dominant one among contemporary cohabiters. Based on in-depth interviews with cohabiters living in New York City at the turn of the 21st century, Sassler (2004) reported that few had discussed marriage prior to moving in with partners. Other qualitative studies of cohabiters—cohabiting couples in Columbus, Ohio, or individuals living with partners on the West Coast (Lamont, 2020; Sassler & Miller, 2017)—suggest that when respondents first begin living together, cohabitation served as a way to share rent while spending cozy time together, rather than a stepping stone toward marriage. Recent surveys conducted by the Pew Research Center suggest that marriage is in mind among cohabiters: between 28% and 50% of cohabiters who were not currently engaged viewed living together as a step toward marriage—but as these data are cross-sectional, it reflects the greater likelihood that the educationally advantaged will transition into marriage overall (Graf, 2019). Yet marriage is still discussed as the implicit reference point, by those doing surveys and the cohabiters themselves, highlighting the persistent hegemony of the institution of marriage, even as declining shares of cohabiting unions are transitioning into marriage.

Perhaps the largest challenge that cohabitation poses to the institution of marriage has emerged from the substantial share of cohabiting couples who enter into cohabiting unions or continue to cohabit (rather than marry) upon becoming pregnant (Lichter et al., 2014, 2016). In the not-so-distant past, many of those couples would have wed before the birth of their child, in what was known as a shotgun marriage. In the past few decades, a conception is more likely to lead to cohabitation than marriage (Lichter et al., 2016). While this may suggest that cohabitation has now become the preferred union status over marriage, that is belied by the sizable share of new parents who assert that they intend to marry—eventually (Gibson-Davis et al., 2005; Sassler & Miller, 2014). Results from the Fragile Families Study finds that only 26% of those who become parents while cohabiting subsequently married within five years of having their child; an equal share (26%) were still cohabiting five years later (Hummer & Hamilton, 2010). For a large segment of cohabiters, living together increasingly serves as an acceptable alternative to marriage for raising children (Lichter et al., 2016). Still, the instability of cohabiting relationships in general challenges the notion that living together has become akin to marriage (Lichter et al., 2016; Musick & Michelmore, 2015), at least in the United States.

Overall, then, research looking at young adults forming relationships in the early years of the 21st century suggest that cohabitation should be assessed as a living relationship unto itself, rather than as a short-term stepping stone toward legal marriage. Cohabitation is certainly more unstable than marriage, although cohabiting unions are lasting longer than in the past (Lamidi et al., 2019). Cohabitation increasingly serves as a location for parenthood, especially among those under age 30. And many cohabiters do go on to marry their partner. But to infer the meaning of cohabitation from the subset of those whose cohabitations transition into marriage is to distort the role that living together serves for a substantial proportion of today's young adults.

Cohabitation's Raison d'Être: Making Ends Meet

Much of the research on cohabitation implicitly places marriage as the end goal of relationships, although that may not be the views of young adults in the United States as we head into the third decade of the 21st century. Various scholars attribute the rise in cohabitation to the growing "economic bar" to marriage (Addo, 2014; Gibson-Davis et al., 2018; Harris, 2021; Ishizuka, 2018). Whereas a lack of "good prospects"—long-term indicators of economic stability such as completing one's schooling, having savings, and a stable job—impedes transitions into marriage, they do not serve as disincentives for cohabiting (Addo, 2014; Sassler & Miller, 2017; Smock et al., 2005). In fact, economic challenges frequently are instigators in decisions to cohabit, at least among the less educated (Sassler & Miller, 2017).

Research has not adequately detailed the extent to which the factors precipitating cohabitation differ by social class. Cohabiters mention that among the reasons they initially moved in with their partner were convenience, finances, and a need for housing (Rhoades et al., 2009; Sassler, 2004; Sassler & Miller, 2011). But the factors influencing entrance into shared living appear to differ in important ways for the more and less advantaged. Among cohabiting couples with less than a college degree, economic challenges, such as job loss, having work hours cut back, inadequate earnings, or difficulty affording rent often served as a backdrop for decisions about living arrangements in newly established relationships (Sassler & Miller, 2017).

Other cohabiters referenced family issues, such as wanting to leave the parental home or discovering they were pregnant, in describing the situations leading to their decision to move in with a partner. About half of these less-educated couples were paying considerably more than a third of their household income in rent. While a few respondents mentioned that they loved their partner, the predominant reasons given for moving in together related to different kind of need: a way to make ends meet, a place to live, or help with a newborn.

College-educated cohabiting couples differed in how their cohabiting unions unfolded in important ways. Reasons for moving in together centered more on economic rationality—the notion that two could live as cheaply as one—although most did not report great difficulty maintaining separate living arrangements. Others described how they'd be able to rent a larger space—a two-bedroom, to provide them with an office, given that they slept in the same room (Sassler & Miller, 2017). A recent national survey conducted by Pew Research Center of cohabiting adults reported that 38% said a major reason they moved in with their partner was because it made sense financially; another 37% said it was more convenient (Graf, 2019; see also Rhoades et al., 2009). In fact, this middle-class narrative of reasons for entering into a cohabiting union with a partner dominates discussions of why couples cohabit in the media.

But this rational choice narrative masks heterogeneity in why couples from more and less advantaged backgrounds cohabit. For starters, it presumes that young adults feel that they can choose their living arrangements. There is abundant evidence that for less educated young adults, options surrounding living arrangements are far more constrained, by a lack of resources, the need to help out families of origin, or an absence of assistance from parents. The majority of Sassler and Miller's (2017) college-educated cohabiters had attended residential colleges where they had begun living apart from families in their late teens; their respondents with less than a college degree were more likely to have moved in with their cohabiting partner from their parent's home. It does make fiscal sense for the person who cannot afford their rent because their hours at work got cut, and they have to decide whether to pay their utilities bill or a credit card debt, to move in with a partner. It also makes sense for two college-educated professionals to move in together. But these justifications for moving in together, while similar, suggest that other aspects of the relationships will be quite different.

Conclusion

Today's young adults are more likely to live with a partner—to shack up, live in sin, or save on rent, depending on your perspective—because it is more acceptable now than it was in the past. But they are also doing so because our society provides many of them with few other options, as they work to transition into adulthood. Some may prefer living on their own, but do not have the means to do so. Many young adults prefer cohabitation because marriage is imbued with weighty responsibilities that a growing share of emerging adults feel are untenable for them. Others would prefer marriage over cohabitation (e.g., Harris, 2021) but are deferring marriage as they work to reach what feels like a stronger foundation for a stable, high-quality union. And others are excited about moving in with a partner—for the companionship, the ability to spend time together, or maybe to assess the strength of their partnership for marriage. The shares of young Americans who actively and willingly eschew marriage, however, remain a select group. Given the hand our society has dealt them, the evidence suggests that many young Americans seem to prefer cohabiting over many other forms of arrangements—living with parents or roommates, for example. Whether they prefer living together over marriage, however, remains an open question. Much additional research is required to help us distinguish between prevalence and preference when it comes to the union formation behaviors of today's young adults. What is clear is that cohabitation has become an important stage in the transition to adulthood—one that is further exacerbating inequality between the more and less advantaged.

References

Addo, F. R. (2012). Ethnoracial differences in early union experiences among young adult women. *The Review of Black Political Economy*, 39(4), 427–444. https://doi.org/10.1007/s12114-012-9138-2

Addo, F. R. (2014). Debt, cohabitation, and marriage in young adulthood. *Demography*, 51(5), 1677–1701. https://doi.org/10.1007/s13524-014-0333-6

Addo, F., & Lichter, D. T. (2013). Marriage, marital history, and Black-White wealth differentials among older women. *Journal of Marriage and Family*, 75(2), 342–362. https://doi.org/10.1111/jomf.12007

Allred, C. (2019). *High school seniors' attitudes toward cohabitation as a testing ground for marriage, 2017*. Family Profiles, FP-19-10. National Center for Family & Marriage Research.

Bloome, D., & Ang, S. (2020). Marriage and union formation in the United States: Recent trends across racial groups and economic backgrounds. *Demography*, *57*(5), 1753–1786. https://doi.org/10.1007/s13524-020-00910-7

Bumpass, L., Sweet, J., & Cherlin, A. (1991). The role of cohabitation in declining rates of marriage. *Journal of Marriage and Family*, *53*, 913–927. https://doi.org/10.2307/352997

Carlson, D. L. (2015). Do differences in expectations and preferences explain racial/ethnic variation in family formation outcomes? *Advances in Life Course Research*, *25*, 1–15. https://doi.org/10.1016/j.alcr.2015.05.002

Casper, L., & Sayer, L. (2002). Cohabitation transitions: Different purposes and goals, different paths. In L. M. Casper and S. M. Bianchi., *Continuity and change in the American family* (pp. 56–60). Sage Publications.

Cate, R. M., & Lloyd, S. A. (1988). Courtship. In S. Duck (Ed.), *Handbook of personal relationships* (pp. 409–427). Wiley.

Cavanagh, S. E., Crissey, S. R., & Raley, R. K. (2008). Family structure history and adolescent romance. *Journal of Marriage and Family*, *70*, 698–714. https://doi.org/10.1111/j.1741-3737.2008.00515.x

Cherlin, A. (2004). The deinstitutionalization of American marriage. *Journal of Marriage and Family*, *66*(4), 848–861. https://doi.org/10.1111/j.0022-2445.2004.00058.x

Coontz, S. (2006). *Marriage, a history: How love conquered marriage*. Penguin Books.

Copen, C., Daniels, K., & Mosher, W. (2013). *First premarital cohabitation in the United States: 2006–2010 National Survey of Family Growth*. National Health Statistics Reports, no. 64. National Center for Health Statistics.

Eickmeyer, K., & Manning, W. (2018). Serial cohabitation in young adulthood: Baby boomers to millennials. *Journal of Marriage and Family*, *80*(4), 826–840. doi:10.1111/jomf.12495

Gibson-Davis, C. M., Edin, K., & McLanahan, S. (2005). High hopes but even higher expectations: The retreat from marriage among low-income couples. *Journal of Marriage and Family*, *67*(5), 1301–1312. https://doi.org/10.1111/j.1741-3737.2005.00218.x

Gibson-Davis, C., Gassman-Pines, A., & Lehrman, R. (2018). "His" and "hers": Meeting the economic bar to marriage. *Demography*, *55*, 2321–2343. https://doi.org/10.1007/s13524-018-0726-z

Graf, N. (2019). *Key findings on marriage and cohabitation in the U.S.* Pew Research Center. https://www.pewresearch.org/fact-tank/2019/11/06/key-findings-on-marriage-and-cohabitation-in-the-u-s/

Guzzo, K. (2014). Trends in cohabitation outcomes: Compositional changes and engagement among never-married young adults. *Journal of Marriage and Family*, *76*(4), 826–842. https://doi.org/10.1111/jomf.12123

Harris, L. E. (2021). Committing before cohabiting: Pathways to marriage among middle-class couples. *Journal of Family Issues*, *42*(8), 1762–1786. https://doi.org/10.1177/0192513x20957049

Hummer, R., & Hamilton, E. (2010). Race and ethnicity in fragile families. *Future of Children*, *20*(2), 113–131. https://doe.org/10.1353/foc.2010.0003

Ishizuka, P. (2018). The economic foundations of cohabiting couples' union transitions. *Demography*, *55*(2), 535–557. https://doi.org/10.1007/s13524-018-0651-1

Kennedy, S., & Bumpass, L. (2008). Cohabitation and children's living arrangements: New estimates from the United States. *Demographic Research*, *19*(47), 1663–1692. doi: 10.4054/DemRes.2008.19.47

Kennedy, S., & Ruggles, S. (2014). Breaking up is hard to count: The rise of divorce in the United States, 1980–2010. *Demography*, *51*(2), 587–598. https://doi.org/10.1007/s13524-013-0270-9

Lamidi, E., Manning, W., & Brown, S. (2019). Change in the stability of first premarital cohabitation among women in the United States, 1983–2013. *Demography*, *56*(2), 427–450. https://doi.org/10.1007/s13524-019-00765-7

Lamont, E. (2020). *The mating game: How gender still shapes how we date*. University of California Press.

Lichter, D., Michelmore, K., Turner, R., & Sassler, S. (2016). Pathways to a stable union? Pregnancy and childbearing among cohabiting and married couples. *Population Research and Policy Review*, *35*, 377–399. https://doi.org/10.1007/s11113-016-9392-2

Lichter, D., Qian, Z., & Mellott, L. (2006). Marriage or dissolution? Union transitions among poor cohabiting women. *Demography*, *43*, 223–240. https://doi.org/10.1353/dem.2006.0016

Lichter, D., & Qian, Z. (2008). Serial cohabitation and the marital life course. *Journal of Marriage and Family*, *70*(4), 861–878. https://doi.org/10.1111/j.1741-3737.2008.00532.x

Lichter, D., Sassler, S., & Turner, R. N. (2014). Cohabitation, post-conception unions, and the rise in nonmarital fertility. *Social Science Research*, *47*, 134–147. doi: 10.1016/j.ssresearch.2014.04.002

Lichter, D., Turner, R., & Sassler, S. (2010). National estimates of the rise in serial cohabitation. *Social Science Research*, *39*(5), 754–756. https://doi.org/10.1016/j.ssresearch.2009.11.002

Manning, W. (2020). Young adulthood relationships in an era of uncertainty: A case for cohabitation. *Demography*, *57*(3), 799–819. doi: https://doi.org/10.1007/s13524-020-00881-9

Manning, W., Brown, S., & Payne, K. K. (2014). Two decades of stability and change in age at first union formation. *Journal of Marriage and Family*, *76*, 247–260. https://doi.org/10.1111/jomf.12090

Manning, W., Longmore, M. & Giordano, P. (2007). The changing institution of marriage: Adolescents' expectations to cohabit and to marry. *Journal of Marriage and Family*, *69*(3), 559–575. https://doi.org/10.1111/j.1741-3737.2007.00392.x

Manning, W., Smock, P., & Fettro, M. (2019). Cohabitation and marital expectations among single millennials in the U.S. *Population Research and Policy Review*, *38*, 327–346. https://doi.org/10.1007/s11113-018-09509-8

Miller, A., Sassler, S., & Kusi-Appouh, D. (2011). The specter of divorce: Views from working- and middle-class cohabitors. *Family Relations*, *60*(5), 602–616. https://doi.org/10.1111/j.1741-3729.2011.00671.x

Musick, K., & Michelmore, M. (2015). Change in the stability of marital and cohabiting unions following the birth of a child. *Demography*, *52*(5), 1463–1485. https://doi.org/10.1007/s13524-015-0425-y

National Institute on Drug Abuse. (2022). *Monitoring the Future*. U.S. Department of Health and Human Services, National Institutes of Health. https://nida.nih.gov/research-topics/trends-statistics/monitoring-future

Parker, E. (2021). Gender differences in the marital plans and union transitions of first cohabitations. *Population Research and Policy Review*, *40*, 673–694. Https://doi.org/10.1007/s11113-020-09579-7

Parker, E., Sassler, S., & Tach, L. (2020). Fatherhood and racial-ethnic differences in the progression of romantic relationships. *Journal of Marriage and Family, 82*, 1–19. https://doi.org/10.1111/jomf.12733

Pew Research Center. (2010). *The decline of marriage and rise of new families.* https://assets.pewresearch.org/wp-content/uploads/sites/3/2010/11/pew-social-trends-2010-families.pdf

Raley, R. K., Sweeney, M. M., & Wondra, D. (2015). The growing racial and ethnic divide in U.S. marriage patterns. *The Future of Children, 25*(2), 89–109. doi: 10.1353/foc.2015.0014

Reed, J. (2006). Not crossing the "extra line": How cohabitors with children view their unions. *Journal of Marriage and Family, 68*, 1117–1131. doi:10.1111/J.1741-3737.2006.00318.X

Rhoades, G., Stanley, S., & Markman, H. (2009). Couples' reasons for cohabitation: Associations with individual well-being and relationship quality. *Journal of Family Issues, 30*(2), 233–258. https://doi.org/10.1177/0192513X08324388

Rindfuss, R., & VandenHeuvel, A. (1990). Cohabitation: A precursor to marriage or an alternative to being single? *Population and Development Review, 16*(4), 703–726. https://doi.org/10.2307/1972963

Sassler, S. (2004). The process of entering into cohabiting unions. *Journal of Marriage and Family, 66*(2), 491–505. https://doi.org/10.1111/j.1741-3737.2004.00033.x

Sassler, S., Addo, F., & Hartmann, E. (2010). The tempo of relationship progression among low-income couples. *Social Science Research, 39*(5), 831–844. https://doi.org/10.1016/j.ssresearch.2010.06.001

Sassler, S., Addo, F., & Lichter, D. T. (2012). The tempo of sexual activity and later relationship quality. *Journal of Marriage and Family, 74*, 708–725. https://doi.org/10.1111/j.1741-3737.2012.00996.x

Sassler, S., and Goldscheider, F. (2004). Revisiting Jane Austen's theory of marriage timing: Union formation among American men in the late 20th century. *Journal of Family Issues, 25*(2), 139–166. https://doi.org/10.1177/0192513X03257708

Sassler, S., & Lichter, D. (2020). Cohabitation and marriage: Complexity and diversity in union-formation patterns. *Journal of Marriage and Family, 82*(1), 35–61. https://doi.org/10.1111/jomf.12617

Sassler, S., Michelmore, K., & Holland, J. (2016). The progression of sexual relationships. *Journal of Marriage and Family, 78*(3), 587–597. https://doi.org/10.1111/jomf.12289

Sassler, S., Michelmore, K., & Qian, Z. (2018). Transitions from sexual relationships into cohabitation and beyond. *Demography, 55*(2), 511–534. https://doi.org/10.1007/s13524-018-0649-8

Sassler, S., & Miller, A. J. (2011). Class differences in cohabitation processes. *Family Relations, 60*(2), 163–177. https://doi.org/10.1111/j.1741-3729.2010.00640.x

Sassler, S., & Miller, A. J. (2014). "We're very careful...": The fertility desires and contraceptive behaviors of cohabiting couples. *Family Relations, 63*(4), 538–553. https://doi.org/10.1111/fare.12079

Sassler, S., & Miller, A. J. (2017). *Cohabitation nation: Gender, class, and the remaking of relationships.* University of California Press.

Sassler, S., & Miller, A. J. (2023). Assessing the deinstitutionalization of marriage thesis: Changes in the meaning of cohabitation over the relationship life course. *Journal of Marriage and Family, 85*(2), 370–390. https://doi.org/10.1111/jomf.12883

Sassler, S., & Schoen, R. (1999). The effect of attitudes and economic activity on marriage behavior. *Journal of Marriage and the Family, 61*(1), 147–159. https://doi.org/10.2307/353890

Smock, P., Manning, W., & Porter, M. (2005). "Everything's there except money": How money shapes decisions to marry among cohabitors. *Journal of Marriage and Family, 67*(3), 680–696. https://doi.org/10.1111/j.1741-3737.2005.00162.x

Smock, P. J. & Schwartz, C. (2020). The demography of families: A review of patterns and change. *Journal of Marriage and Family, 82*, 9–34. https://doi.org/10.1111/jomf.12612

Stepler, R. (2017). *Number of U.S. adults cohabiting with a partner continues to rise, especially among those 50 and older.* Fact Tank, Pew Research Center.

Surra, C., Arizzi, P., & Asmussen, L. (1988). The association between reasons for commitment and the development and outcome of marital relationships. *Journal of Social and Personal Relationships, 5*, 47–63. https://doi.org/10.1177/0265407588051003

Sweeney, S., & Raley, R. K. (2020). Divorce, repartnering, and stepfamilies: A decade in review. *Journal of Marriage and Family, 82*(1), 81–99. https://doi.org/10.1111/jomf.12651

U.S. Census Bureau. (2018). America's families and living arrangements. https://www.census.gov/data/tables/2018/demo/families/cps-2018.html

U.S. Census Bureau. (2021). Historical marital status tables. https://www.census.gov/data/tables/time-series/demo/families/marital.html

Vespa, J. (2014). Historical trends in the marital intentions of one-time and serial cohabitors. *Journal of Marriage and Family, 76*(1), 207–217. https://doi.org/10.1111/jomf.12083

Wang, W., & Parker, K. (2014). *Record share of Americans have never married: As values, economics and gender patterns change.* Social & Demographic Trends Project. Pew Research Center.

Zhang, X., & Sassler, S. (2022). Opting out of coresidential unions? Factors predicting non-marriage by midlife across race, ethnicity, and gender. *Social Currents.* Advance online publication. https://doi.org/10.1177/23294965221142769

4
Being Single in the 21st Century

Reasons and Consequences

Elyakim Kislev

Singlehood's Definitions

Although it is often treated as an intuitive concept, singlehood is not easily defined. Definitions of singlehood are continuously shifting as new patterns of coupling emerge. Currently, there are many different kinds of lifestyle choices and living arrangements that complicate the definition of singlehood and indicate that single people do not form a homogenous group (Lehmann et al., 2015; Pepping et al., 2018). In addition, living alone does not necessarily indicate the absence of a romantic partner, nor does living together necessarily imply an intimate bond (Kislev, 2022b). While the proliferation of different kinds of living arrangements, like celibacy, living together apart (LAT), and extramarital cohabitation is growing, the diversity of singlehood has often been overlooked in policymaking and research (Bernard-Allan, 2016; Moore & Radtke, 2015; Reynolds et al., 2007; Terry, 2012).

The basic distinction between voluntary and involuntary singlehood was initially theorized by Stein (1978). He proposed that singlehood could be understood to fall within four categories: voluntary temporary, voluntary stable, involuntary temporary, and involuntary stable.

In their study of 30 women aged between 30 and 60 years, interviewed between 1998 and 1999, Reynolds et al. (2007) found that individuals may shift between these categories when citing reasons for their singlehood. Drawing on narrative theory—which posits that individuals frame their experience in narrative terms—and employing discourse analysis, Reynolds et al. showed that the distinction between chance and choice was not always clear-cut when it came to defining singlehood. For instance, in their study, "not meeting a suitable partner" was given as a reason for both voluntary and involuntary singlehood. This suggests that participants were ambivalent about whether the reasons for remaining single were down to chance or choice. Another commonly cited reason for choosing singlehood, summarized as "I haven't felt the need," raised other problems, as Reynolds et al. (2007) noted. On the one hand, this assertion served to legitimize the experience of singlehood as a normal part of social life. On the other, however, single people citing this reason positioned themselves as deviating from normal experiences of having the desire for sexual and emotional intimacy, which might be viewed as asexual or "different."

Such studies, in fact, placed the ambivalence that exists around the experience of singlehood in the context of the marginalization of single people in societies rooted in heterosexual norms (as explored in the next section) as well as the increasing popularity of the celebratory narrative of singlehood. The implication of the theory posited by Reynolds et al. (2007) is that single people opt for a narrative of choice to make up for the loss of social stature accompanying the status of singlehood. Voluntary singlehood may, in this view, be thought of as a narrative technique to make sense of a marginalized social experience.

A related conclusion was reached in an earlier study by Lewis and Moon (1997), who studied single women's perspectives on their singlehood across different life stages. They found that single women had ambivalent and unresolved feelings about singlehood and attributed this assertion to three linked findings. First, women gave ambivalent explanations for their singlehood. Second, women were aware of both the pros and cons of being single. And, third, although many women felt content with their singlehood, they simultaneously experienced feelings of loss and grief. Rather than two discrete states of being, voluntary and involuntary singlehood may, therefore, represent flexible categories through which single individuals negotiate their identities (Adamczyk, 2017).

Bernard-Allan (2016) described women's negotiation of singlehood as dialectical. She argued that women come to accept singlehood through a process of "improvisations" whereby they attach positively to their single status. Moore and Radtke (2015), in their study of middle-aged single women, found that women negotiated their identity by moving back and forth between three identity narratives: the singlehood as deficit narrative, the transformative midlife narrative, and the comfortably single at midlife identity (see also in: Kislev, 2023a). They concluded that these women's lives could be described as "an ongoing struggle to create and maintain a space where being single constitutes normalcy, while at the same time having to answer to normative discourses of womanhood" (Moore & Radtke, 2015, p. 317). If they managed to shape an alternative view of singlehood and free themselves from the constraints of heteronormative ideas of family and marriage, this was always a temporary state of autonomy. However, the explanation for this challenge to feel whole with singlehood may not be found within oneself but, rather, with the social pressure, stigmas, and prejudices put on and against singles (DePaulo, 2011; DePaulo & Morris, 2006; Morris et al., 2008). Reynolds et al. (2007) found that, while women struggled to define their single status as the result of choice, they were severely constrained by existing cultural norms.

In his study of single gay men, Hostetler (2009) also challenged the clear-cut notion of voluntary singlehood. His study found that the "celebratory narrative" of singlehood—where singlehood is presented as a choice rather than as the result of external circumstance—was largely an interpretive strategy single men used to make sense of their single status and to assign meaning to their lives retrospectively. Hostetler found that even those men who reported choosing singlehood were dissatisfied with their single status and wished for a different outcome. Yet again, the reason for this often lies with societal pressure that LGBT communities find themselves forced to succumb to. Moreover, the studies that link well-being and mental health to marital status are increasingly being challenged, especially as delayed marriage or the choice not to marry at all is on the increase in the Western world (Adamczyk & Segrin, 2015; Kislev, 2019e). For this reason, the following sections further examine the reasons for being single and the relation of singlehood to mental well-being and other consequences such as sociability and sexuality.

Reasons to Be Single

Reasons for choosing to remain single vary widely (Kislev, 2019a; Pepping et al., 2018; Prabhakar, 2011). Not finding a suitable partner, the pursuit of a career, religious beliefs, and preferences for solitude are cited as reasons for choosing singlehood. In addition, high marital expectations, desire for independence, disappointment in love, parental objection to the choice of marriage, financial constraints, loss of parents, and health and disability play a role in the decision to remain single.

Adamczyk (2017) concluded that there are three main categories of reasons why individuals choose to remain unmarried: personal choice, external circumstances, and personal deficits or self-blame. The first of these categories included options where the adults in question were satisfied with their choice of being single. Reasons in this category included the idea that life would not be improved by being involved in a romantic relationship, wanting freedom, and being on the lookout for new experiences, all of which were found to be related to singles and choosing singlehood (DePaulo, 2015, 2017; Kislev, 2018, 2021a; Klinenberg, 2012). The second category included perceived external barriers to being married, such as career obligations, transnational immigration, and moving to an urban area (Kislev, 2019a). The third category, however, included reasons for choosing singlehood that might be understood as arising from avoidant or anxious attachment: ideas about being unattractive or not "good enough" to find a partner (Pepping et al., 2018).

Indeed, attachment style is emerging as an increasingly popular framework for understanding voluntary and involuntary singlehood (Pepping & MacDonald, 2019; Pepping et al., 2018; Schachner et al., 2008). Broadly speaking, two kinds of attachment anxiety are observed in adults. Avoidant attachment is characterized by a fear of intimacy and excessive feelings of self-reliance, which results in cognitive and behavioral patterns that undermine the establishment of an intimate relationship, while anxious attachment is grounded in fear of abandonment that often results in intense distress when attachment needs are not being met (Hazan & Shaver, 2017). This distress, in turn, gives rise to behavioral patterns like incessant reassurance seeking and hypervigilance to signs of rejection and anxiety, which are detrimental to sustaining intimate partnerships (Pepping & MacDonald, 2019).

Accordingly, Pepping and MacDonald (2019) postulated that a significant percentage of singles display an insecure attachment style, that is, an attachment style that includes both avoidant attachment and anxious attachment. Pepping et al. (2018) found, moreover, that the subjective experience of voluntary singlehood was more likely when individuals' attachment needs were met outside of romantic relationships. In another study, however, Pepping and MacDonald (2019) stressed the impact of attachment style on all kinds of social relationships—including relationships with pets. So, for example, securely attached individuals reaped more benefits from relationships with pets than individuals who were insecurely attached. The meeting of attachment needs outside of romantic relationships was therefore connected with whether individuals were insecurely or anxiously attached, and, as a result, the possible impact of non-romantic relationships or other networks of social support decreased for singles with an insecure attachment style as opposed to those who were securely attached. Attachment style, therefore, may potentially impact not only the perception of whether singlehood is voluntary or involuntary but also individuals' ability to mitigate the negative impacts of singlehood by drawing on a broader range of social relationships.

As the scope of these reasons implies, voluntary singlehood does not necessarily carry a positive valence: While some may consider their singlehood as relating to the importance of other things in life (Kislev, 2018, 2019d), voluntary singlehood may also arise from fear, negative self-image, or unrequited love (Kislev, 2019b). A crucial factor in understanding voluntary singlehood is thus whether singlehood truly reflects a personal choice rather than underlying difficulties in maintaining relationships (Pepping & MacDonald, 2019; Pepping et al., 2018). Yet, in order to better define and identify a personal choice to remain single, one needs to delve into the cultural norms that affect such choices.

The Cultural Norms of Being Single

The cultural definition and subjective perception of singlehood are heavily influenced by the broader concept of heteronormativity: the unquestioned assumption that people are heterosexual and conform to ideals of family life. Because heteronormative coupling and marriage ideals that some call "matrimania" are seen as central to the "normal" life path, singlehood is still viewed as a deviant category or a "deficit identity" that some title as "singlism" (DePaulo, 2011; Kislev, 2019e; Moore & Radtke, 2015; Morris et al., 2008).

These negative stereotypes of singlehood are more often applied to women than to men. Single women are either depicted as leading empty, meaningless lives and as being morally lacking or as occupying a confrontational position against the patriarchy (Lahad, 2017; Moore & Radtke, 2015). Single men generally escape such stereotyping: Unmarried men are assumed to choose their single status (Sandfield & Percy, 2003). Not only are single men and single women perceived in different ways (Moore & Radtke, 2015), but heteronormative ideas about marriage, family life, and valid trajectories also have an influence on the subjective experience of singlehood and identity (Bernard-Allan, 2016). Accordingly, women are more likely than men to describe their singlehood in negative terms. These gender biases are also noticeable in the ways singlehood has been studied: Single women are studied more than single men, and homosexual single men have received almost no scholarly attention (Suen, 2015).

The fact that singlehood is often understood as a passing or preparatory phase is an indication of the stronghold of heteronormative culture on the definition of singlehood (Sandfield & Percy, 2003). Lahad (2017) provided a critical analysis of the expected linear life course trajectory. She argued that singlehood comes into existence through a "hegemonic temporal gaze" that is deeply embedded in social interaction (Lahad, 2017). According to this socially scripted time frame, singlehood is a "non-scheduled status passage." Rather than being viewed as participating in the "normal" life trajectory, single women are viewed as being downwardly mobile. This perspective on singlehood and time has not yet been adequately addressed in empirical research. If it is true that singlehood emerges in time as single individuals increasingly fall out of step with their partnered peers, it is possible that the experience of singlehood will differ dramatically for younger adults and adults in their 30s (Kislev, 2018, 2020b).

These cultural and societal pressures might explain why Poortman and Liefbroer (2010) found that while many singles indicated that they choose singlehood for personal autonomy and individualization, singlehood did not necessarily result in positive feelings about being single. They noted that the research on singlehood and well-being contradict currently circulating ideas about voluntary singlehood: The view that singles are happy with their single status is difficult to reconcile with the research that associates singlehood with decreased happiness and fewer positive health outcomes (Joung et al., 1994; Peters & Liefbroer, 1997). As noted in the discussion earlier, however, this might be due to stigmas and prejudices against singles rather than objective reasons of lacking a romantic partner. Moreover, the research linking singlehood with lower well-being outcomes are increasingly being challenged.

Singlehood and Its Consequences

While earlier studies found a conclusive link between marriage, psychological health, and other factors such as sociability and sexuality (e.g., Waite & Gallagher, 2000), others have reported more complicated findings for people in unmarried romantic relationships (Dush & Amato, 2005; Kislev, 2019e). Some researchers have pointed out the limitations of earlier studies (DePaulo & Morris, 2005). Lehmann et al. (2015), for example, suggested that the research on marriage and well-being has consistently viewed both married and single individuals as homogenous groupings without taking into account individual differences. They further posited that group-level differences between partnered and single people may have been oversimplified and that the effect of other markers of well-being—like gender, personality, work satisfaction, relationship history, relationship satisfaction, relationship length, or a person's social network—have not been taken into account (see, for example, DePaulo, 2015, 2017; Kislev, 2023b, forthcoming). The link between mental health and romantic relationships is therefore not as uncomplicated as previously assumed (Adamczyk & Segrin, 2015).

The literature on voluntary singlehood further complicates the assumed connection between relationship status and mental health and well-being. As singlehood is becoming more widespread and accepted, it is more readily associated with positive effects like personal freedom, independence, and autonomy as opposed to failure or personal deficits (Adamczyk & Segrin, 2015; Kislev, 2018). Lehmann et al. (2015) found that satisfaction with relationship status, independent of relationship status, indicated better life satisfaction and less distress. This means that singles who are satisfied with being single are also satisfied with their life in general (see also in Kislev, 2021a, 2022c). Furthermore, a lack of social support predicted higher levels of distress, regardless of marital status. Similarly, Adamczyk and Segrin (2015) found that social support outweighed relationship status as a determinant of mental health, although those in romantic relationships were more likely to feel supported than single individuals. Despite these findings, the difference in the mental health and well-being of partnered and single individuals was statistically insignificant. They concluded that while being in a romantic relationship did not directly influence well-being and mental health, partnered individuals received more social support than their single counterparts and that the increased sense of social support correlated positively with better health outcomes.

As opposed to the research on well-being and marital status, the literature on the link between relationship status and romantic loneliness seems to be more widely accepted. Adamczyk (2016) concluded, supporting the findings mentioned above, that perceived social support was higher for those in partnered relationships than for single people, and that higher perceived levels of social support acted as a buffer against romantic loneliness. As expected, those in non-relationships were less lonely than single individuals. Single individuals received less support from family than those in romantic partnerships. This may be attributed to heteronormative pressure to conform to a "normal" life trajectory.

Yet, the fact that partnered individuals receive more social support is in question. A study conducted by Amato and colleagues (2007) compared the differences in social behaviors between couples in 1980 with those in the year 2000. Couples in the year 2000 were less likely to participate in social activities, while singles have become increasingly adept at building networks over a similar period of time. Moreover, an analysis of more than 200,000 survey participants from 32 countries (Kislev, 2020b) showed that singles not only present higher social capital, which is positively correlated with higher happiness, but also derive greater happiness from equal levels of social capital. It appears that singles involved in social undertakings can, and often do, boost their well-being in significant ways. In fact, singles who pursue social interactions more proactively than do couples can bypass them in the happiness index.

Furthermore, research aimed at exploring the impact of choosing singlehood on social satisfaction and the importance of friends found that singles with low romantic relationship desire have higher levels of social satisfaction and consider friendships more important (Kislev, 2020b). The study depicted a negative correlation between wanting a relationship and satisfaction from social life as well as friends' importance. Conversely, choosing singlehood was positively correlated with both social indicators. These results are in line with other studies that point to a phenomenon of networked individualism and widening social networks among singles (Kislev, 2019c; Raine & Wellman, 2012; Wellman, 2012). Another study (Kislev, 2021b) showed that voluntary singles are more sexually satisfied; this is not due to having more casual sex, but, rather, this is associated with desiring less sex and, among women, with being less sexually active compared with involuntary single women.

It appears that singles with low relationship desire are those who particularly derive emotional, social, material, and financial support from friendships and make them central to their lives. It might well be that singles with low relationship desire transfer some of the assumed responsibilities of the nuclear family to their networks of friends (Bellotti, 2008; Fileborn et al., 2015). Moreover, it seems that those who more strongly prefer being single are also those who are less interested in sex, on average. In turn, they report on higher levels of sexual satisfaction relative to involuntary singles. They possibly report so because they do not seek sex in high intensity. In turn, they are not frustrated when it is not available to them (Kislev, 2021b).

Indeed, as opposed to the defensive denial of the need for intimacy, which has a detrimental effect on relationships in general, voluntary singlehood is associated with satisfaction with being single, self-fulfillment, and personal autonomy (Kislev, 2021a). Involuntary singlehood, on the other hand, is associated with regret and dissatisfaction with single status (Timonen & Doyle, 2014).

It follows from these findings that satisfaction with single status (voluntary singlehood) will be associated with better outcomes than dissatisfaction with single status (involuntary singlehood). Indeed, regardless of whether perceptions on voluntary and involuntary singlehood are objectively true, Reynolds et al. (2007) showed that the perceptions of singlehood as voluntary or involuntary are associated with different outcomes. Slonim and Schütz (2015) reported that those who viewed themselves as single by choice expected fewer benefits from romantic relationships and were more likely to view romantic relationships as potentially constraining and causing boredom or stress. In their sample, those who viewed their singlehood as caused by circumstance had similar expectations to those of their partnered counterparts as to the cost and benefit of romantic relationships. It follows that those who viewed singlehood as the result of personal choice did not experience the same sense of failure and lack of agency as those who viewed singlehood as involuntary.

Different perceptions of singlehood may, in turn, reflect more general views on autonomy and self-determination—aspects that contribute to physical and psychological well-being (Adamczyk, 2017; Reynolds et al., 2007). Accordingly, Adamczyk (2017) found that chosen singlehood might be associated with greater positive mental health and lower levels of mental health problems and romantic loneliness.

Conclusion

It seems that the convergence of the various social forces that lead to singlehood will only accelerate in the near future (Kislev, 2019e; Klinenberg, 2012). Not only are the proportions changing between married and single people, but the norms and functions of society are also fundamentally shifting to be more inclusive of singles. Given the large number of children expected to never get married (25% of U.S. children: Wang & Parker, 2014), and the increasingly high divorce rates (40%–50% in Europe: Eurostat, 2017), it is essential to start thinking about research designs, policymaking, urban planning, and educational training systems that fit and address the needs of singles in the 21st century.

To some people, the institution of marriage can no longer be the sole supplier of physical, social, emotional, and mental needs. Instead, these needs require a varied network of exchanges to be satisfied. While still not a widely shared belief, more and more people are understanding that traditional marriage, which means living with the same person and trusting them as the main provider for almost all needs throughout a half-century or more, is simply impossible. For this reason, many people turn to adopting single living and developing "networked life." This growingly popular choice challenges the marriage institution at an ever-increasing pace. Thus, varying or dividing the exchange of emotional, intellectual, and even sexual needs is likely to take a larger and more positive role in the lives of singles. Some researchers name this coming reality an age of "post-traditional intimacy" (Budgeon, 2006). This term does not mean that intense emotional exchange or sexual interactions will disappear; rather, there will be multiple streams to form such exchanges.

It is thus expected that the friendship institution will come to the fore in an age of singlehood to fill the void that marriage can no longer fill. For many, meaningful friendships will become a life goal just as important, if not more so, than getting married. Not only will such connections be more diverse, but they will also be more central to singles' lives, serving as a major source for addressing their needs. Thus, a new type of stronger, more intense, and even formally established friendship is expected to be part of an ecosystem surrounding singles.

Moreover, while singles receive support from family and friends, and while they socialize with circles of people, enjoying a diverse range of relationship statuses, some of the most meaningful support can come from other singles organized in groups. Singles stand to gain by establishing communities of like-minded individuals who offer support and camaraderie via shared attitudes, interests, beliefs, and goals.

Moving forward, the growing singles population, particularly in urban communities, also fuels the search for creative solutions that accommodate this demographic change. Urban planning is already adjusting, and several solutions have been offered. Cohousing has already been suggested as a policy solution for aging communities that can benefit from the mutual support and shared spaces (Peace & Holland, 2001). But in the near future, cohousing is expected to be common among younger singles as well. Research already shows that cohousing tends to attract less conventional households (Toker, 2010). Thus, even in cohousing communities not specifically designed for singles, the traditional family unit is not always the norm, making it easier for singles to assimilate.

Furthermore, the rise of the singles demographic is well timed with unprecedented advances in technological innovation, probably not coincidentally. For a dynamic population like singles, technology offers efficient ways to network that overcome the constraints of the immediate family. Today's technology overcomes time and space constraints, allowing singles to expand their reach. New technologies facilitate the choice to enter or exit different types of relationships, making them malleable and diversified (Kislev, 2022a).

Witnessing the above changes and looking ahead, it seems essential to prepare for an age of singlehood. Education systems should be urged to equip children with a social and psychological "toolbox" of how to be singles in the future. Learning about singleness in schools and supporting high-quality solo lifestyles through the health and welfare ministries, exactly as is done with family life, are essential to our society. Social workers, psychologists, and physicians should be trained to serve the singles population. Additionally, special community centers and information points should be set up. Today's children need these services for their own benefit as well as for the welfare of the many singles who will surround them in the future.

References

Adamczyk, K. (2016). An investigation of loneliness and perceived social support among single and partnered young adults. *Current Psychology*, 35(4), 674–689. https://doi.org/10.1007/s12144-015-9337-7

Adamczyk, K. (2017). Voluntary and involuntary singlehood and young adults' mental health: An investigation of mediating role of romantic loneliness. *Current Psychology*, 36(4), 888–904. https://doi.org/10.1007/s12144-016-9478-3

Adamczyk, K., & Segrin, C. (2015). Perceived social support and mental health among single vs. partnered Polish young adults. *Current Psychology*, 34(1), 82–96. https://doi.org/10.1007/s12144-014-9242-5

Amato, P. R., Booth, A., Johnson, D. R., & Rogers, S. J. (2007). *Alone together: How marriage in America is changing*. Harvard University Press. https://doi.org/10.1353/sof.0.0108

Bellotti, E. (2008). What are friends for? Elective communities of single people. *Social Networks, 30*(4), 318–329. https://doi.org/10.1016/j.socnet.2008.07.001

Bernard-Allan, V. Y. (2016). *It is not good to be alone; singleness and the Black Seventh-Day Adventist woman*. University College London.

Budgeon, S. (2006). Friendship and formations of sociality in late modernity: The challenge of "post traditional intimacy." *Sociological Research Online, 11*(3). https://doi.org/10.5153/sro.1248

DePaulo, B. (2011). *Singlism: What it is, why it matters, and how to stop it*. DoubleDoor Books.

DePaulo, B. (2015). *How we live now: Redefining home and family in the 21st century*. Simon and Schuster. https://doi.org/10.1111/jftr.12171

DePaulo, B. (2017). Towards a positive psychology of single life. In B. DePaulo, *Positive Psychology: Established and Emerging Issues* (251–275). Routledge / Taylor & Francis Group. https://doi.org/10.4324/9781315106304-15

DePaulo, B., & Morris, W. (2005). Singles in society and in science. *Psychological Inquiry, 16*(2–3), 57–83. https://doi.org/10.1080/1047840X.2005.9682918

DePaulo, B., & Morris, W. (2006). The unrecognized stereotyping and discrimination against singles. *Current Directions in Psychological Science, 15*(5), 251–254. https://doi.org/10.1111/j.1467-8721.2006.00446.x

Dush, C. M. K., & Amato, P. R. (2005). Consequences of relationship status and quality for subjective well-being. *Journal of Social and Personal Relationships, 22*(5), 607–627. https://doi.org/10.1177/0265407505056438

Fileborn, B., Thorpe, R., Hawkes, G., Minichiello, V., & Pitts, M. (2015). Sex and the (older) single girl: Experiences of sex and dating in later life. *Journal of Aging Studies, 33*, 67–75.

Hazan, C., & Shaver, P. (2017). Romantic love conceptualized as an attachment process. In Rita Zukauskiene (Ed.), *Interpersonal development* (pp. 283–296). Routledge. https://doi.org/10.4324/9781351153683-17

Hostetler, A. J. (2009). Single by choice? Assessing and understanding voluntary singlehood among mature gay men. *Journal of Homosexuality, 56*(4), 499–531. https://doi.org/10.1080/00918360902821486

Joung, I., Van de Mheen, H., Stronks, K., Van Poppel, F., & Mackenbach, J. P. (1994). Differences in self-reported morbidity by marital status and by living arrangement. *International Journal of Epidemiology, 23*(1), 91–97. https://doi.org/10.1093/ije/23.1.91

Kislev, E. (2018). Happiness, post-materialist values, and the unmarried. *Journal of Happiness Studies, 19*(8), 2243–2265. https://doi.org/10.1007/s10902-017-9921-7

Kislev, E. (2019a). The age of singlehood. In E. Kislev, *Happy singlehood* (pp. 13–44). University of California Press. https://doi.org/10.2307/j.ctvd1c7r2.6

Kislev, E. (2019b). Defying social pressure. In Kislev, *Happy singlehood* (pp. 79–102). https://doi.org/10.2307/j.ctvd1c7r2.8

Kislev, E. (2019c). Sleeping alone, bowling together. In Kislev, *Happy singlehood* (pp. 103–124). https://doi.org/10.2307/j.ctvd1c7r2.9

Kislev, E. (2019d). Singling in a postmaterialist world. In E. Kislev, *Happy singlehood* (pp. 125–142). https://doi.org/10.1525/9780520971004-008

Kislev, E. (2019e). *Happy singlehood: The rising acceptance and celebration of solo living.* University of California Press. https://doi.org/10.2307/j.ctvd1c7r2

Kislev, E. (2020a). Does marriage really improve sexual satisfaction? Evidence from the Pairfam data set. *The Journal of Sex Research, 57*(4), 470–481. https://doi.org/10.1080/00224499.2019.1608146

Kislev, E. (2020b). Social capital, happiness, and the unmarried: A multilevel analysis of 32 European countries. *Applied Research in Quality of Life, 15*(5), 1475–1492. https://doi.org/10.1007/s11482-019-09751-y

Kislev, E. (2021a). Reduced relationship desire is associated with better life satisfaction for singles in Germany: An analysis of pairfam data. *Journal of Social and Personal Relationships, 38*(7). https://doi.org/10.1177/02654075211005024

Kislev, E. (2021b). The sexual activity and sexual satisfaction of singles in the second demographic transition. *Sexuality Research and Social Policy, 18*, 726–738. https://doi.org/10.1007/s13178-020-00496-0

Kislev, E. (2022a). *Relationships 5.0: How AI, VR, and robots will reshape our emotional lives.* Oxford University Press US. https://doi.org/10.1093/oso/9780197588253.001.0001

Kislev, E. (2022b). Aging, marital status, and loneliness: Multilevel analyses of 30 countries. *Research on Ageing and Social Policy, 10*(1), 77–103. https://doi.org/ https://doi.org/10.17583/rasp.8923

Kislev, E. (2022c). Relationship desire and life satisfaction among never-married and divorced men and women. *Sexual and Relationship Therapy*, 1–13. https://doi.org/ https://doi.org/10.1080/14681994.2022.2099538

Kislev, E. (2023a). Relationship-status and work-life balance satisfaction: Cross-sectional and longitudinal analyses. *Applied Research in Quality of Life, 18*(2), 1115–1142.

Kislev, E. (2023). Singlehood as an Identity. *European Review of Social Psychology.*

Kislev, E. (Forthcoming). Singles in the workplace: Benefits and challenges. In K. Chowkhani & C. Wynne (Eds.), *Singular Selves: An Introduction to Singles Studies.* Routledge.

Klinenberg, E. (2012). *Going solo: The extraordinary rise and surprising appeal of living alone.* Penguin.

Lahad, L. (2017). *A table for one: A critical reading of singlehood, gender and time.* Manchester University Press. https://doi.org/10.1111/j.1728-4457.2012.00523.x

Lehmann, V., Tuinman, M. A., Braeken, J., Vingerhoets, A. J. J. M., Sanderman, R., & Hagedoorn, M. (2015). Satisfaction with relationship status: Development of a new scale and the role in predicting well-being. *Journal of Happiness Studies, 16*(1), 169–184. https://doi.org/10.1007/s10902-014-9503-x

Lewis, K. G., & Moon, S. (1997). Always single and single again women: A qualitative study. *Journal of Marital and Family Therapy, 23*(2), 115–134.https://doi.org/10.1111/j.1752-0606.1997.tb00238.x

Moore, J. A., & Radtke, H. L. (2015). Starting "real" life: Women negotiating a successful midlife single identity. *Psychology of Women Quarterly, 39*(3), 305–319. https://doi.org/10.1177/0361684315573244

Morris, W., DePaulo, B., Hertel, J., & Taylor, L. C. (2008). Singlism—Another problem that has no name: Prejudice, stereotypes and discrimination against singles In M. A. Morrison & T. G. Morrison (Eds.), *The psychology of modern prejudice* (pp. 165–194). Nova Science Publishers.

Peace, S. M., & Holland, C. (2001). *Inclusive housing in an ageing society: Innovative approaches*. Policy Press. https://doi.org/10.46692/9781847425362.013

Pepping, C. A., & MacDonald, G. (2019). Adult attachment and long-term singlehood. *Current Opinion in Psychology, 25*, 105–109. https://doi.org/https://doi.org/10.1016/j.copsyc.2018.04.006

Pepping, C. A., MacDonald, G., & Davis, P. J. (2018). Toward a psychology of singlehood: An attachment-theory perspective on long-term singlehood. *Current Directions in Psychological Science, 27*(5), 324–331. https://doi.org/10.1177/0963721418 7752106

Peters, A., & Liefbroer, A. C. (1997). Beyond marital status: Partner history and well-being in old age. *Journal of Marriage and the Family, 59*(3), 687–699. https://doi.org/10.2307/353954

Poortman, A.-R., & Liefbroer, A. C. (2010). Singles' relational attitudes in a time of individualization. *Social Science Research, 39*(6), 938–949. https://doi.org/http://dx.doi.org/10.1016/j.ssresearch.2010.03.012

Prabhakar, B. (2011). Causes for remaining single: A comparative study. *Journal of Psychosocial Research, 6*(2), 203.

Raine, L., & Wellman, B. (2012). Networked: The new social operating system. *Massachusetts Institute of Technology*. The MIT Press. https://doi.org/10.7551/mitpress/8358.001.0001

Reynolds, J., Wetherell, M., & Taylor, S. (2007). Choice and chance: Negotiating agency in narratives of singleness. *The Sociological Review, 55*(2), 331–351. https://doi.org/10.1111/j.1467-954x.2007.00708.x

Sandfield, A., & Percy, C. (2003). Accounting for single status: Heterosexism and ageism in heterosexual women's talk about marriage. *Feminism & Psychology, 13*(4), 475–488. https://doi.org/10.1177/09593535030134013

Schachner, D. A., Shaver, P. R., & Gillath, O. (2008). Attachment style and long-term singlehood. *Personal Relationships, 15*(4), 479–491. https://doi.org/10.1111/j.1475-6811.2008.00211.x

Slonim, G., & Schütz, A. (2015). *Singles by choice differ from singles by circumstance in their perceptions of the costs and benefits of romantic relationships*. 27th annual convention of the Association for Psychological Science, Bamberg, Germany.

Stein, Peter J. (1978). The lifestyles and life chances of the never-married. *Marriage & Family Review, 1*(4), 1–11. https://doi.org/10.1300/j002v01n04_01

Suen, Y. T. (2015). What's gay about being single? A qualitative study of the lived experiences of older single gay men. *Sociological Research Online, 20*(3), 1–14. https://doi.org/10.5153/sro.3716

Terry, G. (2012). "I'm putting a lid on that desire": Celibacy, choice and control. *Sexualities, 15*(7), 871–889. https://doi.org/10.1177/1363460712454082

Timonen, V., & Doyle, M. (2014). Life-long singlehood: Intersections of the past and the present. *Ageing & Society, 34*(10), 1749–1770.

Toker, Z. (2010). New housing for new households: Comparing cohousing and new urbanist developments with women in mind. *Journal of Architectural and Planning Research, 27*(4), 325–339.

Wang, W., & Parker, K. C. (2014). *Record share of Americans have never married: As values, economics and gender patterns change*. Pew Research Center, Social & Demographic Trends Project.

Waite, L., & Gallagher, M. (2000). *The case for marriage: Why married people are happier, healthier and better off financially*. Random House.

Wellman, B. (2012). Networked individualism: How the personalized internet, ubiquitous connectivity, and the turn to social networks can affect learning analytics. In *Proceedings of the 2nd International Conference on Learning Analytics and Knowledge*. Association for Computing Machinery. https://doi.org/10.1145/2330601.2330603

PART II
MARRIAGE IN THE 21ST CENTURY

5

Modern Marital Satisfaction

Are We Expecting Too Much?

Daniel Perlman and Rowland S. Miller

Expectations matter. We are typically pleased with the outcomes we receive in life when they exceed our expectations, being better than we thought they would be. In contrast, unmet expectations—that is, outcomes that are poorer than we expected—are disappointing, and they undermine and reduce our contentment. This is generally true: It involves the pay we receive at work (Schnaufer et al., 2022), our experiences with travel (Geeraert et al., 2021), the results of our surgeries (Conner-Spady et al., 2020), and most everything else, including becoming a parent (Mitnick et al., 2022) and the sexual interactions that follow the birth of a child (Rosen et al., 2022).

Indeed, classic conceptualizations of the origins of satisfaction in close relationships make note of this pattern. According to John Thibaut and Harold Kelley's (1959) theory of interdependence (Kelley & Thibaut, 1978), each of us has a personal standard, an idiosyncratic *comparison level*, that describes the value of the outcomes that we have come to expect (and that we feel we deserve) from our dealings with others. Our comparison levels are thought to emerge from our relational histories; those who have enjoyed rewarding past partnerships are likely to expect more of the same and to believe that others should treat them well, whereas those with a history of disappointment and discontent are unlikely to expect as much. Importantly, however, whatever we expect, interdependence theory suggests that *satisfaction* results when partners receive outcomes that exceed their comparison levels, being better than the minimums that they expect and take as their due. *Dis*satisfaction with a partnership occurs when one encounters treatment that is substandard, falling below one's expectations.

This does seem to be the case. People *are* more content when their romantic partners meet their expectations than when they do not (e.g., Lou et al., 2004; Vannier & O'Sullivan, 2017)—and the greater the gap between their expectations and a lover's actual behavior, the more disappointed and less satisfied they are likely to be (Kelley & Burgoon, 1991). Further, because our expectations shape both our appraisals of our partners' behavior (McNulty & Karney, 2002) and our own actions (Neff & Geers, 2013), unreasonable expectations that are hard to fulfill can be problematic. For instance, Neff and Geers found that when newlyweds foolishly expected that they would always agree about family issues, communicate well, never hurt each other, and always have great sex, they were *less* able than other couples to manage conflict constructively and their marital satisfaction eroded more quickly. Unmet expectations are clearly corrosive, and marital frustrations appear to be easier to accept when one's expectations are more modest than grand (McNulty & Karney, 2004).

Two interesting phenomena may also follow from this pattern. First, if one's comparison level is lofty (perhaps being unrealistically high), one can be dissatisfied by unmet expectations even though one has nevertheless objectively been treated very well (and even better than most people). For instance, if people do not regularly expect small sacrifices from their partners (in which one person forgoes a preferred activity in order to benefit the other), they are grateful and satisfied when such sacrifices occur; however, if they *do* expect sacrifices to be routine, they gain no pleasure from the generosity of their partners when they encounter it (Zoppolat et al., 2020). Evidently, one's expectations determine how much gratification and contentment is gleaned from a partner's thoughtful kindness, and one can remain unimpressed with notable munificence if one's expectations are excessive.

Second, interdependency theory suggests that our comparison levels will gradually change over time as they track the outcomes we receive. Thus, when we enjoy some success and a partnership *is* rich and rewarding, we may be delighted and contented at first but slowly come to take our gains for granted as we become accustomed to our good fortune. As we are well loved and treated well, our comparison levels—our expectations and our judgments of our interpersonal worth (Schmitt & Jonason, 2019)—are likely to rise. And as we come to expect better and better treatment from our partners, their ability to exceed our expectations gradually shrinks and our satisfaction slowly declines.

Interdependency theory thus predicts that satisfaction with a relationship can be hard to sustain. When we are content, our delight may slowly but steadily fade as our expectations rise. And whenever one expects too much, satisfaction will be elusive. This all suggests that a pattern of slowly diminishing satisfaction with an intimate relationship may be commonplace. Is that true? Is gradually declining delight with our romances an ordinary experience? Let's consider those questions.

Many Marriages Aren't as Happy as People Expect Them to Be

Remarkable studies have now tracked spouses' satisfaction with their marriages over spans of 16 (Birditt et al., 2012), 20 (Anderson et al., 2010), and 35 years (James, 2015), and their findings are clear: Many marriages turn out to be less satisfying over time than they were when they started. In some cases, that change is dramatic and abrupt; about 10% of newlyweds are already distressed and discontent just a few months after their marriages begin (Schramm et al., 2005). Thereafter, idiosyncrasy prevails; some couples start and stay happily married, others display modest declines in their delight, and still others (who were less fulfilled when they wed, on average) become thoroughly disenchanted (Karney & Bradbury, 2020). Overall, however, gradual, moderate diminishment of the satisfaction of heterosexual spouses is typical (Kurdek, 2008). Indeed, in the Netherlands (Soons et al., 2009), Switzerland (Anusic et al., 2014), and Germany and Great Britain (Lucas, 2007), people are generally more satisfied with their lives when they get married than they will ever be again; getting married usually boosts one's well-being, but those gains in contentment don't last. And down the road, a sizable number of marriages don't just decline; they crash and burn. The latest data from the U.S. Census Bureau (Mayol-García et al., 2021) demonstrate that 43% of Americans aged 55–64 who have ever married have been divorced (at least once). While some couples do live happily ever after, it does appear that many marriages—if not most—are not as happy as people expected them to be. The ordinary outcomes of marriage support the supposition that people often expect too much from their marriages. Why is that the case?

Cultural Exemplars Can Be Misleading

To some extent, we should be forgiven for mistaken marital predictions because misleading examples of marital bliss abound. People who read romance novels (Stern et al., 2019), consume television romantic comedies or soap operas (Segrin & Nabi, 2002), or watch Disney princess films such as *Frozen* (Hefner & Kretz, 2021), for instance, tend to have idealized views of marriage that don't fit real relationships.

Moreover, all of us encounter cultural norms that tend to denigrate unmarried people (see Chapter 4) while simultaneously suggesting standards for fulfilling marriages that are hard, if not impossible, to meet. Those who wish to remain single are often quite incorrectly (DePaulo, 2014) stigmatized as unhealthy, lonely losers (Fisher & Sakaluk, 2020) who would be better off if they wed. Arguably, though, it's harder to have a "good" marriage than it used to be. Whereas our grandparents simply expected love and companionship from their marriages, "we now often want our romances to be magical rather than merely pleasant, and deeply fulfilling instead of just fine" (Miller, 2022, p. 229). An "all-or-nothing" model (Finkel, 2017) that "places a premium on spouses helping each other meet their authenticity and personal-growth needs" (p. 10) and that facilitates their "voyages of *self-discovery*" (p. 13, italics added) now applies. As a result, spouses are expected to be perfect partners who are "our best friends, workout partners, spiritual brethren, likeminded sexual partners, culinary compatriots, parental supporters, financial planners, philanthropic kindred spirits, and travel companions" (DeWall, 2015, p. 31). Those are daunting requirements that are hard to meet (McNulty, 2016), and maladaptive cultural norms are a first source of erroneous marital expectations.

Some Personal Beliefs Are Counterproductive

More idiosyncratic are a variety of personal beliefs about romance and intimacy that are unreasonable and unrealistic. People differ in the extent to which they believe that "if you really loved me, we'd never disagree and I wouldn't have to tell you what I want," but those who do are routinely less satisfied with their marriages than are those who don't hold such naive notions (Topkaya et al., 2023).

Notable among the disadvantageous ideas some people hold are *destiny beliefs* that assume that spouses are either soulmates who are right for each other—and thus destined to live happily ever after—or they're not (Knee & Petty, 2013). When disagreements occur (as they inevitably do), partners with such views respond less constructively than those who think that good relationships result from collaborative compromise and hard work (Weigel et al., 2016)—and over time, lower satisfaction with their relationships results (Goodwin & Gaines, 2004). Thus, individuals' personal misconceptions about the nature of successful intimacy are a second source of specious suppositions about marriage.

Our Partners Are Less Wonderful Than We Think They Are

Further, our perceptions of our partners are routinely less accurate than we believe them to be, and what we (think we) see usually isn't exactly what we get. That's because we're typically well aware of our lovers' deficiencies and faults, but we consider them to be less important and influential than they really are (Neff & Karney, 2003). In turn, we also tend to exaggerate our intimates' positive qualities, so that, for instance, we judge them to be more intelligent than they actually are (Gignac & Zajenkowski, 2019). In general, we tend to maintain *positive illusions* of our partners that, to a degree, are idealized fictions; we think that they're more desirable partners than others judge them to be and that, on the whole, they're better people than they really are (Fletcher et al., 2013).

When they're not too unrealistic, such illusions are actually beneficial: They support benevolent perceptions of a partner's behavior that help sustain one's satisfaction (Fletcher, 2015). But they also open the door to unwelcome surprises that can cause disappointment and disillusionment (Niehuis et al., 2011). Another way our expectations can be incorrect is to idealize our partners in a manner that minimizes or even overlooks characteristics of our partners that will ultimately be intolerable.

Consider, for instance, someone's narcissism, which often takes the form of a "fatal attraction" (which is a quality that seems initially attractive in a potential partner but that later becomes one of the most obnoxious and undesirable things about that person [Felmlee, 2001]). Narcissists are snappy dressers (Holtzman & Strube, 2013) and their self-assurance can be appealing (Giacomin & Jordan, 2019), so they often seem attractive early on—and it can take some time to realize just how greedy, prickly, and abusive they truly are (Rentzsch & Gebauer, 2019). Ultimately, expectations that forecast generosity and thoughtfulness from narcissistic people are likely to go unfulfilled.

It's also routine for lovers to think they have more in common with each other than they really do. Lovers overestimate their similarities; they believe that they share more attitudes, interests, and traits than is truly the case (de Jong & Reis, 2014), so they often expect smoother sailing than they actually experience. In sum, then, unwelcome surprises that stem from misperceptions of one's partner are other common sources of inaccurate expectations.

Adverse Events Occur

Disappointments and setbacks are inevitable in life, and, sooner or later, any lasting relationship will encounter unforeseen stresses and strains. Some of these—such as pandemic lockdowns and rising interest rates that put the purchase of a home out of reach (Xu & Wang, 2022)—may afflict large portions of a population, whereas other difficulties—such as illness (Tracy & Utz, 2020) and financial debt (Ascigil et al., 2020)—are more idiosyncratic. Still, whatever their type, stressful events routinely present burdensome challenges that are usually unanticipated.

The damage done by stressors will depend on the existing vulnerabilities of a couple and the coping skills and strategies with which they respond to their circumstances (Backes et al, 2017; Neff & Karney, 2017). Only rarely, however, are they inconsequential (McNulty et al., 2021). And notably, people often underestimate just how stressful some desired experiences—such as parenthood—will turn out to be. The raising of children, which is commonly more expensive, exhausting, and frustrating than people expect, is undeniably a grand adventure that can be very rewarding. Nevertheless, because parenting absorbs a couple's time and their conflicts increase (Doss et al., 2009), parenthood "is associated with deterioration of relationship functioning for the average couple" (Doss & Rhoades, 2017, p. 27), and couples who expect parenthood to be consistently delightful are almost always fooling themselves. Indeed, *unrealistic optimism*, the belief that one's future outcomes will be more positive than can possibly be true (Shepperd et al., 2015), is commonplace, and it is yet another reason why some of our expectations go unfulfilled.

The Grass Can Seem Greener on the Other Side of the Fence

Compared with those who are presently distressed, contented lovers tend to be uninterested in others who might be potential replacements for their current partners (Ma et al., 2019). They're relatively inattentive; they spend less time monitoring their other options (Miller, 1997a), and they underestimate the attractiveness of desirable others when they do come to mind (Cole et al., 2016). These are handy misperceptions that help to protect existing relationships: Romances are more fragile, being less likely to last (Miller, 2008)—and partners are more likely to cheat and have extradyadic sex (McNulty et al., 2018)—when people do take heed of the attractive alternatives available to them.

Unfortunately, beneficial inattention and disinterest in others may be hard to sustain over time. First, as is the case with other means of managing temptation, diverting one's attention from attractive others requires self-control (Brady et al., 2020), and the ability to control one's impulses in this manner is a limited resource (Luchies et al., 2011). Both the inclination and effort to avoid and/or disparage attractive alternatives can erode when one is fatigued, stressed, or intoxicated, allowing desirable others to seem more compelling. Moreover, inattention covaries with one's satisfaction with one's relationship; any episode of discontent is likely to make alternative potential partners both more noticeable *and* (seemingly) more alluring (Miller, 2008). And importantly, some of us have partners who simply don't even *try* to take no notice of their other options; in one large sample of American collegians, 57% of those in committed partnerships were simultaneously maintaining "back burner" relationships, staying in touch with others "with whom they can see a future romantic or sexual connection" (Dibble et al., 2018, p. 216). Others of us have partners who don't really want to have a monogamous relationship; a full fifth of Americans (Haupert et al., 2017) and Canadians (Fairbrother et al., 2019) have experienced consensual arrangements that allowed both partners to have more than one sexual or romantic relationship at the same time (see Chapter 7). Add all this up, and a good many folks who expect that they and their partners will never be distracted by—and seriously attracted to—someone else will sooner or later be mistaken. Hoping that a lover will always "only have eyes for you" is often another source of unmet expectations.

Intimacy Is More Costly Than We Think It Will Be

Finally, we suggest that in forecasting their futures, partners rarely realize that interdependent intimacy is usually more costly than they think it will be. Because partners spend so much time together and depend on each other for so much, interdependency can be said to be a "magnifying glass" (Miller, 1997b): It accentuates the small-but-inescapable vexations and irritations that inevitably occur in even the best relationships. Consequently, over time, our intimate partners are likely to cause us more frustration than anyone else does, and there are several reasons why. First, once a partnership has developed, people typically work less hard to be consistently charming and decorous than they did when they were making first impressions on their first dates—and that lazy lack of effort often causes intimates to be more selfish and less polite to each other than they are to other people (Miller, 2001). Then, through repetition, trivial annoyances can become genuinely exasperating as one's sensitivity to them grows (Cunningham et al., 2005). And their very personal knowledge of our foibles and eccentricities means that, sooner or later, our intimates will accidentally reveal some secret (Petronio, 2010) or embarrass us (Miller, 1996) in ways that no one else can.

The bottom line is that for these and all the other reasons described, most relationships—even those between quite compatible lovers—routinely turn out to be less magical and enchanted than the partners thought they would be. And that gap between the partners' expectations and their actual outcomes opens the door to corrosive disappointment that is a very influential cause of the failure of modern marriages.

Deleterious Disappointment

Marriages that begin poorly—with ambivalence, frustrating incompatibilities, and other stressors at work—are less satisfying than those with fewer problems, and they tend to remain so, being more likely to quickly end in divorce (Huston et al., 2001). That is, of course, no surprise. Over time, however, existing problems—and lower levels of satisfaction—do not predict divorce as well as does a more potent cause of marital failure: *disillusionment*. Coming to find that marriage is less enchanting and exhilarating than one expected is a particular form of displeasure that is especially destructive (Niehuis et al., 2015). Disappointed spouses become less affectionate and begin to have damaging doubts (Niehuis et al., 2016), and it's those changes in contentment that are caustic. Indeed, couples who divorce after several (8–13) years of marriage are often those who were more passionate and loving than most when their marriages began, and who, notably, are no less loving than most when they decide to break up. What turns out to be ruinous in such cases isn't incompatibility; it's a decrease in the delight the partners expected to share (Huston et al., 2001). Erroneous expectations can lead to detrimental disillusionment that put marriages, and any relationship, at risk.

Conclusions: Turning the Tide in the Pursuit of Happiness

People are disappointed and dissatisfied when the outcomes they encounter in life fail to meet their expectations. And because most marriages evidence declines in the spouses' satisfaction over time, it seems that a lot of expectations are not being met. Perhaps this should be no surprise: As we have seen, a variety of influences can lead lovers to expect more from their marriages—such as smoother sailing, greater compatibility, and longer lasting romantic fascination with one another—than they'll actually get. More annoyances, distractions, and setbacks are likely to occur in a typical marriage than most people think.

Indeed, this all suggests that marital satisfaction can be hard to sustain. However, our analysis of the sources of erroneous expectations also suggests targets for intervention that may allow insight and countervailing strategies to support partners' contentment.

Beneficial Beliefs

It's foolish to believe that after we find our perfect partners—our soulmates—our work is done. It's clearly more profitable and more adaptive to hold a *growth* mindset that conceives of a successful marriage as the product of ongoing investments of effort, creativity, and compromise from both spouses (Knee & Petty, 2013). When difficulties arise, partners who hold growth beliefs tend to remain optimistic that obstacles can be overcome, and they're quick to take action to remedy their woes. Such beliefs, then, embody expectations that support, rather than undermine, spouses' satisfaction.

Benevolent Perceptions

Illusory perceptions of one's partner are risky—but *generous* judgments that portray one's partner in the best possible, but reasonable, light are not. Couples are happier, for instance, when they judge each other's kindnesses to be intentional and habitual (Osterhout et al., 2011) while they consider the other's insensitivity or selfishness to be a temporary, accidental aberration (Walsh & Neff, 2020). Moderation and prudence can be key in this regard; perceptions of a spouse's habits, characteristics, and actions that are charitable but sensible are likely to foster desirable forbearance while avoiding unwelcome foolishness (Fletcher, 2015).

Play (and Other Absorbing Adventures)

Spouses who play together usually stay together. Partners who planfully pursue entertainments and adventures that are novel, playful, and passionate tend to be happier with each other than couples who play together less often (Proyer et al., 2019). The value of play was cleverly established by Arthur Aron, who pioneered a procedure that invited couples to crawl through an obstacle course tied together at their wrists and ankles while pushing a foam cylinder with their heads (Aron et al., 2000). The silly activity left couples feeling closer to each other, which wasn't true when participants engaged in a more mundane endeavor. It's a good thing, then, that playfulness can be increased if partners want it to be (Proyer et al., 2021); spouses are undoubtedly less likely to be distracted by other potential partners if they're enjoying lots of fun together, and the rich rewards to be gained from novelty and play can desirably counterbalance some of the unanticipated costs of intimacy.

It's also useful to take the time to mindfully *savor* positive experiences when they occur. Anticipating special events, consciously appreciating them as they unfold, and then happily reminiscing about them afterward all magnify the value of those experiences and increase the satisfaction of the spouses who share them (Lenger & Gordon, 2019). Thoughtfully and actively creating and pursuing positive experiences—and then attentively milking them for as much pleasure as possible—are clever, strategic ways to reduce the injurious gap between their expectations and outcomes that too many couples encounter. Both initiatives can help sustain some of the excitement and energy—and enjoyable discoveries—that characterized a couple's new relationship when they fell in love in the first place (Aron & Tomlinson, 2019).

In Closing, a Call for Relational Realism

Finally, a particularly valuable tactic that may sustain spouses' satisfaction is to have sensible expectations from the start. We suggest that it can be profitable to be more *realistic* than *romantic* in constructing one's expectations for a long-term relationship. To the extent that lovers anticipate warmth and contentment *and* occasional nuisance instead of bottomless beguilement that is free of frustration, they may find themselves more satisfied and less annoyed as years go by. A generous acknowledgment that nobody's perfect is likely to help. Fundamentally, though, expecting to be happy rather than rapturous, and forbearing rather than blissful, is smart; being more reasonable than romantic is apt to be more correct and thus more advantageous, supporting greater satisfaction over time.

Let us note that we do not consider this to be pessimistic advice. (It certainly is not intended to be!) To the contrary, we simply suggest that spouses who expect some bad along with the good are being more prudent and farsighted—and inarguably more accurate—than those who expect unending delight, and their smarter expectations are likely to serve them well.

Once their marriages begin, spouses often do gradually develop more realistic expectations about what the future holds (Vaterlaus et al., 2017). But experience can be a hard teacher, and dangerous disillusionment can be minimized if spouses hold credible and pragmatic outlooks from the start. In the end, a couple's optimistic hope that they'll live (mostly) happily ever after is likely to be both desirable and beneficial only *if* it is cautious and well informed (Neff & Geers, 2013).

In our view, then, many, if not most people, *do* expect too much out of their marriages, and those naive convictions are troublesome. Satisfaction is more likely to follow when partners hold expectations that recognize both the pluses and minuses of sharing one's life with someone else.

References

Anderson, J. R., Van Ryzin, M. J., & Doherty, W. J. (2010). Developmental trajectories of marital happiness in continuously married individuals: A group-based modeling approach. *Journal of Family Psychology, 24*(5), 587–596. https://doi.org/10.1037/a0020928

Anusic, I., Yap, S. C. Y., & Lucas, R. E. (2014). Testing set-point theory in a Swiss national sample: Reaction and adaptation to major life events. *Social Indicators Research, 119*(3), 1265–1288. https://doi.org/10.1007/s11205-013-0541-2

Aron, A., Norman, C. C., Aron, E. N., McKenna, C., & Heyman, R. E. (2000). Couples' shared participation in novel and arousing activities and experienced relationship quality. *Journal of Personality and Social Psychology, 78*(2), 273–284. https://doi.org/10.1037/0022-3514.78.2.273

Aron, A., & Tomlinson, J. M. (2019). Love as expansion of the self. In R. J. Sternberg & K. Sternberg (Eds.), *The new psychology of love* (2nd ed., pp. 1–24). Cambridge University Press.

Ascigil, E., Selcuk, E., Gunaydin, G., & Ong, A. D. (2020). Integrating models of marital functioning to understand the mental health consequences of the Great Recession. *Journal of Social and Personal Relationships, 37*(7), 2118–2135. https://doi.org/10.1177/0265407520918938

Backes, S., Brandstätter, V., Kuster, M., Nussbeck, F. W., Bradbury, T. N., Bodenmann, G., & Sutter-Stickel, D. (2017). Who suffers from stress? Action-state orientation moderates the effect of external stress on relationship satisfaction. *Journal of Social and Personal Relationships, 34*(6), 894–914. https://doi.org/10.1177/0265407516661045

Birditt, K. S., Hope, S., Brown, E., & Orbuch, T. (2012). Developmental trajectories of marital happiness over 16 years. *Research in Human Development, 9*(2), 126–144. https://doi.org/10.1080/15427609.2012.680844

Brady, A., Baker, L. R., & Miller, R. S. (2020). Look but don't touch?: Self-regulation determines whether noticing attractive alternatives increases infidelity. *Journal of Family Psychology, 34*(2), 135–144. https://doi.org/10.1037/fam0000578

Cole, S., Trope, Y., & Balcetis, E. (2016). In the eye of the betrothed: Perceptual downgrading of attractive alternative romantic partners. *Personality and Social Psychology Bulletin, 42*(7), 879–892. https://doi.org/10.1177/0146167216646546

Conner-Spady, B. L., Bohm, E., Loucks, L., Dunbar, M. J., Marshall, D. A., & Noseworthy, T. W. (2020). Patient expectations and satisfaction 6 and 12 months following total hip and knee replacement. *Quality of Life Research, 29*(3), 705–719. https://doi.org/10.1007/s11136-019-02359-7

Cunningham, M. R., Shamblen, S. R., Barbee, A. P., & Ault, L. K. (2005). Social allergies in romantic relationships: Behavioral repetition, emotional sensitization, and dissatisfaction in dating couples. *Personal Relationships, 12*(2), 273–295. https://doi.org/10.1111/j.1350-4126.2005.00115.x

de Jong, D. C., & Reis, H. T. (2014). Sexual kindred spirits: Actual and overperceived similarity, complementarity, and partner accuracy in heterosexual couples. *Personality and Social Psychology Bulletin, 40*(10), 1316–1329. https://doi.org/10.1177/0146167214542801

DePaulo, B. (2014). A singles studies perspective on Mount Marriage. *Psychological Inquiry, 25*(1), 64–68. https://doi.org/10.1080/1047840X.2014.878173

DeWall, C. N. (2015). Teaching students why a good marriage is hard to find. *Observer, 28*(8), 31–32.

Dibble, J. L., Punyanunt-Carter, N. M., & Drouin, M. (2018). Maintaining relationship alternatives electronically: Positive relationship maintenance in back burner relationships. *Communication Research Reports, 35*(3), 200–209. https://doi.org/10.1080/08824096.2018.1425985

Doss, B. D., & Rhoades, G. K. (2017). The transition to parenthood: Impact on couples' romantic relationships. *Current Opinion in Psychology, 13,* 25–28. https://doi.org/10.1016/j.copsyc.2016.04.003

Doss, B. D., Rhoades, G. K., Stanley, S. M., & Markman, H. J. (2009). The effect of the transition to parenthood on relationship quality: An 8-year prospective study. *Journal of Personality and Social Psychology, 96*(3), 601–619. https://doi.org/10.1037/a0013969

Fairbrother, N., Hart, T. A., & Fairbrother, M. (2019). Open relationship prevalence, characteristics, and correlates in a nationally representative sample of Canadian adults. *Journal of Sex Research, 56*(6), 695–704. https://doi.org/10.1080/00224499.2019.1580667

Felmlee, D. H. (2001). From appealing to appalling: Disenchantment with a romantic partner. *Sociological Perspectives, 44*(3), 263–280. https://doi.org/10.1525/sop.2001.44.3.263

Finkel, E. J. (2017). *The all-or-nothing marriage: How the best marriages work.* Dutton.

Fisher, A. N., & Sakaluk, J. K. (2020). Are single people a stigmatized "group"? Evidence from examinations of social identity, entitativity, and perceived responsibility. *Journal of Experimental Social Psychology, 86,* Article 103844. https://doi.org/10.1016/j.jesp.2019.103844

Fletcher, G. J. O. (2015). Accuracy and bias of judgments in romantic relationships. *Current Directions in Psychological Science, 24*(4), 292–297. https://doi.org/10.1177/0963721415571664

Fletcher, G., & Kerr, P. (2013). Love, reality, and illusion in intimate relationships. In J. Simpson & L. Campbell (Eds.), *The Oxford handbook of close relationships* (pp. 306–320). Oxford University Press.

Geeraert, N., Demes, K. A., & Ward, C. (2021). Sojourner expectations: Are they met and does it matter if they're not? *International Journal of Intercultural Relations, 84,* 27–40. https://doi.org/10.1016/j.ijintrel.2021.06.004

Giacomin, M., & Jordan, C. H. (2019). Misperceiving grandiose narcissism as self-esteem: Why narcissists are well liked at zero acquaintance. *Journal of Personality, 87*(4), 827–842. https://doi.org/10.1111/jopy.12436

Gignac, G. E., & Zajenkowski, M. (2019). People tend to overestimate their romantic partner's intelligence even more than their own. *Intelligence, 73,* 41–51. https://doi.org/10.1016/j.intell.2019.01.004

Goodwin, R., & Gaines, S. O., Jr. (2004). Relationships beliefs and relationship quality across cultures: Country as a moderator of dysfunctional beliefs and relationship quality in three former Communist societies. *Personal Relationships, 11*(3), 267–279. https://doi.org/10.1111/j.1475-6811.2004.00082.x

Haupert, M. L., Gesselman, A. N., Moors, A. C., Fisher, H. E., & Garcia, J. R. (2017). Prevalence of experiences with consensual nonmonogamous relationships: Findings from two national samples of single Americans. *Journal of Sex & Marital Therapy, 43*(5), 424–440. https://doi.org/10.1080/0092623X.2016.1178675

Hefner, V., & Kretz, V. E. (2021). Does the glass slipper fit? Disney princess films and relationship beliefs and attitudes. *Journal of Media Psychology, 33*(3), 125–133. https://doi.org/10.1027/1864-1105/a000290

Holtzman, N. S., & Strube, M. J. (2013). People with dark personalities tend to create a physically attractive veneer. *Social Psychological and Personality Science, 4*(4), 461–467. https://doi.org/10.1177/1948550612461284

Huston, T. L., Caughlin, J. P., Houts, R. M., Smith, S. E., & George, L. J. (2001). The connubial crucible: Newlywed years as predictors of marital delight, distress, and divorce. *Journal of Personality and Social Psychology, 80*(2), 237–252. https://doi.org/10.1037/0022-3514.80.2.237

James, S. L. (2015). Variation in trajectories of women's marital quality. *Social Science Research, 49*, 16–30. https://doi.org/10.1016/j.ssresearch.2014.07.010

Karney, B. R., & Bradbury, T. N. (2020). Research on marital satisfaction and stability in the 2010s: Challenging conventional wisdom. *Journal of Marriage and Family, 82*(1), 100–116. https://doi.org/10.1111/jomf.12635

Kelley, D. L., & Burgoon, J. K. (1991). Understanding marital satisfaction and couple type as functions of relational expectations. *Human Communication Research, 18*(1), 40–69. https://doi.org/10.1111/j.1468-2958.1991.tb00528.x

Kelley, H. H., & Thibaut, J. W. (1978). *Interpersonal relations: A theory of interdependence.* Wiley.

Knee, C. R., & Petty, K. N. (2013). Implicit theories of relationships: Destiny and growth beliefs. In J. A. Simpson & L. Campbell (Eds.), *The Oxford handbook of close relationships* (pp. 183–198). Oxford University Press.

Kurdek, L. A. (2008). Change in relationship quality for partners from lesbian, gay male, and heterosexual couples. *Journal of Family Psychology, 22*(5), 701–711. https://doi.org/10.1037/0893-3200.22.5.701

Lenger, K. A., & Gordon, C. L. (2019). To have and to savor: Examining the associations between savoring and relationship satisfaction. *Couple and Family Psychology: Research and Practice, 8*(1), 1–9. https://doi.org/10.1037/cfp0000111

Lou, V. W. Q., Chow, J. C-C., & Chan, C. L. W. (2004). Impact of expectation fulfillment on post-migration marital happiness among mainland Chinese wives with Hong Kong husbands. *Journal of Social Work Research and Evaluation, 5*(1), 99–112.

Lucas, R. E. (2007). Adaptation and the set-point model of subjective well-being: Does happiness change after major life events? *Current Directions in Psychological Science, 16*(2), 75–79. https://doi.org/10.1111/j.1467-8721.2007.00479.x

Luchies, L. B., Finkel, E. J., & Fitzsimons, G. M. (2011). The effects of self-regulatory strength, content, and strategies on close relationships. *Journal of Personality, 79*(6), 949–977. https://doi.org/10.1111/j.1467-6494.2010.00701.x

Ma, Y., Xue, W., Zhao, G., Tu, S., & Zheng, Y. (2019). Romantic love and attentional biases toward attractive alternatives and rivals: Long-term relationship maintenance among female Chinese college students. *Evolutionary Psychology, 17*(4), 1–14. https://doi.org/10.1177/1474704919897601

Mayol-García, Y., Gurrentz, B., & Kreider, R. M. (2021). *Number, timing, and duration of marriages and divorces: 2016.* Current Population Reports. United States Census Bureau Report Number P70-167. Retrieved from https://www.census.gov/library/publications/2021/demo/p70-167.html

McNulty, J. K. (2016). Should spouses be demanding less from marriage? A contextual perspective on the implications of interpersonal standards. *Personality and Social Psychology Bulletin, 42*(4), 444–457. https://doi.org/10.1177/0146167216634050

McNulty, J. K., & Karney, B. R. (2002). Expectancy confirmation in appraisals of marital interactions. *Personality and Social Psychology Bulletin, 28*(6), 764–775. https://doi.org/10.1177/0146167202289006

McNulty, J. K., & Karney, B. R. (2004). Positive expectations in the early years of marriage: Should couples expect the best or brace for the worst? *Journal of Personality and Social Psychology, 86*(5), 729–743. https://doi.org/10.1037/0022-3514.86.5.729

McNulty, J. K., Meltzer, A. L., Makhanova, A., & Maner, J. K. (2018). Attentional and evaluative biases help people maintain relationships by avoiding infidelity. *Journal of Personality and Social Psychology, 115*(1), 76–95. https://doi.org/10.1037/pspi0000127

McNulty, J. K., Meltzer, A. L., Neff, L. A., & Karney, B. R. (2021). How both partners' individual differences, stress, and behavior predict change in relationship satisfaction: Extending the VSA model. *PNAS, 118*(27), ArtID: e2101402118. https://doi.org/10.1073/pnas.2101402118

Miller, R. S. (1996). *Embarrassment: Poise and peril in everyday life*. Guilford Press.

Miller, R. S. (1997a). Inattentive and contented: Relationship commitment and attention to alternatives. *Journal of Personality and Social Psychology, 73*(4), 758–766. https://doi.org/10.1037/0022-3514.73.4.758

Miller, R. S. (1997b). We always hurt the ones we love: Aversive interactions in close relationships. In R. M. Kowalski (Ed.), *Aversive interpersonal behaviors* (pp. 11–29). Plenum Press. https://doi.org/10.1007/978-1-4757-9354-3_2

Miller, R. S. (2001). Breaches of propriety. In R. M. Kowalski (Ed.), *Behaving badly: Aversive behaviors in interpersonal relationships* (pp. 29–58). American Psychological Association. https://doi.org/10.1037/10365-002

Miller, R. S. (2008). Attending to temptation: The operation (and perils) of attention to alternatives in close relationships. In J. P. Forgas & J. Fitness (Eds.), *Social relationships: Cognitive, affective, and motivational processes* (pp. 321–337). Psychology Press.

Miller, R. S. (2022). *Intimate relationships* (9th ed.). McGraw Hill.

Mitnick, D. M., Heyman, R. E., Slep, A. M. S., Giresi, J., & Shanley, J. E. (2022). Impact of expectation violation on relationship satisfaction across the transition to parenthood. *Journal of Family Psychology, 36*(2), 236–245. https://doi.org/10.1037/fam0000870

Neff, L. A., & Geers, A. L. (2013). Optimistic expectations in early marriage: A resource or vulnerability for adaptive relationship functioning? *Journal of Personality and Social Psychology, 105*(1), 38–60. https://doi.org/10.1037/a0032600

Neff, L. A., & Karney, B. R. (2003). The dynamic structure of relationship perceptions: Differential importance as a strategy of relationship maintenance. *Personality and Social Psychology Bulletin, 29*(11), 1433–1446. https://doi.org/10.1177/0146167203256376

Neff, L. A., & Karney, B. R. (2017). Acknowledging the elephant in the room: How stressful environmental contexts shape relationship dynamics. *Current Opinion in Psychology, 13*, 107–110. https://doi.org/10.1016/j.copsyc.2016.05.013

Niehuis, S., Lee, K., Reifman, A., Swenson, A., & Hunsaker, S. (2011). Idealization and disillusionment in intimate relationships: A review of theory, method, and research. *Journal of Family Theory & Review, 3*(4), 273–302. https://doi.org/10.1111/j.1756-2589.2011.00100.x

Niehuis, S., Reifman, A., Feng, D., & Huston, T. L. (2016). Courtship progression rate and declines in expressed affection early in marriage: A test of the disillusionment model. *Journal of Family Issues, 37*(8), 1074–1100. https://doi.org/10.1177/0192513X14540159

Niehuis, S., Reifman, A., & Lee, K.-H. (2015). Disillusionment in cohabiting and married couples: A national study. *Journal of Family Issues, 36*(7), 951–973. https://doi.org/10.1177/0192513X13498594

Osterhout, R. E., Frame, L. E., & Johnson, M. D. (2011). Maladaptive attributions and dyadic behavior are associated in engaged couples. *Journal of Social and Clinical Psychology, 30*(8), 787–818. https://doi.org/10.1521/jscp.2011.30.8.787

Petronio, S. (2010). Communication privacy management theory: What do we know about family privacy regulation? *Journal of Family Theory & Review, 2*(3), 175–196. https://doi.org/10.1111/j.1756-2589.2010.00052.x

Proyer, R. T., Brauer, K., Gander, F., & Chick, G. (2021). Can playfulness be stimulated? A randomized placebo-controlled online playfulness intervention study on effects on trait playfulness, well-being, and depression. *Applied Psychology: Health and Well-Being, 13*(1), 129–151. https://doi.org/10.1111/aphw.12220

Proyer, R. T., Brauer, K., Wolf, A., & Chick, G. (2019). Adult playfulness and relationship satisfaction: An APIM analysis of romantic couples. *Journal of Research in Personality, 79*, 40–48. https://doi.org/10.1016/j.jrp.2019.02.001

Rentzsch, K., & Gebauer, J. E. (2019). On the popularity of agentic and communal narcissists: The tit-for-tat hypothesis. *Personality and Social Psychology Bulletin, 45*(9), 1365–1377. https://doi.org/10.1177/0146167218824359

Rosen, N. O., Vannier, S. A., Johnson, M. D., McCarthy, L., & Impett, E. A. (2022). Unmet and exceeded expectations for sexual concerns across the transition to parenthood. *Journal of Sex Research*. https://doi.org/10.1080/00224499.2022.2126814

Schmitt, D. P., & Jonason, P. K. (2019). Self-esteem as an adaptive sociometer of mating success: Evaluating evidence of sex-specific psychological design across 10 world regions. *Personality and Individual Differences, 143*, 13–20. https://doi.org/10.1016/j.paid.2019.02.011

Schnaufer, K., Christandl, F., Berger, S., Meynhardt, T., & Gollwitzer, M. (2022). The shift to pay transparency: Undermet pay standing expectations and consequences. *Journal of Organizational Behavior, 43*(1), 69–90. https://doi.org/10.1002/job.2575

Schramm, D. G., Marshall, J. P., Harris, V. W., & Lee, T. R. (2005). After "I do": The newlywed transition. *Marriage & Family Review, 38*(1), 45–67. https://doi.org/10.1300/J002v38n01_05

Segrin, C., & Nabi, R. L. (2002). Does television viewing cultivate unrealistic expectations about marriage? *Journal of Communication, 52*(2), 247–263. https://doi.org/10.1111/j.1460-2466.2002.tb02543.x

Shepperd, J. A., Waters, E. A., Weinstein, N. D., & Klein, W. M. P. (2015). A primer on unrealistic optimism. *Current Directions in Psychological Science, 24*(3), 232–237. https://doi.org/10.1177/0963721414568341

Soons, J. P. M., Liefbroer, A. C., & Kalmijn, M. (2009). The long-term consequences of relationship formation for subjective well-being. *Journal of Marriage and Family, 71*(5), 1254–1270. https://doi.org/10.1111/j.1741-3737.2009.00667.x

Stern, S. C., Robbins, B., Black, J. E., & Barnes, J. L. (2019). What you read and what you believe: Genre exposure and beliefs about relationships. *Psychology of Aesthetics, Creativity, and the Arts, 13*(4), 450–461. https://doi.org/10.1037/aca0000189

Thibaut, J. W., & Kelley, H. H. (1959). *The social psychology of groups*. Wiley.
Topkaya, N., Şahin, E., & Mehel, F. (2023). Relationship-specific irrational beliefs and relationship satisfaction in intimate relationships. *Current Psychology*, 42(2), 1257–1269. https://doi.org/10.1007/s12144-021-01426-y
Tracy, E. L., & Utz, R. L. (2020). For better or for worse: Health and marital quality during midlife. *Journal of Aging and Health*, 32(10), 1625–1635. https://doi.org/10.1177/0898264320948305
Vannier, S. A., & O'Sullivan, L. F. (2017). Passion, connection, and destiny: How romantic expectations help predict satisfaction and commitment in young adults' dating relationships. *Journal of Social and Personal Relationships*, 34(2), 235–257. https://doi.org/10.1177/0265407516631156
Vaterlaus, J. M., Skogrand, L., Chaney, C., & Gahagan, K. (2017). Marital expectations in strong African American marriages. *Family Process*, 56(4), 883–899. https://doi.org/10.1111/famp.12263
Walsh, C. M., & Neff, L. A. (2020). The importance of investing in your relationship: Emotional capital and responses to partner transgressions. *Journal of Social and Personal Relationships*, 37(2), 581–601. https://doi.org/10.1177/0265407519875225
Weigel, D. J., Lalasz, C. B., & Weiser, D. A. (2016). Maintaining relationships: The role of implicit relationship theories and partner fit. *Communication Reports*, 29(1), 23–34. https://doi.org/10.1080/08934215.2015.1017653
Xu, Y., & Wang, F. (2022). The health consequence of rising housing prices in China. *Journal of Economic Behavior & Organization*, 200, 114–137. https://doi.org/10.1016/j.jebo.2022.05.011
Zoppolat, G., Visserman, M. L., & Righetti, F. (2020). A nice surprise: Sacrifice expectations and partner appreciation in romantic relationships. *Journal of Social and Personal Relationships*, 37(2), 450–466. https://doi.org/10.1177/0265407519867145

6
Equity and Gender Roles in Marriage

Are We Finally Equal?

Grace M. Wetzel and Diana T. Sanchez

Gender roles have a long history of impacting many aspects of life in a deeply entrenched manner. The current chapter assesses how these gender roles influence various aspects of romantic relationships, particularly in the context of heterosexual marriage. Research indicates that there are well-established gender disparities between men and women that continue to persist across various domains relevant to romantic relationships and marital life (e.g., household labor, sexuality). In this chapter, we will review the literature on inequities that exist in these domains, namely, household labor and child care, mental labor, income and work responsibility, and sexual pleasure. We will discuss how heteronormative gender roles uphold disparities in these domains, compare outcomes for those in same-gender relationships to those in heterosexual relationships, and provide recommendations that might encourage more equitable marriages for heterosexual couples.

Gender Roles

Men have historically been viewed as the breadwinners of society while women are viewed as the caretakers of the house and family (Eagly, 1987). These societal roles are reflected in the core gender stereotypes of agency and communality, in which men are stereotyped as agentic and women as communal (Williams & Best, 1990). Core traits of communality include an interest in children, sensitivity, cooperation, warmth, and support. Thus, this stereotype is fitting for women's assigned role in family care. Agency is embodied by traits such as being competitive, career oriented, intelligent, ambitious, and assertive, fitting for men's historical role in the professional and political realm. Men and women experience backlash (i.e., negative social repercussions) when they display prohibited gender traits. The largest sources of gender backlash occur when women embody agentic traits perceived as dominant (e.g., aggressive, intimidating) or when men display communal traits perceived as weak (e.g., emotional, insecure; Rudman, 1998; Rudman & Glick, 2001).

Importantly, men are societally prohibited from embodying traits low in status while women experience backlash for embodying traits high in status (Rudman & Glick, 2001). Attributes associated with men have long been associated with higher status than those attributed to women (Gerber, 2009). Thus, these traits serve as a way of reinforcing an unequal gender system by supporting men's continued occupation of high-status roles. Women often face a dilemma when pursuing leadership roles, wherein they must display agency and disconfirm feminine stereotypes in order to be perceived as competent but are seen as less likable when they do so (Rudman & Phelan, 2008). Negative reactions for gender violations (i.e., backlash; Rudman, 1998; Rudman & Glick, 2001) have been documented in the literature starting as early as the 1970s (e.g., Costrich et al., 1975) and persisting in more recent work (Skewes et al., 2018; Xiao et al., 2022).

Gendered expectancies are influenced by racial stereotypes, which shape the type of backlash agentic women receive (e.g., Livingston et al., 2012; Schug et al., 2015). Because Black women are stereotypically expected to behave more aggressively than White women, they may have weaker gender proscriptions discouraging agentic behavior (Livingston et al., 2012; Rosette et al., 2016). However, Asian women may experience even greater feminine expectancies than White women, leading to increased backlash for Asian women's agentic behavior (Rosette et al., 2016). Recent research finds that, regardless of the target's race, perceivers tend to express the greatest backlash toward women in their racial in-groups (Xiao et al., 2022). Thus, it is important to consider the ways in which racial identity intersects with central gender stereotypes. Expectations related to these central stereotypes of agency and communality affect marital outcomes across domains, discussed in detail next.

Household Labor and Child Care

While women have continued to enter the workforce in increasing numbers over the past 50 years, their time dedicated to housework has not reflected this change. Hochschild (1989) argued that working wives and mothers spend far more time on household labor and childcare than their husbands, essentially serving as a second job and creating a leisure gap (i.e., a discrepancy in the amount of time available for leisure, outside of paid or unpaid work). This phenomenon was named "the second shift" (Hochschild, 1989). While the situation has improved since the 1980s, men's and women's contributions are hardly equitable. Recent work finds that women still do almost twice as much housework as men (18 hours of household work per week for wives compared with 10 hours for husbands; Bianchi et al., 2012).

One argument for the unequal division of housework is that the spouse with higher levels of resources (e.g., education, income) has greater power within the relationship and, thus, less responsibility to contribute to housework. The gender–wage ratio between partners has been identified as one of the most important predictors of perceived fairness when it comes to housework distribution (Braun et al., 2008). Because men have historically contributed greater income and still earn more than women (i.e., the gender wage gap; Hegewisch et al., 2014), wives are typically left with greater housework responsibility. However, this hypothesis has not been fully supported. When wives report equal income to or greater income than their husbands, women still report doing over 60% of the housework (Fetterolf & Rudman, 2014). Women's reports of their average housework share only decreased by 10% when earning less versus earning greater income than their husbands (from 72% to 62% of the housework share; Fetterolf & Rudman, 2014).

In a study examining expected and desired housework share, women expected to do substantially more household chores and child care than men, and more than they ideally wanted (Askari et al., 2010). There are also gender divisions regarding the kind of housework that men and women do, with men doing a larger proportion of occasional, discretionary tasks (e.g., yard work, car maintenance) as opposed to routine, everyday chores (e.g., cooking, washing dishes; Coltrane, 2000). Husbands and wives may see this division of household tasks as fair, although women's share of the task division is, in fact, much larger (Hochschild, 1989).

Wives often evaluate fairness in comparison with other wives, and husbands evaluate fairness in comparison with other husbands (Hochschild, 1989). Research finds that women use time availability (e.g., their husbands work more hours), resource dependence (e.g., their husbands make more money), and gender ideology (e.g., housework is part of their role as a woman) as legitimizing principles to shape their perceptions of fairness in doing the majority of the housework (Braun et al., 2008). However, in many couples today, both spouses are likely to work full-time (Blair-Loy, 2010), and women tend to do the majority of housework even when they make an equal or greater contribution to the household income than their husbands, as previously discussed (Fetterolf & Rudman, 2014).

Similar trends emerge with child care specifically, wherein mothers spend substantially more time on child care than fathers (Craig, 2006; Raley et al., 2012). A lack of paternity leave policies hinders women's ability to share the child care responsibilities with men, despite evidence that paternity leave increases women's wages and produces higher household wages overall (Andersen, 2018). Also, as a result of having children, mothers are more likely than fathers to drop out of the workforce, take reduced hours, choose more family-friendly jobs, or decline promotions (Raley et al., 2012). This disparity in child care, as well as household labor, reflects the persistence of gendered roles, such that husbands still have more opportunity in the professional realm, while wives tend to play a greater role in family life.

Social expectations have shifted since the 1970s toward involved fatherhood, with men expected to care for and emotionally connect with their children. However, fathers still retain their expected role as primary income earners (Kay, 2006; Raley et al., 2012). Thus, husbands may be expected to take on new responsibilities (family care) without releasing any old ones (paid work), in a similar manner to wives who work outside the home yet have not released any household responsibilities (Kay, 2006). Ultimately, social trends have led to more involved fatherhood (i.e., fathers spending more time with children), but women's expectations for involved motherhood and men's workplace expectations have increased simultaneously, leaving true equity out of reach (Shaw, 2010).

While the discrepancy in household labor and child care has persisted over the past several decades, recent trends show a decrease in the amount of housework executed by women and an increase in men's contribution to household chores and child care (e.g., Bianchi et al., 2000; Sayer et al., 2004). However, a decrease in women's contribution to housework does not necessarily guarantee a shift toward gender equity. Today, more excess labor is often outsourced beyond the family or is not done at all (Bianchi et al., 2000). Because perceived domestic overburdening is related to marital satisfaction and marital outcomes (Frisco & Williams, 2003), class dynamics play a role in the "divorce divide," in which higher income couples have experienced a decline in divorce rates since the 1980s, while the opposite is true for lower income couples (Blair-Loy et al., 2015; Stevenson & Wolfers, 2007). Upper-class women often have the privilege to pass "invisible" labor to lower class women and, thus, retain marital satisfaction (Blair-Loy et al., 2015).

The division of domestic work is an important marital discrepancy, because unfair domestic labor distributions may account for women's lower marital satisfaction compared with men (Claffey & Mickelson, 2009). Women tend to have greater marital satisfaction when they have a reduced housework load (i.e., husbands share the housework equally or work is outsourced). Women with high expectations for egalitarianism tend to experience more marital strain when engaging in high levels of household labor, which likely reflects a disconnect between women's desire for relational equity and their reality (Claffey & Mickelson, 2009). Individual perceptions of fairness are an important mediator between unequal divisions of household labor and marital and personal stress for wives and mothers. Women who perceive the distribution of household labor as unfair within their marriages are more than twice as likely to be divorced eight years later (Frisco & Williams, 2003; Blair-Loy et al., 2015).

While the "second shift" has improved since the 1980s, the gender imbalance of household labor and child care remains. Thus, to preserve satisfaction within mixed-sex marriages, it may be important to reassess the ways that traditional gender roles have defined housework and child care expectations. Couples should search for a family work and paid work distribution that is considered fair and satisfying to both members of the couple, while keeping in mind that gender norms may shape our very perceptions of what is seen as "fair."

Mental Labor

Related to housework and child care responsibilities, wives, particularly mothers, tend to take on a larger proportion of "mental work" for the household (Robertson et al., 2019). Mental work is defined as the "thinking performed for the sake of accomplishing family goals" (p. 196; Robertson et al., 2019). Mental labor has been described as a sort of "mental spreadsheet," in which individuals keep track of tasks and participate in the thinking needed to accomplish daily activities (Offer, 2014, p. 917). Mental labor is historically understudied (Lee & Waite, 2005) and often remains invisible and unacknowledged, as it intersects with and is disguised within other forms of household and family work (Walzer, 1996).

The mental labor that wives perform for the household is complex and multifaceted. It can range from planning and strategizing (e.g., time management, planning activities, creating contingency plans) to meta-parenting (e.g., developing and executing a parenting philosophy that will guide the parents' decisions; Robertson et al., 2019). A substantial body of research suggests that mothers take on the majority of mental labor for the household (e.g., Meier et al., 2006). Mental labor is intertwined with ideas and expectations about motherhood and gender roles in family life, in which mothers are considered the "default" parent with ultimate responsibility for running the household (Robertson et al., 2019). In one recent sample of 25 mothers, all of them believed themselves to be the primary source of mental labor for the family, regardless of employment status (Robertson et al., 2019). Including mental work modestly widens existing gender disparities in household labor distribution (Lee & Waite, 2005). Additionally, early research on mental work asserted that the gendered division of invisible mental work contributed to marital stress and increased gender differentiation (Walzer, 1996). Some research finds that simply delegating tasks is not effective at reducing mothers' stress compared with sharing mental responsibility with the coparent (Walzer, 1996). Gender inequities in mental work have been established, yet research on its consequences is nascent. This disparity likely contributes to similar consequences for women's health, occupational achievements, and marital outcomes.

Work and Financial Contribution

While women in heterosexual partnerships take on a larger share of domestic work and child care, including mental labor, men have historically taken on a greater share of professional, paid work and have been largely responsible for family income (Eagly, 1987). Today, both members of a heterosexual marriage are likely to work, and women make up half of the U.S. paid workforce (Blair-Loy, 2010; Blair-Loy et al., 2015). However, while the wage gap has decreased since 1970, women still earn a lower income than men overall (Blair-Loy et al., 2015; Hegewisch et al., 2014). The gender pay gap is more usefully framed as a "maternal wage penalty," as women with children make less money than both men and women without children (Cukrowska-Torzewska & Matysiak, 2020; Glauber, 2018). Comparatively, fathers experience an increase in wages, which reflects an opposing phenomenon known as the "paternal boost" (Glauber, 2018). While research has indicated that the maternal wage penalty has decreased since 1980, the paternal wage boost has modestly increased over time (Glauber, 2018). Changes in wage gaps over time are also dependent on class status, with upper- and middle class women experiencing a greater decrease in the motherhood penalty compared with lower class women, and upper class men experiencing the greatest paternal boost (Glauber, 2018). Prejudice and stereotypes about working mothers and fathers shape expectations for parental roles and likely contribute to women getting paid less than men even within the same jobs (Glauber, 2018; Park et al., 2010). Research has shown that mothers are viewed as less competent, less capable, and less committed to their work, and as a result of this bias, mothers may be less likely to be hired, promoted, and compensated fairly as compared with fathers (Benard & Correli, 2010; Correli et al., 2007; Glauber, 2018).

While working fathers typically receive advantages over mothers in the workplace (Williams, 2003), fathers sometimes face a flexibility stigma at work, because they are expected to embody an ideal worker and uphold standards of masculinity related to their work (Blair-Loy et al., 2015). Men and women alike consider men who take leave, request part-time work, or have family care responsibilities to be poor workers, and these evaluations are tied to perceptions of femininity (Rudman & Mescher, 2013; Vandello et al., 2013). In one study, regardless of whether men took leave for child care or elderly parental care, they were seen as less agentic and weaker than men in a control condition, leading to fewer recommendations for rewards (e.g., promotion) and greater recommendations for penalties (e.g., pay cut; Rudman & Mescher, 2013). Thus, men are often discriminated against to a greater extent than women when they take family leave.

Societal expectations about gender and work contribute to different professional penalties for women and men. Working mothers tend to be evaluated negatively, be paid less, and receive fewer professional opportunities, but working fathers also experience professional penalties when they attempt to play a larger role in family care (e.g., take family leave). Much of the research on these effects has been conducted in the past 10 years, indicating that gendered expectations in the workplace and their corresponding penalties for parents have not yet been resolved.

Sexuality

Cultural norms about gender and sexuality create gender-based sexual scripts, which inform individual behaviors in romantic and sexual relationships (Simon & Gagnon, 1986). Review Chapter 10 in this volume for more information on this topic. Fitting with stereotypical gender roles, men are typically expected to be dominant, and women are typically expected to be submissive in sexual and romantic scenarios (Sanchez et al., 2012b). Today, sexual gender roles have become more egalitarian in the sense that women are encouraged to pursue sexual and relationship partners, and women initiate sex more often than in the past, though men still initiate sex more frequently than women (Sanchez et al., 2012a; Vannier & O'Sullivan, 2011). However, sexuality as a domain is one in which people often feel most compelled to enact gendered roles, including dominance and submission (Sanchez et al., 2012a).

Women have been shown to accept and even internalize a submissive sexual role in which their own sexual desires are secondary. Not only do women report more sexually submissive behavior than men, but when primed with sex, women identify submission-related words more easily (e.g., comply, submit). Those with stronger associations between sex and submission also show greater sexual issues, including difficulty with orgasm (Kiefer et al., 2006). The concept of sex appears to prime submission in other domains as well, with women writing a smaller signature, waiting longer to interrupt an experimenter, and complying with obnoxious experimenter demands after being primed with sex. Men, on the other hand, show opposite reactions when primed with sex (Hundhammer & Mussweiler, 2012).

Women's sexual submission has been associated with diminished sexual autonomy, which, in turn, is associated with less sexual satisfaction for women and their partners, even when controlling for related factors such as sexual desire and relationship satisfaction (Kiefer & Sanchez, 2007; Sanchez et al., 2006). On the contrary, women's sexual assertiveness predicts greater sexual satisfaction for both men and women (Kiefer & Sanchez, 2007; Sanchez et al., 2012b). In fact, both men and women suffer from lower arousal and lower orgasm rates when they "perform gender" in the bedroom. In other words, if men and women feel as though they must enact gendered expectations during sexual encounters, they are less able to experience their sexuality authentically and ultimately are less sexually satisfied (Sanchez et al., 2005; Sanchez et al., 2012a).

In addition to the established impact of gender roles on sexual satisfaction, a reliable and large orgasm gap exists between men and women in heterosexual partnerships, with men having substantially more orgasms than women on average (e.g., Frederick et al., 2018; Mahar et al., 2020; Wetzel & Sanchez, 2022). In one recent study of heterosexual adults in committed relationships, 95% of men reported usually or always experiencing orgasm, while only 65% of women reported the same (Frederick et al., 2018). While women have more orgasms in relationships than during casual, "hookup" sex (Armstrong et al., 2012), the orgasm gap persists in long-term relationships and marriages that span many years (Jones et al., 2018; Wetzel et al., 2022).

Biological essentialist explanations for orgasm differences between men and women argue that women are less capable of orgasm, biologically speaking, and that women's orgasm is elusive or difficult to achieve (Matsick et al., 2016). However, there is evidence to the contrary of these claims. The clitoris and the penis are homologous structures with similar form and function, which develop during gestation from the same tissue (Nagoski, 2015). Additionally, women have similar or equal orgasm rates to men in several contexts (e.g., during masturbation, during sex with women, and during sexual encounters that include sufficient clitoral stimulation; Frederick et al., 2018; Kinsey et al., 1953; Wetzel & Sanchez, 2022), pointing to contextual rather than biological causes of the orgasm gap.

Orgasm frequency is a strong predictor of sexual satisfaction, especially for women (e.g., Haning et al., 2007). Additionally, an individual's partner's orgasm rate is correlated with that individual's own sexual satisfaction (Jones et al., 2018; Wetzel et al., 2022). Thus, increasing women's orgasm frequency increases sexual satisfaction for both members of a mixed-sex couple. Orgasm and sexual satisfaction have positive associations with several sexual outcomes for couples, including sex duration, sexual variety, sexual communication, and relationship satisfaction, as well as general psychological well-being (Byers, 2005; Davison et al., 2009; Frederick et al., 2018; Jones et al., 2018). As such, the persistence of orgasm inequity can have expansive costs for marital couples.

While several methods have been established for mixed-sex couples to increase women's orgasm frequency (e.g., sexual communication, clitoral stimulation), some heterosexual women have stopped expecting orgasm in their partnered sexual encounters (Goldey et al., 2016). Women's experience with low orgasm frequency compared with men can shape expectations about the orgasm frequency that should be expected (Wetzel et al., 2022). When women do not feel entitled to take steps to achieve orgasm with their partners, they may begin to redefine what sexual satisfaction means to them, in order to compensate for the inequality (McClelland, 2010). While women may cope with the orgasm gap by adjusting their expectations and redefining their sexual satisfaction, low orgasm frequency for women is still associated with several negative outcomes for couples.

Orgasm is not always the goal of a sexual encounter or the only route to a sexually satisfying experience (Chadwick et al., 2019). However, the persistence of the orgasm gap as one of the largest and most reliable gender differences within heterosexual relationships represents a form of gender inequity that is often overlooked within marital life. Few interventions have been tested to change the underlying beliefs and behaviors that contribute to this gap.

Same-Sex Relationships

Research has found that same-sex couples divide household labor and child care in a more egalitarian manner than mixed-sex couples (Perlesz et al., 2010; Goldberg et al., 2012). However, when disparities exist, the partner with lower income or greater work flexibility tends to take on the larger share of domestic work (Sutphin, 2010). Many lesbian and gay couples assert that their household responsibilities are distributed according to preferences and strengths rather than gendered expectations (Perlesz et al., 2010; Rawsthorne & Costello, 2010). However, many same-sex couples split domestic and paid work arrangements, with one member of the couple taking on a larger proportion of paid work and the other member doing the majority of unpaid work in a manner that mirrors heteronormative gender role divisions (Downing & Goldberg, 2011). Same-sex couples are typically aware of and may have complex relationships with heteronormative divisions of labor (Goldberg, 2013).

In the domain of sexuality, lesbian women experience orgasm at a similar rate to heterosexual and gay men, and significantly more frequently than heterosexual women (Frederick et al., 2018). Lesbian women are more likely to engage in a turn-taking culture that prioritizes clitoral stimulation and equal pleasure of both partners (Frederick et al., 2018). Additionally, lesbian women have a longer length of sexual encounters compared to heterosexual couples (Blair & Pukall, 2014). One study that included a small sample of 14 bisexual women who had engaged in one-night stands found that 64% reported frequently or always experiencing orgasm when their one-night-stand partner was a woman, while only 7% reported the same when their partner was a man (Eschler, 2004; Mahar et al., 2020). Thus, women tend to have greater orgasm frequencies when they have sex with other women than when they have sex with men. These findings emphasize that the current sexual scripts for heterosexual sex can and should be reorganized to account for the clitoral stimulation necessary to facilitate women's equal orgasm frequency.

In general, research comparing lesbian and gay married couples with heterosexual married couples has found that same-sex couples show greater marital satisfaction, more stable relationships, a lower divorce rate, lower levels of conflict, and greater intimacy (Belous & Wampler, 2016, p. 453). In contrast, relationship satisfaction for same-sex couples can be negatively impacted by stigma, internalized homophobia, and a lack of social support (Frost, 2011; Otis et al., 2006). Though same-sex couples face their own unique relationship challenges and are not always free from heteronormative narratives, these relationships provide an example showing that relationship divisions based on gender, and the inequities that result, are not inevitable.

Conclusion

Ultimately, the research reviewed in this chapter finds that, while gender relations in the context of marriage have become more equitable over the past several decades, there is still a long way to go to reach true equity. Substantial disparities persist today in the domains of household responsibility, mental labor, financial contribution, and sexual pleasure. While same-sex partners face their own unique sets of challenges, they consistently report greater equality across traditionally gendered dimensions, as well as greater marital outcomes overall, proving that these inequities are not inevitable. Thus, it is important to continue to dismantle deeply ingrained gender roles, stereotypes, and expectations, as well as enact system-level changes, in order to achieve marital equity for all couples.

References

Andersen, S. H. (2018). Paternity leave and the motherhood penalty: New causal evidence. *Journal of Marriage and Family, 80*(5), 1125–1143. https://doi.org/10.1111/jomf.12507

Armstrong, E. A., England, P., & Fogarty, A. C. K. (2012). Accounting for women's orgasm and sexual enjoyment in college hookups and relationships. *American Sociological Review, 77*(3), 435–462. http://doi.org/10.1177/0003122412445802

Askari, S. F., Liss, M., Erchull, M. J., Staebell, S. E., & Axelson, S. J. (2010). Men want equality, but women don't expect it: Young adults' expectations for participation in household and child care chores. *Psychology of Women Quarterly, 34*(2), 243–252. https://doi.org/10.1111/j.1471-6402.2010.01565.x

Belous, C. K., & Wampler, R. S. (2016). Development of the gay and lesbian relationship satisfaction scale. *Journal of Marital and Family Therapy, 42*(3), 451–465. https://doi.org/10.1111/jmft.12158

Benard, S., & Correli, S. J. (2010). Normative discrimination and the motherhood wage penalty. *Gender & Society, 24*, 616–646. https://doi.org/10.1177/0891243210383142

Bianchi, S. M., Milkie, M. A., Sayer, L. C., & Robinson, J. P. (2000). Is anyone doing the house work? Trends in the gender division of household labor. *Social Forces, 79*(1), 191–228. https://doi.org/10.1093/sf/79.1.191

Bianchi, S. M., Sayer, L. C., Milkie, M. A., & Robinson, J. P. (2012). Housework: Who did, does or will do it, and how much does it matter? *Social Forces, 91*(1), 55. https://doi.org/10.1093/sf/sos120

Blair, K. L., & Pukall, C. F. (2014). Can less be more? Comparing duration vs. frequency of sexual encounters in same-sex and mixed-sex relationships. *The Canadian Journal of Human Sexuality, 23*(2), 123–136. https://doi.org/10.3138/cjhs.2393

Blair-Loy, M. (2010). Moral dimensions of the work-family nexus. In S. Hitlin & S. Vaisey (Eds.), *Handbook of the sociology of morality* (pp. 439–453). New York: Springer.

Blair-Loy, M., Hochschild, A., Pugh, A. J., Williams, J. C., & Hartmann, H. (2015). Stability and transformation in gender, work, and family: Insights from the second shift for the next quarter century. *Community, Work, & Family, 18*(4), 435–454. http://dx.doi.org/10.1080/13668803.2015.1080664

Braun, M., Lewin Epstein, N., Stier, H., & Baumgärtner, M. K. (2008). Perceived equity in the gendered division of household labor. *Journal of Marriage and Family, 70*(5), 1145–1156. https://doi.org/10.1111/j.1741-3737.2008.00556.x

Byers, E. S. (2005). Relationship satisfaction and sexual satisfaction: A longitudinal study of individuals in long-term relationships. *Journal of Sex Research, 42*(2), 113–118. https://doi.org/10.1080/00224490509552264

Chadwick, S. B., Francisco, M., & van Anders, S. M. (2019). When orgasms do not equal pleasure: Accounts of "bad" orgasm experiences during consensual sexual encounters. *Archives of Sexual Behavior, 48*(8), 2435–2459. https://doi.org/10.1007/s10508-019-01527-7

Claffey, S. T., & Mickelson, K. D. (2009). Division of household labor and distress: The role of perceived fairness for employed mothers. *Sex Roles, 60*(11), 819–831. https://doi.org/10.1007/s11199-008-9578-0

Coltrane, S. (2000). Research on household labor: Modeling and measuring the social embeddedness of routine family work. *Journal of Marriage and the Family, 62*(4), 1208–1233. https://doi.org/10.1111/j.1741-3737.2000.01208.x

Correli, S. J., Benard, S., & Paik, I. (2007). Getting a job: Is there a motherhood penalty? *American Journal of Sociology*, *112*(5), 1297–1338. https://doi.org/10.1086/511799

Costrich, N., Feinstein, L., Kidder, L., Maracek, J., & Pascale, L. (1975). When stereotypes hurt: Three studies of penalties for sex-role reversals. *Journal of Experimental Social Psychology*, *11*, 520–530. https://doi.org/10.1016/0022-1031(75)90003-7

Craig, L. (2006). Does father care mean fathers share? A comparison of how mothers and fathers in intact families spend time with children. *Gender & Society*, *20*(2), 259–281. https://doi.org/10.1177/0891243205285212

Cukrowska-Torzewska, E., & Matysiak, A. (2020). The motherhood wage penalty: A meta-analysis. *Social Science Research*, *88*, Article 102416. https://doi.org/10.1016/j.ssresearch.2020.102416

Davison, S. L., Bell, R. J., LaChina, M., Holden, S. L., & Davis, S. R. (2009). The relationship between self-reported sexual satisfaction and general well-being in women. *The Journal of Sexual Medicine*, *6*(10), 2690–2697. https://doi.org/10.1111/j.1743-6109.2009.01406.x

Downing, J. B., & Goldberg, A. E. (2011). Lesbian mothers' constructions of the division of paid and unpaid labor. *Feminism and Psychology*, *21*, 100–120. https://doi.org/10.1177/0959353510375869

Eagly, A. H. (1987). *Sex differences in social behavior: A social-role interpretation*. Erlbaum.

Eschler, L. (2004). The physiology of the female orgasm as a proximate mechanism. *Sexualities, Evolution & Gender*, *6*(2–3), 171–194. https://doi.org/10.1080/14616660412331330875

Fetterolf, J. C., & Rudman, L. A. (2014). Gender inequality in the home: The role of relative income, support for traditional gender roles, and perceived entitlement. *Gender Issues*, *31*(3), 219–237. https://doi.org/10.1007/s12147-014-9126-x

Frederick, D. A., John, S., Kate, H., Garcia, J. R., & Lloyd, E. A. (2018). Differences in orgasm frequency among gay, lesbian, bisexual, and heterosexual men and women in a U.S. national sample. *Archives of Sexual Behavior*, *47*(1), 273–288. https://doi.org/10.1007/s10508-017-0939-z

Frisco, M. L., & Williams, K. (2003). Perceived housework equity, marital happiness, and divorce in dual-earner households. *Journal of Family Issues*, *24*(1), 51–73. https://doi.org/10.1177/0192513X02238520

Frost, D. M. (2011). Stigma and intimacy in same-sex relationships: A narrative approach. *Journal of Family Psychology*, *25*(1), 1–10. https://doi.org/10.1037/a0022374

Gerber, G. L. (2009). Status and gender stereotyped personality traits: Toward an integration. *Sex Roles*, *61*, 297–316. https://doi.org/10.1007/s11199-008-9529-9

Glauber, R. (2018). Trends in the motherhood wage penalty and fatherhood wage premium for low, middle, and high earners. *Demography*, *55*(5), 1663–1680. https://doi.org/10.1007/s13524-018-0712-5

Goldberg, A. E. (2013). "Doing" and "undoing" gender: The meaning and division of housework in same-sex couples. *Journal of Family Theory & Review*, *5*(2), 85–104. https://doi.org/10.1111/jftr.12009

Goldberg, A. E., Smith, J. Z., & Perry-Jenkins, M. (2012). The division of labor in lesbian, gay, and heterosexual new adoptive parents. *Journal of Marriage and Family*, *74*, 812–828. https://doi.org/10.1111/j.1741-3737.2012.00992.x

Goldey, K. L., Posh, A. R., Bell, S. N., & van Anders, S. M. (2016). Defining pleasure: A focus group study of solitary and partnered sexual pleasure in queer and heterosexual women. *Archives of Sexual Behavior*, *45*, 2137–2154. https://doi.org/10.1007/s10508-016-0704-8

Haning, R. V., O'Keefe, S. L., Randall, E. J., Kommor, M. J., Baker, E., & Wilson, R. (2007). Intimacy, orgasm likelihood, and conflict predict sexual satisfaction in heterosexual male and female respondents. *Journal of Sex & Marital Therapy, 33*(2), 93–113. https://doi.org/10.1080/00926230601098449

Hegewisch, A., Williams, C., Hartmann, H., & Hudiburg, S. K. (2014). *The gender wage gap: 2013; Differences by race and ethnicity, no growth in real wages for women*. Institute for Women's Policy Research.

Hochschild, A. (1989). *The second shift: Working parents and the revolution at home*. Viking.

Hundhammer, T., & Mussweiler, T. (2012). How sex puts you in gendered shoes: Sexuality-priming leads to gender-based self-perception and behavior. *Journal of Personality and Social Psychology, 103*(1), 176. https://doi.org/10.1037/a0028121

Jones, A. C., Robinson, W. D., & Seedall, R. B. (2018). The role of sexual communication in couples' sexual outcomes: A dyadic path analysis. *Journal of Marital Family Therapy, 44*(4), 606–623. https://doi.org/10.1111/jmft.12282

Kay, T. (2006). Where's dad? Fatherhood in leisure studies. *Leisure Studies, 25*(2), 133–152. https://doi.org/10.1080/02614360500467792

Kiefer, A. K., & Sanchez, D. T. (2007). Scripting sexual passivity: A gender role perspective. *Personal Relationships, 14*, 269–290. https://doi.org/10.1111/j.1475-6811.2007.00154.x

Kiefer, A. K., Sanchez, D. T., Kalinka, C. J., & Ybarra, O. (2006). How women's nonconscious association of sex with submission relates to their subjective sexual arousability and ability to orgasm. *Sex Roles, 55*, 83–94. https://doi.org/10.1007/s11199-006-9060-9

Kinsey, A. C., Pomeroy, W. B., Martin, C. E., & Gebhard, P. H. (1953). *Sexual behavior in the human female*. W. B. Saunders.

Lee, Y., & Waite, L. J. (2005). Husbands' and wives' time spent on housework: A comparison of measures. *Journal of Marriage and Family, 67*(2), 328–336. https://doi.org/10.1111/j.0022-2445.2005.00119.x

Livingston, R. W., Rosette, A. S., & Washington, E. F. (2012). Can an agentic Black woman get ahead? The impact of race and interpersonal dominance on perceptions of female leaders. *Psychological Science, 23*(4), 354–358. https://doi.org/10.1177/0956797611428079

Mahar, E. A., Mintz, L. B., & Akers, B. M. (2020). Orgasm equality: Scientific findings and societal implications. *Current Sexual Health Reports, 12*, 24–32. https://doi.org/10.1007/s11930-020-00237-9

Matsick, J. L., Conley, T. D., & Moors, A. C. (2016). The science of female orgasms: Pleasing female partners in casual and long-term relationships. In K. Aumer (Ed.), *The psychology of love and hate in intimate relationships* (pp. 47–63). Springer, Cham. https://doi.org/10.1007/978-3-319-39277-6_4

McClelland, S. I. (2010). Intimate justice: A critical analysis of sexual satisfaction. *Social & Personality Psychology Compass, 4*(9), 663–680. https://doi.org/10.1111/j.1751-9004.2010.00293.x

Meier, J. A., McNaughton-Cassill, M., & Lynch, M. (2006). The management of household and childcare tasks and relationship satisfaction in dual earner families. *Marriage and Family Review, 40*, 61–88. https://doi.org/10.1300/J002v40n02_04

Nagoski, E. (2015). *Come as you are: The surprising new science that will transform your sex life*. Simon and Schuster.

Offer, S. (2014). The costs of thinking about work and family: Mental labor, work–family spillover, and gender inequality among parents in dual-earner families. *Sociological Forum, 29*(4), 916–936. https://doi.org/10.1111/socf.12126

Otis, M. D., Rostosky, S. S., Riggle, E. D. B., & Hamrin, R. (2006). Stress and relationship quality in same-sex couples. *Journal of Social and Personal Relationships, 23*(1), 81–99. https://doi.org/10.1177/0265407506060179

Park, B., Smith, J. A., & Correll, J. (2010). The persistence of implicit behavioral associations for moms and dads. *Journal of Experimental Social Psychology, 46*(5), 809–815. https://doi.org/10.1016/j.jesp.2010.04.009

Perlesz, A., Power, J., Brown, R., McNair, R., Schofield, M., Pitts, M., Barrett, A., & Bickerdike, A. (2010). Organizing work and home in same-sex parented families: Findings from the work love play study. *The Australian and New Zealand Journal of Family Therapy, 31*(4), 374–391. https://doi.org/10.1375/anft.31.4.374

Raley, S., Bianchi, S. M., & Wang, W. (2012). When do fathers care? Mothers' economic contribution and fathers' involvement in child care. *American Journal of Sociology, 117*(5), 1422–1459. https://doi.org/10.1086/663354

Rawsthorne, M., & Costello, M. (2010). Cleaning the sink: Exploring the experiences of Australian lesbian parents reconciling work/family responsibilities. *Community, Work, and Family, 13*(2), 189–204. https://doi.org/10.1080/13668800903259777

Robertson, L. G., Anderson, T. L., Hall, M. E. L., & Kim, C. L. (2019). Mothers and mental labor: A phenomenological focus group study of family-related thinking work. *Psychology of Women Quarterly, 43*(2), 184–200. https://doi.org/10.1177/0361684319825581

Rosette, A. S., Koval, C. Z., Ma, A., & Livingston, R. (2016). Race matters for women leaders: Intersectional effects on agentic deficiencies and penalties. *Leadership Quarterly, 27*(3), 429–445. https://doi.org/10.1016/j.leaqua.2016.01.008

Rudman, L. A. (1998). Self-promotion as a risk factor for women: The costs and benefits of counterstereotypical impression management. *Journal of Personality and Social Psychology, 74*(3), 629–645. https://doi.org/10.1037/0022-3514.74.3.629

Rudman, L. A., & Glick, P. (2001). Prescriptive gender stereotypes and backlash toward agentic women. *Journal of Social Issues, 57*(4), 743–762. https://doi.org/10.1111/0022-4537.00239

Rudman, L. A., & Mescher, K. (2013). Penalizing men who request a family leave: Is flexibility stigma a femininity stigma? *Journal of Social Issues, 69*(2), 322–340. https://doi.org/10.1111/josi.12017

Rudman, L. A. & Phelan, J. E. (2008). Backlash effects for disconfirming gender stereotypes in organizations. *Research in Organizational Behavior, 28*, 61–79. https://doi.org/10.1016/j.riob.2008.04.003

Sanchez, D. T., Crocker, J., & Boike, K. R. (2005). Doing gender in the bedroom: Investing in gender norms and the sexual experience. *Personality and Social Psychology Bulletin, 31*(10), 1445–1455. https://doi.org/10.1177/0146167205277333

Sanchez, D. T., Fetterolf, J. C., & Rudman, L. A. (2012a). Eroticizing inequality in the United States: The consequences and determinants of traditional gender role adherence in intimate relationships. *Journal of Sex Research, 49*(2-3), 168–183. https://doi.org/10.1080/00224499.2011.653699

Sanchez, D. T., Kiefer, A., & Ybarra, O. (2006). Sexual submissiveness in women: Costs for autonomy. *Personality and Social Psychology Bulletin, 32*(4), 512–524. https://doi.org/10.1177/0146167205282154

Sanchez, D. T., Phelan, J. E., Moss-Racusin, C. A., & Good, J. J. (2012b). The gender role motivation model of women's sexually submissive behavior and satisfaction in heterosexual couples. *Personality and Social Psychology Bulletin, 38*(4), 528–539. https://doi.org/10.1177/0146167211430088

Sayer, L. C., Bianchi, S. M., & Robinson, J. P. (2004). Are parents investing less in children? Trends in mothers' and fathers' time with children. *American Journal of Sociology, 110,* 1–43. https://doi.org/10.1086/386270

Schug, J., Alt, N. P., & Klauer, K. C. (2015). Gendered race prototypes: Evidence for the non-prototypicality of Asian men and Black women. *Journal of Experimental Social Psychology, 56,* 121–125. https://doi.org/10.1016/j.jesp.2014.09.012

Shaw, S. M. (2010). Diversity and ideology: Changes in Canadian family life and implications for leisure. *World Leisure Journal, 52*(1), 4–13. https://doi.org/10.1080/04419057.2010.9674617

Simon, W., & Gagnon, J. H. (1986). Sexual scripts: Permanence and change. *Archives of Sexual Behavior, 15,* 97–120. https://doi.org/10.1007/BF01542219

Skewes, L., Fine, C., & Haslam, N. (2018). Beyond Mars and Venus: The role of gender essentialism in support for gender inequality and backlash. *PLoS One, 13*(7), e0200921. https://doi.org/10.1371/journal.pone.0200921

Stevenson, B., & Wolfers, J. (2007). Marriage and divorce: Changes and their driving forces. *Journal of Economic Perspectives, 21*(2), 27–52. https://doi.org/10.1257/jep.21.2.27

Sutphin, S. (2010). Social exchange theory and the division of household labor in same-sex couples. *Marriage and Family Review, 46,* 191–206. https://doi.org/10.1080/01494929.2010.490102

Vandello, J. A., Hettinger, V. E., Bosson, J. K., & Siddiqi, J. (2013). When equal isn't really equal: The masculine dilemma of seeking work flexibility. *Journal of Social Issues, 69*(2), 303–321. https://doi.org/10.1111/josi.12016

Vannier, S. A., & O'Sullivan, L. F. (2011). Communicating interest in sex: Verbal and nonverbal initiation of sexual activity in young adults' romantic dating relationships. *Archives of Sexual Behavior, 40,* 961–969. https://doi.org/10.1007/s10508-010-9663-7

Walzer, S. (1996). Thinking about the baby: Gender and divisions of infant care. *Social Problems, 43*(2), 219–234. https://doi.org/10.1525/sp.1996.43.2.03x0206x

Wetzel, G. M., Cultice, R. A., & Sanchez, D. T. (2022). Orgasm frequency predicts desire and expectation for orgasm: Assessing the orgasm gap within mixed-sex couples. *Sex Roles, 86,* 456–470. https://doi.org/10.1007/s11199-022-01280-7

Wetzel, G. M. & Sanchez, D. T. (2022). Heterosexual young adults' experience with and perceptions of the orgasm gap: A mixed methods approach. *Psychology of Women Quarterly, 46*(2), 131–146. https://doi.org/10.1177/03616843221076410

Williams, J. C. (2003). Beyond the glass ceiling: the maternal wall as a barrier to gender equality. *Thomas Jefferson Law Review, 26,* 1.

Williams, J. E., & Best, D. L. (1990). *Measuring sex stereotypes: A multination study.* Newbury Park, CA: Sage.

Xiao, V. L., Lowery, B. S., & Stillwell, A. (2022). Gender backlash and the moderating role of shared racial group membership. *Personality and Social Psychology Bulletin, 29*(4), 554–570. https://doi.org/10.1177/01461672221074543

7

What Is a Marriage?

The Rise of More Diverse Unions

Rhonda N. Balzarini, Karen L. Blair, and Marissa Walter

Introduction

For better or for worse, the last two decades have seen rapid changes in the family system, with the family structure diversifying and people increasingly opting out of or delaying marriage. Questions have arisen about the future of marriage and whether the unfolding trends represent the deterioration or evolution of marriage. The United States is experiencing a precipitous decline in marriage (also see Chapters 4 and 13 in this volume), with rates in recent years lower than at any other point in history. According to census data, in 2021, about half of Americans were married (51%), compared with 72% in 1960. When people do marry, they are much older, with the median age of first marriage in the United States rising by eight years since 1960 (U.S. Census Bureau, 2022). Notably, these trends are not unique to the United States and appear in many parts of the world.

Despite fewer marriages, people continue to have a vast array of relationships (see Chapter 17 in this volume). The number of adults cohabitating with a non-spousal partner, remarrying, or having a kid solo (e.g., single parenthood) has increased substantially (Ortiz-Ospina & Roser, 2020). More people are choosing to cohabitate before marriage or instead of marriage (see Chapter 3 in this volume). While cohabitation once served as a stepping stone to marriage (Guzzo 2014), it now exceeds marriage rates (Horowitz et al., 2019). Indeed, cohabitation among non-married romantic partners is becoming the normative relationship experience among young adults, and fewer cohabiting unions are transitioning into marriages (Guzzo, 2014).

Another illustrative example is that, historically, marriage was a precursor to a couple's decision to procreate. Many people waited until marriage to have

Rhonda N. Balzarini, Karen L. Blair, and Marissa Walter, *What Is a Marriage?* In: *Modern Relationships*. Edited by: Mahzad Hojjat and Anne Moyer, Oxford University Press. © Oxford University Press 2024. DOI: 10.1093/oso/9780197655504.003.0007 children or were married due to pregnancy. However, it has become increasingly common for people to have and raise children outside of marriage, either as single parents or by co-raising children with cohabitating, unmarried partners (Hayford et al., 2014). These examples suggest that marriage rates are decreasing and that pivotal relational and familial decisions are no longer tied to marriage.

What Do Marriages Look Like Today?

The outward appearance of marriage has changed to better reflect the composition of society, with notable increases in interracial, inter-religious, and same-sex marriages (Rosenfeld & Kim, 2005). The 1960s saw a rapid rise in interracial marriages, partially as a reflection of the growing diversity of the United States population. Between 1980 and 2015, the rates of interracial marriages nearly tripled (Livingston & Brown, 2017). In addition to crossing lines of race, marriage is now legal for many same-sex couples in various jurisdictions, including the United States, since 2015. Unsurprisingly, nations with legal same-sex marriage have seen drastic increases in the number of same-sex couples getting married. Despite increased diversification of the family system (Rosenfeld & Kim, 2005), prejudices remain toward any relationship that does not fit the standard "norm" of heterosexual, intraracial marriage. Indeed, some forms of nontraditional relationships, such as consensually non-monogamous (CNM) relationships, are still under great scrutiny and denied access to the privilege of having their relationships recognized. In this chapter, we will discuss the impact of the diversification of the family structure on the current state of marriage and the specific forms of prejudice encountered by those in interracial, LGBTQ+, and CNM relationships.

Interracial Marriages

An increase in interracial relationships has occurred within the context of various social and political factors that have reduced the barriers to marrying across racial lines (see Chapter 8 in this volume). In the United States, the percentage of interracial or interethnic married-couple households increased from 7.4% in 2000 to 10.2% in 2016 (Rico et al., 2018), and 17% of all new marriages in 2015 were between people of different racial backgrounds (Livingston & Brown, 2017). Direct comparisons across countries can be challenging, as the definition of interracial relationships tends to vary. For example, scholars often rely on census surveys not designed to measure interracial relationships to generate population estimates.

Drawing specific attention to sexual relationships between members of different races dates back to 1864 when an anonymous author first coined the term "miscegenation." The term combined the Latin roots for "mix" (*miscere*) and "race" (*genus*) to provide a seemingly more scientific term for the more colloquial phrasing of "race-mixing" (Sussman, 2019). Although the term became commonly used in formal and informal settings, such as the anti-miscegenation laws, the original pamphlet argued that such relationships should be encouraged and viewed as capable of producing racially superior offspring. While abolitionists initially praised the pamphlet, those who favored continuing slavery in the United States condemned the publication. The result was a series of publications arguing against miscegenation. Indeed, the original pamphlet was an anti-abolitionist hoax aimed at making the abolitionist agenda appear more radical (e.g., suggesting that abolitionists supported *forced* marriage between races). The pamphlet left a lasting mark on views toward interracial marriage in the United States and directly contributed to the generation of laws that would prohibit "miscegenation" (Sussman, 2019). Formal and informal barriers to interracial marriage were blatant throughout much of the 20th century across North America and beyond (e.g., "immorality laws" in South Africa). Many American states had anti-miscegenation laws forbidding cohabitation, marriage, or sexual relations between racial groups. Such laws remained in place until the 1967 United States Supreme Court Ruling in *Loving v. Virginia*, which deemed such laws a violation of the 14th Amendment (Bryant & Duncan, 2019).

Families were frequent sources of disapproval for interracial couples. In 1939, Velma Demerson's father had her arrested for the crime of being "incorrigible." Such a charge fell under the Canadian Female Refuges Act of 1897, which allowed the incarceration and detention of women who failed to follow the societal status quo. For Velma, her crime was being an unwed, pregnant, White woman living with the soon-to-be father of her child, a Chinese man (Demerson, 2004). The consequences for Velma were vast; she was incarcerated for 10 months and subjected to abusive medical treatments and solitary confinement. The Canadian government stripped Velma of her Canadian citizenship under the 1946 Citizenship Act, which dictated that women who married men of foreign citizenship were assumed to have relinquished being Canadian. Consequently, Velma was stateless until 2004, when her citizenship was finally reinstated (Fleet, 2011).

Much has changed over the past century in North America, including attitudes concerning interracial marriages. According to Bibby (2007), "most social scientists maintain that there is probably no better index of racial and cultural integration than intermarriage" (p. 1), leading many sociologists to note the importance of tracking changes in the prevalence of interracial relationships because this metric can provide insight into broader societal trends of racial integration, assimilation, and prejudices (Hou et al., 2015). Indeed, attitudes have also improved with the increased prevalence of interracial relationships. In Canada, the approval of interracial relationships has risen from approximately 55% in the mid-1970s to 92% in the early 2000s (Bibby, 2007). Positive attitudes vary, by time and place, and remain lower in the United States, where a 2007 U.S. Gallop Poll identified that while 77% of Americans approved of marriages between Black and White individuals, nearly a quarter (23%) withheld such approval (17% disapproving and 6% reporting no opinion; Carroll, 2007).

Despite increased engagement in and acceptance of interracial relationships, specific challenges remain. For example, people in interracial relationships often report reduced social support, more significant stigma from friends and family (Rosenthal & Starks, 2015), and feeling that others more closely scrutinize their relationship (Wieling, 2003). People in interracial relationships often report a lack of support from parents, which, in turn, can be a source of conflict within the relationship (Bell & Hastings, 2015). Any relationship met with greater disapproval from parents and friends can subsequently experience reduced relationship well-being, which can have detrimental effects on the mental and physical well-being of those in the relationship (Blair & Holmberg, 2008; Blair et al., 2018). Furthermore, society grants less approval to interracial relationships, thereby generating stigma associated with the *nature* of the relationship rather than its unique qualities. Experiencing this stigma is, in turn, associated with reduced mental well-being (Rosenthal et al., 2019) and can be associated with lower levels of relationship investment (Lehmiller & Agnew, 2006).

Relationship stigma has many consequences. Interracial couples can feel undue pressure to make their relationship appear as a "model" relationship, fearing that onlookers will judge all interracial relationships negatively if their relationship fails. Additionally, some interracial couples experience "visual dislocation," in which others do not automatically see them as being in a relationship together (Steinbugler, 2005). Potentially in response to visual dislocation, those in interracial relationships engage in more actions that indicate that they are together in a romantic relationship. Such behaviors, such as holding hands, are associated with better mental health, relationship satisfaction, and closeness (Mederos, 2015).

Same-Sex Marriage

Social and legal arguments supporting same-sex marriage have focused on declaring that they are *no different* from traditional, heterosexual marriages. There are meaningful differences between same- and mixed-sex marriages, but the focus on achieving "marriage equality" led to near-willful blindness to differences. To understand the emphasis on arguing for "sameness," we must provide a brief history of how society has treated same-sex relationships over time.

For much of the 20th century, *homosexuality* was a criminal form of sexual deviance (see Chapter 11 in this volume). Over time, viewing homosexuality as a *chosen* criminal activity gave way to seeing it as an *affliction* or mental illness. While today it is considered prejudiced to think of homosexuality (or sexual diversity as we might say today) as a mental illness, the transition from chosen crime to mental affliction represented a positive step. Individuals with a "mental illness" could potentially "recover" with treatment; if not, it seemed cruel to criminally punish them for something that was "no fault of their own." Consequently, throughout the 1900s, the medical professions subjected gay men and lesbians to ineffective treatments that we would now consider torture, ranging from extreme aversion therapy to lobotomies and chemical castration. The legal prohibitions against homosexuality often remained, making it challenging for gay men and lesbians to conceive of fighting for marriage rights when they lacked fundamental rights of freedom and self-determination.

Dr. Evelyn Hooker's work in the late 1960s was instrumental in defining same-sex attraction as a natural variation in human sexuality (Hooker, 1993). The American Psychiatric Association removed homosexuality from the Diagnostic and Statistics Manual of Mental Illnesses (DSM) in 1973. The famous Stonewall Riots of 1969 and the decriminalization of homosexuality (e.g., Canada: 1969, California: 1976) contributed to gay men's sexual liberation in the 1970s, sparking motivation to fight for equal marriage rights. In 1970, a county clerk denied Richard Baker and James McConnell a marriage license (Ekholm, 2015). Their challenge of the ruling failed, rendering marriage rights a matter to be handled by individual states rather than U.S. federal law for decades to come.

Much of this momentum for relationship recognition was lost when the HIV/AIDS epidemic struck the community. The government left the community alone to handle the fatal fallout of the epidemic, which cost the lives of more than 330,000 gay and bisexual men in the United States alone (Linley et al., 2019). The lack of legal recognition for same-sex relationships throughout the 1980s and 90s resulted in institutions denying gay men the right to visit their dying partners, participate in their partner's treatment decisions, or even maintain ownership of their property after a partner's death. Although some places, like San Francisco, made exceptions, the United States did not grant legal hospital visitation rights to same-sex couples until 2010 (Shapiro, 2010).

The HIV/AIDs epidemic placed the marriage equality movement on the back burner for decades in many jurisdictions worldwide. The Canadian Supreme Court heard the first legal case for marriage in Canada in 1995. The court denied access to legal marriage for Jim Egan and his partner of 47 years, Jack Nesbit, but the ruling resulted in the inclusion of sexual orientation as a protected category within Canada's Charter of Rights and Freedoms. The same court redefined "spouse" to include same-sex partners in 1998, followed by a case in 2003 that required the federal government to legalize same-sex marriage, which was completed by 2005. Canada was the third country to legalize same-sex marriage, following the Netherlands in 2001 and Belgium in 2003. The United States lagged many years behind as individual states fought to extend or restrict the definition of marriage, but eventually, the U.S. Supreme Court legalized same-sex marriage in 2015. It is within this context that research on same-sex relationships emerged.

Lawrence Kurdek provided one of the earliest attempts to systematically study same-sex relationships through longitudinal research comparing the relationships of gay men and lesbians with mixed-sex heterosexual dating and married couples. By comparing Rusbult et al.'s (1998) investment model of relationship commitment across same-sex and mixed-sex couples, Kurdek (2007) found that same-sex couples often had similar conceptions and levels of commitment as their mixed-sex counterparts. Kurdek argued that inconsistent commitment findings concerning same-sex relationships could likely be attributed to the lack of legal recognition available to same-sex couples (Kurdek, 2006) and to a reduced number of barriers to leaving a same-sex relationship (Kurdek, 1998).

Over a decade later, Rosenfeld (2014) found that relationship dissolution rates between same-sex and mixed-sex couples in committed "marriage or marriage-like" relationships were similar. Thus, researchers prioritized providing evidence that same-sex relationships were "similar" to heterosexual marriages to "warrant" the extension of equal marriage rights. Lawyers often referred to such research in their legal arguments for marriage equality (e.g., Lau & Strohm, 2011) and the American Psychological Association relied heavily upon Kurdek's research in preparing their amicus briefs supporting same-sex marriage (Pollitt et al., 2023). Differences that did emerge were often linked to stigma and discrimination, including the lack of access to legal spousal recognition.

The minority stress model (Meyer, 2003) became a focal theoretical framework to explain the differences between mixed- and same-sex relationships. The model helps explain LGBTQ+ health disparities, arguing that the additional day-to-day stressors associated with managing one's minority (and stigmatized) identity can take a cumulative toll on an individual's well-being. The model can also shed light on "couple-level" stressors that affect the relationship (LeBlanc et al., 2015). For example, two gay men walking down the street may not draw any negative attention from strangers until the specific moment when onlookers come to perceive the two men as being in a same-sex relationship, potentially due to sharing affection, such as holding hands. The relationship becomes the target of stigma and the tool through which the men's sexual identities become known (Blair et al., 2022).

Through the lens of the minority stress model, it becomes salient how a stigmatized identity or relationship type can contribute to reduced relationship well-being and, in turn, health and well-being consequences. Couples who perceive less social support for their relationships from their friends and family report lower relationship well-being and, in turn, reduced mental and physical health (Blair et al., 2018). While this is true for *all* relationship types, individuals in same-sex relationships consistently perceive lower levels of support for their relationships than those in mixed-sex relationships (Holmberg & Blair, 2016). The slow rollout of legal same-sex marriage in the Western world has provided opportunities for comparing relational outcomes between those with and without access to marriage. In 2011,

Badgett and Herman concluded that individuals in same-sex relationships with access to legal relationship recognition had lower levels of relationship dissolution, potentially due to a greater ability to garner support for their relationship from outsiders. Relatedly, Ogolsky et al. (2019) reported a decrease in psychological distress and an increase in general life satisfaction among LGBTQ+ people following the U.S. Supreme Court's ruling on marriage equality in 2015.

These findings are not limited to the United States; the legalization of same-sex marriage is associated with positive well-being outcomes for sexual minorities worldwide (e.g., Boertien & Vignoli, 2019). Indeed, the focus on marriage equality as a *primary* goal of LGBTQ+ community activism has lessened attention to advancing the rights of gender minorities and LGBTQ+ individuals who experience other sources of marginalization, such as racism, ableism, or femmephobia (see Chapter 11, this volume). Consequently, researchers and LGBTQ+ communities have questioned whether the general approach of basing the argument for marriage equality on "similarity" may have unjustly held monogamous heterosexual marriage up as a "gold standard" to which all other relationships must be measured. By focusing on the similarities between same-sex relationships and married heterosexual couples, scholars have given less attention to the areas in which same-sex relationships may be unique or face challenges unrelated to discrimination and stigma.

More recent research has begun to examine the strengths associated with same-sex relationships, such as how their freedom from sexual scripts provides greater sexual flexibility (Blair et al., 2015) or how the removal of gendered power structures results in more equal divisions of labor (van der Vleuten et al., 2021). Same-sex couples tend to maintain a sense of humor during conflicts, which is associated with relationship well-being and stability (Gottman et al., 2003). While these are positive differences, deficits also emerge. In fighting for one's legal rights, it can be difficult to shed light on perceived negative experiences for fear that outsiders will use such experiences against the community. With a more solid footing in the world of equal rights, research on negative differences between same-sex and mixed-sex relationships is now emerging. For example, some forms of intimate partner violence may be more prevalent within same-sex relationships (e.g., Messinger, 2011). Moving through the world with a marginalized identity and the associated lack of social safety (Diamond & Alley, 2022) likely contributes to such discrepancies.

Nonetheless, relationship scholars need to be open to studying the "skeletons in the closet" so that the field can better identify the needs of same-sex couples and develop tailored interventions. Love is love, but conflict is also conflict, and all relationship types can encounter difficulties. If there are meaningful differences in how those difficulties emerge or the processes best suited to ameliorating their effects, researchers must extend the use of research methods that are LGBTQ+ inclusive to all areas of relationship research.

CNM Relationships—What Is Next for Legal Recognition of Relationships?

Throughout the battle for legal recognition of same-sex relationships, one of the common reprieves from those opposed to "redefining" marriage was that the extension of relationship rights to same-sex couples was the beginning of a slippery slope that would eventually lead to the recognition of other "non-normative" relationships, including those between multiple consenting adults. When a journalist asked Stanley Kurtz, a senior fellow at the Ethics and Public Policy Center, about his objection to the legalization of same-sex marriage, he replied that "the core issue here is not homosexuality; it is marriage.... Up to now, with all the changes in marriage, the one thing [we have] been sure of is that marriage means monogamy" (Kurtz, 2003, p. 9). When opponents challenged President Barack Obama on his support of legalizing same-sex marriage, he described thinking "about members of [his] own staff ... in incredibly committed *monogamous* relationships, same-sex relationships" and about "those soldiers or airmen or Marines or sailors who are out there fighting on my behalf and yet feel constrained, ... because they are not able to *commit themselves in a marriage*" (Earnest, 2012, emphasis added). In both cases, the argument for extending marriage rights to same-sex couples rested upon their participation in monogamous, committed relationships. Such sentiments also made clear that policymakers at the highest level viewed CNM as an unacceptable sexual deviancy that would deteriorate the validity of marriage. Consequently, advocacy for same-sex marriage walked a fine line of holding same-sex relationships up to a "heterosexual norm" to demonstrate sameness while simultaneously denying the legitimacy of what we now refer to as CNM relationships.

While monogamy remains the most common romantic relationship arrangement in North America and Europe, scholars have recently posited that the family system and the rules regarding romantic relationships are changing, with increased interest in, and awareness of, CNM relationships—relationships in which all partners give explicit consent to engage in romantic, intimate, and/or sexual relationships with multiple people. The desire to seek out and maintain relationships that deviate from the monogamous dyad reflects a cultural shift away from traditional Christian values and marital arrangements. Indeed, public interest in options beyond the monogamous dyad has increased dramatically (Moors, 2017). Such interest is reflected by heightened media attention, with shows like *You, Me, and Her* and *Shameless* including CNM storylines and providing exposure to relationship options beyond the monogamous dyad. Popular dating sites like OkCupid now allow users to identify as CNM, providing greater accessibility to finding others interested in non-monogamous relationship formations.

In the United States and Canada, approximately 4%–5% of individuals are currently in some form of CNM relationship, and 21.9% say that they have engaged in a CNM relationship at some point in their life (Haupert et al., 2017). According to a recent poll, about one-third (32%) of U.S. adults say their ideal relationship is non-monogamous to some degree, particularly among younger generations (Ballard, 2020). Although research on CNM is still relatively scarce, individuals in CNM relationships report high-quality relationships. That is, they tend to report high levels of relationship satisfaction, open communication, honesty, and trust coupled with low levels of jealousy, and they report highly satisfying sex lives with their partners (Balzarini et al., 2019b, 2021; Balzarini & Muise, 2020, for a review). Interestingly, the same qualities that characterize CNM relationships are analogous to those that characterize a secure attachment (Hazan & Shaver, 1987), the gold standard for relationships, according to adult attachment theory (Shaver & Mikulincer, 2009), representing the healthiest attachment style. However, across the research, stigma is one component of CNM relationships that sets them apart from monogamous unions (Moors et al., 2013).

Stigma toward CNM is robust, with 26%–43% of people in CNM relationships reporting experiences of stigma and discrimination (Fleckenstein et al., 2012). Such stigma is pervasive and extends beyond simply judging non-monogamists on their relationships. For example, in addition to viewing non-monogamists as less trustworthy, less passionate, and more distant from their partners, research participants also judge non-monogamists to be less likely to pay their taxes on time, have good oral hygiene, or routinely walk their dogs (Conley et al., 2013). Thus, individuals in CNM relationships still face a great deal of stigma that influences how their relationships are perceived and how others judge them as individuals across multiple facets of life.

CNM relationships also lack legal rights and recognition. Historically, diverse relationship configurations and families (e.g., same-sex, interracial) have been criminalized and declared unfit to raise children. While many jurisdictions now protect the right to parenthood for same-sex or interracial couples, no protections specifically relate to a person's relationship orientation (e.g., monogamous vs. CNM) or status (e.g., single, one partner, multiple partners). As such, despite the frequent experiences of discrimination and stigma associated with their relationship type, individuals in CNM relationships have no legal protections or recourse when they experience discrimination. The lack of legal recognition alongside the lack of acceptance from friends and families results in many CNM individuals opting to keep their relationship structure secret or hiding aspects of their relationship from the public (e.g., passing as monogamous by hiding aspects of their relationships with others; Balzarini et al., 2017, 2019a).

The stigma that people in CNM relationships face can have detrimental effects on their health and well-being, as well as their relationships. Experiences of minority stress and stigma can be turned inward and subsequently internalized in the form of internalized negativity. Internalized CNM negativity includes fear of one's CNM identity becoming known publicly, discomfort with having a CNM lifestyle, and discomfort associating with other CNM individuals. Perhaps it is not surprising that CNM negativity is associated with diminished relationship functioning and a lower degree of relationship satisfaction (Moors et al., 2021). Furthermore, the internalized negativity and experiences of minority stress associated with a marginalized sexual identity are associated with adverse physical health implications and mental health concerns.

Research examining the effects of CNM suggests that CNM relationships are not harmful to the individuals who engage in them or to society, and yet, these relationships are not legally protected or afforded the same rights as others. Indeed, intermarriage, such as interracial marriage and same-sex marriage, was considered illegal in the United States and other countries, and there is now greater acceptance and rights for these relationships than ever before. As acceptance of CNM relationships grows, approaches to legalizing and distributing rights based on relationship status may change to become more inclusive and adaptable to the realities of human relationships. Given research on the link between legal recognition and well-being for same-sex marriages, access to spousal rights, privileges, protections, and obligations would likely have a similar outcome for those in CNM relationships.

Conclusion

While marriage has not ended, it has starkly declined and has reached historically low rates in the United States and many other countries. Despite this, the institution of marriage has evolved to accommodate increased diversity and to maintain relevance in an ever-evolving family system. The diversification of marriage is apparent in the acceptance of and rise in interracial and same-sex marriages in the United States and many other countries (Rosenfeld & Kim, 2005). For those who have access, marriage continues to provide positive outcomes. One of the most robust findings in the literature is the role that our social relationships, including marriages, play in predicting our overall health and well-being (Umberson & Montez, 2010). Even recent research suggests that married people reap the rewards and benefits over and above individuals in unmarried relationships. For example, married people report greater trust and satisfaction with their partners than those who cohabitate (Horowitz et al., 2019).

Consequently, it is not surprising that policymakers have suggested that increasing the marriage rate could lead to greater societal well-being (e.g., Aber et al. 2015). However, the perks of marriage are not universal. Indeed, the positive links between marriage, health, and well-being are not equally distributed. People in poor-quality marriages often experience more health problems than single people or those who leave unhealthy relationships (Lawrence et al., 2018). The benefits of marriage also differ based on demographics, such that women often benefit less than men, and the effects of marriage are unequal across socioeconomic status and race (e.g., Drabble et al., 2021; Liu & Umberson, 2008). Indeed, the positive associations between marriage and well-being may reflect more the demographic composition of people who are more apt to get married. White, more educated, and financially well-off individuals are more likely to get married (e.g., Elliott et al., 2012), and thus these demographics may tip the balance in calculating the potential benefits of marriage itself.

If marriage does, indeed, provide benefits above and beyond other forms of relationship commitment (e.g., cohabitation), we must seek to understand the source of such benefits better. This chapter has focused on how marriage has changed and adapted over time, but it is also essential to consider the function of marriage in society and to understand what is unique to marriage that affords such perks. Is it that the *word* "marriage" and the title that accompanies it influence people's sense of commitment? Is it the legal rights and benefits that help secure these relationships? Could it be the resulting recognition and social support from peers and society? Alternatively, perhaps it is a combination of these things. We know that legitimizing a relationship is an important milestone and ritual event for many couples. Indeed, when individuals in stigmatized relationships (e.g., same-sex or CNM relationships) have commitment ceremonies or get married, this may positively influence the opinion of those who attend the ceremony (Liddle & Liddle, 2004). We also know that social support for relationships is an important predictor of relationship well-being and better health and well-being. The marriage ritual and legal recognition may help social network members "slot" a relationship into a well-understood script of commitment, thereby providing the schematic structure necessary for outsiders to understand and subsequently support a marginalized relationship (Pollitt et al., 2023).

As this chapter has discussed, the family system has diversified, and the institution of marriage has evolved to become more inclusive of the greater diversity in society and diverse relationships. Recent and historical changes to the institution of marriage demonstrate that social institutions can, and often do, change quite quickly. Indeed, the legalization of same-sex marriage, interracial marriage, and women's rights to end a marriage are developments of the last century. With the additional advancements in gender equality, fertility science, and drastic increases in life expectancy, it is unsurprising to see the fundamental structure of human relationships continue to change. CNM relationships are becoming more common but remain restricted in terms of access to the legal protections afforded by the institution of marriage. Although it seems unlikely that humans will forego the ritual and celebration associated with marriage any time soon, as we look ahead to the future, the boundaries around marriage are likely to continue shifting as humans continue to reconfigure and explore a multitude of relationship structures and experiences. With an eye to these future possibilities, researchers must continue to be novel in their approach to relationship science and seek to generate adaptive research methods that can accurately reflect and include all the diversity that currently exists, as well as the diversity yet to come—did someone mention robots?

References

Aber, L., Butler, S., Danziger, S., Doar, R., Ellwood, D., Gueron, J., Haidt, J., Haskins, R., Holzer, H. J., Hymowitz, K., Mead, L., Mincy, R., Reeves, R. V., Strain, M. R., & Waldfogel, J. (2015). *Opportunity, responsibility, and security: A consensus plan for reducing poverty and restoring the American dream*. American Enterprise Institute for Public Policy Research/Brookings Institution.

Badgett, M. V. L., & Herman, J. L. (2011). Patterns of relationship recognition by same-sex couples in the United States. In A. Baumle (Ed.), *International handbook on the demography of sexuality* (Vol. 5, pp. 331–362). Springer. https://doi.org/10.1007/978-94-007-5512-3_17

Ballard, J. (2020). *One-third of Americans say their ideal relationship is non-monogamous*. YouGovAmerica. https://today.yougov.com/topics/society/articles-reports/2020/01/31/millennials-monogamy-poly-poll-survey-data

Balzarini, R. N., Campbell, L., Kohut, T., Holmes, B. M., Lehmiller, J. J., Harman, J. J., & Atkins, N. (2017). Perceptions of primary and secondary relationships in polyamory. *PloS ONE*, *12*(5), https://doi.org/10.1371/journal.pone.0177841

Balzarini, R. N., Dharma, C., Kohut, T., Campbell, L., Lehmiller, J. J., Harman, J. J., & Holmes, B. M. (2019a). Comparing relationship quality across different types of romantic partners in polyamorous and monogamous relationships. *Archives of Sexual Behavior*, *48*(6), 1749–1767. https://doi.org/10.1007/s10508-019-1416-7

Balzarini, R. N., Dharma, C., Muise, A., & Kohut, T. (2019b). Eroticism versus nurturance: How eroticism and nurturance differ in polyamorous and monogamous relationships. *Social Psychology*, *50*(3), 185–200. https://doi.org/10.1027/1864-9335/a000378

Balzarini, R. N., McDonald. J., Kohut, T., Harman, J. J., Lehmiller, J. J., & Holmes, B. M. (2021). Compersion: When jealousy-inducing situations don't (just) induce jealousy. *Archives of Sexual Behavior*, *50*(4), 1311–1324. https://doi.org/10.1007/s10508-020-01853-1

Balzarini, R. N., & Muise, A. (2020). Beyond the dyad: A review of the novel insights gained from studying consensual non-monogamy. *Current Sexual Health Reports*, *12*(4), 398–404. https://doi.org/10.1007/s11930-020-00297-x

Bell, G. C., & Hastings, S. O. (2015). Exploring parental approval and disapproval for Black and White interracial couples. *Journal of Social Issues*, *71*(4), 755–771. https://doi.org/10.1111/josi.12147

Bibby, R. (2007, August 29). *Racial intermarriage: Canada and the US*. University of Lethbridge [Project Canada press release no. 9]. Retrieved October 30, 2022, from http://www.reginaldbibby.com/images/PC_9_RACIAL_INTERMARRIAGE_AUG2907.pdf

Blair, K. L., & Holmberg, D. (2008). Perceived social network support and well-being in same-sex versus mixed-sex romantic relationships. *Journal of Social and Personal Relationships*, *25*(5), 769–791. https://doi.org/10.1177/0265407508096695

Blair, K. L., Holmberg, D., & Pukall, C. F. (2018). Support processes in same-and mixed-sex relationships: Type and source matters. *Personal Relationships*, *25*(3), 374–393. https://doi.org/10.1111/pere.12249

Blair, K. L., McKenna, O., & Holmberg, D. (2022). On guard: Public versus private affection-sharing experiences in same-sex, gender-diverse, and mixed-sex relationships. *Journal of Social and Personal Relationships*, *39*(9), 2914–2938. https://doi.org/10.1177/02654075221090678

Blair, K. L., Pukall, C. F., Smith, K. B. & Cappell, J. (2015). Differential associations of communication and love in heterosexual, lesbian, and bisexual women's perceptions and experiences of chronic vulvar and pelvic pain. *Journal of Sex and Marital Therapy*, *41*(5), 498–524. https://doi.org/10.1080/0092623X.2014.931315

Boertien, D., & Vignoli, D. (2019). Legalizing same-sex marriage matters for the subjective well-being of individuals in same-sex unions. *Demography*, *56*(6), 2109–2121. https://doi.org/10.1007/s13524-019-00822-1

Bryant, C. M., & Duncan, J. C. (2019). Interracial marriages: Historical and contemporary trends. *Biracial Families: Crossing Boundaries, Blending Cultures, and Challenging Racial Ideologies*, 81–104.

Carroll, J. (2007). *Most Americans approve of interracial marriages*. Gallup. https://news.gallup.com/poll/28417/most-americans-approve-interracial-marriages.aspx

Conley, T. D., Moors, A. C., Matsick, J. L., & Ziegler, A. (2013). The fewer the merrier?: Assessing stigma surrounding consensually non-monogamous romantic relationships. *Analyses of Social Issues and Public Policy*, *13*, 1–30. https://doi.org/10.1111/j.1530-2415.2012.01286.x

Diamond, L. M., & Alley, J. (2022). Rethinking minority stress: A social safety perspective on the health effects of stigma in sexually-diverse and gender-diverse populations. *Neuroscience & Biobehavioral Reviews*, *138*, 104720.

Demerson, V. (2004). *Incorrigible*. Wilfrid Laurier University Press.

Drabble, L. A., Mericle, A. A., Munroe, C., Wootton, A. R., Trock, K. F., & Hughes, T. L. (2021). Examining perceived effects of same-sex marriage legalization among sexual minority women: Identifying demographic differences and factors related to alcohol use disorder, depression, and self-perceived health. *Sexuality Research and Social Policy*, *19*(3), 1285–1299. https://doi.org/10.1007/s13178-021-00639-x

Earnest, J. (2012). *President Obama supports same-sex marriage*. The White House. https://obamawhitehouse.archives.gov/blog/2012/05/10/obama-supports-same-sex-marriage

Eckholm, E. (2015). *The same-sex couple who got a marriage license in 1971*. New York Times.

Elliott, D. B., Krivickas, K., Brault, M. W., & Kreider, R. M. (2012, May 3–5). *Historical marriage trends from 1890-2010: A focus on race differences* [Paper presentation]. Annual meeting of the Population Association of America, San Francisco, CA, United States. https://www.census.gov/content/dam/Census/library/working-papers/2012/demo/SEHSD-WP2012-12.pdf

Fleckenstein, J., Bergstrand, C. R., & Cox, D. W. (2012). *What do Polys want?: An overview of the 2012 Loving More survey*. Loving More. https://www.lovingmorenonprofit.org/polyamory-articles/2012-lovingmore-polyamory-survey/

Fleet, D. (2011, March 1). Lost Canadian Velma Demerson's tragic story of love and loss. *Vancouver Observer*. https://www.vancouverobserver.com/world/canada/2011/02/28/lost-canadian-velma-demersons-tragic-story-love-and-loss.html#:~:text=Demerson's%20marriage%20fell%20apart%20under,The%20two%20never%20reconciled

Gottman, J. M., Levenson, R. W., Gross, J., Frederickson, B. L., McCoy, K., Rosenthal, L., Ruef, A., & Yoshimoto, D. (2003). Correlates of gay and lesbian couples' relationship satisfaction and relationship dissolution. *Journal of Homosexuality*, 45(1), 23–43. https://doi.org/10.1300/J082v45n01_02

Guzzo, K. B. (2014). Trends in cohabitation outcomes: Compositional changes and engagement among never-married young adults. *Journal of Marriage and Family*, 76(4), 826–842. https://doi.org/10.1111/jomf.12123

Haupert, M., Gesselman, A., Moors, A., Fisher, H., & Garcia, J. (2017). Prevalence of experiences with consensual non-monogamous relationships: Findings from two nationally representative samples of single Americans. *Journal of Sex and Marital Therapy*, 43(5), 424–440. https://doi.org/10.1080/0092623X.2016.1178675

Hayford, S. R, Guzzo, K. B, & Smock, P. J. (2014). The decoupling of marriage and parenthood? Trends in the timing of marital first births, 1945–2002. *Journal of Marriage and Family*, 76(3), 520–538. https://doi.org/10.1111/jomf.12114

Hazan C, & Shaver P. (1987). Conceptualizing romantic love as an attachment process. *Journal of Personality and Social Psychology*, 52(3), 511–524. https://doi.org/10.1037/0022-3514.52.3.511

Holmberg, D., & Blair, K. L. (2016). Dynamics of perceived social network support for same-sex versus mixed-sex relationships. *Personal Relationships*, 23(1), 62–83. https://doi.org/10.1111/pere.12111

Hooker, E. (1993). Reflections of a 40-year exploration: A scientific view on sexuality. *American Psychologist*, 48, 450–453.

Horowitz, J. M., Graf, N., & Livingston, G. (2019, November 6). Marriage and cohabitation in the U.S. *Pew Research Center*. https://www.pewresearch.org/social-trends/2019/11/06/marriage-and-cohabitation-in-the-u-s/#:~:text=Cohabiting%20adults%20(82%25)%20are,as%20well%20as%20married%20couples

Hou, F., Wu, Z., Schimmele, C., & Myles, J. (2015). Cross-country variation in interracial marriage: A USA-Canada comparison of metropolitan areas. *Ethnic and Racial Studies*, 38(9), 1591–1609. https://doi.org/10.1080/01419870.2015.1005644

Kurdek, L. A. (1998). Relationship outcomes and their predictors: Longitudinal evidence from heterosexual married, gay cohabiting, and lesbian cohabiting couples. *Journal of Marriage and the Family*, 60(3), 553–568.

Kurdek, L. A. (2007). Avoidance motivation and relationship commitment in heterosexual, gay male, and lesbian partners. *Personal Relationships*, 14(2), 291–306.

Kurtz, S. (2003). Beyond gay marriage: The road to polyamory. *The Weekly Standard*, 8(45). https://pages.pomona.edu/~vis04747/h21/readings/Kurz_Beyond_gay_marriage.pdf

Lau, H. S. & Strohm, C. Q. (2011). The effects of legally recognizing same-sex unions on health and well-being. *Law and Inequality: A Journal of Theory and Practice*, 29, 107–148. Retrieved October 30, 2022, fromhttps://scholarship.law.unc.edu/cgi/viewcontent.cgi?article=1190&context=faculty_publications

Lawrence, E. M., Rogers, R. G., Zajacova, A., & Wadsworth, T. (2018). Marital happiness, marital status, health, and longevity. *Journal of Happiness Studies*, 20(5), 1539–1561. https://doi.org/10.1007/s10902-018-0009-9

LeBlanc, A. J., Frost, D. M., & Wight, R. G. (2015). Minority stress and stress proliferation among same-sex and other marginalized couples. *Journal of Marriage and Family*, 77(1), 40–59. https://doi.org/10.1111/jomf.12160

Lehmiller, J. J., & Agnew, C. R. (2006). Marginalized relationships: The impact of social disapproval on romantic relationship commitment. *Personality and Social Psychology Bulletin*, *32*(1), 40–51. https://doi.org/10.1177/0146167205278710

Liddle, K., & Liddle, B. J. (2004). VI. In the meantime: Same-sex ceremonies in the absence of legal recognition. *Feminism & Psychology*, *14*(1), 52–56. https://doi.org/10.1177/0959353504040303

Linley, L., Johnson, A. S., Song, R., Wu, B., Hu, S., Singh, S., Siddiqi, A., Green, T. A., Hall, H. I., Hernandez, A., Morgan, M., & Friend, M. (2019). *Estimated HIV incidence and prevalence in the United States, 2010–2016*. HIV Surveillance Supplemental Report, *24*(1). https://stacks.cdc.gov/view/cdc/76252

Liu, H., & Umberson, D. (2008). The times they are a changin': Marital status and health differentials from 1972 to 2003. *Journal of Health and Social Behavior*, *49*(3), 239–253. https://doi.org/10.1177/00221465080490030

Livingston, G., & Brown, A. (2017). Intermarriage in the U.S. 50 years after Loving v. Virginia. *Pew Research Center*. https://www.pewresearch.org/social-trends/2017/05/18/intermarriage-in-the-u-s-50-years-after-loving-v-virginia/

Mederos, M. (2015). *Expressions of affection and the tie signs in interracial and intraracial romantic relationships* (Publication No. 1598346) [Master's thesis, San Diego State University]. ProQuest Dissertations Publishing. https://www.proquest.com/openview/2aec0d9d6dbf65aa2c4dbbcf78401c76/1?pq-origsite=gscholar%26cbl=18750%26diss=y

Messinger, A. M. (2011). Invisible victims: Same-sex IPV in the National Violence Against Women Survey. *Journal of Interpersonal Violence*, *26*(11), 2228–2243. https://doi.org/10.1177/0886260510383023

Meyer, I. H. (2003). Prejudice, social stress, and mental health in lesbian, gay, and bisexual populations: Conceptual issues and research evidence. *Psychological Bulletin*, *129*(5), 674–697. https://doi.org/10.1037/0033-2909.129.5.674

Moors, A. C. (2017). Has the American public's interest in information related to relationships beyond "the couple" increased over time? *Journal of Sex Research*, *54*(6), 677–684. https://doi.org/10.1080/00224499.2016.1178208

Moors, A. C., Matsick, J. L., Ziegler, A., Rubin, J. & Conley, T. D. (2013). Stigma toward individuals engaged in consensual non-monogamy: Robust and worthy of additional research. *Analyses of Social Issues and Public Policy*, *13*(1), 52–69. https://doi.org/10.1111/asap.12020

Moors, A., Schechinger, H., Balzarini, R. N., & Flicker, S. (2021). Internalized consensual non-monogamy negativity and relationship quality among people engaged in polyamory, swinging, and open relationships. *Archives of Sexual Behavior*, *50*(4), 1389–1400. https://doi.org/10.1007/s10508-020-01885-7

Ogolsky, B. G., Monk, J. K., Rice, T. M., & Oswald, R. F. (2019). As the states turned: Implications of the changing legal context of same-sex marriage on well-being. *Journal of Social and Personal Relationships*, *36*(10), 3219–3238. https://doi.org/10.1177/0265407518816883

Ortiz-Ospina, E., & Roser, M. (2020). *Marriages and divorces*. Our World in Data. https://ourworldindata.org/marriages-and-divorces

Pollitt, A. M., Blair, K. L., & Lannutti, P. (2023). A review of two decades of LGBTQ-inclusive research in JSPR and PR. *Personal Relationships*, 1–30. Advance online publication. https://doi.org/10.1111/pere.12432

Rico, B., Kreider, R. M., & Anderson, L. (2018). *Growth in interracial and interethnic married-couple households*. United States Census Bureau. https://www.census.gov/library/stories/2018/07/interracial-marriages.html

Rosenfeld, M. J. (2014). Couple longevity in the era of same-sex marriage in the United States. *Journal of Marriage and Family*, 76(5), 905–918. https://doi.org/10.1111/jomf.12141

Rosenfeld, M. J., & Kim, B. (2005). The independence of young adults and the rise of interracial and same-sex unions. *American Sociological Review*, 70(4), 541–562. https://doi.org/10.1177/0003122405070004

Rosenthal, L., Deosaran, A., Young, D., & Starks, T. (2019). Relationship stigma and well-being among adults in interracial and same-sex relationships. *Journal of Social and Personal Relationships*, 36(11–12), 3408–3428. https://doi.org/10.1177/0265407518822781882278

Rosenthal, L., & Starks, T. J. (2015). Relationship stigma and relationship outcomes in interracial and same-sex relationships: Examination of sources and buffers. *Journal of Family Psychology*, 29(6), 818–830. https://doi.org/10.1037/fam0000116

Rusbult, C. E., Martz, J. M., & Agnew, C. R. (1998). The investment model scale: Measuring commitment level, satisfaction level, quality of alternatives, and investment size. *Personal Relationships*, 5, 357–387.

Shapiro, A. (2010, April 16). Obama: Hospitals must grant same-sex visitation rights. *National Public Radio*. https://www.npr.org/templates/story/story.php?storyId=126034014

Shaver, P. R., & Mikulincer, M. (2009). An overview of adult attachment theory. In J. H. Obegi & E. Berant (Eds.), *Attachment theory and research in clinical work with adults* (pp. 17–45). Guilford Press.

Steinbugler, A. C. (2005). Visibility as privilege and danger: Heterosexual and same-sex interracial intimacy in the 21st century. *Sexualities*, 8(4), 425–443. https://doi.org/10.1177/1363460705056618

Sussman, M. (2019, February 20). The "miscegenation" troll. *JSTOR Daily*. https://daily.jstor.org/the-miscegenation-troll/

Umberson, D., & Montez, J. K. (2010). Social relationships and health: A flashpoint for health policy. *Journal of Health and Social Behavior*, 51(Suppl.), S54–S66. https://doi.org/10.1177/00221465103835

U.S. Census Bureau. (2022). *Historical marital status tables*. https://www.census.gov/data/tables/time-series/demo/families/marital.html

Van der Vleuten, M., Jaspers, E., & van der Lippe, T. (2021). Same-sex couples' division of labor from a cross-national perspective. *Journal of GLBT Family Studies*, 17(2), 150–167. https://doi.org/10.1080/1550428X.2020.1862012

Wieling, E. (2003). Latino/a and White marriages: A pilot study investigating the experiences of interethnic couples in the United States. *Journal of Couple & Relationship Therapy*, 2(2–3), 41–55. https://doi.org/10.1300/J398v02n02_04

8

Marriage and Ethnicity Around the World

Marrying Someone From a Different Race, Religion, or Nationality

Stanley O. Gaines, Jr.

> Many of us have inherited an element of anger or fear of familial links with people who are different—those who in some way are not like us, those who are the "other." Sometimes it is religion that is perceived as a barrier to keep us apart. More often nowadays it is the colour of our skin. Over the centuries and across cultures marriages, or proposed marriages, between members of different racial groups cause small explosions of irritation, disappointment or anger, even in the most harmonious societies...
>
> —June Duncan Owen,
> *Mixed Matches: Interracial Marriage in Australia* (2002, p. 1)

Throughout the development of relationship science, from its "greening" phase (Berscheid, 1999) to its "ripening" phase (Reis, 2007) and its "blossoming" phase (L. Campbell & Simpson, 2013), the topic of *interethnic marriage* (i.e., marriage between persons who differ in their presumed biological and/or cultural heritage) has been relatively under-studied (for example, see E. M. Clark et al., 2015; and Gaines et al., 2015, concerning research on interethnic marriage in the United States). Although interethnic marriage stands at the crossroads between interpersonal relations and intergroup relations, reviews of the respective literatures on interpersonal relations (e.g., Berscheid, 1985; Berscheid & Reis, 1998; Leary, 2010) and intergroup relations (e.g., Brewer & Brown, 1998; Stephan, 1985; Yzerbyt & Demoulin, 2010) have tended not to mention interethnic marriage (see also Clark & Lemay, 2010). In any event, as the opening quote from Owen's (2002) book-length study of more than 100 interethnic (and, specifically, interracial) marriages within Australia illustrates, interethnic marriage retains the potential to stir negative intergroup attitudes (and, not infrequently, negative intergroup behavior) among many individuals across the world.

Like other "hot" topics within the field of relationship science, interethnic marriage reflects the ongoing dialectic between social change and social stability across generations in various societies (e.g., see Finkel et al., 2014a, 2014b, for provocative accounts of individuals' evolving expectations about marriages fulfilling growth-related versus deficit-related needs). Within the United States, the percentage of married couples who identified themselves as interethnic doubled from the 1990s (i.e., approximately 5%; Gaines, 1997) to the 2010s (i.e., approximately 10%; Gaines, 2017/2018)—a dramatic increase that clearly is fueled by demographic trends (particularly among younger couples) but nonetheless underscores the fact that the overwhelming majority of married couples continue to identify themselves as intraethnic. Furthermore, although exact percentages of interethnic versus intraethnic marriages are not so easily documented outside the United States, demographic trends appear to be driving comparable increases in interethnic marriages around the world (e.g., compare Goodwin, 1999, with Goodwin, 2009). We hasten to add that the one-time prevalence of anti-"miscegenation" laws historically presented unique barriers to interethnic marriage in the United States (Spickard, 1989).

In the present chapter, we draw upon Allport's (1954/1979) conceptualization of intergroup attitudes and intergroup behavior (Fiske, 1998), followed by Goffman's (1963) conceptualization of social stigma (Crocker et al., 1998), as we consider the impact of experiences with stereotyping, prejudice, and discrimination upon marginalization that individuals may experience with interethnic marriages around the world (Frost, 2011). Next, we provide in-depth reviews of 21st-century qualitative articles on (1) interracial marriage in Singapore (Wise & Velayutham, 2008), (2) interreligious marriage in Australia (Ata & Furlong, 2005), and (3) international marriage in Thailand (P. Statham, 2020). Lastly, we invoke Goffman's (1959) interactionist role theory as we propose future research on stigma in interethnic marriage. We note that, not only is *interracial marriage* (i.e., marriage between persons who differ in their presumed biological heritage) under-researched, especially outside the United States; but also *interreligious marriage* (i.e., marriage between persons who differ in their presumed "faith-based" cultural heritage) and *international marriage* (i.e., marriage between persons who differ in their presumed "state-based" cultural heritage) are under-researched to an even greater extent, within *and* outside the United States (Gaines, 2017/2018).

From Intergroup Attitudes and Intergroup Behavior to Social Stigma Concerning Interethnic Marriage

Like other attitudes, *intergroup attitudes* (i.e., individuals' evaluation of persons who presumably belong to socially defined groups other than their own group) include cognitive/thinking and affective/feeling aspects that may or may not be reflected in individuals' behavior (Allport, 1954/1979). In turn, the cognitive aspect of intergroup attitudes is known as *stereotyping*; the affective aspect of intergroup attitudes is known as *prejudice*; and the potentially resulting intergroup behavior is known as *discrimination* (Fiske, 1998). From the standpoint of intergroup relations, many members of societal in-groups (including European-descent, Christian persons, and/or non-immigrant persons in "Western" nations) tend to think, feel, and behave negatively toward members of societal out-groups (including non-European-descent, non-Christian, and/or immigrant persons within "Western" nations; Fiske & Tablante, 2015). Moreover, from the standpoint of interpersonal relations, perceptions of intergroup competition (whether held by members of societal ingroups *or* members of societal outgroups) might prevent many individuals from establishing a basis for trust toward members of socially defined groups other than their own group (Van Lange & Balliet, 2015).

Social stigma refers to target persons' possession of devalued physical and/or psychological characteristics, in the view of social observers (Goffman, 1963). Unlike the constructs of intergroup attitudes and intergroup behavior (which tend to be examined from the standpoint of individuals who hold negative attitudes and engage in negative behavior), the construct of social stigma tends to be explored from the vantage point of individuals who are the *targets* of negative attitudes and negative behavior (Crocker et al., 1998). From the perspective of intergroup relations, many members of societal out-groups (e.g., non-European-descent, non-Christian, and/or immigrant persons within "Western" nations) experience marginalization by societal institutions, which tend to be represented formally or informally by members of societal in-groups (e.g., European-descent, Christian persons, and/or non-immigrant persons in "Western" nations; Barreto, 2015). Additionally, from the standpoint of interpersonal relations, members of ethnic minority groups are likely to experience a greater variety of stressors (and possibly a greater intensity of social anxiety) than will members of ethnic majority groups *within the same relationships* (see Diamond, 2015).

We do not mean to imply that, around the world, interethnic relationships are inherently beset with difficulties or destined to fail; results from a large body of research on interracial friendships (inspired largely by the "contact hypothesis" of Allport, 1954/1979) suggest that interethnic relationships can flourish under certain circumstances (e.g., the perception of *equal-status contact* between minority-group and majority-group partners; Shelton & Richeson, 2015). Nevertheless, to the extent that minority-group and majority-group partners within interethnic *romantic* relationships experience marginalization, those partners may also experience a lack of relationship commitment (see Lehmiller & Agnew, 2006). For the purposes of the present chapter, Frost's (2011) commentary on marginalization and interethnic marriage is especially relevant: Even individuals from ethnic majority groups (e.g., European-descent, Christian persons, and/or non-immigrant persons in "Western" nations) may experience marginalization within a given society, if and when they marry individuals from ethnic minority groups (e.g., non-European-descent, non-Christian, and/or immigrant persons within "Western" nations). Thus, the "tribal stigmas" of race, religion, and nationality that Goffman (1963) identified 60 years ago remain intact today.

Cases in Point: Interethnic Marriage Around the World

Profile #1: Interracial Marriage in Singapore. Our first profile ostensibly consists of Wise and Velayutham's (2008) case study involving a marriage between an Asian-descent man from India (i.e., Selvaraj) and a European-descent woman from Australia (i.e., Amanda), with the five-day wedding ceremony taking place in Singapore. We say "ostensibly" because Wise and Velayutham's study actually focuses on the complex negotiations occurring between the spouses' families and, crucially, negotiations occurring *within* the groom's family (including a large number of extended family members and immediate family members alike) that were designed to maximize pride and minimize shame among all parties to the wedding ritual. Indeed, Wise and Velayutham reported that exchanges involving *tangible* resources (i.e., money, goods, services, information) were explicitly transacted, within and across families before and during the wedding event (and expected to continue afterward); whereas readers are left to infer that the spouses at the center of the wedding event probably engaged in their own exchanges involving *intangible* resources (i.e., affection and respect) before, during, and after the event (for details concerning *resource exchange theory*, see U. G. Foa & E. B. Foa, 1974).

Although the groom in Wise and Velayutham's (2008) case study was not the first member of his village to pursue interethnic marriage, he was the first to propose *interracial* marriage—a prospect that, though not explored at length, may help in explaining the unusually elaborate set of negotiations that the groom's father undertook to ensure that the wedding event proceeded in a village-approved manner. Conversely, the prospect of interracial marriage did not seem to loom as a source of concern for the bride's family (though the case study is virtually silent regarding the thoughts, feelings, or behavior of the bride's handful of family members who attended the wedding event). We are tempted to speculate that the lack of apparent protest from the Australian-born bride's family may be rooted in the rapidly rising percentage of individuals who are linked via immediate or extended family to interracial married couples in Australia (with estimates of 75% by 2030; Owen, 2002). However, it might be more prudent of us to conclude that—given the greater investment that the groom's immediate and extended family members placed in the success of the wedding event—the responsibility for counteracting possible stigmatization and ostracism against the couple simply weighed more heavily upon the groom's family.

In their case study of interracial marriage in Singapore, Wise and Velayutham (2008) cited Goffman's (1963) construct of stigma, as well as Goffman's (1967) construct of *face-work* (i.e., individuals' attempts at conveying a positive impression of themselves via social interaction; Perakyla, 2015), in the process of documenting efforts by members of the groom's immediate and extended family to promote a rare example of "out-marriage" involving a member of their village as a source of pride. As it turns out, stigma and face-work are major constructs within Goffman's *interactionist role theory*, which emphasizes the impact of society upon individuals' behavior (and, hence, individuals' self-definitions), with the caveat that individuals retain the ability to construct some of their own self-definitions (and to behave purposefully in many respects, if not to try to "make a difference" within their societies; Hancock & Garner, 2015). However, Wise and Velayutham did not specifically refer to Goffman's interactionist role theory.

At a minimum, we may conclude that results of the study in question are consistent with Goffman's view that individuals' *identities* (i.e., aggregates of individuals' self-definitions) are sustained within particular societal and interpersonal contexts (see also Stryker & A. Statham, 1985).

Profile #2: Interreligious Marriage in Australia. Our second profile consists of Ata and Furlong's (2005) observations regarding the social and psychological experiences of individuals within Christian–Muslim marriages in Australia. Ata and Furlong analyzed interview data from 106 individuals (19 Christian husbands, 44 Muslim husbands, 10 Christian wives, and 33 Muslim wives); couple-level data were not available. Individuals in Ata and Furlong's study identified particular challenges within interreligious marriages (e.g., Christian spouses were more likely to view their marriages as ideally closed to scrutiny from the public, including family and friends, whereas Muslim spouses were more likely to view their marriages as ideally open to scrutiny from the public, including family and friends—if not acquaintances and strangers). By the same token, individuals in Ata and Furlong's study also identified particular opportunities within interreligious marriages (e.g., individuals tended to report that they and their spouses shared a pro-relationship perspective on *interdependence*, or partners' mutual influence upon each other's thoughts, feelings, and behavior (for details regarding *interdependence theory*, see Kelley, 1979; Kelley & Thibaut, 1978; Thibaut & Kelley, 1959).

Given their interest in advising psychotherapists regarding sensitivity when working with individuals whose marriages are interreligious in nature, perhaps it should not be surprising that Ata and Furlong (2005) cautioned *therapists* against stigmatizing their own clients. Nevertheless, Ata and Furlong's advice underscores the degree to which therapists must consciously refrain from abusing their authority—whether as agents of social stability (e.g., openly questioning the morality of interreligious marriage) *or* as agents of social change (e.g., casting individuals' adherence to a given faith as evidence of "backward" thinking and, thus, creating barriers to social equality between husbands and wives). Ata and Furlong were especially concerned that therapists might wittingly or unwittingly communicate pro-Christian and anti-Muslim attitudes to clients in interreligious marriages, within the broader context of the "Anglo" (i.e., British- and North American-influenced) society that constitutes Australia. Ata and Furlong went so far as to contend that therapists likely bear most (and, perhaps, all) of the blame for the apparently high percentage of clients from "diverse" backgrounds who discontinue therapy without obtaining a successful outcome, although "diversity" is by no means limited to marriage across religious boundaries.

Although they did not cite Goffman's (1963) book on stigma, Ata and Furlong (2005) *did* invoke Goffman's construct of stigma when referring to societal marginalization of Muslim husbands (presumably on the basis of the husbands' religious group membership) and Christian wives (presumably on the basis of the wives' gender) in Christian–Muslim marriages. Interestingly, Ata and Furlong did not allude to the "double whammy" that Muslim wives in Christian–Muslim marriages might experience as targets of stereotyping, prejudice, and discrimination (whether inside or outside the therapy setting). In any event, not only did Ata and Furlong display familiarity with Goffman's construct of stigma, but they also invoked Goffman's (1969) construct of face-work when informing therapists that the "Anglo" or "Western" norm of directness in interpersonal communication between strangers might be counterproductive when interacting with clients from diverse cultural (including, but not limited to, religious) backgrounds. Finally, although Ata and Furlong did not mention Goffman's (1959) interactionist role theory, it is clear that individuals possess the capacity to "ad-lib" their performances as actors on metaphorical social stages (even as individuals enact their social roles; Stryker & A. Statham, 1985).

Profile #3: International Marriage in Thailand. Our third and final profile consists of Statham's (2020) study of the social and psychological experiences of Thai women who had been married to "Western" men for seven years or longer in Thailand. A total of 20 women provided interview data for Statham's study, reflecting upon the ways in which they (and their marriages) evolved over time. Approximately half of the women's marriages ended in divorce; among individuals whose marriages remained intact, some of the women noted that aging had taken such a toll on the physical and mental capacities of their husbands (who were more than a decade older than the wives on average) that the balance of power had shifted away from their husbands and toward themselves. Furthermore, Statham alluded to *social exchange* (Merton, 1941) regarding the status differentials that initially characterized the marriages (i.e., younger, upwardly mobile Thai wives pairing with older, financially well-to-do "Western" men). However, a more nuanced set of exchange-related dynamics also was evident in Statham's analysis, such that reciprocity of affection and respect served as the socioemotional glue that held many of the marriages together over time (as one would expect from the resource exchange theory of Foa & Foa, 1974).

Statham (2020) frequently used terms such as "partnering" and "partnership" when describing the highly transactional series of interactions between Thai women and "Western" men that culminated in marriage. However, the phrase "arranged marriage" does not accurately capture (1) the active role of Thai women in pursuing "partnerships" with "Westerners" or (2) the informal nature of social network members' efforts toward identifying available men. Rather, the "narrative arc" that Statham uncovered was the common occurrence of a life-altering event that led the women to conclude that their last, best hope for socioeconomic advancement was to signal their interest in pursuing tangible exchanges with "Western" men over the short term (via informal "partnership") that, optimally, would lead to intangible as well as tangible exchanges over the long term (via formal marriage). Despite the lack of any acknowledgment concerning interdependence theory as relevant to his study, certain constructs that Statham mentioned (e.g., *trust, power, exit*) are familiar to interdependence theorists (e.g., Kelley et al., 1983/2002, 2003).

Statham (2020) did not refer specifically to Goffman's *Stigma* (1963) when describing the potential stigmatization of those Thai women who had entered into informal "partnerships" with "Western" men without having entered into formal marriage—even though some social perceivers' inaccurate and unflattering depiction of those women as "prostitutes" clearly invokes the stereotypical "blemishes of character" attributes that (along with "physical deformities" and the "tribal stigmas" of race, religion, and nationality that can adversely affect individuals *and family members*, including spouses) best exemplify stigmas (Goffman, 1963, p. 14). (Interestingly, those "Western" men who are involved as unmarried partners seemingly avoid getting stigmatized as "sugar daddies.") As it happens, Statham's only citation of Goffman involved methodology—that is, *frame analysis* (Goffman, 1974). Additionally, Statham did not overtly mention Goffman's (1959) interactionist role theory. Nonetheless, results of Statham's study regarding international marriages between Thai women and "Western" men are compatible with Goffman's assumption that individuals possess limited autonomy concerning their self-definitions and corresponding behavior, in the wake of far-reaching societal constraints on individuals' behavior.

Putting It All Together. Taking (1) Wise and Velayutham's (2008) study of interracial marriage in Singapore, (2) Ata and Furlong's (2005) study of interreligious marriage in Australia, and (3) Statham's (2020) study of international marriage in Thailand as a whole, we are struck by the lack of empirical data from both spouses within any couple. (We have already commented on the lack of any data from *either* spouse in the study by Wise and Velayutham.) In the absence of data from both spouses, we are left with results that generally lend themselves to individual-level (rather than dyad-level) analyses—a scenario that has been commonplace throughout the history of relationship science (Berscheid, 1999) but likewise has been criticized as impeding progress within the field (Berscheid, 1986). Nevertheless, results of the studies that we have reviewed consistently indicate that *reinforcement-oriented theories* (all of which owe a debt to the operant reinforcement theory of Skinner, 1938) not only are relevant to close relationship processes in general (Berscheid, 1985) but also are relevant to interethnic marriage processes in particular. It remains to be seen whether the qualitative results of the studies in question will enable researchers to design quantitative studies to test a priori hypotheses concerning interethnic marriage processes.

Just as results from the studies by Wise and Velayutham (2008), Ata and Furlong (2005), and P. Statham (2020) point toward the usefulness of reinforcement-based theories (which are based on the assumption that individuals will tend to remain in social as well as physical environments that provide a preponderance of rewards over costs; Skinner, 1938) in interpreting individuals' behavior within interethnic marriage, so too do the results from those studies serve to direct researchers' attention toward the utility of identity-related theories in understanding individuals' self-definitions as potential influences on behavior within interethnic marriage (as anticipated by Gaines, 2017/2018). So far, we have limited our commentary to Goffman's (1959) interactionist role theory, especially as articulated in Goffman's *Stigma* (1963). However, it turns out that Goffman's interactionist role theory was derived from Mead's (1934/1967) *social behaviorism* (which proposes that individuals and societies may influence each other over time, with the dual influence mediated via individuals' behavior; Schellenberg, 1978). Compared with Mead's social behaviorism, Goffman's interactionist role theory places greater importance upon the impact of societies on individuals' self-definitions by way of individuals' behavior (rather than the impact of individuals' self-definitions upon societies by way of individuals' behavior; Stryker & Statham, 1985).

In the following section, drawing upon the results of the previously mentioned studies by Wise and Velayutham (2008), Ata and Furlong (2005), and Statham (2020) in combination with the aforementioned theories by Goffman (1959), Thibaut and Kelley (1959; Kelley, 1979; Kelley & Thibaut, 1978), and Mead (1934/1967), we shall propose a dyadic model of *individuals'*

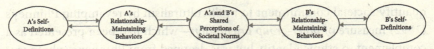

Figure 8.1 Dyadic Model of Identities, Interdependence, and Shared Perception of Societal Norms within Interethnic Marriages.

self-definitions (i.e., racial, religious, and national identities; Gaines et al., 2013), *individuals' relationship-maintaining behaviors* (i.e., accommodation-related responses to partners' anger or criticism; Rusbult et al., 1991), and *couples' shared perceptions regarding societal norms* (i.e., perceptions of society's commitment to multiculturalism; see Phinney, 1992) within interethnic marriages around the world. Although Gaines's (2017/2018) book on identity and interethnic marriage in the United States directly inspired the development of our model, we note that much of our conceptualization is unique to the present chapter (particularly our operationalization of societal influences in terms of couples' shared multiculturalist ethos). By the same token, we view the model (presented in Figure 8.1) as ripe for theory-driven quantitative research on interethnic marriage.

Toward a Dyadic Model of Identities, Interdependence, and Shared Perceptions of Societal Norms Within Interethnic Marriages

At the center of our model is couples' shared perceptions of societal norms. Both Mead's (1934/1967) social behaviorism and Goffman's (1959) interactionist role theory envision enduring influences of societal norms on individuals' behavior over time (Stryker & Statham, 1985). However, Mead and Goffman were concerned primarily with *individuals' own perceptions* of societal norms, whereas we are concerned mainly with couples' shared perceptions of those norms, following Thibaut and Kelley's (1959; Kelley 1979; Kelley & Thibaut, 1978) interdependence theory as adapted by Gaines (2017/2018). We reasoned that, *if* interethnic married couples can lay claim to a particular society as the context within which they live together (which may not be the case; Schueths, 2015), then couples' joint belief that the society upholds a multicultural ethos will tend to elicit relationship-promoting behavior from both spouses. In turn, future researchers might wish to quantify societal commitment to multiculturalism by revamping Phinney's (1992) measure of *other-group orientation*—which had been presented as a complement to ethnic identity but was dropped from Phinney's subsequent surveys (e.g., Phinney & Ong, 2007; R. E. Roberts et al., 1999)—to reflect perceived societal promotion of a multicultural ethos.

Emanating directly from couples' shared perception of societal norms within our model are individuals' relationship-maintaining behaviors. Unlike Mead's (1934/1967) social behaviorism or Goffman's (1959) interactionist role theory, Thibaut and Kelley's (1959) interdependence theory as revised by Kelley and Thibaut (1978) and refined by Kelley (1979) posits that individuals may choose to refrain from acting in a self-interested manner toward partners' relationship-threatening behavior over the short term, instead acting in ways that promote the survival of their relationships over the long term (Gaines, 2017/2018). One of the most intensively studied interdependence processes is individuals' *accommodation in response to partners' anger or criticism* (Rusbult et al., 1991), which includes high levels of *voice* (an active, constructive response), high levels of *loyalty* (a passive, constructive response), low levels of *exit* (an active, destructive response), and low levels of *neglect* (a passive, destructive response). Although various individual-difference variables promote accommodation (e.g., secure attachment style, positive femininity, "we-oriented" cultural values), we are unaware of any studies that have examined the potentially positive impact of perceived societal commitment to multiculturalism (see Gaines, 2016/2018).

Lastly, emanating from individuals' relationship-maintaining behaviors within our model are individuals' self-definitions. In contrast to Thibaut and Kelley's (1959; Kelley, 1979; Kelley & Thibaut, 1978) interdependence theory, Mead's (1934/1967) social behaviorism and Goffman's (1959) interactionist role theory comment at length upon individuals' self-definitions (Gaines, 2017/2018). Additionally, in contrast to Mead's social behaviorism, Goffman distinguished among *racial, religious, and national identities* (i.e., those self-definitions that are associated with individuals' presumed biological heritage, presumed "faith-based" cultural heritage, and presumed "state-based" cultural heritage; Goffman, 1963). To our knowledge, no published study of interdependence processes has examined the impact of individuals' accommodation-related behaviors upon those aspects of individuals' ethnic identity, or vice versa (see Gaines, 2016/2018). In fact, we are not aware of any studies within relationship science—whether examining relationship maintenance processes or not—in which Goffman's distinction among racial, religious, and national identities has been acknowledged (for an exception outside relationship science, see Gaines et al., 2013).

So far, we have focused on paths from couples' shared perception of societal norms to individuals' self-definitions over time, mediated by individuals' relationship maintenance behaviors—in other words, paths that anticipate *social stability*. However, both Mead's (1934/1967) social behaviorism and (to a lesser extent) Goffman's (1959) interactionist role theory suggest that we should also consider paths from individuals' self-definitions to couples' shared perception of societal norms over time, similarly mediated by individuals' relationship-maintenance behaviors—namely, paths that anticipate *social change* (Stryker & A. Statham, 1985). Indeed, at any given point in time, one might argue that the paths from individuals' self-definitions to individuals' relationship maintenance behaviors (if not the paths from individuals' relationship maintenance behaviors to couples' shared perception of social norms) make the most sense at an intuitive level (i.e., positivity regarding racial, religious, and national aspects of ethnic identity will lead individuals within interethnic marriages to reject the temptation to interpret their spouses' anger or criticism as evidence of the spouses' hard-wired "otherness," instead interpreting spouses' as evidence of the spouses' transitory "having a bad day;" see Gaines, 2017/2018).

In addition to pondering the directionality of links among individuals' self-definitions, individuals' relationship maintenance behaviors, and couples' perception of societal norms among interethnic couples according to our interpretation of Mead's (1934/1967) social behaviorism and Goffman's (1959) interactionist role theory, we acknowledge that Thibaut and Kelley's (1959; Kelley, 1979; Kelley & Thibaut, 1978) interdependence theory would lead us to consider a correlation (or, alternatively, bidirectional paths) linking the relationship maintenance behaviors *between* the partners (and *within* a set of couples; see Gaines, 2017/2018). Ideally, one should compare the goodness of fit concerning rival models via covariance structure analyses (first testing the model without the covariance between individuals' relationship maintenance behavior, then testing the model with the covariance between individuals' relationship maintenance behavior, and finally determining whether adding the cross-partner behavioral covariance leads to a model with a significantly better fit to the data; see Kline, 2016). In order to provide adequate tests regarding goodness of fit for the initial versus final models, one would need moderately large samples (i.e., no fewer than 100 couples, and optimally 200 or more couples; Schumacker & Lomax, 2016).

Notwithstanding the challenges that relationship scientists may face when trying to assemble large samples of interethnic married couples at a single point in time (Afful et al., 2015), the sequence of paths from individuals' self-definitions to individuals' relationship-maintaining behaviors to couples' shared perceptions of societal norms (and in the opposite direction as well) ideally should be tested using longitudinal data, with a minimum of three time points (see Kline, 2016). Of course, the creation of a sufficiently large data set may be easier said than done, with attrition likely to reduce the sample size over time (see Craig-Henderson & Lewis, 2015, for a discussion of methodological difficulties that may be especially pronounced in longitudinal research on interethnic marriages, as distinct from comparable research on intraethnic marriages). Nevertheless, longitudinal quantitative research is conspicuous in its absence from the literature on interethnic marriages (see Gaines et al., 2015). Particularly where tests of hypotheses derived from interdependence theory (Kelley, 1979; Kelley & Thibaut, 1978; Thibaut & Kelley, 1959) are concerned, such research would be useful (E. M. Clark et al., 2015).

Concluding Thoughts

At the beginning of the present chapter, we cited page 1 of Owen's *Mixed Matches* (2002) as support for our argument that stereotyping, prejudice, and discrimination as antecedents of spouses' marginalization in interracial and other interethnic marriages were prevalent in "Western" nations such as Australia. It is noteworthy that Owen ultimately expressed optimism regarding the future of interracial marriage in Australia, given that changes in societal attitudes and intermarriage patterns had made the social-psychological climate increasingly hospitable for interracial couples in that nation (although results of survey research in the United States suggest that individuals' own willingness to marry outside their racial group lags behind individuals' acceptance of hypothetical other persons entering into interethnic marriage; M. E. Campbell & Herman, 2015). Nonetheless, it is evident from a recent review of the literature on support communication within "culturally diverse" families (including, but not limited to, interethnic married couples) that—across "Western" nations, and around the world— spouses in interethnic marriage remain targets of negative intergroup attitudes, negative intergroup behaviors, and stigmatization (Gaines &

Mickelson, 2022). In closing, we encourage relationship scientists to dig deeper into stigma in interethnic marriage.

References

Afful, S. E., Taff, C. W., & Stoelting, S. M. (2015). Beyond *"difference"*: Examining the process and flexibility of racial identity in interracial marriages. *Journal of Social Issues, 71,* 659–674. doi:10.1111/josi.12142

Allport, G. W. (1979). *The nature of prejudice.* Addison-Wesley. (Original work published 1954.)

Ata, A., & Furlong, M. (2005). Researching Moslem-Christian marriages: Extrapolating from mixed-faith couples towards the practices of *Convivencia. Australian and New Zealand Journal of Family Therapy, 26,* 200–209. doi: 10.1002/j.1467-8438.2005.tb00675.x

Barreto, M. (2015). Experiencing and coping with social stigma. In M. Mikulincer & P. R. Shaver (Eds.), *APA handbook of personality and social psychology. Vol. 2: Group processes* (pp. 473–506). American Psychological Association.

Berscheid, E. (1985). Interpersonal attraction. In G. Lindzey & E. Aronson (Eds.), *The handbook of social psychology* (3rd ed., Vol. 2, pp. 413–484). Random House.

Berscheid, E. (1986). Mea culpas and lamentations: Sir Francis, Sir Isaac, and "The slow progress of soft psychology." In R. Gilmour & S. Duck (Eds.), *The emerging field of personal relationships* (pp. 267–286). Erlbaum.

Berscheid, E. (1999). The greening of relationship science. *American Psychologist, 54,* 260–266. doi: 10.1037/0003-066X.54.4.260

Berscheid, E., & Reis, H. T. (1998). Attraction and close relationships. In D. T. Gilbert, S. T. Fiske., & G. Lindzey (Eds.), *The handbook of social psychology* (4th ed., Vol. 2, pp. 193–281). McGraw-Hill.

Brewer, M. B., & Brown, R. J. (1998). Intergroup relations. In D. T. Gilbert, S. T. Fiske, & G. Lindzey (Eds.), *Handbook of social psychology* (4th ed., pp. 554–594). McGraw-Hill.

Campbell, L., & Simpson, J. A. (2013). The blossoming of relationship science. In J. A. Simpson & L. Campbell (Eds.), *The Oxford handbook of close relationships* (pp. 3–10). Oxford University Press.

Campbell, M. E., & Herman, M. R. (2015). Both personal and public: Measuring intermarriage attitudes. *Journal of Social Issues, 71,* 712–732. doi: 10.1111/josi.12145

Clark, E. M., Harris, A. L., Hasan, M., Votaw, K. L. B., & Fernandez, P. (2015). Concluding thoughts: Interethnic marriage through the lens of interdependence theory. *Journal of Social Issues, 71,* 821–833. doi: 10.1111/josi.12151

Clark, M. S., & Lemay, E. P., Jr. (2010). Close relationships. In S. T. Fiske, D. T. Gilbert, & G. Lindzey (Eds.), *Handbook of social psychology* (5th ed., Vol. 2, pp. 898–940). John Wiley & Sons.

Craig-Henderson, K., & Lewis, R.; Jr. (2015). Methodological considerations and challenges to conducting research on interethnic relationships: Using the right took kit! *Journal of Social Issues, 71,* 675–692. doi: 10.1111/josi.12143

Crocker, J., Major, B., & Steele, C. (1998). Social stigma. In D. T. Gilbert, S. T. Fiske, & G. Lindzey (Eds.), *Handbook of social psychology* (Vol. 2, pp. 504–553). McGraw-Hill.

Diamond, L. M. (2015). Sexuality and same-sex sexuality in relationships. In M. Mikulincer & P. R. Shaver (Eds.), *APA handbook of personality and social psychology. Vol. 3: Interpersonal relations* (pp. 523–553). American Psychological Association.

Finkel, E. J., Hui, C. M., Carswell, K. L., & Larson, G. M. (2014). The suffocation of marriage: Climbing Mount Maslow without enough oxygen. *Psychological Inquiry, 25*, 1–41. doi: 10.1080/1047840X.2014.863723

Finkel, E. J., Larson, G. M., Carswell, K. L., & Hui, C. M. (2014). Marriage at the summit: Response to the commentaries. *Psychological Inquiry, 25*, 120–145. 10.1080/1047840X.2014.890512

Fiske, S. T. (1998). Prejudice, stereotyping, and discrimination. In D. T. Gilbert, S. T. Fiske, & G. Lindzey (Eds.), *Handbook of social psychology* (4th ed., pp. 357–411). McGraw-Hill.

Fiske, S. T., & Tablante, C. B. (2015). Stereotyping: Processes and content. In M. Mikulincer & P. R. Shaver (Eds.), *APA handbook of personality and social psychology. Vol. 1: Attitudes and social cognition* (pp. 457–507). American Psychological Association.

Foa, U. G., & Foa, E. B. (1974). *Societal structures of the mind*. Charles C. Thomas.

Frost, D. M. (2011). Social stigma and its consequences for the socially stigmatized. *Social and Personality Psychology Compass, 5*, 824–839. doi: 10.1111/j.1751-9004.2011.00394.x

Gaines, S. O., Jr. (2018). *Identity and interethnic marriage in the United States*. Routledge. (Original work published 2017)

Gaines, S. O., Jr. (2018). *Personality and close relationship processes*. Cambridge University Press. (Original work published 2016)

Gaines, S. O., Jr. (with R. Buriel, J. H. Liu, & D. I. Rios). (1997). *Culture, ethnicity, and personal relationship processes*. Routledge.

Gaines, S. O., Jr., Clark, E. M., & Afful, S. E. (2015). Interethnic marriage in the United States: An introduction. *Journal of Social Issues, 71*, 647–658. doi: 10.1111/josi.12141

Gaines, S. O., Jr., Marelich, W. D., Bunce, D., Robertson, T., & Wright, B. C. (2013). MEIM expansion: Racial, religious, and national aspects of sense of ethnic identity within the United Kingdom. *Identity: An International Journal of Theory and Research, 13*, 289–317. doi:10.1080/15283488.2013.780973

Gaines, S. O., Jr, & Mickelson, K. D. (2022). Support communication in culturally diverse families: The role of stigma, revisited. In A. L. Vangelisti (Ed.), *Routledge handbook of family communication* (3rd ed., pp. 187–200). Routledge.

Goffman, E. (1959). *The presentation of self in everyday life*. Doubleday.

Goffman, E. (1963). *Stigma: Notes on the management of spoiled identity*. Prentice-Hall.

Goffman, E. (1967). *Interaction ritual: Essays on face-to-face behavior*. Anchor Books.

Goffman, E. (1969). *Where the action is: Three essays*. Allen Lane.

Goffman, E. (1974). *Frame analysis: An essay on the organization of experience*. Harvard University Press.

Goodwin, R. (1999). *Personal relationships across cultures*. Routledge.

Goodwin, R. (2009). *Changing relations: Achieving intimacy in a time of social transition*. Cambridge University Press.

Hancock, B. H., & Garner, R. (2015). Theorizing Goffman and Freud: Goffman's interaction order as a social-structural underpinning for Freud's psychoanalytic self. *Canadian Journal of Sociology, 40*, 417–444. doi: 10.29173/cjs21639

Kelley, H. H. (1979). *Personal relationships: Their structures and processes*. Erlbaum.

Kelley, H. H., Berscheid, E., Christensen, A., Harvey, J. H., Huston, T. L, Levinger, G., McClintock, E., Peplau, L. A., & Peterson, D. R. (2002). *Close relationships*. Percheron Press. (Original work published 1983)

Kelley, H. H., Holmes, J. G., Kerr, N. L., Reis, H. T., Rusbult, C. E., & Van Lange, P. A. M. (2003). *An atlas of interpersonal situations*. Cambridge University Press.

Kelley, H. H., & Thibaut, J. W. (1978). *Interpersonal relations: A theory of interdependence*. Wiley.

Kline, R. B. (2016). *Principles and practice of structural equation modeling* (4th ed.). Guilford Press.

Leary, M. R. (2010). Affiliation, acceptance, and belonging: The pursuit of interpersonal connection. In S. T. Fiske, D. T. Gilbert, & G. Lindzey (Eds.), *Handbook of social psychology* (3rd ed., Vol. 2, pp. 864–897). John Wiley & Sons.

Lehmiller, J. J., & Agnew, C. R. (2006). Marginalized relationships: The impact of social disapproval on romantic relationship commitment. *Personality and Social Psychology Bulletin, 32*, 40–51. doi: 10.1177/0146167205278710

Mead, G. H. (1967). *Mind, self and society from the standpoint of a social behaviorist*. University of Chicago Press. (Original work published 1934)

Merton, R. K. (1941). Intermarriage and the social structure: Fact and theory. *Psychiatry, 4*, 361–374. doi: 10.1080/00332747.1941.11022354

Owen, J. D. (2002). *Mixed matches: Interracial marriage in Australia*. UNSW Press.

Perakyla, A. (2015). From narcissism to face work: Two views on the self in social interaction. *American Journal of Sociology, 121*, 445–474. doi: 10.1086/682282

Phinney, J. S. (1992). The Multigroup Ethnic Identity Measure: A new scale for use with diverse groups. *Journal of Adolescent Research, 7*, 156–176. doi: 10.1177/074355489272003

Phinney, J. S., & Ong, A. D. (2007). Conceptualization and measurement of ethnic identity: Current status and future directions. *Journal of Counseling Psychology, 54*, 271–281. doi: 10.1037/0022-0167.54.3.271

Reis, H. T. (2007). Steps toward the ripening of relationship science. *Personal Relationships, 14*, 1–23. doi: 10.1111/J.1475-6811.2006.00139.X

Roberts, R., Phinney, J., Masse, L., Chen, Y., Roberts, C., & Romero, A. (1999). The structure of ethnic identity in young adolescents from diverse ethnocultural groups. *Journal of Early Adolescence, 19*, 301–322. doi: 10.1177/0272431699019003001

Rusbult, C., Verette, J., Whitney, G., Slovik, L., & Lipkus, I. (1991). Accommodation processes in close relationships: Theory and preliminary evidence. *Journal of Personality and Social Psychology, 60*, 53–78. doi: 10.1037/0022-3514.60.1.53

Schellenberg, J. A. (1978). *Masters of social psychology*. Oxford University Press.

Schueths, A. M. (2015). Barriers to interracial marriage? Examining policy issues concerning U.S. citizens married to undocumented Latino/a immigrants. *Journal of Social Issues, 71*, 805–821. doi: 10.1111/josi.12150

Schumacker, R. E., & Lomax, R. G. (2016). *A beginner's guide to structural equation modelling* (4th ed.). Erlbaum.

Shelton, J. N., & Richeson, J. A. (2015). Interacting across racial lines. In M. Mikulincer & P. R. Shaver (Eds.), *APA handbook of personality and social psychology. Vol. 2: Group processes* (pp. 395–422). American Psychological Association.

Skinner, B. F. (1938). *The behaviour of organisms: An experimental analysis*. D. Appleton Century Company.

Spickard, P. R. (1989). *Mixed blood: Intermarriage and ethnic identity in twentieth-century America*. University of Wisconsin Press.

Statham, P. (2020). Living the long-term consequences of Thai-Western marriage migration: The radical life-course transformations of women who partner older Westerners. *Journal of Ethnic and Migration Studies, 46*, 1562–1587. doi: 10.1080/1369183X.2019.1565403

Stephan, W. G. (1985). Intergroup relations. In G. Lindzey & E. Aronson (Eds.), *Handbook of social psychology* (3rd ed., Vol. 2, pp. 599–658). Random House.

Stryker, S., & Statham, A. (1985). Symbolic interaction and role theory. In G. Lindzey & E. Aronson (Eds.), *Handbook of social psychology* (3rd ed., Vol. 1, pp. 311–378). Random House.

Thibaut, J. W., & Kelley, H. H. (1959). *The social psychology of groups*. Wiley.

Van Lange, P. A. M., & Balliet, D. (2015). Interdependence theory. In M. Mikulincer & P. R. Shaver (Eds.), *APA handbook of personality and social psychology. Vol. 3: Interpersonal relations* (pp. 65–92). American Psychological Association.

Wise, A., & Velayutham, S. (2008). Second-generation Tamils and cross-cultural marriage: Managing the translocal village in a moment of cultural rupture. *Journal of Ethnic and Migration Studies, 34*, 113–131. doi: 10.1080/13691830701708718

Yzerbyt, V., & Demoulin, S. (2010). Intergroup relations. In S. T. Fiske, D. T. Gilbert, & G. Lindzey (Eds.), *Handbook of social psychology* (5th ed., Vol. 2, pp. 1024–1083). John Wiley & Sons.

9
Conscious Uncoupling
Divorce in the 21st Century

Abdullah S. Salehuddin, Tamara D. Afifi, and Jade Salmon

In 2014, celebrities Gwyneth Paltrow and Chris Martin terminated their romantic relationship by moving forward in love and friendship. This example encapsulates the concept of *conscious uncoupling*—a constructive approach to relational termination with positive implications for those involved (Thomas, 2016). Since 2014, conscious uncoupling, both as an ideology and a practice, has gained traction in popular culture and, more recently, attracted scholarly investigations. Understanding positive approaches to relational dissolution, given the high rates of divorce estimated at 50% (Centers for Disease Control and Prevention, 2017) in the United States, is essential. Divorce is the legal dissolution of marital relationships (Price & McKenry, 1988), which may detrimentally impact mental and physical well-being (Kalmijn & Monden, 2006) and child development (Sands et al., 2017). Nonetheless, how constructively or destructively partners terminate romantic relationships and, by extension, form new, non-romantic partnerships likely influences these outcomes.

In this chapter, we unpack *conscious uncoupling* to better understand its ideology and practice. The chapter proceeds in four parts. First, we trace the development of conscious uncoupling by discussing the historical evolution of marital ideology relative to life expectancy. Second, we identify certain predictors and positive outcomes associated with conscious uncoupling in romantic relationships. Third, we underscore the implications of conscious uncoupling on children. Finally, we offer suggestions for future research related to conscious uncoupling, like measurement development, and applications in resilience, coping, and culture.

History of Conscious Uncoupling

Conscious uncoupling—an approach to relational termination grounded in tremendous amounts of goodwill, generosity, and respect between the separating partners—is a modern phenomenon that challenges traditional perceptions and practices of relational dissolution (Thomas, 2016). Traditional marital perspectives, rooted in the language of "happily ever after" and "until death do us part," have for a large part of human history influenced cultural perceptions of marital ideology and praxis. Evidence suggests that traditional worldviews on marriage were not necessarily about love, commitment, and unity between marital partners but, rather, life expectancy and survival in early history (Sadeghi & Sami, 2014; Thomas, 2016). To unpack historical associations between marital ideology and life expectancy, as well as gain a deeper understanding of the emergence of conscious uncoupling in the modern era, this section will proceed in two parts. First, we discuss the historical evolution of marital ideology from the Paleolithic period to the modern era. Second, we reconceptualize belief structures surrounding marriage by unpacking conscious uncoupling.

Life Expectancy

Conscious uncoupling, in many ways, counters the assumption that married individuals should/will remain together until death—an assumption associated with life expectancy and survival in early human history. In the upper Paleolithic period, the average human life expectancy was 33 years (Kotre & Hall, 1997). As such, the average pair bonding would approximately last for a decade and, if fortunate, two at most. In the 1900s, the average life expectancy for both women and men ranged from 48 to 51— roughly a two-decade increase (Kinsella, 1992). Life expectancy from the upper Paleolithic period to the inception of the 20th century rose by roughly 15 years. Fast-forward to the contemporary era, a 2020 National Center for Health Statistics (NCHS) report reveals that life expectancy is now 77 years (Arias et al., 2021). From the 1900s to the contemporary era— a period marked by immense technological and medical advancements— life expectancy rose by roughly 43 years for men, and for women, 48 years (Sadeghi & Sami, 2014). This means that, depending on the time of marriage, married individuals are expected to endorse and practice traditional notions of marriage, grounded in the lexicon of "happily ever after" and "until death do us part," for multiple decades.

The historical evolution of life expectancy coupled with modern-day divorce rates in the United States, however, suggests that the rhetoric of traditional marital ideology may have outlived its applicability. According to several reports (National Marriage Project, 2019), roughly 40%–50% of all first-time marriages in the United States will end in divorce. Cross-cultural research also suggests that divorce and remarriage are highly commonplace (Brown & Wright, 2019; Fisher, 2016). The high rates of divorce underscore that romantic partners have struggled to uphold the socially-constructed, ideological fascination with, and practice of, eternal monogamy in marital contexts. What seems more consistent with lived experiences and (inter) national statistics is the practice of serial monogamy, or "having multiple partnerships (or marriages) in sequence—where one relationship ends before the next relationship begins" (Snopkowski, 2016, p. 395), without any overlap between the two. Serial monogamy, by default, assumes that "most of us will also go through one or two significant romantic endings as well" (Thomas, 2016, p. 42). In fact, scholars have argued that serial monogamy is becoming the norm, giving weight to the notion that most individuals will experience at least two to three serious romantic partnerships and, by extension, one or two major relational dissolution(s) (Fisher, 2016). To be clear, living "happily ever after" is not impossible by any means, as many married couples have achieved such relational milestones. However, evidence suggests that living "happily ever after" with one individual forever is seemingly the *exception*, not the rule by which marriage should be defined.

Using an evolutionary-psychological framework, scholars have argued that human beings are perhaps not meant to remain in monogamous relationships for durations exceeding several decades. "Our biology and psychology are not set up to be with one person for four, five, or six decades" (Sadeghi & Sami, 2014, n.p.). Fisher (2012) similarly argues that considerable data—comprised of evidence for serial monogamy in conjunction with the rates of adultery—suggest that human beings may not be biologically and psychologically wired to be with one individual forever. Infidelity in marital and dating contexts has been widespread not only in the 21st century (Allen & Baucom, 2006; Buunk & Dijkstra, 2006), but also in most decades in preceding centuries (Fisher, 1992; Hunt, 1974; Lawrence, 1989). Furthermore, international data (from several countries) on divorce rates between 1947 and 1981 indicate that the average length of marriage was roughly four years (Fisher, 1989), which has since then increased to eight years in the contemporary era. Despite this increase, statistics coupled with evolutionary perspectives suggests that belief structures surrounding marriage, rooted in traditional marital ideology, necessitate reconceptualization through the concept of conscious uncoupling.

What Is Conscious Uncoupling?

Conscious uncoupling is a concept that reconceptualizes traditional belief structures surrounding marriage and divorce using a positive lens. Marital belief structures rooted in the lexicon of traditional marital ideology shape socially-constructed perceptions of divorce as a negative phenomenon. Thomas (2016) explains, "If a romantic relationship ends for any reason other than one or both people die, we [as a society] assume the relationship to be a failure" (n.p.). Because married individuals are expected to remain together for eternity regardless of circumstantial severity, there are negative connotations associated with marital termination (Thomas, 2016). For instance, marital dissolution has been associated with undesirable perceptions, as children view divorce as a highly destructive event with traumatic impact, especially when there is low post-divorce adjustment (van der Wal et al., 2019), and adults associate this type of relational termination with guilt (Kalmijn, 2020). Blood and Blood (1979) explain that traditional divorce is typically perceived as acrimonious, where the offended individuals are plagued with feelings of bitterness, anger, and resentment caused by their partners' marital betrayal. Essentially, traditional divorce insinuates relational failure, individual shame and guilt, and partner blame. Under the conscious uncoupling perspective, however, divorce need not be perceived in such a negative way and, therefore, necessitates reconceptualization.

The notion of conscious uncoupling promotes the extrapolation of positive elements in relational termination in a manner beneficial to the separating parties and, importantly, others involved (i.e., children, family, friends, etc.). In her book, *Conscious Uncoupling: 5-Steps to Living Happily Even After*, Thomas (2016) coins the term *conscious uncoupling* and breaks down its five-step process, which includes: (1) "find emotional freedom," (2) "reclaim your power and your life," (3) "break the pattern, heal your heart," (4) "become a love alchemist," and (5) "create your happily-*even*-after life." Ultimately, conscious uncoupling assumes a sense of wholeness and coming together despite relational termination and separation. The remainder of the section will offer a glimpse into each step by providing a brief overview (for an elaborate discussion on each step, please see Thomas, 2016).

The first step, "find emotional freedom," encourages conscious uncouplers to look internally at their emotions and use them to help transform disappointing and destructive patterns of perceived love into endless supplies of individual strength, stability, and support. Second, to "reclaim your power and your life," Thomas (2016) suggests that conscious uncouplers retrospectively craft a holistic and accurate narrative of the relational termination but mainly focus on the area of self-improvement. The third step, "break the pattern, heal your heart," promotes the learning of new skills/capacities that facilitate imminent, successful relationships by first identifying core beliefs that sabotaged the conscious uncouplers' love life to begin with. Fourth, to "become a love alchemist," Thomas (2016) argues that conscious uncouplers must learn more about what aspects of themselves they are releasing versus aspects they are creating; moreover, they should also dissolve and resolve any feelings of residual anger or hurt between the separating parties. Lastly, the fifth step, "create your happily-*even*-after life," motivates conscious uncouplers to generate novel agreements appropriate for the new relationship being developed and discover wholesome, healthy, and cooperative ways to handle relational processes, whether navigating legal procedures, dividing property, or caretaking for children (if applicable). Taken together, these aspects of conscious uncoupling may significantly impact romantic partners and their newly formed non-romantic relationships after relational termination.

Conscious Uncoupling in Romantic Relationships

Despite the novelty of the term "conscious uncoupling" (Thomas, 2016), research has examined similar constructs for decades. Blood and Blood (1979) described *amicable divorce* as ending a marital relationship without pinning blame, rather, perceiving the divorce as an opportunity for ex-romantic partners to pursue their respective life paths freely. Indeed, relationship dissolution is often characterized by pain. However, this perspective treats such pain as a signal to make positive changes that will benefit both exes' lives (Cohen, 2021). As such, Rollie and Duck (2006) argued for a greater emphasis on relational *change* versus relational *ending* in investigating relationship dissolution. The remainder of this section will review the divorce and relationship dissolution literature to present predictors and positive outcomes associated with conscious uncoupling.

Predictors: Who Consciously Uncouples and How?

Although there is a lack of research on who is most likely to consciously uncouple and the behaviors involved, the literature on post-dissolution relationships provides insight. Griffith et al. (2017) found that individuals who are male, LGBTQ+, high in the Big Five traits of extraversion and agreeableness, and less anxiously attached are more likely to stay friends with an ex-romantic partner. Madey and Jilek (2012) found similar tendencies in those with secure attachment. That said, individual factors (i.e., agreeableness, extraversion, neuroticism, etc.) represent weak predictors for dissolution in non-marital (i.e., dating) relationships in general (Le et al., 2010). Regarding cognitions, likelihood to reconcile with an ex-romantic partner is associated with positive, or even ambivalent, evaluations of one's ex (Dailey et al., 2020). The probability of engaging in conscious uncoupling may even be a question of *personal dedication*; that is, the desire and action to improve a relationship's quality to benefit both parties. While conscious uncoupling was initially theorized as a feature of commitment, it also involves efforts to sacrifice for the relationship and prioritize the well-being of both the self and partner (Righetti et al., 2020). It could be argued that individuals who are personally dedicated to their relationship with their soon-to-be ex may choose to sacrifice the romantic aspect of their connection to allow both parties to grow—this would correspond with the viewpoint of amicable divorce (Blood & Blood, 1979; Cohen, 2021).

Beyond individual characteristics, there are a selection of intra- and interpersonal behaviors that may promote conscious uncoupling. *Benefit finding*, which describes the process of reflecting on the positive outcomes of stressful life events, is linked to positive post-dissolution adjustment (Samios et al., 2014). During the dissolution process, individuals may transition from mourning the end of the relationship to appreciating what it provided, as well as their own emotional strength in dissolving it. Similarly, considering one's romantic partner's point of view can help shift the stereotypical feelings of anger and hurt into a reflection of how *both* parties feel about the dissolution and what would make *both* comfortable in the process (Cohen, 2021).

Interpersonally, taking a team-oriented approach to relationship dissolution is associated with an amicable breakup and, therefore, conscious uncoupling. Historically, mutual initiation of the breakup predicts more positive emotional reactions to dissolution (Wilmot et al., 1985). Contemporarily, such effects are long-lasting, as mutual initiation is also a predictor of positive mental health outcomes and growth for years after a divorce (Miller, 2009; Symoens et al., 2013). A possible explanation for this can be extrapolated from the post-divorce adjustment literature: Wang and Amato (2000) argued that breakup initiators are better adjusted because they engage in emotional processing and mourning prior to the termination event. Likewise, mutual initiation may provide an opportunity for joint processing, such that both partners work through the relationship dissolution together from the start. Of course, not every breakup is initiated mutually. Still, being thoughtful of the other party facilitates conscious uncoupling. When discussing breaking up, the use of strategies involving a more positive tone and less manipulation predicts a greater probability of being amicable after the breakup (Metts et al., 1989). Vangelisti (2006) recommends *direct, other-oriented* strategies (i.e., those that confront the topic while considering the other's thoughts and feelings) as mutually beneficial in highly intimate relationships. Altogether then, conscious uncoupling is a rather thoughtful and intentional means of relationship dissolution that should benefit both parties involved.

Positive Outcomes: The Benefits of Conscious Uncoupling

Research suggests that the careful process of conscious uncoupling pays off for both ex-partners. By focusing on cooperatively transitioning out of a romantic relationship, exes are likely to leave the dissolution process feeling a sense of fairness. For instance, exes who remain on good terms are more likely to maintain frequent, mutually initiated communication than those who hold primarily negative feelings (Villella, 2010). Amicable divorce is characterized by equitable division of property, due to the ability of exes to negotiate the terms directly (Blood & Blood, 1979). Indeed, perceiving a fair division of property is associated with better mental health outcomes post divorce (Symoens et al., 2013). Mutual good intentions in conscious uncoupling are linked to maintaining shared friendships, as well. That is, these ex-romantic partners are less likely to obligate their friends to "pick" between the two of them (Blood & Blood, 1979).

In fact, as suggested by the post-divorce relationship literature, conscious uncoupling often leaves the door open for exes to remain friends. From a social exchange perspective, the reception of desirable and satisfying resources (e.g., love, information, goods) from an ex-romantic partner predicts a higher-quality post-dissolution friendship (Busboom et al., 2002; Mogilski & Welling, 2017). Furthermore, Griffith et al. (2017) found that people who stay friends with an ex for security and practical reasons were more likely to experience positive affective outcomes. Amicable exes also often report greater relational satisfaction than those who create distance from each other (Villella, 2010). These findings lend themselves to the benefits of conscious uncoupling, such that proactive relationship dissolution can serve as a couple's way of "salvaging their love" (Blood & Blood, 1979, p. 493) from falling victim to a destructive romantic relationship. In this way, they can still experience the rewards of the relationship. In fact, queer women are often inclined to maintain friendships with exes because (1) they provide one another with a sense of community within their marginalized group, and (2) they have developed such a deep sense of intimacy from their romantic relationship that they can maintain a connection and effectively support one another (Fitzgerald, 2004). In other words, terminating a romantic relationship cooperatively and optimistically can help buffer the distress that tends to characterize divorce (Dailey et al., 2020) by leveling the playing field, so that ex-romantic partners can move on happily, with or without each other. Ultimately, conscious uncoupling may have positive implications for ex-partners with children.

Effects of Conscious Uncoupling on Children

Parental divorce is typically considered an adverse childhood event that can negatively influence children long into adulthood (Becher et al., 2019). However, it does not have to be. In fact, research shows that children vary considerably in their responses to divorce, with some children being harmed by their parents' divorce, others not being affected at all, and still others benefiting from being removed from a turbulent environment (Amato, 2010; Sands et al., 2017; Thomas, 2018). In addition, unlike what the popular press suggests, most couples have amicable relationships after a divorce (Haddad et al., 2016). Parents' communication is central to determining how well children function after a divorce (Xerxa et al., 2020). Conscious uncoupling could be used by parents to redefine their boundaries from couples to co-parents, allowing for a greater awareness of how they communicate. Even though there is no empirical research on the term "conscious uncoupling," to our knowledge, the idea is evidenced in the divorce literature on interparental conflict and co-parenting.

Interparental Conflict and Co-Parenting

Interparental conflict and co-parenting are two crucial communication processes that contribute to risk and resilience in children's and parents' functioning after a divorce. Interparental conflict has been shown to be a stronger predictor of children's personal and relational well-being than divorce per se, with children whose parents stay married and who have a highly conflicted relationship being worse off than children whose parents have a conflicted relationship and divorce (Amato & Afifi, 2006; Amato & Sobolewski, 2001). Interparental conflict is arguably the most important factor in determining how well children function after a divorce (Xerxa et al., 2020). This is particularly the case when the conflict is intense, long-lasting, and involves the children, and when the children feel caught in the middle. Children feel caught between their parents when parents disclose inappropriate information about the other parent, talk badly about the other parent, or ask the child to carry information to the other parent (Afifi, 2003). Feeling caught has been associated with weakened parent–child relationships and diminished mental health (Amato & Afifi, 2006; O'Mara & Schrodt, 2017; Schrodt & Afifi, 2006). Children often respond to feeling caught by avoiding talking about one parent to the other, mimicking the parents' conflict behaviors, or directly confronting their parents about conflict (Afifi, 2003). Feelings of being caught can go unresolved for years because children are too afraid to tell their parents to stop putting them in the middle, and parents are therefore largely unaware of the negative impact their interparental conflict is having on their child's mental health and their relationship with them and the other parent. Being more consciously aware of one's feelings toward the other parent, the source of those feelings, and how one communicates those feelings to one's children could dramatically improve relationships within the entire family system.

Part of effective conscious uncoupling also likely involves former partners renegotiating their boundaries from once being romantic partners to now transitioning into co-parents. It is important for former partners to shift their thinking of each other as romantic partners to co-parents of their children to successfully parent their children together.

Effective co-parenting has often been shown to be a protective factor that is essential to children's resilience. The majority of the research has demonstrated that positive co-parenting improves child and family outcomes in divorced (step)families (Ganong et al., 2021). Co-parenting is conceptualized as "the reciprocal and conjoint involvement of both parents in education, childrearing and planning of children's life decisions" (Lamela et al., 2016, p. 151). Co-parenting is a multidimensional construct, consisting of a variety of active parenting behaviors, expectations, and beliefs. According to Feinberg (2003), there are four primary characteristics of effective co-parenting: (1) an agreement on how children should be parented, (2) a sharing of household responsibilities, support, and validation of the other's parenting abilities (versus undermining them), (3) managing overt and covert conflict, and (4) joint family management or regulation of family roles and responsibilities. Often, co-parenting changes throughout the divorce process. Some partners have a good relationship and effective communication from the very beginning of the divorce process, other partners struggle during the divorce and then their relationship improves over time, and still others have a relationship that becomes more conflicted, as co-parenting grows increasingly difficult over time (Becher et al., 2019).

In divorced (step)families, a strong co-parenting alliance has been associated with positive outcomes for young adult children, whereas a strained co-parenting alliance has been associated with negative outcomes. For instance, Schrodt and Afifi (2018) found that supportive co-parental communication helped young adults' mental health, whereas antagonistic co-parental communication hurt young adults' well-being when they felt caught between their parents. This mediating effect was applicable for both children of divorced and continuously married families and evidenced the strongest effect in the mother–child relationship. Likewise, children in stepfamilies fare better when their parents and stepparents work together to create a parenting plan that benefits the children, agree on parenting rules, communicate those rules clearly and consistently abide by them, and communicate warmth (Ganong et al., 2021). In addition, Herrero et al. (2020) found that effective co-parental communication and broader family communication patterns were positively associated with psychological adjustment and fewer economic consequences for children after a divorce, such as negotiations of pension and child support. When parents attempted to co-parent under high-conflict circumstances, however, co-parenting was associated with worse adjustment in children.

Interparental conflict and co-parenting are likely interdependent in terms of conscious uncoupling being successful. It is difficult to create a strong parental alliance when conflict levels are high between the parents (Becher et al., 2019). Research shows that co-parenting tends to benefit both the parents' and children's mental and relational health when conflict is kept to a minimum between parents (Becher et al., 2019). When conflict levels are high, attempts at co-parenting can backfire and escalate further conflict in the family (Hardesty et al., 2008). Therefore, when parents have a contentious relationship, shared physical custody is not always the best custody plan (Becher et al., 2019). Conflict is also an interpersonal process, and successful conscious uncoupling would require that both parents be willing to be mindful of their perceptions and communication patterns. This will allow conflict to be managed more effectively, providing an opportunity for successful co-parenting to exist.

Future Research Directions

While the official coinage of the term *conscious uncoupling* is relatively new (Thomas, 2016), research examining the process by which romantic partners terminate relationships in a positive manner has received decent amounts of scholarly attention. Concepts like amicable divorce and co-parenting closely resemble certain dimensions of conscious uncoupling. However, there are subtle differences between these concepts, which make conscious uncoupling unique and more applicable in various contexts. For instance, amicable divorce seemingly applies only to those individuals who are legally married (Blood & Blood, 1979), whereas conscious uncoupling does not assume marriage as a prerequisite (Thomas, 2016). Co-parenting—which can be a positive approach to managing relationships post dissolution—exclusively includes relationships in which children are involved (Schoppe et al., 2001).

Conscious uncoupling, by contrast, may broadly apply to both parental and non-parental relationships. To truly examine conscious uncoupling, how can we, as scholars, imminently differentiate between conscious uncoupling and other closely related concepts?

Measurement Development

Given these distinctions between concepts that closely resemble similar relational termination processes, future research should focus on developing methodological instruments to precisely measure conscious uncoupling. Researchers may investigate conscious uncoupling using qualitative and quantitative instruments. Qualitatively, in-depth interviews or communicated narrative sense-making (CNSM; Kellas, 2018) may be used as instruments to better understand the challenges with enacting conscious uncoupling and, once enacted, the corresponding effects for those involved and the relationships they maintain. Quantitatively, however, there is a need for researchers to develop an actual scale of conscious uncoupling that captures its five dimensions as outlined by Thomas (2016). Once an official conscious uncoupling scale has been developed, researchers may then quantify the concept to better understand the general and temporal effects of conscious uncoupling through longitudinal studies in various contexts, some of which may include coping and resilience.

Coping, Resilience, and Culture

After developing measurement instruments for conscious uncoupling, researchers should then investigate how conscious uncoupling unfolds in relationships to influence relational outcomes. In romantic relationships, scholars may investigate how conscious uncoupling impacts coping and resilience. Using the extended theoretical model of communal coping (TMCC; Afifi et al., 2020), scholars may research how conscious uncouplers and ex-partners cope with shared stressors affecting children (i.e., life-altering medical diagnoses, major transitions in life, etc.). Researchers could also utilize the theory of resilience and relational load (TRRL; Afifi et al., 2016) to assess conscious uncouplers' ability to positively adapt in the face of adversity or stressful situations. There are many avenues for research in the social sciences on conscious uncoupling given its relatively novel coinage.

Another avenue for future research should focus on the interaction between conscious uncoupling and culture. Hofstede (1980) dichotomized culture by identifying two distinct dimensions: (1) individualism and (2) collectivism. Individualistic cultures centralize values, beliefs, and practices primarily driven by self-goals as opposed to group goals (Hofstede, 1980, 2001). As such, people from individualistic cultures may be more likely to terminate unhappy marriages given the strong sense of individual goal-orientation (Toth & Kemmelmeier, 2009). By contrast, collectivistic cultures tend to prioritize group goals over individual objectives (Hofstede, 1980). Research shows that individuals from collectivistic cultures are more likely to remain in marriages despite higher levels of marital dissatisfaction (Levinger, 1999). Future research should compare individualistic groups to collectivistic ones to examine variability influenced by conscious uncoupling on relational outcomes, such as relational satisfaction, communal orientation, and relational load post conscious uncoupling, to name just a few.

Conclusion

In this chapter, we unpacked conscious uncoupling to better understand positive and constructive approaches to relational termination that ultimately benefit both parties involved. Traditional ideologies surrounding marriage have generated unrealistic expectations for married individuals to eternally remain together, which seems inconsistent with modern-day divorce rates, remarriages, and evidence toward the practice of serial monogamy. Conscious uncoupling provides avenues for ex-partners to maintain new forms of healthy and positive relationships post relational termination. In turn, people who practice conscious uncoupling may be better suited to offer a meaningful life to their children by co-parenting in equitable ways. Although on the opposite end of the spectrum of love often lies heartbreak, conscious uncoupling challenges the notion that relational termination must result in negative, destructive, and undesirable outcomes. Taken together, conscious uncoupling captures the end of any relationship as the beginning of self-growth, acceptance, and love.

References

Afifi, T. D. (2003). "Feeling caught" in stepfamilies: Managing boundary turbulence through appropriate communication privacy rules. *Journal of Social and Personal Relationships, 20*(6), 729–755. http://dx.doi.org/10.1177/0265407503206002

Afifi, T. D., Basinger, E. D., & Kam, J. A. (2020). The extended theoretical model of communal coping: Understanding the properties and functionality of communal coping. *Journal of Communication, 70*(3), 424–446. http://dx.doi.org/10.1093/joc/jqaa006

Afifi, T. D., Merrill, A. F., & Davis, S. (2016). The theory of resilience and relational load. *Personal Relationships, 23*(4), 663–683. http://dx.doi.org/10.1007/978-3-319-15877-8_852-1

Allen, E. S., & Baucom, D. H. (2006). Dating, marital, and hypothetical extradyadic involvements: How do they compare? *Journal of Sex Research, 43*(4), 307–317. https://psycnet.apa.org/doi/10.1080/00224490609552330

Amato, P. R. (2010). Research on divorce: Continuing trends and new developments. *Journal of Marriage and Family, 72*(3), 650–666. https://doi.org/10.1111/j.1741-3737.2010.00723.x

Amato, P. R., & Afifi, T. D. (2006). Feeling caught between parents: Adult children's relations with parents and subjective well-being. *Journal of Marriage and Family, 68*(1), 222–235. https://psycnet.apa.org/doi/10.1111/j.1741-3737.2006.00243.x

Amato, P. R., & Sobolewski, J. M. (2001). The effects of divorce and marital discord on adult children's psychological well-being. *American Sociological Review, 66*(6), 900–921. https://doi.org/10.2307/3088878

Arias, E., Tejada-Vera, B., Ahmad, F., & Kochanek, K. D. (2021). *Provisional life expectancy estimates for 2020*. National Center for Health Statistics. https://dx.doi.org/10.15620/cdc:107201

Becher, E. H., Kim, H., Cronin, S. E., Deenanath, V., McGuire, J. K., McCann, E. M., & Powell, S. (2019). Positive parenting and parental conflict: Contributions to resilient coparenting during divorce. *Family Relations, 68*(1), 150–164. https://doi.org/10.1111/fare.12349

Blood, R. O., & Blood, M. C. (1979). Amicable divorce: A new lifestyle. *Alternative Lifestyles, 2*(4), 483–498. https://doi.org/10.1007/BF01082681

Brown, S. L., & Wright, M. R. (2019). Divorce attitudes among older adults: Two decades of change. *Journal of Family Issues, 40*(8), 1018–1037. https://doi.org/10.1177/0192513X19832936

Busboom, A. L., Collins, D. M., Givertz, M. D., & Levin, L. A. (2002). Can we still be friends? Resources and barriers to friendship quality after romantic relationship dissolution. *Personal Relationships, 9*(2), 215–223. https://doi.org/10.1111/1475-6811.00014

Buunk, A. P., & Dijkstra, P. (2006). Temptations and threat: Extradyadic relations and jealousy. In A. L. Vangelisti & D. Perlman (Eds.), *The Cambridge handbook of personal relationships* (pp. 533–555). Cambridge University Press.

Centers for Disease Control and Prevention. (2017). FastStats—Marriage and divorce. https://www.cdc.gov/nchs/fastats/marriage-divorce.htm

Cohen, E. (2021). *Light on the other side of divorce: Discovering the new you*. Mango.

Dailey, R. M., Zhong, L., Pett, R., & Varga, S. (2020). Post-dissolution ambivalence, breakup adjustment, and relationship reconciliation. *Journal of Social and Personal Relationships, 37*(5), 1604–1625. https://doi.org/10.1177/0265407520906014

Feinberg, M. (2003). The internal structure and ecological context of coparenting: A framework for research and intervention. *Parent Science Practice*, *3*, 95–131. http://dx.doi.org/10.1207/S15327922PAR0302_01

Fisher, H. E. (1989). Evolution of human serial pair-bonding. *American Journal of Physical Anthropology*, *78*(3), 331–354. https://doi.org/10.1002/ajpa.1330780303

Fisher, H. E. (1992). *Anatomy of love*. WW Norton.

Fisher, H. E. (2012). Serial monogamy and clandestine adultery: Evolution and consequences of the dual human reproductive strategy. In S. C. Roberts (Ed.), *Applied evolutionary psychology* (pp. 93–111). Oxford University Press.

Fisher, H. (2016). *Anatomy of love: A natural history of mating, marriage, and why we stray*. WW Norton and Company.

Fitzgerald, S. B. (2004). Making the transition: Understanding the longevity of lesbian relationships. *Journal of Lesbian Studies*, *8*(3–4), 177–192. https://doi.org/10.1300/J155v08n03_29

Ganong, L., Sanner, C., Berkley, S., & Coleman, M. (2021). Effective coparenting in stepfamilies: Empirical evidence of what works. *Family Relations*, *71*(3), 918–934. https://doi.org/10.1111/fare.12607

Griffith, R. L., Gillath, O., Zhao, X., & Martinez, R. (2017). Staying friends with ex-romantic partners: Predictors, reasons, and outcomes. *Personal Relationships*, *24*(3), 550–584. https://doi.org/10.1111/pere.12197

Haddad, L., Phillips, K. D., & Bone, J. M. (2016). High-conflict divorce: A review of the literature. *American Journal of Family Law*, *29*(4), 243–258. https://www.proquest.com/scholarly-journals/high-conflict-divorce-review-literature/docview/1773809787/se-2

Hardesty, J., Khaw, L., Chung, G., & Martin, J. (2008). Coparenting relationships after divorce: Variations by type of marital violence and fathers' role differentiation. *Family Relations: An Interdisciplinary Journal of Applied Family Studies*, *57*(4), 479–491. https://psycnet.apa.org/doi/10.1111/j.1741-3729.2008.00516.x

Herrero, M., Martínez-Pampliega, A., & Alvarez, I. (2020). Family communication, adaptation to divorce and children's maladjustment: The moderating role of coparenting. *Journal of Family Communication*, *20*(2), 114–128. https://doi.org/10.1080/15267431.2020.1723592

Hofstede, G. (1980). *Culture's consequences: International differences in work-related values*. Sage.

Hofstede, G. (2001). *Culture's consequences: Comparing values, behaviors, institutions, and organizations across nations*. Sage.

Hunt, M. (1974). *Sexual behavior in the 1970s*. Playboy Press.

Kalmijn, M. (2020). Feelings of guilt in the family: The case of divorced parents. In D. Mortelmans (Ed.), *Divorce in Europe* (pp. 271–289). Springer, Cham.

Kalmijn, M., & Monden, C. W. (2006). Are the negative effects of divorce on well-being dependent on marital quality? *Journal of Marriage and Family*, *68*(5), 1197–1213. https://doi.org/10.1111/j.1741-3737.2006.00323.x

Kellas, J. K. (2018). Communicated narrative sense-making theory: Linking storytelling and well-being. In D. O. Braithwaite, E. A. Suter, & K. Floyd (Eds.), *Engaging theories in family communication: Multiple perspectives* (pp. 62–74). Routledge.

Kinsella, K. G. (1992). Changes in life expectancy 1900–1990. *American Journal of Clinical Nutrition*, *55*(6), 1196–1202. https://doi.org/10.1093/ajcn/55.6.1196s

Kotre, J. N., & Hall, E. (1997). *Seasons of life: The dramatic journey from birth to death*. University of Michigan Press.

Lamela, D., Figueiredo, B., Bastos, A., & Feinberg, M. (2016). Typologies of post-divorce coparenting and parental well-being parenting quality and children's psychological adjustment. *Child Psychiatry and Human Development, 47,* 716–728. https://doi.org/10.1007/s10578-015-0604-5

Lawrence, R. J. (1989). *The poisoning of Eros: Sexual values in conflict.* Augustine Moore Press.

Le, B., Dove, N. L., Agnew, C. R., Korn, M. S., & Mutso, A. A. (2010). Predicting nonmarital romantic relationship dissolution: A meta-analytic synthesis. *Personal Relationships, 17*(3), 377–390. https://doi.org/10.1111/j.1475-6811.2010.01285.x

Levinger, G. (1999). Duty to whom? Reconsidering attractions and barriers as determinants of commitment in relationship. In J. M. Adams & W. H. Jones (Eds.), *Handbook of interpersonal commitment and relationship stability* (pp. 37–52). Kluwer Academic/Plenum.

Madey, S. F., & Jilek, L. (2012). Attachment style and dissolution of romantic relationships: Breaking up is hard to do, or is it? *Individual Differences Research, 10*(4), 202–210. http://dx.doi.org/10.25669/h5i4-2ykd%20processed,%20response:%20201

Metts, S., Cupach, W. R., & Bejlovec, R. A. (1989). "I love you too much to ever start liking you": Redefining romantic relationships. *Journal of Social and Personal Relationships, 6*(3), 259–274. https://doi.org/10.1177/0265407589063002

Miller, M. R. (2009). *Growth following romantic relationship dissolution.* Stony Brook.

Mogilski, J. K., & Welling, L. L. (2017). Staying friends with an ex: Sex and dark personality traits predict motivations for post-relationship friendship. *Personality and Individual Differences, 115,* 114–119. https://psycnet.apa.org/doi/10.1016/j.paid.2016.04.016

National Marriage Project. (2019). State of our unions 2019. http://nationalmarriageproject.org/wp-content/uploads/2019/07/SOU2019.pdf

O'Mara, C., & Schrodt, P. (2017). Parents' negative relational disclosures and young adult children's perceptions of appropriateness and feelings of being caught. *Communication Quarterly, 65*(5), 565–579. https://doi.org/10.1080/01463373.2017.1321563

Price, S. J., & McKenry, P. C. (1988). *Divorce.* Sage.

Righetti, F., Sakaluk, J. K., Faure, R., & Impett, E. A. (2020). The link between sacrifice and relational and personal well-being: A meta-analysis. *Psychological Bulletin, 146*(10), 900–921. https://psycnet.apa.org/doi/10.1037/bul0000297

Rollie, S. S., & Duck, S. (2006). Divorce and dissolution of romantic relationships: Stage models and their limitations. In M.A. Fine & J. H. Harvey (Eds.), *Handbook of divorce and relationship dissolution* (pp. 223–240). Lawrence Erlbaum.

Sadeghi, H., & Sami, S. (2014). Changing the concept of divorce. Be hive of healing. https://behiveofhealing.com/conscious-uncoupling/

Samios, C., Henson, D. F., & Simpson, H. J. (2014). Benefit finding and psychological adjustment following a non-marital relationship breakup. *Journal of Relationships Research, 5,* Article e6. https://psycnet.apa.org/doi/10.1017/jrr.2014.6

Sands, A., Thompson, E., & Gaysina, D. (2017). Long-term influences of parental divorce on offspring affective disorders: A systematic review and meta-analysis. *Journal of Affective Disorders, 218,* 105–114. https://doi.org/10.1016/j.jad.2017.04.015

Schoppe, S. J., Mangelsdorf, S. C., & Frosch, C. A. (2001). Coparenting, family process, and family structure: Implications for preschoolers' externalizing behavior problems. *Journal of Family Psychology, 15,* 526–545. https://psycnet.apa.org/doi/10.1037/0893 3200.15.3.526

Schrodt, P., & Afifi, T. D. (2006). Communication processes that predict young adults' feelings of being caught and their associations with mental health and family satisfaction. *Communication Monographs, 74*(2), 200–228. https://doi.org/10.1080/036377 50701390085

Schrodt, P., & Afifi, T. D. (2018). Untying the ties that bind: Dispositional and relational patterns of negative relational disclosures and family members' feelings of being caught. *Journal of Family Issues, 39*(7), 1962–1983. https://doi.org/10.1177/0192513x1 7739050

Snopkowski, K. (2016). Marital dissolution and child educational outcomes in San Borja, Bolivia. *Human Nature, 27*(4), 395–421. https://doi.org/10.1007/s12110-016-9265-8

Symoens, S., Bastaits, K., Mortelmans, D., & Bracke, P. (2013). Breaking up, breaking hearts? Characteristics of the divorce process and well-being after divorce. *Journal of Divorce and Remarriage, 54*(3), 177–196. https://doi.org/10.1080/10502 556.2013.773792

Thomas, J. (2018). Dimensions of family disruption: Coincidences, interactions, and impacts on children's educational attainment. *Longitudinal and Life Course Studies, 9*(2), 157–187. https://doi.org/10.14301/llcs.v9i2.436

Thomas, K. W. (2016). *Conscious uncoupling: 5 steps to living happily even after.* Harmony.

Toth, K., & Kemmelmeier, M. (2009). Divorce attitudes around the world: Distinguishing the impact of culture on evaluations and attitude structure. *Cross-Cultural Research, 43*, 280–297. http://dx.doi.org/10.1177/1069397109336648

van der Wal, R. C., Finkenauer, C., & Visser, M. M. (2019). Reconciling mixed findings on children's adjustment following high-conflict divorce. *Journal of Child and Family Studies, 28*(2), 468–478. https://psycnet.apa.org/doi/10.1007/s10826-018-1277-z

Vangelisti, A. L. (2006). Relationship dissolution: Antecedents, processes, and consequences. In P. Noller & J. A. Feeney (Eds.), *Close relationships* (pp. 353–379). Psychology Press.

Villella, S. (2010). Broken up but not broken: Satisfaction, adjustment, and communication in post-dissolutional relationships. *Communication and Theater Association of Minnesota Journal, 37*(1), 27–46.

Wang, H., & Amato, P. R. (2000). Predictors of divorce adjustment: Stressors, resources, and definitions. *Journal of Marriage and Family, 62*(3), 655–668. https://doi.org/ 10.1111/j.1741-3737.2000.00655.x

Wilmot, W. W., Carbaugh, D. A., & Baxter, L. A. (1985). Communicative strategies used to terminate romantic relationships. *Western Journal of Communication, 49*(3), 204–216. https://doi.org/10.1080/10570318509374195

Xerxa, Y., Rescorla, L. A., Serdarevic, F., Van IJzendorn, M. H., Jaddoe, V. W., Verhulst, F. C., Luijk, M. P. C. M., & Tiemeier, H. (2020). The complex role of parental separation in the association between family conflict and child problem behavior. *Journal of Clinical Child and Adolescent Psychology, 49*(1), 79–93. https://doi.org/10.1080/15374 416.2018.1520118

PART III
GENDER AND SEXUALITY IN THE 21ST CENTURY

PART III

10

Sexuality in the 21st Century

A Feminist and Queer Theoretical Perspective on Sex and Sexuality in Emerging Adulthood

Jasna Jovanovic and Jean Calterone Williams

Young adults are at the forefront of negotiating new ways of expressing sexual and gender identities, pushing both heteronormative and homonormative boundaries in order to define themselves (Goldberg et al., 2020; Morandini et al., 2017). While exploring identities such as queer and pansexual, emerging adults are questioning whether and how sexuality may be understood as fluid, ambiguous, and multidimensional. This fluidity in gender and sexual identities shapes the context for interpreting trends in sexual and relationship choices and behaviors among young adults across sexual identities.

Emerging adulthood is a key developmental period that involves making meaning of identities and intimate relationships. Flexible sexual behavior norms can be linked to identity formation during emerging adulthood (Arnett, 2015). Sex is more normative during emerging adulthood than adolescence; most youth experience first intercourse by their late teens (Martinez & Abma, 2020). Given that the average age of first marriage in the United States is nearly 29 for women and 30 for men (U.S. Census Bureau, 2021), the majority of sexual activity among young adults is happening outside of marriage. Yet while sexual activity in emerging adults has declined (South & Lei, 2021), experimentation with non-committed relationships has increased, including consensual non-monogamy (Sizemore & Omstead, 2017) and sex with a friend (Machia et al. 2020; Monto & Carey 2014).

In this chapter, we begin by reviewing current trends in emerging adult sexual activity with a particular focus on casual sexual activity and the impact of new forms of social media. We then use the lenses provided by feminist and queer theories to provide an understanding of new developments in sex and sexuality in this age group. These theories allow us to contextualize and make sense of the trends, providing a range of explanations for the significance of sexual identities and behaviors.

Trends in Emerging Adult Sexual Behavior

Emerging adults' likelihood of having sex outside of a committed relationship, as well as their number of sexual partners, is similar to that of 20 years ago (Monto & Carey, 2014; Netting & Reynolds, 2018); the majority of young adults have experienced various forms of sexual behavior by age 24. However, between 2000–2002 and 2016–2018, the proportion of 18- to 24-year-olds reporting no sexual activity in the past year had increased (Ueda et al., 2020). This was particularly true among men identifying as heterosexual (18.9% vs. 30.9%) but less so among women (15.1% vs. 19.1%; see also Johnston et al., 2021). While the percent of young adult males reporting multiple sex partners in the prior year has been declining—from 27% in 2005 to 24.6% in 2020—this has held steady among females, from 22% in 2005 to 22.7% in 2020 (Johnston et al., 2021). Explanations for the decline in sexual activity include greater numbers of young adults co-residing with parents (Payne, 2019), the increase in Internet-based entertainment that limits unstructured socializing (Arnett, 2018), and a decrease in alcohol consumption (Schulenberg et al., 2021). In fact, South and Lei (2021) found that one quarter of the drop in casual sex in young women was due to a decline in their frequency of drinking alcohol.

However, casual sexual relationships occur regularly on college campuses, with 53%–84% of students engaging in hookups and 60%–64% experiencing friends with benefits (FWB) relationships (Kuperberg & Padgett, 2015; Williams & Jovanovic, 2015). Kalish and Kimmel (2010) found that among over 14,000 students at 19 colleges, the majority of heterosexual students hooked up by their senior year, on average seven times. Similarly, among 13,000 heterosexual college women, 69% reported hooking up, with a median of three times (Armstrong et al., 2012). Most sexually active students have both casual and committed sex (Fielder et al., 2013; Netting & Reynolds, 2018), and most prefer romantic relationships to hookups (Garcia et al., 2012). Monto and Carey (2014) suggest that the term "hooking up" is ambiguous, contributing to the misconception that college students have more intercourse than they actually do. Although most studies on casual sexual activity are largely heteronormative (Watson et al., 2017), one study of 274 gay men and 5,106 heterosexual men found that gay men were more likely to hookup: 74% versus 64%, respectively (Barrios & Lundquist, 2012).

Social norms reinforce the expectation that the college years represent a time to sexually experiment and may encourage same-sex hookups even among those who identify as straight. Kuperberg and Walker (2018) found in the Online College Life Survey data set of over 24,000 undergraduate students that most who engaged in same-sex hookups but identified as heterosexual could be described as privately experimenting and/or having religious conflicts that stymied their ability to outwardly identify as LGBTQ. In data gathered by the CDC, a larger percentage of young women than men reported engaging in same-sex sexual contact (Copen et al., 2016). The college hookup scene may be an opportunity for female students to experiment with and affirm LGBTQ sexual identities or to confirm a heterosexual one (Rupp et al., 2014).

Hookups

Hookups are "brief uncommitted sexual encounters among individuals who are not romantic partners or dating each other" (Garcia et al., 2012, p. 161) and may occur between those who are strangers or acquaintances. Netting and Reynolds (2018) note that the following relate to the likelihood of participating: pre-college history of frequent casual sex, heavy alcohol use, and membership in the Greek system or male athletic teams. Those who abstain are more religious and/or are from racial and ethnic minority, conservative, and immigrant groups. College students of color are less likely to participate in these relationships, not for lack of desire but because of lack of opportunities resulting from racial preferences among potential partners that favor Whites (Spell, 2017). Those with more economic privilege versus less-economically privileged college women are more at ease with hooking up (Uecker & Martinez, 2017). On the other hand, young adults who did not have a high school degree, or individuals with some college experience, had more lifetime and recent casual sex partners (Lyons et al., 2013).

On most college campuses, a higher percentage of men than women report hooking up (Fielder & Carey, 2010). In heterosexual hookups, women are found to be sexually submissive, less likely to report sexual pleasure, and less likely to be sexually satisfied than in a more committed relationship (Armstrong et al., 2012; Brugman et al., 2010; Wade, 2017). Both men and women reported that men were less concerned with women achieving orgasm in hookups, but men were attentive to women's sexual pleasure in more committed relationships (Armstrong et al., 2012). Bay-Cheng and Eliseo-Arras (2008) argue that gender norms leave young women feeling obligated to satisfy their male partner's desires regardless of their own wishes. Kettrey (2018) found that when young women prioritize their own orgasm equally with their heterosexual partners, it decreases the odds of performing sexual acts to please their most recent hookup partner. Inequality in sexual satisfaction also explains a large portion of the gender difference in hookup regret (Uecker & Martinez, 2017). Moreover, Kettrey (2018) found that women who initiated sex with their most recent hookup partner were less likely to perform sexual acts simply to please their partner or to succumb to verbal pressure for undesired sexual intercourse.

As we noted, the literature on casual sexual relationships remains largely heteronormative. Research specifically on LGBTQ casual sexual relationships suggests that there may be differences in sexual and emotional satisfaction when comparing heterosexual and queer men and women (Mark et al., 2015). LGBTQ emerging adults report experiencing hookups as mostly positive, with some variation across lesbian, gay, and bisexual–identified youth, and with gay men expressing the most sexual and emotional satisfaction (Watson et al., 2019).

Exploring one's sexual identity, making friends, and establishing ties to the community are all part of LGBTQ hookup culture (Rupp et al., 2014; Kuperberg & Walker, 2018). In a national sample, Jaffe et al. (2021) found that lesbian and bisexual women reported that hookups allowed them to increase their sense of connection with and participation in LGBTQ communities. In this sense, the authors define hooking up as having a "protective" function: "sexual minority women who hooked up more frequently reported less subsequent minority stress, indicating that hookups contributed to effective coping with minority stress" (Jaffe et al., 2021, p. 1608).

Hookup culture can also have negative associations for LGBTQ young people. Lamont et al. (2018) found that "same-sex sexual behaviors on college campuses are still embedded in and interpreted through dominant meanings of gendered sexualities . . . LGBTQ students feel alienated by and excluded from the dominant hookup scene on campuses" (p. 1001). LGBTQ emerging adults receive offers of casual sexual relationships from other queer-identified young people as well as those who are "straight-but-curious" (SBC) or are straight-identified females performing "public kissing" for an assumed straight male audience (Kuperberg & Walker, 2018; Matsick et al., 2021). Given the stereotypes associated particularly with gay male relationships as hypersexualized, gay men reported being aware of more social stigma when casual sexual relationships are between two gay men, rather than those including a bisexual or SBC male-identified person (Matsick et al., 2021).

Friends With Benefits

FWB relationships suggest a greater level of intimacy than a hookup. Specifically, the "friendship" aspect of the relationship, the presumption of repeated sexual contact, and an ongoing connection to another person shape the relationship: "Because these situations represent a greater entanglement of friendship, trust, and emotional comfort, FWBs are distinct from notions of hooking up in some aspects" (Garcia et al. 2012, p. 163). Mongeau et al. (2013) found, however, that some were based upon a friendship while others were basically serial hookups with little prior or subsequent emotional connection. Thus, both "friends with benefits" and "hookup" are ambiguous terms that overlap (Mongeau et al., 2013). Still other FWBs provide a transition into or out of a more conventional romantic relationship (Owen & Fincham, 2012). Machia et al. (2020) found that among FWB partners, those who wanted their relationship to transition to a friendship were more likely to achieve this goal. Those who wanted their FWB to transition into a romantic relationship were unlikely to obtain their desired outcome *unless* both partners agreed and communicated similar intentions: Lack of communication appears to be detrimental.

Unlike hookups, heterosexual FWB relationships may provide a form of casual intimacy that allows women to express their sexual desires more freely because they feel safer (Jovanovic & Williams, 2018). In a study of 411 emerging adults who indicated current involvement in an FWB relationship, Lehmiller et al. (2011) found that women reported sexual desire as a motive for initiating an FWB. Bay-Cheng et al. (2009) found that FWB relationships were associated with the highest level of "desire, wanting, and pleasure" compared with all other serious and casual relationship experiences reported by women: "FWBs may enable individuals to enjoy the stability, familiarity, and egalitarian balance of platonic friendships as a means of sexual experimentation and gratification" (p. 520). In a study using focus groups with heterosexual college students, we found that some viewed FWB relationships as a promising venue for heterosexual women to sexually experiment and to practice sexual agency. Most students believed, however, that the social context for FWB relationships was shaped by a sexual double standard, and thus such relationships did not differ much from the gendered assumptions governing other heterosexual forms of intimacy (Jovanovic & Williams, 2018).

There is some evidence that in heterosexual FWB relationships, women put emphasis on friends while men tend to view the relationship as more casual with an emphasis on sexual benefits (McGinty et al., 2007). Women are more likely to report unmet expectations than men (Gusarova et al., 2012). Although men and women similarly have more positive than negative emotional reactions in a heterosexual FWB relationship, the difference is larger for men (Owen & Fincham, 2011). Moreover, men are more likely to perceive their FWB as primarily focused on sex, while women are more likely to report that FWBs were attempts—often failed—to move into a romantic relationship (Mongeau et al., 2013; Williams & Jovanovic, 2015).

Overall, the research literature contains few mentions of FWBs among LGBTQ emerging adults, and FWBs have been conceptualized in terms of heterosexual actors and expectations. The language of "friends with benefits" likewise is used by college students mainly to describe heterosexual relationships (Jovanovic & Williams, 2018). The few studies to explore FWB as a primary relationship type among LGBTQ respondents suggest that such terminology is used loosely and in the context of relationship fluidity in terms of the depth of the friendship or ongoing connection to a sexual partner (Bauermeister, 2014; Sullivan, et al., 2018).

The Role of Social Media

Social media, particularly dating apps such as Tinder or Grindr, represents a relatively new but ubiquitous aspect of sex and sexuality. Online media (see Chapter 2 this volume) have become one means of fulfilling the developmental need of finding intimacy (Lefebvre, 2018). Young adults have the highest social media and dating site or app use at 84% and 48%, respectively (Pew Research Center, 2020, 2021).

Traditional face-to-face relationship development is being supplemented—if not supplanted—by computer-mediated communications

(Brody et al., 2016). LeFebvre (2018) specifically found that 46% of emerging young adults said using Tinder increased their current accessibility to partners. When asked what Tinder was designed for, 51.5% said hookups and 33.5% said dating. LeFebvre (2018) argues that although Tinder is often used as a means to hook up among emerging adults, it does not always result in vaginal or anal intercourse and instead is more multifaceted, suggesting dating apps now have a unique influence on interpersonal relationships. Sumter et al. (2016) found that young adults' motivations for using Tinder include love, casual sex, communication, validation of self-worth, thrill of excitement, and popularity. Men tend to use the app more for sex, while women and older participants used the app more for love, communication, and casual sex (Sumter et al. 2016).

Indeed, dating apps are not exclusively used to form sexual and romantic connections, but are also used particularly by LGBTQ people to meet new friends and establish social networks (Duguay, 2019; Pond & Farvid, 2017). Bryon et al. (2021) found that dating apps were used by queer youth to find friendships that would allow for intimacy and support and a sense of safety. Such online relationships can increase sexual self-acceptance, thereby positively impacting sexual health, mental health, self-esteem, and overall quality of life for LGBTQ youth (Hillier & Harrison, 2007; Magee et al., 2012). In their study of 32 ethnically diverse 16- to 24-year-olds, Dehann et al. (2013) found that the anonymity of dating apps allowed participants a greater ability to experiment not only with same-sex desires, but also with other aspects of themselves such as their gender identity and interpersonal interactions. They suggested that some youth began such explorations before doing so offline, because of the anonymity or the perception that online contexts were more supportive or affirming of an LGBTQ identity.

Like dating apps, consensual sexting, the sharing of personal, sexually suggestive text messages, has become a common behavior among emerging adults. In a meta-analysis Mori et al. (2020) found that consensual sexting among emerging adults was a common behavior; on average, 38% reported sending a sext, 42% reported receiving a sext, and 48% reported engaging in reciprocal sexting. Therefore, although sexual intercourse in emerging adults may be on the decline, sexting may be increasing (Madigan et al., 2018). It is possible that, in the current digital era, sexting could be considered a type of sexual activity that can occur on its own or serve as foreplay for future sexual activity.

Using Feminist and Queer Theory to Understand Sexual Activity

Largely missing from the research on emerging adult sexual behavior are explicit theoretical frameworks to make sense of current trends. Lenses provided by feminist and queer theories allow us to analyze sexual behavior and relationships among emerging adults that create a more nuanced and complete understanding of the trends. These theories deconstruct the cultural and social forces that shape and delimit relationships such as hookups and FWBs. We turn to those theories, grounded in the concepts of sexual agency, the gendered double standard, sexual fluidity, heteronormativity, and homonormativity, to analyze young people's sexual relationships and behaviors.

Sexual Agency and the Gendered Double Standard

A social construction approach to defining sexuality suggests that meanings for sexuality are constructed, defined, and made real through cultural norms and political and social institutions. As Butler (2006) states, gender and sexuality are best understood as "the effects of institutions, practices, discourses with multiple and diffuse points of origin" (p. ix). Sexuality and gender are constructed in terms of one another and thus are intertwined: "Heterosexuality, like gender identity, must be constantly achieved and reproduced in daily life by habitually enacting social practices associated with cultural gendered ideals" (Fischer, 2013, p. 504; Butler, 2006). Black feminist theorists have led the way in arguing that these processes are racialized, and thus gender, race, and sexuality must be understood to be mutually constituted (e.g., Crenshaw, 1989; Hill Collins, 2021). They argue for using an intersectional lens to explore sexuality and gender, decentering White, upper class, cisgender, straight women as the norm.

One of the seeds for today's broad participation in hookups, FWBs, and use of dating apps such as Tinder and Grindr can be found in feminist theory since the 1990s, which advocates for the embrace of desire and sexual experimentation. Feminists critique a dominant social construction of female sexuality that argues that women have less sexual desire than men (e.g.,

Baumgardner & Richards, 2010; hooks, 2000). Instead, young women's sexual desire is championed and normalized. Noting the pervasiveness of sexual stigma for young women, feminists also argue that young women face a social context that inhibits their ability to seek sexual agency, as their sexuality continues to be repressed and silenced in a variety of ways that structure their choices. Most notably, a sexual double standard still exists, where sexual girls, particularly those in casual sexual relationships, risk being labeled as "sluts" or even as "pathological" (e.g., Conley et al., 2013; Fetterolf & Sanchez 2015; Williams & Jovanovic, 2015).

Notwithstanding a college culture where a majority of the students experiment with hooking up or FWBs, sexual double standards prevail on campus (Jovanovic & Williams, 2018). Men may be viewed as sexual agents and women as sexual objects; relatedly, students may rely on the "virgin–slut" dichotomy to interpret women's sexuality (Delgado-Infante & Ofreneo, 2014). Bay-Cheng (2015) posits that the double standard has become more complicated than the historic virgin–slut dichotomy; now, girls must navigate simultaneously both a "virgin–slut continuum" and an "agency line." Being labeled as a slut does not necessarily translate to presumptions of promiscuity but, rather, refers to those who seek "male desire and approval" and are unable to control sexual interactions (p. 282). Our research has found that the threat of being called a slut may serve to undermine young women's ability to seek sexual pleasure, to articulate sexually permissive beliefs, or to openly seek information about their sexuality, thus operating as a form of social control that stunts sexual agency (Jovanovic & Williams, 2018).

The lack of information provided by parents and school-based sexuality education constrains the avenues available to learn about sex, sexual pleasure, and contraception (Brugman et al., 2010). Abstinence-only education, taught in about a third of public high schools that teach sex education, not only undermines access to knowledge but also teaches that girls' virginity is a "gift" to be given and should be closely guarded (Doan & Williams, 2008). Moreover, because curricula use a heterosexual lens to define and discuss sexuality, LGBTQ sexualities are made invisible in school sexuality education (McNeill, 2013; Torkelson, 2012). Laws and policies limiting access to reproductive healthcare operate in tandem with restricted information to impede young women's ability to explore and understand their own desires.

Deconstructing Sexuality and Heteronormativity

Queer theory and feminist theory overlap as they define and deconstruct sexuality. Like feminist theory, queer theory explores the relationships between sexuality and gender through an intersectional lens, argues for a notion of sexuality as fluid and ambiguous as opposed to biological and clearly definable, and strives to decenter reproduction in sex. In other ways, queer theory establishes a focus on elements of sexuality that feminist theory addresses less centrally. Using the frames of heteronormativity and homonormativity, queer theory argues that some identities, behaviors, and bodies are defined as "normal" while others are defined as "pathological" (e.g., Duggan, 2002; Halperin, 2019). In denaturalizing and deconstructing sexuality, queer theory seeks to undermine seemingly coherent categories such as gay, straight, bisexual, and the like (Morandini et al., 2017). The term "queer" functions to question such categories and the associated limits of existing language, concepts, and identities in understanding sexualities, and it serves to underscore the ambiguity and malleability in sexual identities (Meek, 2012).

The critique of heteronormativity and homonormativity in understanding sexuality and the formation of queer relationships is a central tenet of queer theory (Halperin, 2019). The state, social institutions, and cultural norms broadly endorse and advocate for heterosexuality while marginalizing queerness (Bond, 2014; Duggan, 2002; Torkelson, 2012). With heterosexuality constructed as "monogamous, marital, middle class and white" (McNeill, 2013, 826), heteronormativity contributes to making queer sexualities invisible and deeming them "abnormal" (Fischer, 2013). Homonormativity is related to heteronormativity, as queer relationships that mimic straight relationships are perceived as more normative and tend to dominate representations of LGBTQ relationships (Halperin, 2019; Macapagel et al., 2015).

For LGBTQ emerging adults, heteronormativity and homonormativity may shape the formation of sexual identities and sexual experimentation. Macapagel et al. (2015) suggest that since many LGBTQ young people lack meaningful cultural images, role models, and sexual scripts that align with their sexual preferences, heterosexual relationships can become the default model for LGBTQ relationships. Expressions of queerness may be denied or challenged by educational institutions, social systems, family members, and the like, which "highlights the degree to which existing social forms do not fit the specificities of lesbian and gay male love" (Halperin, 2019, p. 397).

In the face of normative and static views of sexualities inherent in homo- and heteronormativity, queer theory has advocated for an understanding of sexualities that embraces ambiguity and fluidity (e.g., Meek, 2012). Researchers have explored sexual identities such as queer and pansexual that move beyond lesbian, gay, and straight (Callis, 2014; Kuper et al., 2012) and examined the rejection of binary notions of sexuality (Better, 2014). Some research has suggested that younger people, women, and transgender people indicate the most interest in queerness and pansexuality that purposely eschew easy categorization (Goldberg et al., 2020; Morandini et al., 2017). Thus, accounting for queerness is particularly important in understanding emerging adult sexuality.

Conclusion

Trends in sexual behavior among emerging adults show some consistency over time, and at the same time reveal new dynamics in how young adults experiment with intimacy and identity. Currently, much of the sexuality literature describes behaviors, providing specifics about new forms of casual relationships among emerging adults. We know what young people are doing, particularly heterosexual, White young people on college campuses. Descriptive research on trends, however important, often does not analyze those trends, and we argue that feminist and queer theories provide an essential entrée into such an examination. These theories deconstruct such key issues as sexual agency and heteronormativity, enabling us to unpack how sexuality is organized and sexual behavior is experienced by emerging adults. When we use concepts like sexual agency or heteronormativity to explore emerging adults' sexual behavior, or when we recognize fluidity in sexual identity, or power and the sexual double standard, we can better comprehend the meaning and impact of emerging adult sexual behaviors. Thus, using queer and feminist theories to contextualize and analyze sexual behavior and identity trends is a crucial next step for understanding emerging adult sexuality.

Wedding queer and feminist theory with behavioral trends makes clear how often the literature relies on research with heterosexual young people exclusively. We argue that the FWB and hookup literature are shaped by heteronormativity in that they create "knowledge" about these forms of sexual behavior that marginalizes or makes invisible LGBTQ individuals, as well as same-sex sexual behavior, regardless of the identities used by the participants. Many of the studies on FWB and hookups, moreover, fail to address their use of a heteronormative lens. Understanding sexual behavior requires deconstructing normative sexuality. This means we must consider more explicit assessments of the power of heteronormativity in constructing sexual and identity development of emerging adults, both for those who are queer and straight (Torkelson, 2012). Analyzing the impact of normative heterosexuality undermines heteronormativity and allows us to "queer" the study of emerging adult sexual behavior, potentially expanding our understanding of the meanings of sex and sexuality during this developmental period.

Acknowledgments

We are grateful for the help we received in compiling the literature from our undergraduate assistants, Sarah Sager and Ariadne Kaylor, as well as Sara Hata, Katarina Reyes, and Ivy Villnow.

References

Armstrong, E. A., England, P., & Fogarty, A. C. (2012). Accounting for women's orgasm and sexual enjoyment in college hook ups and relationships. *American Sociological Review, 77*(3), 435–462. http://doi.org/10.1177/0003122412445802

Arnett, J. J. (2015). *Emerging adulthood: The winding road from the late teens through the twenties* (2nd ed.). Oxford University Press.

Arnett, J. J. (2018). Getting better all the time: Trends in risk behavior among American adolescents since 1990. *Archives of Scientific Psychology, 6*(1), 87–95. http://dx.doi.org/10.1037/arc0000046

Barrios, R. J., & Lundquist, J. H. (2012). Boys just want to have fun? Masculinity, sexual behaviors, and romantic intentions of gay and straight males in college. *Journal of LGBT Youth, 9*(4), 271–296. http://doi.org/10.1080/19361653.2012.716749

Bauermeister, J. A. (2014). Sexual partner typologies among single young men who have sex with men. *AIDS Behavior, 19*(6), 1116–1128. http://doi.org/10.1007/s10461-014-0932-7

Baumgardner, J., & Richards, A. (2010). *Manifesta: Young women, feminism, and the future*. Picador.

Bay-Cheng, L. (2015). The agency line: A neoliberal metric for appraising young women's Sexuality. *Sex Roles, 73*(7–8), 279–291. http://doi.org/10.1007/s11199-015-0452-6

Bay-Cheng, L. Y., & Eliseo-Arras, R. K. (2008). The making of unwanted sex: Gendered and neoliberal norms in college women's unwanted sexual experiences. *The Journal of Sex Research*, *45*(4), 386–397. http://doi.org/10.1080/00224490802398381

Bay-Cheng, L. Y., Robinson, A. D., & Zucker, A. N. (2009). Behavioral and relational contexts of adolescent desire, wanting, and pleasure: Undergraduate women's retrospective accounts. *The Journal of Sex Research*, *46*(6), 511–524. http://doi.org/10.1080/00224490902867871

Better, A. (2014). Redefining queer: Women's relationships and identity in an age of sexual fluidity. *Sexuality & Culture*, *18*(1), 16–38. http://doi.org/10.1007/s12119-013-9171-8

Bond, B. (2014). Sex and sexuality in entertainment media popular with lesbian, gay, and bisexual adolescents. *Mass Communication and Society*, *17*(1), 98–120. http://doi.org/10.1080/15205436.2013.816739

Brody, N., LeFebvre, L., & Blackburn, K. (2016). Online relationship behaviors: Measurement and association with relational development and dissolution. *Social Media & Society*, *2*(4), 1–16. http://doi.org/10.1177/2056305116680004

Brugman, M., Caron, S. L., & Rademakers, J. (2010). Emerging adolescent sexuality: A comparison of American and Dutch college women's experiences. *International Journal of Sexual Health*, *22*(1), 32–46. https://doi.org/10.1080/19317610903403974

Butler, J. (2006.) *Gender trouble: Feminism and the subversion of identity*. Routledge.

Byron, P., Albury, K., & Pym, T. (2021). Hooking up with friends: LGBTQ+ young people, dating apps, friendship, and safety. *Media, Culture & Society*, *43*(3), 497–514. https://doi.org/10.1177/0163443720972312

Callis, A. S. (2014). Bisexual, pansexual, queer: Non-binary identities and the sexual borderlands. *Sexualities*, *17*(1/2), 63–80. https://doi.org/10.1177/1363460713511094

Conley, T. D., Ziegler, A., & Moors, A. C. (2013). Backlash from the bedroom: Stigma mediates gender differences in acceptance of casual sex offers. *Psychology of Women Quarterly*, *37*(3), 392–407. https://doi.org/10.1177/0361684312467169

Copen, C. E., Chandra, A., Febo-Vazquex, I. (2016). *Sexual behavior, sexual attraction, and sexual orientation among adults aged 18–44 in the United States: Data from the 2011–2013 National Survey of Family Growth*. National health statistics reports no. 88. National Center for Health Statistics.

Crenshaw, K. (1989). Demarginalizing the intersection of race and sex: A Black feminist critique of antidiscrimination doctrine, feminist theory and antiracist politics. *University of Chicago Legal Forum*, *1* (8), 139–167.

DeHaan, S., Kuper, L. E., Magee, J. C., Bigelow, L., & Mustanski, B. S. (2013). The interplay between online and offline explorations of identity, relationships, and sex: A mixed-methods study with LGBT youth. *Journal of Sex Research*, *50*(5), 421–434. https://doi.org/10.1080/00224499.2012.661489

Delgado-Infante, M. L., & Ofreneo, M. A. P. (2014). Maintaining a "good girl" position: Young Filipina women constructing sexual agency in first sex within Catholicism. *Feminism & Psychology*, *24*(3), 390–407. https://doi.org/10.1177/0959353514530715

Doan, A., & Williams, J. C. (2008). *The politics of virginity: Abstinence in sex education*. Praeger.

Duggan, Lisa. (2002). *The new homonormativity: The sexual politics of neoliberalism*. Duke University Press, 2002.

Duguay, S. (2019). "There's no one new around you": Queer women's experiences of scarcity in geospatial partner-seeking on Tinder. In C. J. Nash & A. Gorman-Murray (Eds.), *The geographies of digital sexuality* (pp. 93–114). Springer Singapore.

Fetterolf, J., & Sanchez, D. (2015). The costs and benefits of perceived sexual agency for men and women. *Archives of Sexual Behavior*, *44*(4), 961–970. https://doi.org/10.1007/s10508-014-0408-x

Fielder, R. L., & Carey, M. P. (2010). Predictors and consequences of sexual "hookups" among college students: A short-term prospective study. *Archives of Sexual Behavior*, *39*(5), 1105-1119. https://doi.org/10.1007/s10508-008-9448-4

Fielder, R. L., Carey, K. B., & Carey, M. P. (2013). Are hookups replacing romantic relationships? A longitudinal study of first year female college students. *Journal of Adolescent Health*, *52*(5), 657–659. https://doi.org/10.1016/j.jadohealth.2012.09.001

Fischer, N. (2013.) Seeing "straight," contemporary critical heterosexuality studies and sociology: An introduction. *The Sociological Quarterly*, *54*(4), 501–510. https://www.jstor.org/stable/24581871

Garcia, J. R., Reiber, C., Massey, S. G., & Merriwether, A. M. (2012). Sexual hookup culture: A review. *Review of General Psychology*, *16*(2), 161–176. https://doi.org/10.1037/a0027911

Goldberg, S., Rothblum, E., Russell, S., & Meyer, I. (2020). Exploring the Q in LGBTQ: Demographic characteristic and sexuality of queer people in a U.S. representative sample of sexual minorities. *Psychology of Sexual Orientation and Gender Diversity*, *7*(1), 101–112. https://doi.org/10.1037/sgd0000359

Gusarova, I., Fraser, V., & Alderson, K. G. (2012). A quantitative study of "friends with benefits" relationships. *The Canadian Journal of Human Sexuality*, *21*(1), 41–59.

Halperin, D. (2019). Queer love. *Critical Inquiry*, *45*(2), 396–419. https://doi.org/10.1086/700993

Hill Collins, P. (2021). *Black feminist thought: Knowledge, consciousness, and the politics of empowerment*. Routledge.

Hillier, L., & Harrison, L. (2007). Building realities less limited than their own: Young people practicing same-sex attraction on the Internet. *Sexualities*, *10*(1), 82–100. https://doi.org/10.1177/1363460707072956

hooks, b. (2000). *Feminism is for everybody: Passionate politics*. Pluto Press.

Jaffe, A. E., Duckworth, J., Blayney, J. A, Lewis, M. A., & Kaysen, D. (2021). A prospective study of predictors and consequences of hooking up for sexual minority women. *Archives of Sexual Behavior*, *50*(4), 1599–1612. https://doi.org/10.1007/s10508-020-01896-4

Johnston, L. D., Schulenberg, J. E., O'Malley, P. M., Patrick, M. E., Miech, R. A., & Bachman, J. G. (2021). *HIV/AIDS: Risk & protective behaviors among adults ages 21 to 30 in the U.S., 2004–2020*. Institute for Social Research, The University of Michigan.

Jovanovic, J., & Williams, J. C. (2018.) Gender, sexual agency, and friends with benefits relationships. *Sexuality & Culture*, *22*(2), 555–576. https://doi.org/10.1007/s12119-017-9483-1

Kalish, R., & Kimmel, M. (2011). Hooking up: Hot hetero sex or the new numb normative? *Australian Feminist Studies*, *26*(67), 137–151. https://doi.org/10.1080/08164649.2011.546333

Kettrey, H. H. (2018). "Bad Girls" say no and "Good Girls" say yes: Sexual subjectivity and participation in undesired sex during heterosexual college hookups. *Sexuality & Culture*, *22*(3), 685–705. https://doi.org/10.1007/s12119-018-9498-2

Kuper, L. E., Nussbaum, R., & Mustanski, B. (2012). Exploring the diversity of gender and sexual orientation identities in an online sample of transgender individuals. *Journal of Sex Research*, *49*(2–3), 244–254. https://doi.org/10.1080/00224499.2011.596954

Kuperberg, A., & Padgett, J. E. (2015). Dating and hooking up in college: Meeting contexts, sex, and variation by gender, partner's gender, and class standing. *Journal of Sex Research*, 52(5), 517–531. https://doi.org/10.1080/00224499.2014.901284

Kuperberg, A., & Walker, A. M. (2018). Heterosexual college students who hookup with same-sex partners. *Archives of Sexual Behavior*, 47(5), 1387–1403. https://doi.org/10.1007/s10508-018-1194-7

Lamont, E., Roach, T., & Kahn, S. (2018). Navigating campus hookup culture: LGBTQ students and college hookups. *Sociological Forum*, 33(4), 1000–1022. https://doi.org/10.1111/socf.12458

Lefebvre, L. E. (2018). Swiping me off my feet: Explicating relationship initiation on Tinder. *Journal of Social and Personal Relationships*, 35(9), 1205–1229. https://doi.org/10.1177/0265407517706419

Lehmiller, J., VanderDrift, L., & Kelly, J. (2011). Sex differences in approaching friends with benefits relationships. *Journal of Sex Research*, 48(2–3), 275–284. https://doi.org/10.1080/00224491003721694

Lyons, H. A., Manning, W. D., Giordano, P. C., & Longmore, M. A. (2013). Predictors of heterosexual casual sex among young adults. *Archives of Sexual Behavior*, 42(4), 585–593. https://doi.org/10.1007/s10508-012-0051-3

Macapagel, K., Greene, G., Rivera, Z., & Mustanski, B. (2015). "The best is always yet to come": Relationship stages and processes among young LGBT couples. *Journal of Family Psychology*, 29(3), 309–320.

Machia, L. V., Proulx, M. S., Ioerger, M., Lehmiller, J. J. (2020). A longitudinal study of friends with benefits relationships. *Personal Relationships*, 27, 47–60.

Madigan, S., Ly, A., Rash, C. L., Van Ouytsel, J., & Temple, J. R. (2018). Prevalence of multiple forms of sexting behavior among youth: A systematic review and meta-analysis. *JAMA Pediatrics*, 172(4), 327–335. https://doi.org/10.1001/jamapediatrics.2017.5314

Magee, J. C., Bigelow, L., DeHaan, S., & Mustanski, B. S. (2012). Sexual health information seeking online: A mixed-methods study among lesbian, gay, bisexual, and transgender young people. *Health Education and Behavior*, 39(3), 276–89. https://doi.org/10.1177/1090198111401384

Mark, K. P., Garcia, J. R., & Fisher, H. E. (2015). Perceived emotional and sexual satisfaction across sexual relationship contexts: Gender and sexual orientation differences and similarities. *Canadian Journal of Human Sexuality*, 24(2), 120–130. https://doi.org/10.3138/cjhs.242-A8

Martinez, G. M., & Abma, J. C. (2020). *Sexual activity and contraceptive use among teenagers aged 15–19 in the United States, 2015–2017*. NCHS Data Brief, no 366. National Center for Health Statistics.

Matsick, J. L., Kruk, M., Conley, T. D., Moors, A. C., & Ziegler, A. (2021). Gender similarities and differences in casual sex acceptance among lesbian women and gay men. *Archives of Sexual Behavior*, 50(3), 1151–1166. https://doi.org/10.1007/s10508-020-01864-y

McGinty, K., Knox, D., & Zusman, M. E. (2007). Friends with benefits: Women want "friends," men want "benefits." *College Student Journal*, 41(4), 1128–1131.

McNeill, T. (2013). Sex education and the promotion of heteronormativity. *Sexualities*, 16(7), 826–846. https://doi.org/10.1177/1363460713497216

Meek, J. B. (2012). "Being queer is the luckiest thing": Investigating a new generation's use of queer within lesbian, gay, bisexual, transgender, and queer (LGBTQ) student groups. In E. R. Meingers & T. Quinn (Eds.), *Counterpoints: Vol. 367. Sexualities in Education: A Reader* (pp. 187–198). Peter Lang.

Mongeau, P. A., Knight, K., Williams, J., Eden, J., & Shaw, C. (2013). Identifying and explicating variation among friends with benefits relationships. *Journal of Sex Research*, 50(1), 37–47. https://doi.org/10.1080/00224499.2011.623797

Monto, M. A., & Carey, A. G. (2014). A new standard of sexual behavior? Are claims associated with the "hookup culture" supported by General Social Survey data? *Journal of Sex Research*, 51(6), 605–615. https://doi.org/10.1080/00224499.2014.906031

Morandini, J., Blaszczynski, A., & Dar-Nimrod, I. (2017). Who adopts queer and pansexual sexual identities? *The Journal of Sex Research*, 54(7), 911–922. https://doi.org/10.1080/00224499.2016.1249332

Mori, C., Cooke, J. E., Temple, J. R., Ly, A., Lu, Y., Anderson, N., Rash, C., & Madigan, S. (2020). The prevalence of sexting behaviors among emerging adults: A meta-analysis. *Archives of Sexual Behavior*, 49, 1103–1119. https://doi.org/10.1007/s10508-020-01656-4

Netting, N. S., & Reynolds, M. K. (2018). Thirty years of sexual behavior at a Canadian university: Romantic relationships, hooking up, and sexual choices. *The Canadian Journal of Human Sexuality*, 27(1), 55–68. https://doi.org/10.3138/cjhs.2017-0035

Owen, J., & Fincham, F. D. (2011). Effects of gender and psychosocial factors on "friends with benefits" relationships among young adults. *Archives of Sexual Behavior*, 40(2), 311–320. https://doi.org/10.1007/s10508-010-9611-6

Owen, J., & Fincham, F. D. (2012). Friends with benefits relationships as a start to exclusive romantic relationships. *Journal of Social and Personal Relationships*, 29(7), 982–996. https://doi.org/10.1177/0265407512448275

Payne, K. K. (2019). *Young adults in the parental home, 2007 & 2018*. Family Profiles, FP-19-04. National Center for Family & Marriage Research. https://doi.org/10.25035/ncfmr/fp-19-04

Pew Research Center. (2020). *The virtues and downsides of online dating*.https://www.pewresearch.org/internet/2020/02/06/the-virtues-and-downsides-of-online-dating/

Pew Research Center. (2021). *Social media use in 2021*. https://www.pewresearch.org/internet/2021/04/07/social-media-use-in-2021/

Pond, T., & Farvid, P. (2017). "I do like girls, I promise": Young bisexual women's experiences of using Tinder. *Psychology of Sexualities Review*, 8(2), 6–24.

Rupp, L. J., Taylor, V., Regev-Messalem, S., Fogarty, A. C. K., England, P. (2014). Queer women in the hookup scene: Beyond the closet? *Gender and Society*, 28(2), 212–235. https://doi.org/10.1177/0891243214556952

Schulenberg, J. E., Patrick, M. E., Johnston, L. D., O'Malley, P. M., Bachman, J. G., & Miech, R. A. (2021). *Monitoring the Future national survey results on drug use, 1975–2020: Volume II, College students and adults ages 19–60*. Institute for Social Research, The University of Michigan. https://monitoringthefuture.org/results/publications/monographs/

Sizemore, K. M., & Olmstead, S. B. (2017). Willingness to engage in consensual nonmonogamy among emerging adults: A structural equation analysis of sexual identity, casual sex attitudes, and gender. *Journal of Sex Research*, 54(9), 1106–1117. https://doi.org/10.1080/00224499.2016.1243200

South, S. J., & Lei, L. (2021). Why are fewer young adults having casual sex? *Socius: Sociological Research for a Dynamic World*, 7, 1–12. https://doi.org/10.1177/2378023121996854

Spell, S. A. (2017). Not just black and white: How race/ethnicity and gender intersect in hookup culture. *Sociology of Race and Ethnicity*, 3(2), 172–187. https://doi.org/10.1177/2332649216658296

Sullivan, S. P., Pingel, E. S., Stephenson, R., & Bauermeister, J. A. (2018). "It was supposed to be a onetime thing": Experiences of romantic and sexual relationship typologies among young gay, bisexual, and other men who have sex with men. *Archives of Sexual Behavior*, 47, 1221–1230. https://doi.org/10.1007/s10508-017-1058-6

Sumter, S. R., Vandenbosch, L., & Ligtenberg, L. (2016). Love me Tinder: Untangling emerging adults' motivations for using the dating application Tinder. *Telematics and Informatics*, 34(1), 67–78. https://doi.org/10.1016/j.tele.2016.04.009

Torkelson, J. (2012.) A queer vision of emerging adulthood: Seeing sexuality in the transition to adulthood. *Sexuality Research and Social Policy*, 9(2), 132–142. https://doi.org/10.1007/s13178-011-0078-6

Uecker, J. E., & Martinez, B. C. (2017) When and why women regret sex in hookups more than men do: An analysis of the Online College Social Life Survey. *The Sociological Quarterly*, 58(3), 470–494. https://doi.org/10.1080/00380253.2017.1331716

Ueda, P., Mercer, C. H., Ghaznavi, C., & Herbenick, D. (2020). Trends in frequency of sexual activity and number of sexual partners among adults aged 18 to 44 years in the US, 2000–2018. *JAMA Network Open*, 3(6), 1–15. https://doi.org/10.1001/jamanetworkopen.2020.3833

U.S. Census Bureau. (2021). *Current population survey*. March and annual social and economic supplements, Table MS-2. U.S. https://www.census.gov/data/datasets/time-series/demo/cps/cps-asec.html

Wade, L. (2017). *American hookup: The new culture of sex on campus*. W.W. Norton & Co.

Watson, R. J., Shahin, Y. M., & Arbeit, M. R. (2019). Hookup initiation and emotional outcomes differ across LGB young men and women. *Sexualities*, 22(5–6), 932–950. https://doi.org/10.1177/1363460718774528

Watson, R. J., Snapp, S., & Wang, S. (2017). What we know and where we go from here: A review of lesbian, gay, and bisexual youth hookup literature. *Sex Roles*, 77(11), 801–811. https://doi.org/10.1007/s11199-017-0831-2

Williams, J. C., & Jovanovic, J. (2015). Third wave feminism and emerging adult sexuality: Friends with benefits relationships. *Sexuality & Culture*, 19(1), 157–171. https://doi.org/10.1007/s12119-014-9252-3

11

Who Do We Love?

Shifts in Attitudes About Gender Identity, Sexual Orientation, and Same-Sex Close Relationships

Karen L. Blair, Erin L. Courtice, and Rhea Ashley Hoskin

Attitudes toward sexual and gender diversity have shifted dramatically over the past century and not always in a linear direction. Same-sex sexuality has moved in and out of various forms of social acceptability. Today, the full spectrum of attitudes, from total acceptance and celebration to punishment by death, remains. At the same time, but not always in parallel, attitudes toward same-sex relationships, gender diversity, and gender (non)conformity have also shifted. This chapter provides a modern understanding of the lesser-known historical roots of 20th-century attitudes toward sexual orientation, gender identity, and same-sex relationships. We also examine how people's attitudes toward same-sex relationships and gender identity have shifted since the early 1900s. Although Western cultures have made significant progress toward accepting gender and sexual diversity—including substantial reductions in levels of societal sexism, homophobia, and transphobia—prejudice remains. We provide recommendations for researchers in this field and outline a lesser known social prejudice that remains virulent today and continues to spur discrimination against individuals of all sexual and gender identities: femmephobia.

Historical Attitudes Toward Sexual and Gender Diversity

Attitudes toward sexual and gender diversity have perhaps varied far more over time than the traditional narrative of "linear progress" may lead one to expect. While we do not have the space to trace changes in attitudes through the millennia, same-sex relationships have existed across many historical cultures. However, by the turn of the 20th century, same-sex sexuality and relationships were generally not accepted and were explicitly outlawed by many jurisdictions. Legal prohibitions against same-sex relationships date back to those created in Europe during the Middle Ages with the urging of the clergy, who viewed such acts as representing sinful behavior. Through colonization, Europeans exported many such laws around the globe (for detailed tracing of attitudes toward gay men and lesbians, see Crompton, 2003). However, there have always been cultural variations in attitudes toward sexual and gender minorities. For example, while Europe punished homosexuality severely during and beyond the Middle Ages, love between two men or two women was more naturalized and celebrated in ancient China and Japan (Crompton, 2003). Today, the tables have turned. Same-sex relationships are often legal and celebrated in the West but illegal and sometimes criminalized in most parts of Asia, with a few exceptions (e.g., Taiwan).

In general, sentiments that vilified and persecuted same-sex relations before the 20th century were rooted in religious doctrine, whether Judaism, Christianity, Islam, or even Buddhism. While organized religion would remain a strong adversary to the civil liberties and acceptance of sexual minorities, attitudes began to shift at the turn of the 20th century. They were no longer solely rooted in religious doctrine, but scholars from the nascent field of psychology also began to offer justifications. One such scholar was Lewis Terman (1877–1956), who, although not often credited as such, can be considered the father of "modern" scientific homophobia, sexual prejudice, and, as we will argue at the end of this chapter, femmephobia. Terman is best known for his contribution to the study of intelligence. Modern scholars often criticize his work for the racist assumptions he imbued into intelligence research by developing the Stanford-Binet Intelligence Quotient (IQ) Test. However, they have paid much less attention to how his views of femininity shaped a century of negative attitudes toward sexual and gender diversity (Hegarty, 2007).

Terman described himself as an outsider among his peers who were "far from providing any stimulus to intellectual development" (Terman, 1930, p. 301). Nevertheless, Terman described feeling a sense of awe and admiration for his peers' strength, agility, and skill—all traits that he would later classify as "masculine." Although perhaps not relatable today, in the early 1900s, high intelligence was an undesirable trait associated with weakness, eccentricity, and homosexuality (Hegarty, 2007). In men, society viewed giftedness as a form of effeminacy and a sign of immature development.

Thus, the prevailing views of intelligence presented a personal challenge for Terman. He longed for his intelligence to not preclude him from the requisite physical mastery and bravado he observed among his male peers. Thus, in 1919, Terman turned his attention to studying intelligence in children to disprove the link between giftedness and effeminacy.

However, Terman faced a hurdle: At the time, there was no means of measuring masculinity (or femininity). From his experience developing IQ tests, he knew that he could devise a measure of masculinity by identifying the statistical norms within the population. Thus, he developed a "masculinity index" in which a child could be scored based upon how their toy preferences aligned with the proportion of boys and girls who liked each activity. Masculinity was ascribed to the activities picked by "most boys," while femininity was ascribed to the activities enjoyed by "most girls," thereby defining both in "entirely relative terms" (Hegarty, 2007, p. 139). Terman revised the test in 1927, referring to it as the "Masculinity–Femininity" (M–F) test, with scores ranging from −100 (feminine) to +100 (masculine), such that Terman's "construction of gender encoded masculinity as presence and femininity as its absence" (Hegarty, 2007, p. 139). If masculinity scores were equal between genius/gifted boys and average boys, Terman could scientifically lay to rest the accusations of giftedness being a sign of "weakness" or effeminacy and consequently rehabilitate his self-view as an intelligent man.

To expand his work's applicability beyond the study of gifted children, Terman and his collaborator, Catherine Cox, revised and expanded the M–F test so that it was not limited to children. Terman and Cox published the revised M–F test in *Sex and Personality* (1936). The book explored the association between marital satisfaction and masculinity/femininity (submissive wives were happy wives) and the purported ability of the M–F test to detect homosexuality. Terman approached several correctional facilities seeking access to men incarcerated for homosexuality and, in pitching his research to the wardens, noted the ability of the test's true purpose to go undetected. The notion of having a pen and paper test that could identify "sexual deviants" without them knowing the true meaning of the test was appealing to those charged with removing homosexuals from society. Terman identified "true" homosexuals as those who participated in "feminine" (receptive) sex acts while scoring highly on the femininity scale of the revised M–F test. Terman's conclusions and conflations of gender expression with sexual identity perhaps did more than any single scholar of the 20th century to solidify the association between femininity and homosexuality.

Curiously, Terman tended to cherry-pick his findings. For example, when a sample of "56 army prisoners in Alcatraz, serving sentences for sodomy, scored on average +66.2, almost identical to the mean for male college students," Terman concluded that these men were "just" bisexual (like the Ancient Greeks) and that they did not represent "true" inverts or homosexuals (Hegarty, 2007, p. 141). Throughout Terman's work, he viewed any homosexual man with lower femininity scores as "capable of redemption" due to simply being "stalled" in their process of maturation toward heterosexual masculinity. Thus, Terman also provided a basis for inventing conversion therapy practices to convert homosexuals into heterosexuals. Modern research has identified significant harms associated with conversion therapy, and several jurisdictions have therefore begun to outlaw its practice (Drescher et al., 2016). Indeed, harking back to his original research interests, it appears that Terman saw individuals with both high intelligence and proclivities toward homosexuality as being a "higher form of 'sexual inverts,' [capable of rehabilitating] ... into normal heterosexuality" (Hegarty, 2007, p. 143).

The influence of Terman's work on defining and measuring masculinity and femininity cannot be understated. His work laid the foundation for the century of research that followed. Views of homosexuality (in men and women) would change in various manners over time, while views toward femininity would remain largely the same—devalued and heavily regulated. Terman's constructs influenced the development of subsequent measures, such as the Minnesota Multiphasic Personality Inventory (MMPI). Hegarty (2007) has argued that our very notions of what masculinity and femininity are, conceptually, have been derived from Terman's work. Terman helped solidify the idea of a homosexual as a "gender invert."

Consequently, his work contributed to theories that conflate gender expression with sexual identity, setting the stage for viewing femininity as a commodity to be consumed by men, and masculinity as the measure of a true man. Any man lacking in masculinity could be assumed gay, while any woman possessing too much masculinity could be presumed lesbian. At the same time, Terman's work also solidified the association between masculinity and intelligence, thereby instilling the ostensible juxtaposition of femininity and competency in ways that can still be felt today.

Terman's creation of measures that could presumably identify homosexuality and his development and application of such measures within the criminal justice system set the stage for a large portion of the 20th century to view homosexuality as a sexually deviant crime[1]. With few exceptions, gay men and lesbians faced disproportionate levels of incarceration in prisons or mental asylums throughout the early to mid-1900s. In addition, neurosurgeons used lobotomies to "treat" sexual deviance, particularly among lesbians, which escalated after World War II and continued into the late 1960s (Morgan & Nerison, 1993). Despite this, there were pockets of time and space within the first half of the 20th century in which sexual and gender minorities carved out significant freedoms. For example, in the interwar period Berlin, Germany, grew to be the home of a burgeoning queer community that some may say has yet to be rivaled by even the queerest of modern cities, including San Francisco and New York City (Beachy, 2014). However, as a stark reminder that progress is not linear, the rise of the Nazi party in Germany brought an end to the growing freedoms enjoyed by Berlin's queer community.

Although Terman conducted most of his work at Stanford University, his conflation of gender expression and sexuality reached all the way to Germany. Many nations in the 1930s and '40s viewed male homosexuality as a criminal form of sexual deviance. However, the Nazi conceptualization of the threats posed by gay men stands out for its emphasis on femininity as the true root of such a threat (Setterington, 2013). Even during the high points of Berlin's queer scene, Paragraph 175 of the German Criminal Code legally prohibited sodomy in Germany, but authorities rarely enforced the law. When Hitler came to power, the Nazi party increased the enforcement and severity of Paragraph 175 under the premise that gay men threatened the *virility* of the race and, therefore, the Reich. In other words, the greatest threat posed by gay men in Nazi Germany was their femininity and associated weakness. Indeed, the Nazis applied the same reasoning as Terman in separating the "true" homosexuals for persecution based on their femininity. Gay men who were less feminine, who could "pass" as straight, and willing to be "reformed," could avoid the extreme degrees of persecution that their more feminine counterparts could not outrun.

Ultimately, between 1933 and 1945, it is estimated that the Nazis arrested roughly 100,000 men, 53,000 of whom were convicted of "homosexual indecency" (Newsome, 2014). It is unknown precisely how many of these men died in concentration camps. Upon liberation by the Allied Forces, gay men were among the few categories of concentration camp inmates remanded to prisons assuming that they were "legitimate" criminals who had violated Paragraph 175. Given that many of the Allied nations had similar sanctions against homosexuality and that a version of Paragraph 175 predated the Nazis, the Allied Forces viewed the "crimes" of gay men as a legitimate cause for incarceration. West Germany went on to convict nearly 60,000 more men under Paragraph 175 *after* WWII ended (Newsome, 2014). Indeed, well past WWII, Allied nations continued to persecute gay men and lesbians, particularly within the military and civil services. Known as the Lavender Scare in the United States and the LGBTQ Purge in Canada, thousands of men and women were removed from their professions during the Cold War due to concerns that their homosexuality would make them easy targets for foreign agents. During the same era, femme lesbians were seen as a threat to national security and assumed to be potential foreign spies due to their "deceptive" identities. Their femininity was considered to grant them an ability to "pass" or be otherwise indistinguishable from heterosexual women (Corber, 2011), making it more difficult to easily "detect" lesbians. Throughout the 1950s, '60s, and '70s, and even stretching into the '80s and '90s in some professions, gay men and lesbians often had to keep their relationships a secret to protect their careers. Witch hunts to roust homosexuality from the military and the civil service rested upon the same conflations of gender and sexuality provided by Terman's work, resulting in gender nonconformity, especially "misplaced femininity," triggering investigations. Self-perpetuating gender norms that prevented men from expressing any degree of femininity for fear of being accused of homosexuality and similarly tempered women's masculinity served to solidify the profoundly ingrained link between homosexuality and gender inversion throughout the latter half of the 20th century.

The levity and freedom of the homosexual movements from the interwar years are a stark reminder that simply achieving any degree of acceptance or tolerance does not guarantee that such sentiments will remain or that future generations will not "turn back the clocks." Indeed, the HIV/AIDS epidemic had a similarly chilling effect on attitudes toward sexual diversity in the 1980s. While responses to HIV/AIDS varied worldwide, in North America, it was painted as a "gay" disease and even referred to as "GRID"—gay-related immunodeficiency—for some time. Thus, governments and health-funding bodies largely ignored the disease instead of viewing HIV/AIDS as the dangerous pandemic that it was—capable of infecting individuals of any gender or sexuality. Consequently, somewhat dormant religious objections to homosexuality returned to the forefront, with some describing AIDS as God's punishment for gay men's sinful promiscuity.

The stigma of HIV/AIDS continues to color societal attitudes toward LGBTQ people and their relationships today. As discussed in Chapter 7, the pandemic significantly delayed advances in LGBTQ civil rights, including the legalization of same-sex marriage. Nonetheless, marriage debates did begin to take place in earnest in the last few years of the 20th century. Depending on the time and place in which such debates emerged, they often brought to the surface hostile public discourses that laid bare the lingering influence of Terman's contributions toward shaping society's views of homosexuality and femininity as deviant, immature, and threatening.

Current Attitudes Toward Same-Sex and Gender-Diverse Relationships

Sexual prejudice has historically focused on the sexual component of same-sex relationships as a rallying point. For example, many organizations have expressed concerns about children's content depicting same-sex relationships or family structures, arguing that such content is "inappropriate" or "sexual" (Hoskin, 2018). However, similar portrayals of heterosexual couples or parenting have always been present in children's content (e.g., the inevitable kiss between prince and princess at the end of Disney movies). Thus, it is not the presence of romance itself that is deemed inappropriate—but, rather, it is the act of *same-sex* romance that is labeled inappropriate or over-sexualized. These arguments suggest that individuals high in sexual prejudice view same-sex relationships as nothing more than their associated sexual acts, thereby reinforcing the narrative of "sexual deviancy" that resonated before and throughout Terman's work. Consequently, attitudes concerning same-sex relationships and their access to institutional legitimacy are essential for understanding attitudes toward sexual minorities more broadly.

As of 2022, 31 countries have legalized same-sex marriage, representing significant progress since 2000, when same-sex marriage was only legal in the Netherlands (HRC, 2022). At the same time, support among citizens of Western countries for same-sex relationships has significantly increased. For example, between 2002 and 2010, European countries with legal recognition of same-sex marriage also reported more positive attitudes toward gay men and lesbians (Hooghe & Meeusen, 2013). Similarly, in the United States, Americans' implicit and explicit anti-gay biases began to improve more quickly following the federal legalization of same-sex marriage in the Obergefell (2015) U.S. Supreme Court decision (Osofu et al., 2019).

Of course, the legalization of same-sex marriage is not the sole explanation for positive shifts in people's attitudes toward sexual minorities and their relationships. Furthermore, legalization has not always had wholly positive outcomes. For example, when the legalization of same-sex marriage has been driven by the courts rather than through legislative processes, public attitudes sometimes regress, representing a reactive backlash response to top-down approaches to extending LGBTQ civil liberties (Flores & Barclay, 2016). In the more conservative states that did not independently legislate same-sex marriage before Obergefell, anti-gay attitudes worsened following the Supreme Court's decision (Ofosu et al., 2019). Thus, individual factors also play a role in people's attitudes toward same-sex relationships. Demographic shifts, including reduced religiosity, increased access to education, and more frequent contact with sexual minorities, may explain some of the positive trends in accepting attitudes toward sexual minorities and their relationships (e.g., Lee & Mutz, 2019). More specifically, positive attitudes toward same-sex marriage are most common among individuals who are younger rather than older, women rather than men, and those residing within higher socioeconomic statuses (e.g., Perales & Campbell, 2018). Notably, attitudes toward sexual minorities are not equal across sexual minority identities. For example, although attitudes have improved considerably toward same-sex relationships (including those between two men), such approval is often reserved for sexual minorities who conform to societal gender norms. In other words, societal and familial acceptance of same-sex relationships and sexual minority identities often hinges upon not straying too far from societal gender expectations (i.e., masculine men, properly feminine women). Consequently, much of the lingering homonegativity directed at men within society is often associated with negative perceptions of femininity in men (Jewell & Morrison, 2012).

Individuals with a family member in a same-sex relationship express improved attitudes toward same-sex marriage and sexual minorities. Even the experience of attending a family member's same-sex wedding can positively impact an individual's support for same-sex relationships more broadly (e.g., Kenndey et al., 2018). Of course, this does not mean that individuals in same-sex relationships do not still face negative attitudes from family members. Indeed, when family members (close and extended) disapprove of same-sex relationships, they often decline to attend a loved one's same-sex wedding, creating stress for those within the relationship and their more supportive family members (Riggle et al., 2018). Thus, for the experience of *attending* a same-sex wedding to influence an individual's attitudes toward same-sex relationships, they must first possess some degree of openness and willingness to attend. In general, though, familial support for same-sex marriage and relationships has increased in recent years (Ogolsky et al., 2019). Despite these increases, individuals in same-sex relationships consistently perceive less social support and approval for their relationships than individuals in mixed-sex relationships (Blair et al., 2018). This finding is particularly stark when exploring perceptions of support from family members (Holmberg & Blair, 2016).

In addition to lower perceptions of support for one's relationship, individuals in same-sex relationships continue to face the dangerous consequences of remaining sexual prejudice. In 2019, over 15% of all hate crimes committed in the United States targeted LGBTQ+ people (Federal Bureau of Investigation, 2019). This percentage is relatively high, considering that only 5.6% of people are estimated to identify as LGBTQ+ in the United States (Jones, 2021). Unsurprisingly, hate crimes motivated by LGBTQ+ bias negatively impact LGBTQ+ people. For instance, following the 2016 Pulse nightclub shooting, LGBTQ+ people reported increased safety concerns (Stults et al., 2017).

Furthermore, overt acts of aggression toward LGBTQ+ people persist, ranging from anti-LGBTQ+ bullying to the disproportionately high murder rates of transgender women (Nadal, 2018). Minority stress refers to the additional stress LGBTQ+ individuals experience due to managing their identity, confronting safety concerns, and discrimination (Meyer, 2003). Such stressors are associated with adverse psychological health outcomes (Pellicane & Ciesla, 2021) and contribute to LGBTQ+ health disparities. Minority stress also applies at the couple level, such as when same-sex couples experience more significant concerns for their safety when in public due to negative attitudes and actions directed at their relationship (LeBlanc & Frost, 2020). One way in which couple-level minority stressors become salient is by engaging in public affection sharing (i.e., public displays of affection; PDAs), such as holding hands. Compared with those in mixed-sex relationships, individuals in same-sex and gender-diverse relationships report engaging in PDAs less frequently and being less comfortable doing so.

When same-sex and gender-diverse couples do share affection in public, they report experiencing higher levels of PDA-related vigilance, or a sense of unease and hyperawareness of their surroundings, knowing that their affection can be the catalyst for violence (Blair et al., 2022). Furthermore, individuals in a same-sex relationship who report having a feminine partner and feminine men experience exacerbated PDA-related vigilance (Matheson et al., 2021).

Attitudes Concerning Gender-Diverse Relationships

Researcher interest in same-sex relationships has grown over the past two decades; however, there is still much left to be explored alongside improved understandings (particularly in Western countries) of the nuances of gender, transness, and nonbinary identities. For instance, people have become more aware of and increasingly identified with trans and nonbinary genders in the past 15 years (Nolan et al., 2019). These shifts have created new questions about how people construe and define their own sexual identity alongside their gender identity. For example, cisgender (someone for whom gender aligns with sex) partners of trans individuals may feel that their partner's transition requires them to change or modify their own sexual identity to affirm their partner's gender (Platt & Bolland, 2017). At the same time, many people have eschewed traditional sexual minority labels (e.g., lesbian, gay, bisexual) in favor of more expansive terminology, such as queer and pansexual. This developing area of research suggests that people's—including heterosexual people's—understandings of their sexual identity may evolve and expand in the next two decades.

Gender-diverse individuals face unique challenges within the context of romantic relationships. Simply being told that another person is transgender or nonbinary (whether true or not) reduces cisgender individuals' reported feelings of attraction (Mao et al., 2019). Transgender people are also more likely to experience intimate partner violence, including being up to 2.2 times more likely to experience physical violence from a partner and 2.5 times more likely to experience sexual violence from a partner (Peitzmeier et al., 2020). Trans women are particularly at risk for intimate partner violence and are vastly overrepresented in each year's transgender day of remembrance (Namaste, 2011). Trans men, however, are not immune to violence, both within and outside of their close relationships. When targeted by strangers, many trans men and nonbinary individuals identify perceived femininity as placing them within the crosshairs of their aggressors (Hoskin, 2019, 2020). Thus, across transgender and nonbinary identities, femmephobia contributes to the negative attitudes directed at gender-diverse individuals and the violence they encounter. Given such real threats of danger, it is no surprise that trans individuals report difficulty deciding if, when, and how to disclose their gender identity to potential romantic partners, an experience that is unique to the trans and nonbinary community (e.g., Lloyd & Finn, 2017). Such concerns are not unfounded. One study reported that 87.5% of the cisgender people in the study's sample would not consider dating a transgender person (Blair & Hoskin, 2019). This number included 96.9% of the cisgender heterosexual participants and 76.1% of the gay and lesbian cisgender participants. Those whose sexual attractions were already blind to gender were the most willing to consider dating trans individuals; 55.2% of queer and bisexual individuals were willing to consider dating a transgender partner. To a disproportionate extent, trans women were the least likely to be included in the hypothetical dating pools of others, providing further support for societal denigration and regulation of "misplaced" or "unwarranted" femininity.

The Invisible Hurdle: Femmephobia

It is impossible to determine what attitudes toward sexual and gender diversity will be most prevalent in the coming decades. There are already legal attempts to limit or roll back some forms of LGBTQ+ civil liberties in the United States. Same-sex relations remain illegal in 71 countries, and the trajectory toward acceptance is reversing in others. For example, the growing conflict between Russia, the European Union, and ultimately, "The West" is, in part, premised upon the proposed necessity of protecting Russia from the disintegration of the family structure that has become commonplace in Western nations. In other words, Russia's leaders argue that the progression of LGBTQ+ rights in the West threatens Russia's values. They subsequently have used the perception of such threats to provide justification and cover for their political and military transgressions (Snyder, 2018). In the United States, legislators have signed controversial bills that limit the discussion of LGBTQ+ identities within the classroom (Izaguirre, 2022). Thus, while attitudes toward sexual and gender diversity have improved, this is no guarantee that they will continue to do so.

Despite generally improving attitudes toward sexual and gender diversity, femmephobia stands apart as a prejudice unfamiliar to many, even within LGBTQ+ communities. The legacy of Terman's denigration and devaluing of femininity is so ubiquitous that femmephobia remains prevalent in terms of attitudes directed *toward* LGBTQ+ communities by outsiders and attitudes expressed *within* the community itself. Consequently, one of the most relevant hurdles to be cleared in the coming decades concerning attitudes toward sexual and gender diversity is eradicating or at least lessening femmephobic sentiments.

Femmephobia, as articulated by Femme Theory, refers to the systematic devaluation and regulation of femininity. Femmephobia describes negative sentiments and attitudes directed at individuals perceived as feminine and those whom society does not view as appropriate feminine subjects. Femme theory emerged from theoretical understandings of 1940s lesbian communities, which often included butch–femme partnerships (Hoskin, 2021). However, as articulated by Hoskin (2017, 2021), femme theory has expanded to explore the treatment of femininity across contexts and identities. Femme theory allows for an understanding of how societal attitudes concerning femininity (many of which trace back to Terman's original work) function to ensure the continued placement of femininity beneath masculinity while maintaining strict confines around *who* can be feminine and what is considered *proper* femininity.

We see femmephobia within the LGBTQ+ community itself through a variety of instances. While outsiders often invoke Terman's conflation of femininity and male homosexuality to denigrate gay men, gay men themselves perpetuate this sentiment against each other by articulating dating preferences that exclude more feminine men (Miller & Behm-Morawitz, 2016). Indeed, the very term "queer" was adopted in the early 1900s by more masculine or "straight-acting" gay men as a way of differentiating themselves from the more feminine "pansies" and "fairies," whom society so virulently hated (Hoskin, 2017; Taywaditep, 2002). Within lesbian communities, feminine lesbians are often excluded and made to feel invisible. Their femininity renders their sexuality inauthentic, and they are assumed to be curious visitors incapable of genuine or permanent attraction to other women (Blair & Hoskin, 2015). Even LGBTQ+ communities' revered and respected champions—drag queens—serve to highlight the deeply ingrained nature of femmephobia, such that many drag queens report being rejected as prospective dating partners precisely because of their femininity or their willingness to perform femininity within their drag queen personas (Levitt et al., 2018). At the same time, while drag celebrates gender diversity and "misplaced" femininity on a large stage, the very appeal of drag queens as a source of entertainment can be seen as a further invocation of femmephobia, such that drag presents femininity as something to be "put on" rather than anything that could be agentic or authentic (Hoskin, 2019, 2020).

Consequently, a prejudice borne out of a desire to equate sexual minorities with sexual deviancy has thus become one of the strongest and most prevalent prejudices expressed by sexual minorities toward each other. Such a shift is perhaps not as surprising as it may initially sound. Terman's work uncovered many examples of gay men who did not score highly on his measure of femininity. Given the degree of persecution that sexual minorities faced throughout the 20th century, is it any wonder that some may try to set themselves apart from what they (and society) understood to be the *truest* or most transgressive of their sins: femininity?

While LGBTQ+ communities have been working to undo the lingering legacy of Terman's denigration of femininity, what makes femmephobia particularly relevant as an "attitude" to watch over the coming decades is that it stretches far beyond the issue of sexual and gender diversity. Femmephobia has implications for many facets of life and cuts across identities, bodies, and sexualities. Terman's conflation of intelligence with masculinity presents itself today in the denigration of femininity within any "serious" work environment. Feminine scientists are taken less seriously and assumed to be less intelligent (Banchefsky et al., 2016), and women in STEM are accepted only so far as they can adhere to masculine norms of intelligence and competency (Menendez, 2019). Female politicians must walk the ever-so-fine line of navigating a sexist world that requires them to master a near-impossible balance of warmth and competence (Bordo, 2019) while carefully ensuring that they do not wade too far into the realm of femininity, which would render them frivolous, too emotional, and incapable of the "serious" matters of governing (Menendez, 2019). Somewhat more than sexism and misogyny, femmephobic sentiments shape the experiences of individuals across all sexual and gender identities. Gay men must navigate the same challenges of not allowing "femininity" to leak into their personae if they wish to be considered competent within masculine realms, and even straight men's ability to express nurturance, affection, or vulnerability is constrained by societal dictates that they not fall into the negative numbers of Terman's M–F test.

Thus, we are still grappling with the fallout nearly 100 years after Terman developed the M–F test with its embedded assumptions about gender expression and identity. Although we have progressed in rehabilitating attitudes toward same-sex relationships and sexual and gender diversity, such progress often hinges upon agreements to not violate the assumptions of acceptable femininity. When one looks to identify the areas in which LGBTQ+ individuals and their relationships still struggle to garner positive attitudes from themselves and others, some transgression of femininity is often nearby. Whether it is the heightened vigilance associated with having a feminine partner, the cruelty of violence directed at trans women, or the ability to instantly express contempt for another by associating them with feminine qualities, femmephobia diverges from other prejudices as requiring much greater attention than it has to date. Indeed, Hoskin (2020) has argued that femmephobia is the thread that weaves through and anchors many other societal prejudices, including homophobia, transphobia, sexism, and "toxic masculinity."

In looking ahead, we hope that readers and scholars alike will challenge Terman's assumptions about gender and sexuality by beginning to imagine our future world as one in which we value femininity on equal footing with masculinity. Such a world would be one in which we equally associate femininity and masculinity with the potential for intelligence, competency, and strength and would allow us to celebrate the feminine qualities of nurturance, emotion, and vulnerability regardless of an individual's sex or gender or sexuality. What would the implications of such a world be for all human relationships? What would it mean for how the world views sexual and gender minorities and their relationships? These are just some of the questions that we are excited to see researchers explore with respect to attitudes toward the relationships of sexual and gender minorities in the coming years.

Note

1. As discussed in Chapter 7, it would not be until the pioneering work of Dr. Evelyn Hooker that the negative consequences of Terman's work would begin to be undone, allowing for gay men and lesbians to be viewed as natural sources of diversity within the spectrum of human sexuality.

References

Banchefsky, S., Westfall, J., Park, B., & Judd, C. M. (2016). But you don't look like a scientist!: Women scientists with feminine appearance are deemed less likely to be scientists. *Sex Roles*, *75*(3), 95–109. https://doi.org/10.1007/s11199-016-0586-1

Beachy, R. (2014). *Gay Berlin: Birthplace of a modern identity*. Alfred A. Knopf Incorporated.

Blair, K. L., Holmberg, D., & Pukall, C. F. (2018). Support processes in same- and mixed-sex relationships: Type and source matters. *Personal Relationships*, *25*(3), 374–393. https://doi.org/10.1111/pere.12249

Blair, K. L., & Hoskin, R. A. (2019). Transgender exclusion from the world of dating: Patterns of acceptance and rejection of hypothetical trans dating partners as a function of sexual and gender identity. *Journal of Social and Personal Relationships*, *36*(7), 2074–2095. https://doi.org/10.1177/0265407518779139

Blair, K. L., & Hoskin, R. A. (2015). Experiences of femme identity: Coming out, invisibility and femmephobia. *Psychology & Sexuality*, *6*(3), 229–244. https://doi.org/10.1080/19419899.2014.921860

Blair, K.L., McKenna, O., & Holmberg, D. (2022). On guard: Public versus private affection-sharing experiences in same-sex, gender-diverse and mixed-sex relationships. *Journal of Social and Personal Relationships*, *39*(9), 2939–2963. https://doi.org/10.1177/02654075221090678

Bordo, S. (2019). *The destruction of Hillary Clinton*. Melville House.

Corber, R. J. (2011). *Cold war femme*. Duke University Press.

Crompton, L. (2003). *Homosexuality & civilization*. Belknap Press of Harvard University Press.

Drescher, J., Schwartz, A., Casoy, F., McIntosh, C. A., Hurley, B., Ashley, K., Barber, M., Goldenberg, D., Herbert, S. E., Lothwell, L. E., Mattson, M. R., McAfee, S. G., Pula, J., Rosario, V., & Tompkins, D. A. (2016). The growing regulation of conversion therapy. *Journal of Medical Regulation*, *102*(2), 7–12. https://doi.org/10.30770/2572-1852-102.2.7

Federal Bureau of Intelligence. (2019). *2019 hate crime statistics*. FBI Uniform Crime Reporting. https://ucr.fbi.gov/hate-crime/2019/resource-pages/tables/table-1.xls

Flores, A. R., & Barclay, S. (2016). Backlash, consensus, legitimacy, or polarization: The effect of same-sex marriage policy on mass attitudes. *Political Research Quarterly*, *69*(1), 43–56. https://doi.org/10.1177/1065912915621175

Hegarty. (2007). From genius inverts to gendered intelligence: Lewis Terman and the power of the norm. *History of Psychology*, *10*(2), 132–155. https://doi.org/10.1037/1093-4510.10.2.132

Holmberg, D., & Blair, K. L. (2016). Dynamics of perceived social network support for same-sex versus mixed-sex relationships. *Personal Relationships*, *23*(1), 62–83. https://doi.org/10.1111/pere.12111

Hooghe, M., & Meeusen, C. (2013). Is same-sex marriage legislation related to attitudes toward homosexuality? *Sexuality Research and Social Policy*, *10*(4), 258–268. https://doi.org/10.1007/s13178-013-0125-6

Hoskin, R. A. (2017). Femme theory: Refocusing the intersectional lens. *Atlantis: Critical Studies in Gender, Culture & Social Justice*, *38*(1), 95–109.

Hoskin, R. A. (2018). Westernization and the transmogrification of Sailor Moon. *InterAlia: Pismo Poświęcone Studiom Queer*, (13), 78–89. https://doi.org/10.51897/interalia/dsgq4165

Hoskin, R. A. (2019). Femmephobia: The role of anti-femininity and gender policing in LGBTQ+ people's experiences of discrimination. *Sex Roles*, *81*(11), 686–703. https://doi.org/10.1007/s11199-019-01021-3

Hoskin, R. A. (2020). "Femininity? It's the aesthetic of subordination": Examining femmephobia, the gender binary, and experiences of oppression among sexual and gender minorities. *Archives of Sexual Behavior*, *49*(7), 2319–2339. https://doi.org/10.1007/s10508-020-01641-x

Hoskin, R. A. (2021). Can femme be theory? Exploring the epistemological and methodological possibilities of femme. *Journal of Lesbian Studies*, *25*(1), 1–17. https://doi.org/10.1080/10894160.2019.1702288

Human Rights Campaign. (n.d.). *Marriage equality around the world*. Retrieved February 14, 2022, from https://www.hrc.org/resources/marriage-equality-around-the-world

Izaguirre, A. (2022, March 28). "Don't Say Gay" bill signed by Florida Gov. Ron DeSantis. *AP News*. https://apnews.com/article/florida-dont-say-gay-law-signed-56aee61f075a1 2663f25990c7b31624d

Jewell, L. M., & Morrison, M. A. (2012). Making sense of homonegativity: Heterosexual men and women's understanding of their own prejudice and discrimination toward gay men. *Qualitative Research in Psychology*, *9*(4), 351–370. https://doi.org/10.1080/14780887.2011.586098

Jones, J. M. (20214). *LGBT identification rises to 5.6% in latest U.S. estimate*. *Gallup*. https://news.gallup.com/poll/329708/lgbt-identification-rises-latest-estimate.aspx

Kennedy, H. R., Dalla, R. L., & Dreesman, S. (2018). "We are two of the lucky ones": Experiences with marriage and wellbeing for same-sex couples. *Journal of Homosexuality*, *65*(9), 1207–1231. https://doi.org/10.1080/00918369.2017.1407612

LeBlanc, A. J., & Frost, D. M. (2020). Couple-level minority stress and mental health among people in same-sex relationships: Extending minority stress theory. *Society and Mental Health*, *10*(3), 276–290. https://doi.org/10.1177/2156869319884724

Lee, H. Y., & Mutz, D. C. (2019). Changing attitudes toward same-sex marriage: A three-wave panel study. *Political Behavior*, *41*(3), 701–722. https://doi.org/10.1007/s11 109-018-9463-7

Levitt, H. M., Surace, F. I., Wheeler, E. E., Maki, E., Alcántara, D., Cadet, M., Cullipher, S., Desai, S., Sada, G. G., Hite, J., Kosterina, E., Krill, S., Lui, C., Manove, E., Martin, R. J., & Ngai, C. (2018). Drag gender: Experiences of gender for gay and queer men who perform drag. *Sex Roles*, *78*(5), 367–384. https://doi.org/10.1007/s11199-017-0802-7

Lloyd, C. E., & Finn, M. D. (2017). Authenticity, validation and sexualization on Grindr: An analysis of trans women's accounts. *Psychology & Sexuality*, *8*(1–2), 158–169. https://doi.org/10.1080/19419899.2017.1316569

Mao, J. M., Haupert, M. L., & Smith, E. R. (2019). How gender identity and transgender status affect perceptions of attractiveness. *Social Psychological and Personality Science*, *10*(6), 811–822. https://doi.org/10.1177/1948550618783716

Matheson, L., Ortiz, D. L., Hoskin, R. A., Holmberg, D., & Blair, K. L. (2021). The feminine target: Gender expression in same-sex relationships as a predictor of experiences with public displays of affection. *The Canadian Journal of Human Sexuality*, *30*(2), 205–218. https://doi.org/10.3138/cjhs.2021-0024

Menendez, A. (2019). *The likeability trap: How to break free and succeed as you are.* HarperCollins.

Meyer, I. H. (2003). Prejudice, social stress, and mental health in lesbian, gay, and bisexual populations: Conceptual issues and research evidence. *Psychological Bulletin, 129,* 674–697. https://doi.org/10.1037/0033-2909.129.5.674

Miller, B., & Behm-Morawitz, E. (2016). "Masculine guys only": The effects of femmephobic mobile dating application profiles on partner selection for men who have sex with men. *Computers in Human Behavior, 62,* 176–185. https://doi.org/10.1016/j.chb.2016.03.088

Morgan, K. S., & Nerison, R. M. (1993). Homosexuality and psychopolitics: An historical overview. *Psychotherapy: Theory, Research, Practice, Training, 30*(1), 133. https://doi.org/10.1037/0033-3204.30.1.133

Nadal, K. L. (2018). A decade of microaggression research and LGBTQ communities: An introduction to the special issue. *Journal of Homosexuality, 66*(10), 1309–1316. https://doi.org/10.1080/00918369.2018.1539582

Namaste, V. (2011). *Sex change, social change: Reflections on identity, institutions, and imperialism.* Canadian Scholars' Press.

Newsome, W. J. (2014). Liberation was only for others: Breaking the silence in Germany surrounding the Nazi persecution of homosexuals. *The Holocaust in History and Memory, 7,* 53–71.

Nolan, I. T., Kuhner, C. J., & Dy, G. W. (2019). Demographic and temporal trends in transgender identities and gender confirming surgery. *Translational Andrology and Urology, 8*(3), 184–190. https://doi.org/10.21037/tau.2019.04.09

Obergefell v. Hodges, 576 U.S. (2015). https://supreme.justia.com/cases/federal/us/576/14-556/

Ofosu, E. K., Chambers, M. K., Chen, J. M., & Hehman, E. (2019). Same-sex marriage legalization associated with reduced implicit and explicit antigay bias. *Proceedings of the National Academy of Sciences, 116*(18), 8846–8851. https://doi.org/10.1073/pnas.1806000116

Ogolsky, B. G., Monk, J. K., Rice, T. M., & Oswald, R. F. (2019). Personal well-being across the transition to marriage equality: A longitudinal analysis. *Journal of Family Psychology, 33*(4), 422. https://doi.org/10.1037/fam0000504

Peitzmeier, S. M., Malik, M., Kattari, S. K., Marrow, E., Stephenson, R., Agénor, M., & Reisner, S. L. (2020). Intimate partner violence in transgender populations: Systematic review and meta-analysis of prevalence and correlates. *American Journal of Public Health, 110*(9), e1–e14. https://doi.org/10.2105/AJPH.2020.305774

Pellicane, M. J., & Ciesla, J. A. (2021). Associations between minority stress, depression, and suicidal ideation and attempts in transgender and gender diverse (TGD) individuals: Systematic review and meta-analysis. *Clinical Psychology Review, 91,* Article 102113. https://doi.org/10.1016/j.cpr.2021.102113

Perales, F., & Campbell, A. (2018). Who supports equal rights for same-sex couples? *Family Matters, (100),* 28–41.

Platt, L. F., & Bolland, K. S. (2017). Trans* partner relationships: A qualitative exploration. *Journal of GLBT Family Studies, 13*(2), 163–185. https://doi.org/10.1080/1550428X.2016.1195713

Riggle, E. D., Drabble, L., Veldhuis, C. B., Wootton, A., & Hughes, T. L. (2018). The impact of marriage equality on sexual minority women's relationships with their families of origin. *Journal of Homosexuality, 65*(9), 1190–1206. https://doi.org/10.1080/00918369.2017.1407611

Setterington, K. (2013). *Branded by the pink triangle.* Second Story Press.
Snyder, T. (2018). *The road to unfreedom: Russia, Europe, America.* Tim Duggan Books.
Stults, C. B., Kupprat, S. A., Krause, K. D., Kapadia, F., & Halkitis, P. N. (2017). Perceptions of safety among LGBTQ people following the 2016 Pulse nightclub shooting. *Psychology of Sexual Orientation and Gender Diversity, 4*(3), 251–256. https://doi.org/10.1037/sgd0000240
Taywaditep, K. J. (2002). Marginalization among the marginalized: Gay men's anti-effeminacy attitudes. *Journal of Homosexuality, 42*(1), 1–28. https://doi.org/10.1300/j082v42n01_01
Terman, L. M. (1930). Autobiography of Lewis M. Terman. *History of Psychology in Autobiography, 2,* 297–331. https://doi.org/10.1037/11082-012
Terman, L. M., & Cox, C. (1936). *Sex and personality: Studies in masculinity and femininity.* McGraw-Hill.

PART IV
FRIENDSHIP IN THE 21ST CENTURY

PART IX

FRIENDSHIP IN THE 21ST CENTURY

12

Modern Friendships

Mixing Multiple Media and Affordances When Communicating With Friends

Kelly Sweeney, Daniel A. Lee, and Andrew C. High

The prevalence of Internet-connected devices has led many friendships to be developed and maintained in part via online spaces (Pouwels et al., 2021). Parks (2017) defined relationships maintained across multiple channels as mixed-media relationships, or "social relationships that parties conduct in whole or in part through the use of multiple media, including face-to-face" (p. 506). Modern friendships often have multiple means of communicating, including texting, phone calls, video chat, and social media. Consequently, people cultivate friendships via a combination of online and face-to-face exchanges. Although early research considered face-to-face (FtF) to be the most effective environment for relational development and maintenance, digital technologies afford certain capabilities that allow people to extend the boundaries of communication and conduct interactions in different, perhaps even beneficial ways (Walther, 1996).

Research on computer-mediated-communication (CMC) is beginning to focus on people's use of multiple channels within relationships (e.g., Caughlin & Sharabi, 2013), yet rapid advancements in communication technology make it difficult to integrate research on technology with theory and research on social relationships. This endeavor is especially difficult when considering multiple channels simultaneously, each with their own set of features and perceived affordances (Fox & McEwan, 2017). In this chapter, we follow the lead of other researchers and distinguish the features, or material technological properties, of channels from affordances, or what users perceive that the channels enable them to do (Evans et al., 2017). Most of the research on features and affordances of channels assumes the use of single channels, even though that does not match the reality of contemporary relationships. By considering the features and affordances that define channels, and theorizing how they are utilized in combination for social outcomes, scholars can achieve a deeper understanding of how the landscape of modern communication technology shapes friendships.

The rise of mixed-media friendships highlights the need for explanations of how using multiple channels influences the development and maintenance of social relationships. We know friendships are important to various aspects of well-being (Fehr, 2012; Vanzetti & Duck, 1996), and we know interactions between friends are often technologically mediated (Anderson & Jiang, 2018; Chan, 2020; Ramirez & Broneck, 2009). Although online channels are often thought to benefit relationships, some scholars have reported that the overuse of technology can harm friendships based on factors such as entrapment, jealousy, or fear of missing out (Hall & Baym, 2012). To clarify these associations, this chapter addresses how a combination of channels might impact friendships. We begin our chapter by discussing the nature and function of friendships while accounting for the prevalence of mixed-media friendships. Next, we review prominent theories and frameworks used to understand mixed-media relationships. Subsequent sections explore potentially relevant affordances of channels of CMC along with how they might be managed or balanced within contemporary friendships.

Mixed-Media Friendships

Whereas family relationships may be seen as "given" relationships, friendships are often viewed as "chosen" (Pahl & Spencer, 2004). They are voluntarily selected and developed. Friendships are developed through reciprocal exchanges of resources and disclosures, which depend on the efforts of both parties (Fehr, 2012; Vanzetti & Duck, 1996). Most friendships lack the formalization and expectations associated with family, coworker, or romantic relationships, yet they provide social support, a sense of belonging, and perspective that shapes people's values and beliefs (Vanzetti & Duck, 1996). Based in part on their chosen or voluntary nature, friendships also require maintenance to advance or sustain relational bonds. Dindia and Canary (1993) defined relational maintenance as behaviors used "to keep a relationship in existence, to keep a relationship at a specific state or condition, to keep a relationship in satisfactory condition, or to keep a relationship in repair" (p. 163). Activities that maintain friendships often involve simple acts, including mutual supportiveness, positive interactions, sharing activities, and self-disclosure (Fehr, 2012). Many of these maintenance behaviors can be managed via both in-person and online settings, and the emergence of new technologies has changed the ways that people maintain their friendships.

Although friendships can persist across the lifespan, they often experience periods of transition. For example, when high school students move to college, they often reassess the costs and rewards of older friendships as they form new networks in college. Oswald and Clark (2003) reported that high school best friendships become increasingly costly to maintain during the transition to college and the rewards and investments of those relationships often decrease. Yet, individuals who communicated more frequently and engaged in more maintenance behaviors were more likely to remain friends and did not report the decrease in satisfaction or rewards noted by friendships that lacked communication. These findings align with research that found few or no differences in closeness, maintenance, or commitment between long-distance and geographically close friends who used technology to stay in touch (Johnson et al., 2009; Ruppel et al., 2018). Communication technology can be used to sustain and maintain friendships across divides in space or time. The numerous, unique, and low-cost ways to engage with friends across multiple channels may explain why over 80% of young people report feeling strongly connected to friends via social media (Anderson & Jiang, 2018).

The presence of friends shapes how people communicate online. Although certain channels are rife with selective self-presentation, research indicates that people present themselves more modestly with friends than strangers online (DeAndrea, 2014). Despite overarching concerns about deception, people generally trust the information sent by their friends online (Perfumi et al., 2019). Many contexts of CMC (e.g., social media) contain a mixture of strong, weak, or latent ties, but research suggests that users are most influenced by their actual friends (Ellison et al., 2014) or their strongest audience group online (Marder et al., 2016). Individuals also engage in large amounts of disclosure with friends online but lower personal disclosure with strangers (Acquisti et al., 2015), and venues on which people have large numbers of friends elicit greater disclosure (Taddicken, 2014). People are even willing to disclose private information online, especially when their friends disclose similar information (Taddicken, 2014). Thus, people use online channels to communicate with friends, and their communication is shaped by both their relationships and aspects of the channels in which they interact.

Beyond opportunities to interact, technology confers relational benefits for friends. People who use multiple channels to maintain their friendships experience heightened feelings of interdependence and closeness (Ledbetter, 2009). Vitak and Ellison (2013) reported that the number of people's "actual" friends on social media corresponds with heightened bridging capital, and users receive several types of support and capital from their friends on social media (High & Buehler, 2019). In this context, bridging capital refers to access to relatively distant social ties that often provide diverse resources and information (Putnam, 2000). Technology provides people with opportunities to maintain their relationships outside of face-to-face interactions, and those in more satisfying relationships use CMC to strengthen friendships (Pouwels et al., 2021), enact friendship maintenance strategies (Ramirez & Broneck, 2009), and provide support to friends (Nabi et al., 2013). Along these lines, maintaining contact with friends on Facebook increases life satisfaction, even after controlling for variables related to offline networks (Nabi et al., 2013). Phone calls, text messages, social media, video chat, and a multitude of other channels have encouraged the prevalence of using multiple communication channels to connect with friends. Such options allow mixed-media friendships to be "flexible," such that friends adjust to a range of options for relational maintenance (Ramirez & Broneck, 2009).

Theoretical Foundations

After establishing that modern friendships are often maintained using multiple channels, we now discuss three frameworks used to explain mixed-media relationships. We review media multiplexity theory (MMT; Haythornthwaite, 2005) and the communicative interdependence perspective (Caughlin & Sharabi, 2013) to summarize theories that can inform an understanding of mixed-media friendships. We then integrate research on affordances to extend this thinking and explain what it is about channels that might produce different results for friends.

Media Multiplexity Theory

One perspective used to understand how social relationships integrate and manage multiple communication channels is Haythornthwaite's

(2005) MMT. MMT argues that people use a greater variety of media when communicating with stronger social ties and fewer channels with weaker ties. Specifically, MMT categorizes strong-tie relationships as relationships between friends, romantic partners, and relatives who have a willingness to share information and access to resources. Weak ties, in contrast, are relationships with people who we know but would not consider to be close associations.

Three key assumptions underlie the predictions of MMT. First, it assumes that "characteristics of ties hold in the mediated environment as they do in the offline environment" (Haythornthwaite, 2002, p. 388). In other words, friendships that exist both on and offline can be described using the same variables, and the nature of ties between friends remains whether they are communicating in person or online. Second, the theory assumes "online exchanges are as real in terms of their impact on the tie as are offline exchanges" (p. 388). That is, CMC is viewed to be just as influential for relational outcomes as in-person exchanges. The third assumption is that "it is the tie that drives the number and types of exchanges, not whether the tie is maintained on or offline, or via any combination of the two" (p. 388). More than the channel of communication, differences in relational ties (i.e., co-worker vs. friend) explain why there are discrepancies in communication frequency and relational outcomes, and relationships (i.e., friendships) can attain equivalent outcomes regardless of the channels used for communication.

Beyond these assumptions, MMT offers simple and well-supported predictions (Chan, 2020; Haythornthwaite, 2005; Ruppel et al., 2018). It asserts a positive relationship between tie strength and media use. Specifically, MMT predicts that strong-tie relationships share more channels and communicate more frequently with one another than those with weaker ties (Haythornthwaite, 2005). Although tie strength is expected to affect media use, the theory also recognizes a reciprocal relationship, wherein media use affects relationships over time. For instance, MMT predicts that as people expand the media they share and communicate more frequently, they perceive increased closeness in their relationships. These predictions have been applied to multiple strong-tie relationships, including family ties (Balayar & Langlais, 2021), friendships (Chan, 2020), and romantic relationships (Caughlin & Sharabi, 2013).

Findings concerning friendships, in particular, demonstrate that the strength of one's friendship (e.g., just friends, good friends, best friends) can influence the amount and type of channels people use. For instance, a study focusing on communication and friendship among youth in Hong Kong found that a greater number of and more private communication channels are used among close friends compared with more distant friends (Chan, 2020). Research on MMT also establishes that as individuals get closer, they broaden their range of communication channels. Ramirez and Broneck's (2009) study on everyday maintenance behaviors found that instant messaging, talking on the phone, emailing, and talking in person were positively correlated. These findings suggest that partners expand their shared communication channels as relationships develop. Finally, research demonstrates that online settings provide sufficient opportunities to develop intimacy. Igarashi et al. (2005) found that friendships involving in-person and text-message exchanges predicted greater perceptions of closeness compared with those of friends who only interacted in person. In other words, mixed-media friendships were perceived to be closer compared with friendships that only engaged in face-to-face interactions.

In general, MMT reveals interesting patterns regarding mixed-media relationships and demonstrates that close friends often use a variety of channels to interact (Chan, 2020; Ledbetter, 2009; Ruppel et al., 2018). However, the theory offers a limited account regarding how media are used within social relationships. More contemporary theorizing has provided insight into those issues.

Communicative Interdependence Perspective

Caughlin and Sharabi's (2013) communicative interdependence perspective (CIP) expands upon MMT and adds to our understanding of mixed-media relationships. CIP is founded on the assumption that online and offline communication have become nearly inseparable as technology becomes commonplace in social exchanges (Sharabi & Hall, 2021). CIP analyzes mixed-media relationships by capturing interdependence, which is defined as "the process by which interacting persons influence one another's experiences—the effects individuals exert on other persons' motives, preferences, behavior, and outcomes" (Rusbult & Van Lange, 1996, p. 564). Interdependence has long been thought to shape relational outcomes, though CIP provides a unique take on that notion by examining interdependence of communication *channels*, specifically examining ways that communication in one channel depends upon or influences exchanges in other channels (Caughlin & Sharabi, 2013).

CIP focuses on three forms of channel interdependence. First, CIP accounts for instances when communication is *integrated* across channels (Caughlin & Sharabi, 2013). Sometimes conversation topics extend across multiple exchanges, like when friends share a funny photo via text message and then talk about it during a later phone call. Instances when communication originating in one channel bleeds into a discussion in another reflect channel integration. CIP also addresses occasions when communication topics are *segmented* to particular channels. For instance, due to the lack of social cues and difficulties conveying tone, friends may be uncomfortable having an argument through text message, instead waiting until they can talk in person to resolve a conflict. In this example, conflict is segmented to in-person discussions. In addition, CIP considers when people experience *difficulty transitioning* between channels. Especially when people have a large number of media at their disposal, traversing between channels may not always be a smooth experience. CIP focuses on integrating, segmenting, and difficulty transitioning as three forms of interdependence to better understand how communication in one channel relates to or depends upon communication in another. Utilizing a variety of communication channels can result in both positive and negative outcomes, depending on how those channels are used interdependently. Generally, greater integration; less segmentation, perhaps unless topics are segmented to face-to-face; and less difficulty transitioning predict more satisfying relational outcomes (Caughlin & Sharabi, 2013; Sharabi & Hall, 2021).

Recently, Sharabi and Hall (2021) advanced conceptualizations of CIP by further defining integration. Two types of constructive integration involve the use of technology to *preserve continuity* in the relationship and *facilitate togetherness*. Technology can preserve continuity by providing opportunities for friends to keep in contact even when physically apart (2021). For instance, when apart, friends may preserve continuity by sending a text, interacting on social media, or documenting memories to share later. Another positive example of integration is when technology is used to facilitate togetherness and enhance FtF conversation by allowing friends to pull information from outside of the relationship (e.g., photos, text message, social media posts) and bring it into the conversation. When spending time together, friends may entertain themselves by discussing a social media post, watching a funny video, or recording a TikTok. These examples illustrate that friends can use technology to bridge physical distance when apart and facilitate social activities when together.

Apart from these benefits, recent iterations of CIP document three ways that technological integration interferes with relationships. First, technology can be destructive when it is used to *perpetuate conflict*. CIP defines perpetuating conflict as using technology to continue or revisit a dispute over a period of time (Sharabi & Hall, 2021). If it is used to further arguments or ruminate on resolved disagreements, technology can exacerbate relationship problems (Pusateri et al., 2015). Technology can also be used to *turn away* from FtF conversations. When spending time in person, friends may use technology as a form of entertainment or distraction. This behavior is not inherently negative; however, it can be problematic when technology is used to avoid or detach from conversations taking place in person. Technology can also have a negative impact on relationships when it is used to *create tension* during FtF interactions. Sharabi and Hall (2021) defined using technology to create tension as "using technology to start and engage in FtF conflict via proving a point, evidencing grievances, or surveilling one's partner with the goal of using that information against them" (p. 6). Indeed, research suggests that technology can interfere with and intensify social exchanges when used to provide evidence in a dispute (Pusateri et al., 2015) or instigate a fight (Toma & Sarmiento, 2018). In these ways, CIP illustrates how technology can strain or harm people's relationships.

Overall, CIP explores mixed-media relationships through a unique lens focused on interdependent use of channels. Despite its advances, CIP does not tell us much about what it is about channels that may prompt different patterns of usage, interdependence, or outcomes. We turn to research on technological affordances to explain how or why channels might be used in particular ways by friends.

Affordances

The theories outlined here help to explain patterns of relationship development and maintenance using multiple channels. Considering the affordances of these channels allows researchers to understand what it is about channels that make them useful in isolation or in combination. Even though scholars sometimes report on communication phenomena in particular channels (e.g., email, Facebook), focusing on affordances that span channels creates more durable theorizing that can be employed across a range of channels.

Although there are different ways of considering affordances, they can be defined as the perceived action possibilities that users believe are present in a channel (Fox & McEwan, 2017; Karahanna et al., 2018), and they can help to explain why and how people use different channels. Affordances are not objective features of channels; rather, they are perceptions based on the properties of a channel and the experience of a user (Evans et al., 2017). Analyses of *perceived* social affordances address the social implications (e.g., privacy, anonymity, etc.) people understand to be present or believe are important in a channel for effective and convenient interactions (Fox & McEwan, 2017). For example, text messaging is often perceived to be easily *accessible* and to allow a person to communicate directly and *asynchronously* with another person. Comparatively, phone calls are often perceived to allow individuals to convey tone or emotion effectively (i.e., *bandwidth*), while providing less *privacy* than a text message because others can overhear and even record the conversations (Fox & McEwan, 2017). Thus, affordances are distinct from both features of channels and outcomes of their use (Evans et al., 2017).

Fox and McEwan (2017) argued that "channel attributes vary, and emerging communication technologies have attributes unlike other interpersonal or mass communication channels . . . and as such, they have distinct social implications" (p. 298). They also defined perceived social affordances, several of which are relevant for using CMC to maintain friendships. *Synchronicity* describes a central affordance of communication channels. Synchronous channels transmit (non)verbal messages in real time (e.g., phone call, FaceTime), whereas asynchronous channels afford a gap in time between messages (e.g., email, text message). If a person reaches out to their best friend for an important reason, such as a birthday greeting or condolences after a breakup, they might select a synchronous channel to increase feelings of closeness. Meanwhile, text messaging (asynchronous) the same friend about lunch plans for next week is likely more convenient than a synchronous phone call that might interrupt their day.

The *bandwidth* of a channel reflects the degree to which channels disseminate various (non)verbal cues (Fox & McEwan, 2017). For example, weekend plans with your best friend can be scheduled easily without extra social cues; therefore, a text message might be sufficient. Conversely, a serious conversation about a recent argument might be better handled over Facetime where facial expressions and vocal tones are available. *Network association* describes how visible CMC connections are between social circles. For example, users are connected to several social groups, such as friends and family, on Instagram, and these otherwise separate groups can view interactions with others. Meanwhile, an online gaming account holds *less* network association if family members are not invited to join a live chat among friends.

Social presence describes perceived closeness between interactants, such that channels with higher levels of social presence make communication partners feel like they are closer with one another when interacting. Friends might select a channel with more social presence when trying to feel near or remove the perception of mediation from an interaction. The affordance of *privacy* describes how some CMC settings allow people to restrict access to their messages. Friends are likely to consider the privacy of an interaction when sharing sensitive information that would be inappropriate for others to see (Fox & McEwan, 2017). Thus, different channels are perceived to contain different affordances that might shape the communication and outcomes experienced between friends.

Balancing Affordances Across Multiple Channels Within Friendships

With a foundational understanding of affordances, we can consider the role of technologically mediated platforms in maintaining friendships. Friends have an abundance of channels available, each affording their users a different set of options. To this point, although we have noted that people use multiple channels to maintain their friendships, and that each channel possesses affordances that users perceive to be more or less valuable to an interaction, we know less about how people consider or attempt to manage affordances across the network of channels they use to communicate. When people integrate, segment, or otherwise manage multiple channels, they might need to balance effective, efficient, or ideal levels of affordances. Researchers might achieve the best understanding of how technology shapes relationships by considering how affordances are perceived and balanced across a collection of channels.

The idea of balancing affordances across a collection of channels combines our focus on multiple channels and outcomes from MMT and the CIP with research on the importance of affordances for understanding people's selection, use, and outcomes of interacting in different channels. Although researchers relate technological affordances to outcomes (Evans et al., 2017), scholars have yet to identify how individuals may select unique collections of channels and their corresponding affordances to develop or maintain friendships. In a preliminary attempt to move research on the balancing of affordances across multiple channels forward, we present three hypotheses that aim to explore some possibilities regarding how friends select unique sets of channels and affordances to maintain connections. These hypotheses represent a dynamic set of preferences that can vary in any given user based on variations in individual differences or social situations. In particular, we suggest that people balance affordances across a variety of channels in ways that are motivated by a complementary, maximization, or minimization view of affordances.

Complementary Hypothesis

Scholars have claimed that people select channels to meet specific interpersonal needs or goals (O'Sullivan, 2000). In line with that thinking, our first hypothesis posits that friends select channels with a complementary combination of affordances. More specifically, we suggest that people select channels with affordances that work together to generate desired social outcomes or complement the needs of an exchange. People might have ideal levels of an affordance and work to meet those desires across a range of channels with some channels possessing greater or lower amounts of the affordance but averaging to the desired level in a complementary way across channels.

From a complementary perspective, friends might choose communication channels based on their friendship or goals for a particular interaction or outcome. Along these lines, Dimmick and colleagues (2000) found that friends often used multiple communication channels to fulfill different needs. For instance, phone calls and text messages can fulfill motivations for connection, but in different ways. Friends may use text messaging to coordinate a get-together, benefiting from the ability to view and respond to a message at their leisure (i.e., asynchronicity, accessibility) and easily see a record of the exchange (i.e., persistence). However, if friends plan to have a serious or intimate discussion, they might complement their needs by selecting channels that allow for synchronous and socially present interactions. Compared with text messages, phone calls are viewed as a more personal form of communication, providing users with synchronous, cue-rich conversation, and friends might value this mix of affordances across channels (Yang et al., 2014). Supported by research on long-distance friends, phone calls are often used for intimate conversations over text-based communication (Utz, 2007), although texting and its related affordances likely complement phone calls for other relational goals. Research has identified that phone calls are a superior option for maintaining personal relationships because they allow for more effective expression of emotion, advice, and information. In contrast, when coordinating plans and activities, phone calls are limited by different time zones and work schedules, and e-mail or text is a preferred form of communication because it allows friends to communicate when convenient (Dimmick et al., 2000). In a similar vein, research on social sharing observes that people prefer channels like Twitter or texting to share positive events, whereas they use phone calls and face-to-face interactions with their respective affordances to share negative information (Choi & Toma, 2014). This research documents that people consider and balance relevant affordances across the collection of channels they use to maintain their relationships.

In sum, our first hypothesis suggests that people select channels with complementary affordances. That is, they desire certain action possibilities within their friendships, and they balance those affordances across an array of channels. Research often focuses on comparing different channels; however, researchers could uncover interesting results by examining the combination of affordances offered by multiple channels.

Maximization Hypothesis

Our maximization hypothesis posits that people select channels to maximize the affordances they think will produce beneficial relational outcomes. This hypothesis proposes that people maximize the affordances they value across all of the channels they use. For example, if friends who are geographically separated want to feel present and emotionally connected in each other's lives, they might communicate through a collection of channels that maximize social presence and bandwidth. They might privilege Skype, Zoom, FaceTime, and phone calls. Along similar lines, the cue cumulation effect argues that there is an additive effect of certain social cues based on an accumulation of content overtime (Sundar et al, 2007).

People might maximize affordances by choosing channels with more options for interaction and impression management over channels with comparatively fewer options. For instance, Abeele and collaborators (2017) documented that friends use mobile devices for a variety of communication tasks because those technologies afford accessibility, privacy, and the ability to control the phrasing of a message before it is sent (i.e., editability). In a similar vein, Karahanna and colleagues (2018) observed that Facebook can gratify needs for autonomy, relatedness, and expression of self-identity through affordances that allow users to passively browse content posted by friends (i.e., persistence), establish relationships and communicate with their network (i.e., network association), and selectively self-present and share content (i.e., editability, information control). Other research contends that the affordance of anonymity can be useful for voicing complaints because it brings about a perception of safety (Mao & DeAndrea, 2019), so if people perceive face threats related to communicating a message, they might elect to maximize anonymity across a range of channels. Those channels that provide access to multiple affordances make it easy to maximize a variety of affordances, especially when used in combination with other channels.

Under the maximization hypothesis, channels that provide a variety of modalities for interaction should be used by those who seek a wide range of affordances. Overall, this hypothesis suggests that friends attempt to maximize their desired affordances across a combination of channels.

Minimization Hypothesis

Scholars traditionally claimed that more complex messages require a rich channel to communicate effectively (Daft & Lengel, 1986); however, there are also instances when people may prefer to communicate through leaner media. Likewise, our third hypothesis proposes that there are circumstances when people select channels to minimize or reduce the presence of affordances. Research has claimed advantages to communicating in spaces where verbal and nonverbal cues are limited (Caplan, 2003; Caplan & Turner, 2007). In fact, fewer cues related to the affordances of social presence or bandwidth are the foundation of the hyperpersonal perspective (Walther, 1996). In social media, due to the reduction of social cues, individuals may be less concerned about how others perceive them (Valkenburg & Peter, 2009). When seeking social support or disclosing sensitive information, people also prefer the reduced cues or privacy afforded by some channels (Caplan, 2003), and reduced bandwidth and social presence allow communicators to reallocate cognitive resources to effective message construction (Walther, 1996).

From a minimization perspective, there are occasions when friends may appreciate the ability to reduce the presence or impact of particular affordances when interacting with one another. By reducing affordances such as bandwidth and social presence, people may use technology to control their verbal and nonverbal expressions (i.e., information control) and mask certain aspects of themselves. Reducing affordances that convey personal information or cues appeals to people who are seeking to express important aspects of themselves without fear of repercussion (Caplan & Turner, 2007; DeAndrea, 2015). For instance, research notes that channels that convey reduced presence help promote self-disclosure about stigmatized health topics (DeAndrea, 2015). People with higher social anxiety also experience more positive interaction outcomes when they communicate in channels with lower levels of bandwidth and social presence (High & Caplan, 2009).

People report advantages to maintaining friendships through social media in part because of their reduction in particular affordances (Anderson & Jiang, 2018). Research supports that short, frequent, asynchronous exchanges through social media can provide people with a high sense of social support from their network (Lu & Hampton, 2017). People often select channels with fewer cues, perhaps including private chat on social media, when they need to reveal negatively valanced personal information because they perceive these channels to provide a buffer between them and their partners (O'Sullivan, 2000). These examples demonstrate instances when people benefit by selecting a collection of channels that minimize certain affordances.

Conclusion

Many contemporary friendships are maintained through a mix of channels, often involving a combination of online and offline options. This chapter reviewed theory relevant to mixed-media friendships and established affordances as a mechanism that explains why certain channels are more or less useful or valued among friends. Moreover, we offered three hypotheses to explain how friends can balance the channels and corresponding affordances at their disposal when maintaining relationships across channels. These hypotheses are dynamic, such that they are not tied to people but vary based on friendship qualities, desired characteristics, and situational goals. Scholars have noted the importance of considering the role affordances play in shaping social interactions and maintaining relational ties (Fox & McEwan, 2017; Karahanna et al., 2018; Ruppel et al., 2018). By investigating the hypotheses offered in this chapter and considering affordances in combination across channels, we can advance our understanding of how people use a number of communication channels to establish, develop, and maintain friendships.

References

Abeele, M. V., Schouten, A. P., & Antheunis, M. L. (2017). Personal, editable, and always accessible: An affordance approach to the relationship between adolescents' mobile messaging behavior and their friendship quality. *Journal of Social and Personal Relationships*, 34(6), 875–893. https://doi.org/10.1177%2F0265407516660636

Acquisti, A., Brandimarte, L., & Loewenstein, G. (2015). Privacy and human behavior in the age of information. *Science*, 347(6221), 509–514. http://www.jstor.org/stable/24745782

Anderson, M., & Jiang, J. (2018). Teens' social media habits and experiences. Pew Research Center. https://www.pewinternet.org/2018/11/28/teens-social-media-habits-and-experiences/

Balayar, B. B., & Langlais, M. R. (2021). Parental support, learning performance, and socioemotional development of children and teenagers during the COVID-19 pandemic. *The Family Journal*, 30(2), 174–183. https://doi.org/10.1177/10664807211052496

Caplan, S. E. (2003). Preference for online social interaction: A theory of problematic Internet use and psychosocial well-being. *Communication Research*, 30, 625–648. https://doi.org/10.1177/0093650203257842

Caplan, S. E., & Turner, J. S. (2007). Bringing theory to research on computer-mediated comforting communication. *Computers in Human Behavior*, 23, 985–998. https://doi.org/10.1016/j.chb.2005.08.003

Caughlin, J. P., & Sharabi, L. L. (2013). A communicative interdependence perspective of close relationships: The connections between mediated and unmediated interactions matter. *Journal of Communication*, 63, 837–893. https://doi.org/10.1111/jcom.12046

Chan, G. H. (2020). Intimacy, friendship, and forms of online communication among Hidden Youth in Hong Kong. *Computers in Human Behavior*, 111(1), Article 106407. https://doi.org/10.1016/j.chb.2020.106407

Choi, M., & Toma, C. L. (2014). Social sharing through interpersonal media: Patterns and effects on emotional well-being. *Computers in Human Behavior*, 36, 530–541. https://doi.org/10.1016/j.chb.2014.04.026

Daft, R. L., and Lengel, R. J. (1986). Organizational information requirements, media richness and structural design. *Management Science*, 32, 554–571. https://doi.org/10.1287/mnsc.32.5.554

DeAndrea, D. C. (2014). Advancing warranting theory. *Communication Theory, 24*(2), 186–204. https://doi.org/10.1111/comt.12033

DeAndrea, D. C. (2015). Testing the proclaimed affordances of online support groups in a nationally representative sample of adults seeking mental health assistance. *Journal of Health Communication, 20*, 147–156. https://doi.org/10.1080/10810730.2014.914606

Dimmick, J., Kline, S., & Stafford, L. (2000). The gratification niches of personal e-mail and the telephone: Competition, displacement, and complementarity. *Communication Research, 27*(2), 227–248. https://doi.org/10.1177/009365000027002005

Dindia, K., & Canary, D. J. (1993). Definitions and theoretical perspectives on maintaining relationships. *Journal of Social and Personal Relationships, 10*(2), 163–173. https://doi.org/10.1177/0265407593010002 01

Ellison, N. B., Vitak, J., Gray, R., & Lampe, C. (2014). Cultivating social resources on social network sites: Facebook relationship maintenance behaviors and their role in social capital processes. *Journal of Computer-Mediated Communication, 19*(4), 855–870. https://doi.org/10.1111/jcc4.12078

Evans, S. K., Pearce, K. E., Vitak, J., & Treem, J. W. (2017). Explicating affordances: A conceptual framework for understanding affordances in communication research. *Journal of Computer-Mediated Communication, 22*, 35–52. https://doi.org/10.1111/jcc4.12180

Fehr, B. (2012). Friendship. In V. S. Ramachandran (Ed.), *Encyclopedia of human behavior* (2nd ed., pp. 205–213). Elsevier. https://doi.org/10.1016/b978-0-12-375000-6.00174-9

Fox, J., & McEwan, B. (2017). Distinguishing technologies for social interaction: The perceived social affordances of communication channels scale. *Communication Monographs, 84*(3), 298–318. https://doi.org/10.1080/03637751.2017.1332418

Hall, J. A., & Baym, N. K. (2012). Calling and texting (too much): Mobile maintenance expectations, (over)dependence, entrapment, and friendship satisfaction. *New Media & Society, 14*, 316–331. https://doi.org/10.1177%2F1461444811415047

Haythornthwaite, C. (2002). Strong, weak and latent ties and the impact of new media. *The Information Society, 18*(5), 385–401. https://doi.org/10.1080/01972240290108195

Haythornthwaite, C. (2005). Social networks and internet connectivity effects. *Information, Communication & Society, 8*(2), 125–147. https://doi.org/10.1080/13691180500146185

High, A. C., & Buehler, E. M. (2019). Receiving supportive communication from Facebook friends: A model of social ties and supportive communication in social network sites. *Journal of Social and Personal Relationships, 36*(3), 719–740. https://doi.org/10.1177%2F0265407517742978

High, A. C., & Caplan, S. E. (2009). Social anxiety and computer-mediated communication during initial interactions: Implications for the hyperpersonal perspective. *Computers in Human Behavior, 25*, 475–482. https://doi.org/10.1016/j.chb.2008.10.011

Igarashi, T., Takai, J., & Yoshida, T. (2005). Gender differences in social network development via mobile phone text messages: A longitudinal study. *Journal of Social and Personal Relationships, 22*, 691–713. https://doi.org/10.1177/0265407505056492

Johnson, A. J., Haigh, M. M., Craig, E. A., & Becker, J. A. (2009). Relational closeness: Comparing undergraduate college students' geographically close and long-distance friendships. *Personal Relationships, 16*, 631–646. https://doi.org/10.1111/j.1475-6811.2009.01243.x

Karahanna, E., Xu, S. X., Xu, Y., & Zhang, N. A. (2018). The needs–affordances–features perspective for the use of social media. *MIS Quarterly, 42*(3), 737–756. https://doi.org/10.25300/MISQ/2018/11492

Ledbetter, A. M. (2009). Patterns of media use and multiplexity: Associations with sex, geographic distance and friendship interdependence. *New Media & Society, 11*, 1187–1208. https://doi.org/10.1177%2F1461444809342057

Lu, W., & Hampton, K. N. (2017). Beyond the power of networks: Differentiating network structure from social media affordances for perceived social support. *New Media & Society, 19*(6), 861–879. https://doi.org/10.1177/1461444815621514

Mao, C. M., & DeAndrea, D. C. (2019). How anonymity and visibility affordances influence employees' decisions about voicing workplace concerns. *Management Communication Quarterly, 33*(2), 160–188. https://doi.org/10.1177%2F0893318918813202

Marder, B., Joinson, A., Shankar, A., & Thirlaway, K. (2016). Strength matters: Self-presentation to the strongest audience rather than lowest common denominator when faced with multiple audiences in social network sites. *Computers in Human Behavior, 61*, 56–62. https://doi.org/10.1016/j.chb.2016.03.005

Nabi, R. L., Prestin, A., & So, J. (2013). Facebook friends with (health) benefits? Exploring social network site use and perceptions of social support, stress, and well-being. *CyberPsychology, Behavior, and Social Networking, 16*, 1–7. https://doi.org/10.1089/cyber.2012.0521

O'Sullivan, B. (2000). What you don't know won't hurt me: Impression management functions of communication channels in relationships. *Human Communication Research, 26*(3), 403–431. https://doi.org/10.1111/j.1468-2958.2000.tb00763.x

Oswald, D. L. & Clark E. M. (2003). Best friends forever? High school best friendships and the transition to college. *Personal Relationships, 10*, 187–196. https://doi.org/10.1111/1475-6811.00045

Pahl, R., & Spencer, L. (2004). Personal communities: Not simply families of "fate" or "choice." *Current Sociology, 52*(2), 199–221. https://doi.org/10.1177/0011392104041808

Parks, M. R. (2017). Embracing the challenges and opportunities of mixed-media relationships. *Human Communication Research, 43*(4), 505–517. https://doi.org/10.1111/hcre.12125

Perfumi, S. C., Bagnoli, F., Caudek, C., & Guazzini, A. (2019). Deindividuation effects on normative and informational social influence within computer-mediated-communication. *Computers in Human Behavior, 92*, 230–237. https://doi.org/10.1016/j.chb.2018.11.017

Pouwels, J. L., Valkenburg, P. M., Beyens, I., van Driel, I. I., & Keijsers, L. (2021). Social media use and friendship closeness in adolescents' daily lives: An experience sampling study. *Developmental Psychology, 57*(2), 309–323. http://dx.doi.org/10.1037/dev0001148

Pusateri, K. B., Roaché, D. J., & Wang, N. (2015). The role of communication technologies in serial arguments: A communicative interdependence perspective. *Argumentation & Advocacy, 52*(1), 44–60. https://doi.org/10.1080/00028533.2015.11821860

Putnam, R. D. (2000). *Bowling alone: The collapse and revival of American community*. Simon & Schuster.

Ramirez, A., & Broneck, K. (2009). "IM me": Instant messaging as relational maintenance and everyday communication. *Journal of Social and Personal Relationships, 26*(2–3), 291–314. https://doi.org/10.1177/0265407509106719

Ruppel, E. K., Burke, T. J., & Cherney, M. R. (2018). Channel complementarity and multiplexity in long-distance friends' patterns of communication technology use. *New Media & Society, 20*(4), 1564–1579. https://doi.org/10.1177/1461444817699995

Rusbult, C. E., & Van Lange, P. A. M. (1996). Interdependence processes. In E. T. Higgins & A. W. Kruglanski (Eds.), *Social psychology: Handbook of basic principles* (pp. 564–596). Guilford.

Sharabi, L. L., & Hall, E. D. (2021). Conceptualizing and measuring communication interdependence: The technology and face-to-face integration scale. *Communication Methods and Measures, 15*(3), 222–242. https://doi.org/10.1080/19312458.2021.1894325

Sundar, S. S., Knobloch-Westerwick, S., & Hastall, M. R. (2007). News cues: Information scent and cognitive heuristics. *Journal of the American Society for Information Science and Technology, 58*, 366–378. https://doi.org/10.1002/asi.20511

Taddicken, M. (2014). The "privacy paradox" in the social web: The impact of privacy concerns, individual characteristics, and the perceived social relevance on different forms of self-disclosure. *Journal of Computer-Mediated Communication, 19*(2), 248–273. https://doi.org/10.1111/jcc4.12052

Toma, C. L., & Sarmiento, I. G. (2018). Connection, conflict, and communication technologies: How romantic couples use the media for relationship management. In Z. Papacharissi (Ed.), *A networked self and love* (pp. 62–85). Routledge.

Utz, S. (2007). Media use in long-distance friendships. *Information, Communication & Society, 10*, 694–713. https://doi.org/10.1080/13691180701658046

Valkenburg, P. M., & Peter, J. (2009). Social consequences of the Internet for adolescents: A decade of research. *Current Directions in Psychological Science, 18*(1), 1–5. https://doi.org/10.1111/j.1467-8721.2009.01595.x

Vanzetti, N., & Duck, S. (Eds.). (1996). *A lifetime of relationships*. Thomson Brooks/Cole Publishing Co.

Vitak, J., & Ellison, N. B. (2013). "There's a network out there you might as well tap": Exploring the benefits of and barriers to exchanging informational and support-based resources on Facebook. *New Media & Society, 15*(2), 243–259. https://doi-org.ezaccess.libraries.psu.edu/10.1177/1461444812451566

Walther, J. B. (1996). Computer-mediated communication: Impersonal, interpersonal, and hyperpersonal interaction. *Communication Research, 23*(1), 3–43. https://doi.org/10.1177%2F009365096023001001

Yang, C., Brown, B. B., & Braun, M. T. (2014). From Facebook to cell calls: Layers of electronic intimacy in college students' interpersonal relationships. *New Media & Society, 16*, 5–23. https://doi.org/10.1177%2F1461444812472486

13
The New and Significant Role of Friendship in the 21st Century

Emily T. Beauparlant, Mahzad Hojjat,
Nicole Melancon, and Laura V. Machia

The typical timeline for milestones in adulthood has changed; postponing marriage and staying single longer have become the norm rather than the exception in many countries around the world. Considering the declining rates of marriage and an increase in single-person households (OECD, 2019; Ortiz-Ospina, 2019), a considerable percentage of the adult population today lives without a romantic partner (Kislev, 2019). Past research suggests that despite the importance of romantic relationships for individuals, friends and family can play significant roles in fulfilling individuals' emotional, social, material, and economical needs in lieu of a romantic partner (Bellotti, 2008; Carbery & Buhrmester, 1998). In this chapter, we will provide an overview of the current research concerning the postponement of marriage, increase in singlehood, and need fulfillment in single adults. Further, we will explore in more detail the notion that single adults may be able to satisfy their psychological needs through other means, for example, alternative social relationships such as friendships.

Changes in Relational Value System

Many developed countries have witnessed a fundamental and multifaceted transformation in their intimate relationships within the last few decades (Kislev, 2020; Roseneil & Budgeon, 2004). The direction of these changes has been away from traditional institutionalized relationships like marriage and toward more temporary and decentralized relationships such as cohabitation (see Chapter 3) and friendship. Scholars have suggested that these transformations are due to a significant cultural shift to increasingly individualistic norms and attitudes (Kislev, 2018; Sassler & Lichter, 2020) and reinforced by the process of globalization, which creates new geographical opportunities and increased mobility but also amplifies the problem of fragmentation, especially in urban settings (Bellotti, 2008). Never-married-before individuals are especially drawn to urban environments in order to connect with communities of singles and take advantage of what has been called "social capital" (Coleman, 1988; Gautier et al., 2010; Kislev, 2018). In this context, social capital is the notion that "individuals and groups can gain resources from their connections to one another" (Paxton, 1999, p. 89). Social capital includes mutually beneficial exchanges of social and instrumental support as well as the opportunity to participate in social activities together and feel that one belongs to a larger community (Leung et al, 2011).

In our increasingly "networked society," the Internet revolution has diminished permanent group boundaries and has expanded our ability to form interpersonal ties with ease and speed, transitory as they may be (McEwen & Wellman, 2013). Accordingly, scholars across disciplines have lauded the rising importance of friendship (Bellotti, 2008; Hojjat & Moyer, 2017; Huxhold, 2019) and its function "as a social glue of contemporary Western society" (McEwen & Wellman, 2013, p. 168). Friendship, as a relationship that is characterized as informal, non-obligatory, non-exclusive, and often temporary, is considered the "archetype of affective relationship" today (Bellotti, 2008, p. 318).

Traditional marriage, on the other hand, is undergoing a process of further deinstitutionalization as the social norms associated with marriage are being challenged by a rise in individualism (Kislev, 2018). More specifically, the emphasis on institutional unionization has decreased, while the importance of personal choice and self-development has increased (Cherlin, 2020). This trend is part of what has been called a "postmaterialist" or "postmodern" value system, which places great emphasis on subjective well-being and self-expression (Inglehart & Baker, 2000). Similarly, other research (Timonen & Doyle, 2014) has found that those who remain single by choice associate singlehood with values such as independence, autonomy, and self-fulfillment throughout their lives, including during their older years. Relatedly, Kislev (2018) conducted an analysis of the data from the European Social Survey collected between 2002 and 2014. Utilizing the Schwartz Values Inventory (Schwartz, 1992, 2003) with a focus on aspects of post-materialism values that are relevant to singlehood (i.e., self-actualization and self-expression), he reported that post-materialist views were associated with greater levels of happiness for singles than for partnered individuals.

In a recent online study, Beauparlant and colleagues (2021) examined young adults' personal values as well as their attitudes about marriage, including the motivation to pursue alternatives, in particular higher education and career. Participants were 372 individuals from across the United States between the ages of 18 and 39 ($M = 27.23$, $SD = 6.34$). The participants self-identified as White (67.74%), Black (12.37%), Asian (6.99%), multiracial (6.99%), Latinx (4.57%), and Native American (0.27%), and 1.08% self-identified as another race. Personal values were measured using the Schwartz Values Inventory (Schwartz, 1992). The findings regarding three values—achievement, self-direction, and universalism—are relevant here. Schwartz (2012) defines the goal of achievement to be obtaining personal success through demonstrating competence and the associated characteristics to include ambitious, successful, and influential. The goal of self-direction is to pursue independent thought and action and to create as well as explore. Finally, universalism includes tolerance and appreciation of all living things and nature. The value items associated with universalism include broad-mindedness, social justice, and equality (Schwartz, 2012). The results indicated that individuals who scored higher on achievement and self-direction were more likely to report a preference to postpone marriage to pursue career goals. Moreover, universalism was associated with a preference to cohabit before marriage. The results of this study are consistent with findings from previous research (Kislev, 2018) suggesting that the rise of post-materialist values such as independence and self-fulfillment are associated with the desire to postpone marriage. At the same time, the association between universalism and a preference to cohabit before marriage may signal a shift towards embracing alternative and transitory lifestyles as opposed to more traditional relationships such as a formal courtship or marriage.

Postponement of Marriage

As people's personal values and social networks have evolved, it has become normative to postpone marriage until later in adulthood. The median age of first marriage in the United States has steadily risen over the past several decades (Smock & Schwartz, 2020). In 1990, the median age at first marriage was 26.1 and 23.9 for men and women, respectively; in 2021, the median age at first marriage was 30.4 years for men and 28.6 years for women (U.S. Census Bureau, 2021). The decline in marriage rates in the United States is due to a combination of postponement of marriage, increases in singlehood, and nonmarital cohabitation (Manning et al., 2014). Some scholars have suggested that several social, economic, and cultural factors may influence the decision to delay marriage, for example, women's increasing economic independence, a rise in divorce and cohabitation, and the increase in childbearing outside of marriage (Smock, 2004).

Further, according to Wilson's (1987) "marriageable male" hypothesis, the decline in marriage is at least partially due to the decline in employment and earnings prospects for men. Indeed, women's educational levels now surpass men's (Van Bavel et al., 2018) such that women are now less financially dependent on spouses compared with previous generations and more likely to marry someone with lower educational attainment (Gibson-Davis et al., 2005; Lichter et al., 2004). In fact, due to this surplus of highly educated women, there are an insufficient number of demographically similar men for heterosexual women to marry (Lichter et al., 2020). This is what Lichter and colleagues (2020) refer to as the "marriage market shortage," which they posit is one explanation for the decline in marriage rates. As a result of this imbalance, an increasing number of women either choose to delay marriage or forego it altogether (Gibson-Davis et al., 2005; Lichter et al., 2004).

Increase in Singlehood

Unsurprisingly, while the rate of marriage has been decreasing, there has also been an increase in the number of single adults. The proportion of unmarried adults in the United States has increased rapidly over the past several decades. In 1970, approximately 28% of the U.S. population was unmarried, but by 2010, this increased to nearly 44% (U.S. Census Bureau, 1970, 2011). This is partially due to the increase in nonmarital cohabitation, but even so, there has also been a substantial increase in single-person households (OECD, 2019), suggesting that many unmarried adults are also unpartnered. This substantial increase in unpartnered adults raises some concerns considering long-term singles report greater depression and anxiety compared with those who are partnered (Schachner et al., 2008). However, it is important to recognize that singles are a heterogenous group (see Chapter 4 of this volume). Some scholars have suggested that there are three subgroups of long-term singles: those who are single due to attachment system deactivation, attachment system hyperactivation, or personal preference (Pepping et al., 2018). Regarding those who are single for attachment style reasons, some research suggests that single people tend to be higher in attachment insecurity compared withthose with partners (Chopik et al., 2013). Further, singles with avoidant attachment tendencies are unlikely to fulfill their intimacy needs with other social relationships (Mikulincer & Shaver, 2012).

On the other hand, some people are happily single by choice (DePaulo, 2014). Lehmann and colleagues (2015) report that a minority of singles, about 13.2%, report not wanting to be in a relationship (Lehmann et al., 2015). Chosen singlehood is associated with several well-being outcomes including satisfaction with being single, self-fulfillment, and personal autonomy, whereas involuntary singlehood is associated with regret and dissatisfaction with singlehood (Timonen & Doyle, 2014). Relatedly, satisfaction with singlehood is associated with higher life satisfaction and less distress (Lehmann et al., 2015). Past research suggests that single people can successfully meet their attachment needs through nonromantic relationships (Doherty & Feeney, 2004; Fraley et al., 2011). In fact, Spielmann and colleagues (2013) found that the most common reason for *not* fearing singlehood was having friends and family to rely on.

The Increasing Importance of Friendship

As the number of single adults has increased, people's social networks have also shifted. In recent work, scholars have considered the roles of broader contextual and societal factors in the development of individuals' social networks (Huxhold, 2019; Suanet & Antonucci, 2017). According to the social convoy model (Antonucci et al., 2014), changes in one's social network are partially due to contextual differences, for example, historical changes. Considering ongoing societal changes, including the increase in singlehood, postponement of marriage, and deinstitutionalization of marriage (Cherlin, 2020), there is greater flexibility in the composition of social networks (Allan, 2008). Some studies suggest that the maintenance of friendships is increasing in importance among adults (Wang & Wellman, 2010). Recent studies on older adults also suggest that later-born cohorts have larger social networks with a greater proportion of friends compared with earlier-born cohorts (Huxhold, 2019; Suanet & Huxhold, 2020; Suanet et al., 2013). For example, Suanet and Antonucci (2017) found cohort differences in network types among older adults (aged 55–64), such that those born in the latest cohort (1948–1957) were more likely to have a friend-focused social network compared with those born in earlier cohorts (1928–1937 and 1938–1947). They also found that the latest-born cohort had friends who were more likely to fulfill needs typically met by family members (Suanet & Antonucci, 2017). Relatedly, there is a growing population of childless adults in the United States and Europe (Rowland, 2007), and childfree people are also reliant on friends for support (Basten, 2009). This is seen across the life span, as evidence suggests that older, childless adults rely on friends in place of family members (Klaus & Schnettler, 2016). Taken together, friends appear to be increasing in importance in many adults' lives.

Need Fulfillment and Singlehood Satisfaction

As more people live without partners, it is important to understand how their needs are being met. People have universal psychological needs that, when met, will increase subjective well-being (Costanza et al, 2007). Close relationships are fundamental to psychological need fulfillment, and romantic relationships specifically are well suited to meet psychological needs (Finkel et al., 2014). According to interdependence theory (IT) (Rusbult & Van Lange, 2003; Thibaut & Kelley, 1959), psychological need fulfillment fosters two types of outcomes that promote relationship well-being: concrete and symbolic outcomes. For example, a concrete outcome is the experience of pleasure or pain (Rusbult & Van Lange, 2003). An example of a symbolic outcome is feeling confident that a need fulfillment source will be available in the future, for example, a person feeling confident their partner will be available to meet their needs in the future. Considering the importance of romantic relationships in the context of need fulfillment and well-being, it is imperative to understand need fulfillment processes in single adults. When people perceive that their needs have been met, they are more satisfied with their relationships (Drigotas & Rusbult, 1992), and satisfaction with one's social life is a strong predictor of subjective well-being (Argyle, 2001).

Whereas romantic partners are typically the preferred source of psychological need fulfillment for adults (Finkel et al., 2014), friends, family, and other relationships are also able to fulfill those same needs. For single adults, friends and family members can fulfill a person's need for companionship and emotional intimacy, decreasing the need for a romantic relationship (Felmlee, 2001). In recent work, Machia and Proulx (2020) found that need fulfillment from outside of a person's romantic relationship was indirectly but positively associated with relationship dissolution consideration via the increase in the perceived quality of alternatives to their relationship. This provides further support for the notion that friends and romantic partners can fulfill similar psychological needs for individuals. Moreover, if a person feels that their needs can be met through alternative means, they may choose to seek another partner or choose to remain single. Thus, it is plausible that single adults may find fulfillment through alternative relationships, including friendships.

Individuals' ability to meet their needs outside of a romantic relationship will likely influence their satisfaction with singlehood. Park and colleagues (2021) examined how having a satisfactory social or sex life is associated with satisfaction with singlehood and the desire to marry. They found that single individuals with higher sexual satisfaction had less desire to marry, believed that unmarried people could be happy, and were less interested in a romantic partner and more satisfied with singlehood. Further, they found that having high-quality friendships was associated with the belief that unmarried people could be happy and satisfied with singlehood. This was unique to friendship, as there was no significant association between satisfaction with family relationships and singlehood satisfaction (Park et al., 2021). Other recent work by Oh and colleagues (2021) yielded similar results. Using a longitudinal design, they found that among individuals who were inconsistently single, that is, those who were going in and out of romantic relationships, satisfaction with friendships and familial relationships were both predictors of singlehood and life satisfaction (Oh et al., 2021). Conversely, for people who were consistently single, that is, those who were not involved in any romantic relationships, their satisfaction with friendships and familial relationships predicted life satisfaction, but not singlehood satisfaction (Oh et al., 2021). Collectively, these studies demonstrate the impact of sexual and social need fulfillment on singlehood and life satisfaction and highlight the importance of friendships.

The Investment Model as Applied to Single Adults

It is likely that need fulfillment and singlehood satisfaction are also related to *commitment* to singlehood. The investment model of commitment (Rusbult, 1980) suggests that there are three factors that predict commitment level in a relationship: satisfaction, quality of alternatives, and investment size. According to the investment model, relationship commitment is highest when relationship satisfaction is high, perceived quality of alternatives to the relationship is low, and relationship investment is high. This model is a powerful predictor of commitment across romantic relationships, including marital relationships and friendships (Rusbult et al., 1998). More broadly, the investment model provides a useful framework for predicting commitment to someone or something (Rusbult et al., 2012). According to the investment model, single individuals who are highly satisfied with singlehood, perceive their alternatives to singlehood (e.g., a potential romantic relationship) as less desirable, and are highly invested in being single should be more committed to staying single. In regard to need fulfillment, those who are able to successfully meet their needs without a romantic partner will likely be more satisfied with being single (Oh et al., 2021; Park et al., 2021) and in turn, more committed to singlehood.

Currently, there is a dearth of research on both need fulfillment processes among single adults and commitment to singlehood. A recent online study (Beauparlant & Machia, 2021) sought to explore how single adults fulfill their needs outside of romantic relationships. Specifically, the researchers measured the fulfillment of the three innate needs according to self-determination theory: autonomy, competence, and relatedness (Patrick et al., 2007), as well as self-expansion (Aron & Aron, 1986). They also included a version of the investment model scale (Rusbult et al., 1998) adapted for singles, to capture satisfaction with and commitment to singlehood, and associations with various well-being measures. The sample included 193 young adults from the Northeastern United States. Participants were 40.93% men and 59.07% women between the ages of 18 and 23 ($M = 18.76$, $SD = 1.04$). The racial composition of the sample was 61.66% White, 20.21% Asian, 8.81% Hispanic/Latino, 5.70% Black, 0.52% Native American/Alaska Native, and 0.52% Native Hawaiian/Pacific Islander; 2.07% self-identified as another race and 0.52% did not provide their race.

To measure need fulfillment (adapted from VanderDrift & Agnew, 2012; Machia & Proulx, 2020), participants were given brief definitions of four needs (autonomy, relatedness, competence, and self-expansion) and were asked to list up to five sources that they thought could meet this particular need, including both actual and potential sources. Each need fulfillment source was categorized using the following groups: Partner (in the context of this sample, a potential partner), Friends, Structured Social Group (e.g., Fraternity), Hobby, Education, Job/Profession, Family, or Other interpersonal relationships (e.g., teachers, therapists, mentors). For each source given, participants also reported the percentage of their need that they *wanted* each source to meet in an average week (see Table 13.1). Averaged across the four needs, it appeared that participants wanted 22.65% of their overall need fulfillment (the largest percentage) to come from friends. Participants also wanted a considerable portion of their needs to come from family; specifically, they wanted 18.70% of their overall need fulfillment to come from family members. Overall, the findings support the notion that single individuals seek to fulfill their psychological needs through nonromantic relationships, most notably friends and family members. As predicted, single participants desired a substantial portion of their needs be met by their friends, which is in line with other recent findings (Oh et al., 2021; Park et al., 2021).

Further, using the newly adapted Investment Model Scale for Singles, the findings indicated that a person's satisfaction with singlehood and their investment in singlehood were both positively associated with their commitment to singlehood; conversely, a person's perceived quality of alternatives to singlehood was negatively correlated with commitment to singlehood. These results mirror the expected correlations from the original Investment Model

Table 13.1. Percentage of Need Fulfillment Desired by Source

Source	Autonomy M (SD)	Self-expansion M (SD)	Relatedness M (SD)	Competence M (SD)
Friends	21.18 (18.24)	24.48 (22.40)	32.28 (25.55)	13.18 (16.67)
Partner	3.59 (11.92)	3.86 (9.31)	5.51 (11.40)	1.42 (6.37)
Social group	0.83 (5.06)	1.74 (6.25)	1.88 (6.92)	1.14 (6.10)
Hobby	15.91 (20.17)	24.44 (25.43)	14.12 (24.15)	20.74 (26.25)
Education	12.20 (15.24)	13.47 (17.19)	8.03 (15.27)	23.87 (23.75)
Job	7.00 (11.76)	5.21 (10.62)	4.15 (9.61)	9.48 (15.18)
Family	23.50 (24.67)	14.15 (18.90)	22.22 (20.31)	14.93 (21.38)
Other interpersonal	2.28 (8.18)	4.18 (11.13)	4.16 (11.88)	5.76 (14.65)

Scale (Rusbult et al., 1998), which is typically used for partnered individuals. Finally, satisfaction with singlehood was positively associated with positive affect, partially supporting the prediction that singlehood satisfaction would be associated with well-being outcomes.

These preliminary results should be interpreted in light of their limitations. First, this study relied on a modestly sized convenience sample of undergraduate students. Future research should include a more diverse sample of participants, particularly in terms of age. For example, it is plausible that friendship is especially salient to college aged students, so it would be important to include participants from a broader age range in future work. Future research should also include *actual* need fulfillment in addition to desired need fulfillment, which is a significant limitation of this work. This would provide important insight into how a person's level of need fulfillment is associated with their satisfaction with singlehood and overall well-being. Another possible avenue for future research would be to compare the desired sources of need fulfillment of single versus partnered adults to see whether there are differences in the percentage desired from friends between the two groups.

Future Directions

In a broader sense, future research should distinguish between singles by choice and singles by circumstance in the context of need fulfillment. Scholars have suggested that singles are a heterogeneous group (Pepping et al., 2018), and it is plausible that whether a single person desires a partner may impact their satisfaction with their need fulfillment sources. As such, if a person desires their needs be met by a partner, they may be less satisfied with a friend meeting that same need. Future research may also consider a network perspective and examine whether it matters what percentage of a person's social network is partnered versus single. This may matter for need fulfillment because of the symmetrical nature of need fulfillment for both partners (VanderDrift & Agnew, 2012). For example, if a single person has a single friend, they may both respectively meet a larger percentage of each other's needs compared with if one of them were partnered. This is because romantic partners are typically a person's preferred source of need fulfillment (Finkel et al., 2014). Further, if a person is the *only* single individual in their social network, they may feel isolated by their single status or feel pressured to find a partner; in a similar vein, previous work demonstrates that family pressures to marry can make singles feel frustrated with their relationship status (Himawan et al., 2018). Finally, it is essential for future research to explore the nuances of need fulfillment for different groups of single individuals. For instance, subgroups of singles (e.g., women, sexual or ethnic minorities, older individuals) may have different needs (e.g., physical, psychological, emotional, informational) that could be satisfied by different means (e.g., friends, family, pets, hobbies, volunteering, traveling).

Conclusion

The current literature clearly demonstrates the growing importance of nonromantic relationships, particularly friendships, among single adults. As people postpone marriage and spend substantial portions of their lives unpartnered, friends can play an important role in a person's life and partially fulfill a person's important psychological needs. Need fulfillment is crucial to well-being outcomes, and as the number of single adults grows in the Western world, it is increasingly important to understand need fulfillment processes among this population.

References

Allan, G. (2008). Flexibility, friendship, and family. *Personal Relationships, 15*, 1–16. http://doi.org/10.1111/j.1475-6811.2007.00181.x

Antonucci, T. C., Ajrouch, K. J., & Birditt, K. S. (2014). The convoy model: Explaining social relations from a multidisciplinary perspective. *The Gerontologist, 54*, 82–92. https://doi.org/10.1093/geront/gnt118

Argyle, M. (2001). *The psychology of happiness* (2nd ed.). Routledge.

Aron, A., & Aron, E. N. (1986). *Love and the expansion of self: Understanding attraction and satisfaction.* Hemisphere Publishing Corp/Harper & Row Publishers.

Basten, S. (2009). *Voluntary childlessness and being childfree.* The Future of Human Reproduction: Working Paper No. 5, 1–23.

Beauparlant, E. T., Hojjat, M., & Machia, L.V. (2021). *Marriage can wait: Attitudes toward postponing marriage* [Unpublished manuscript, Department of Psychology, University of Massachusetts Dartmouth].

Beauparlant, E. T., & Machia, L. V. (2021). *Need fulfillment among single adults* [Unpublished manuscript, Department of Psychology, Syracuse University].

Bellotti, E. (2008). What are friends for? Elective communities of single people. *Social Networks, 30*, 318–329. https://doi.org/10.1016/j.socnet.2008.07.001

Carbery, J., & Buhrmester, D. (1998). Friendship and need fulfillment during three phases of young adulthood. *Journal of Social and Personal Relationships*, *15*(3), 393–409. https://doi.org/10.1177/0265407598153005

Cherlin, A. J. (2020). Degrees of change: An assessment of the deinstitutionalization of marriage thesis. *Journal of Marriage and Family*, *82*(1), 62–80. https://doi.org/10.1111/jomf.12605

Chopik, W. J., Edelstein, R. S., & Fraley, R. C. (2013). From the cradle to the grave: Age differences in attachment from early adulthood to old age. *Journal of Personality*, *81*, 171–183. https://doi.org/10.1111/j.1467-6494.2012.00793.x

Coleman, J. M. (1988). Social capital in the creation of human capital. *American Journal of Sociology*, *94*(Suppl.), S95–S120.

Costanza, R., Fisher, B., Ali, S., Beer, C. C., Bond, L., Boumans, R., Danigelis, N. L., Dickinson, J., Elliott, C., Farley, J., Gayer, D., Glenn, L. M., Hudspeth, T. R., Mahoney, D., McCahill, L., Mcintosh, B., Reed, B. V., Rizvi, S., Rizzo, D., . . . Snapp, R. (2007). Quality of life: An approach integrating opportunities, human needs, and subjective well-being. *Ecological Economics*, *61*, 267–276. https://doi.org/10.1016/j.ecolecon.2006.02.023

DePaulo, B. (2014). A singles studies perspective on mount marriage. *Psychological Inquiry*, *25*, 64–68. https://doi.org/10.1080/1047840X.2014.878173

Doherty, N. A., & Feeney, J. A. (2004). The composition of attachment networks throughout the adult years. *Personal Relationships*, *11*, 469–488. https://doi.org/10.1111/j.1475-6811.2004.00093

Drigotas, S. M., & Rusbult, C. E. (1992). Should I stay or should I go? A dependence model of breakups. *Journal of Personality and Social Psychology*, *62*(1), 62–87. https://doi.org/10.1037/0022-3514.62.1.62

Felmlee, D. H. (2001). No couple is an island: A social network perspective on dyadic stability. *Social Forces*, *79*(4), 1259–1287. https://doi.org/10.1353/sof.2001.0039

Finkel, E. J., Hui, C. M., Carswell, K. L., & Larson, G. M. (2014). The suffocation of marriage: Climbing Mount Maslow without enough oxygen. *Psychological Inquiry*, *25*(1), 1–41. https://doi.org/10.1080/1047840X.2014.863723

Fraley, R. C., Heffernan, M. E., Vicary, A. M., & Brumbaugh, C. C. (2011). The experiences in close relationships—Relationship Structures Questionnaire: A method for assessing attachment orientations across relationships. *Psychological Assessment*, *23*, 615–625. https://doi.org/10.1037/a0022898

Gautier, P. A., Svarer, M., & Teulings, C. N. (2010). Marriage and the city: Search frictions and sorting of singles. *Journal of Urban Economics*, *67*(2), 206–218. https://doi.org/10.1016/j.jue.2009.08.007

Gibson-Davis, C. M., Edin, K., & McLanahan, S. (2005). High hopes but even higher expectations: The retreat from marriage among low-income couples. *Journal of Marriage and Family*, *67*(5), 1301–1312. https://doi.org/10.1111/j.1741-3737.2005.00218.x

Himawan, K. K., Bambling, M., & Edirippulige, S. (2018). The Asian single profiles: Discovering many faces of never married adults in Asia. *Journal of Family Issues*, *39*, 3667–3689. https://doi.org/10.1177/0192513X18789205

Hojjat, M., & Moyer, A. (Eds.) (2017). *The psychology of friendship*. Oxford University Press. https://oxford.universitypressscholarship.com/view/10.1093/acprof:oso/9780190222024.001.0001/acprof-9780190222024

Huxhold, O. (2019). Gauging effects of historical differences on aging trajectories: The increasing importance of friendships. *Psychology and Aging*, *34*(8), 1170–1184. https://doi.org/10.1037/pag0000390

Inglehart, R., & Baker, W. E. (2000). Modernization, cultural change, and the persistence of traditional values. *American Sociological Review*, 19–51, 65(1), https://doi.org/10.2307/2657288

Kislev, E. (2018). Happiness, post-materialist values, and the unmarried. *Journal of happiness Studies*, 19(8), 2243–2265. https://doi.org/10.1007/s10902-017-9921-7

Kislev, E. (2019). *Happy singlehood: The rising acceptance and celebration of solo living.* University of California Press.

Kislev, E. (2020). Social capital, happiness, and the unmarried: A multilevel analysis of 32 European countries. *Applied Research in Quality of Life*, 15(5), 1475–1492. https://doi.org/10.1007/s11482-019-09751-y

Klaus, D., & Schnettler, S. (2016). Social networks and support for parents and childless adults in the second half of life: Convergence, divergence, or stability? *Advances in Life Course Research*, 29, 95–105. https://doi.org/10.1016/j.alcr.2015.12.004

Lehmann, V., Tuinman, M. A., Braeken, J., Vingerhoets, A. J., Sanderman, R., & Hagedoorn, M. (2015). Satisfaction with relationship status: Development of a new scale and the role in predicting well-being. *Journal of Happiness Studies*, 16, 169–184. https://doi.org/10.1007/s10902-014-9503-x

Leung, A., Kier, C., Fung, T., Fung, L., & Sproule, R. (2011). Searching for happiness: The importance of social capital. *Journal of Happiness Studies*, 12, 443–462. https://doi.org/10.1007/s10902-010-9208-8

Lichter, D. T., Batson, C. D., & Brown, J. B. (2004). Welfare reform and marriage promotion: The marital expectations and desires of single and cohabiting mothers. *Social Service Review*, 78(1), 2–25. https://doi.org/10.1086/380652

Lichter, D. T., Price, J. P., & Swigert, J. M. (2020). Mismatches in the marriage market. *Journal of Marriage and Family*, 82(2), 796–809. https://doi.org/10.1111/jomf.12603

Machia, L. V., & Proulx, M. L. (2020). The diverging effects of need fulfillment obtained from within and outside of a romantic relationship. *Personality and Social Psychology Bulletin*, 46(5), 781–793. https://doi.org/10.1177/0146167219877849

Manning, W. D., Brown, S. L., & Payne, K. K. (2014). Two decades of stability and change in age at first union formation. *Journal of Marriage and Family*, 76(2), 247–260. https://doi.org/10.1111/jomf.12090

McEwen, R., & Wellman, B. (2013). Relationships, community, and networked individuals. In R. Teigland & D. Power (Eds.), *The immersive internet: Reflections on the entangling of the virtual with society, politics and the economy* (pp. 168–179). Macmillan.

Mikulincer, M., & Shaver, P. R. (2012). Adult attachment orientations and relationship processes. *Journal of Family Theory & Review*, 4, 259–274. https://doi.org/10.1111/j.1756-2589.2012.00142.x

OECD. (2019). *SF3.1: Marriage and divorce rates.* https://www.oecd.org/els/family/SF_3_1_Marriage_and_divorce_rates.pdf

Oh, J., Chopik, W., & Lucas, R. (2021). Happiness singled out: Bidirectional associations between singlehood and life satisfaction. *Personality & Social Psychology Bulletin.* Advance online publication. https://doi.org/10.1177/01461672211049049

Ortiz-Ospina, E. (2019). *The rise of living alone: How one-person households are becoming increasingly common around the world.* Our World in Data. https://ourworldindata.org/living-alone

Park, Y., Impett, E. A., & MacDonald, G. (2021). Singles' sexual satisfaction is associated with more satisfaction with singlehood and less interest in marriage. *Personality and Social Psychology Bulletin*, 47(5), 741–752. https://doi.org/10.1177/0146167220942361

Patrick, H., Knee, C. R., Canevello, A., & Lonsbary, C. (2007). The role of need fulfillment in relationship functioning and well-being: A self-determination theory perspective. *Journal of Personality and Social Psychology*, *92*(3), 434–457. https://doi.org/10.1037/0022-3514.92.3.434

Paxton, P. (1999). Is social capital declining in the United States? A multiple indicator assessment. *American Journal of Sociology*, *105*(1), 88–127. https://doi.org/10.1086/210268

Pepping, C. A., MacDonald, G., & Davis, P. J. (2018). Toward a psychology of singlehood: An attachment-theory perspective on long-term singlehood. *Current Directions in Psychological Science*, *27*(5), 324–331. https://doi.org/10.1177/0963721417752106

Roseneil, S., & Budgeon, S. (2004). Cultures of intimacy and care beyond "the family": personal life and social change in the early 21st century. *Current Sociology*, *52* (2), 135–159. http://dx.doi.org/10.1177/0011392104041798

Rowland, D. T. (2007). Historical trends in childlessness. *Journal of Family Issues*, *28*(10), 1311–1337. https://doi.org/10.1177/0192513X07303823

Rusbult, C. E. (1980). Commitment and satisfaction in romantic associations: A test of the investment model. *Journal of Experimental Social Psychology*, *16*(2), 172–186. https://doi.org/10.1016/0022-1031(80)90007-4

Rusbult, C. E., Agnew, C. R., & Arriaga, X. B. (2012). The investment model of commitment processes. In P. A. M. Van Lange, A. W. Kruglanski, & E. T. Higgins (Eds.), *Handbook of theories of social psychology* (Vol. 2, pp. 218–231). Sage.

Rusbult, C. E., Martz, J. M., & Agnew, C. R. (1998). The Investment Model Scale: Measuring commitment level, satisfaction level, quality of alternatives, and investment size. *Personal Relationships*, *5*(4), 357–391. https://doi.org/10.1111/j.1475-6811.1998.tb00177.x

Rusbult, C. E., & Van Lange, P. A. (2003). Interdependence, interaction, and relationships. *Annual Review of Psychology*, *54*, 351–375. https://doi.org/10.1146/annurev.psych.54.101601.145059

Sassler, S., & Lichter, D. (2020). Cohabitation and marriage: Complexity and diversity in union-formation patterns. *Journal of Marriage and Family*, *82*(1), 35–61. https://doi.org/10.1111/jomf.12617

Schachner, D. A., Shaver, P. R., & Gillath, O. (2008). Attachment style and long-term singlehood. *Personal Relationships*, *15*, 479–491. https://doi.org/10.1111/j.1475-6811.2008.00211.x

Schwartz, S. H. (1992). Universals in the content and structure of values: Theory and empirical tests in 20 countries. In M. Zanna (Ed.), *Advances in experimental social psychology* (Vol. 25, pp. 1–65). Academic Press. http://dx.doi.org/10.1016/S0065-2601(08)60281-6

Schwartz, S. H. (2003). *A proposal for measuring value orientations across nations*. NSD—Norwegian Centre for Research Data.

Schwartz, S. H. (2012). An overview of the Schwartz theory of basic values. *Online Readings in Psychology and Culture*, *2*(1), Article 11. http://dx.doi.org/10.9707/2307-0919.1116

Smock, P. J. (2004). The wax and wane of marriage: Prospects for marriage in the 21st century. *Journal of Marriage and Family*, *66*(4), 966–973. https://doi.org/10.1111/j.0022-2445.2004.00066.x

Smock, P. J., & Schwartz, C. R. (2020). The demography of families: A review of patterns and change. *Journal of Marriage and Family, 82*(1), 9–34. https://doi.org/10.1111/jomf.12612

Spielmann, S. S., MacDonald, G., Maxwell, J. A., Joel, S., Peragine, D., Muise, A., & Impett, E. A. (2013). Settling for less out of fear of being single. *Journal of Personality and Social Psychology, 105*, 1049–1073. https://doi.org/10.1037/a0034628

Suanet, B., & Antonucci, T. C. (2017). Cohort differences in received social support in later life: The role of network type. *The Journals of Gerontology: Series B, Psychological Sciences and Social Sciences, 72*, 706–715. https://doi.org/10.1093/geronb/gbw075

Suanet, B., & Huxhold, O. (2020). Cohort difference in age-related trajectories in network size in old age: Are networks expanding? *The Journals of Gerontology: Series B: Psychological Sciences and Social Sciences, 75*(1), 137–147. https://doi.org/10.1093/geronb/gbx166

Suanet, B., van Tilburg, T. G., & van Groenou, M. I. B. (2013). Nonkin in older adults' personal networks: More important among later cohorts? *The Journals of Gerontology: Series B: Psychological Sciences and Social Sciences, 68*(4), 633–643. https://doi.org/10.1093/geronb/gbt043

Thibaut, J. W., & Kelley, H. H. (1959). *The social psychology of groups*. John Wiley.

Timonen, V., & Doyle, M. (2014). Life-long singlehood: Intersections of the past and the present. *Ageing and Society, 34*, 1749–1770. https://doi.org/10.1017/S0144686X13000500

U.S. Census Bureau. (1970). *Marital status of the population by sex, race, and Hispanic origin*. Retrieved from https://www.allcountries.org/uscensus/53_marital_status_of_the_population_by.html

U.S. Census Bureau. (2011). *Statistical abstract. Table 56: Marital status of the population by sex, race, and Hispanic origin: 1990 to 2010*. Retrieved from ftp://ftp.census.gov/library/publications/2011/compendia/statab/131ed/tables/12s0056.pdf

U.S. Census Bureau. (2021). *Historical marital status tables*. U.S. Census Bureau. Retrieved from https://www.census.gov/data/tables/time-series/demo/families/marital.html

Van Bavel, J., Schwartz, C. R., & Esteve, A. (2018). The reversal of the gender gap in education and its consequences for family life. *Annual Review of Sociology, 44*(1), 341–360. https://doi.org/10.1146/annurev-soc-073117-041215

VanderDrift, L. E., & Agnew, C. R. (2012). Need fulfillment and stay–leave behavior: On the diagnosticity of personal and relational needs. *Journal of Social and Personal Relationships, 29*(2), 228–245. https://doi.org/10.1177/0265407511431057

Wang, H., & Wellman, B. (2010). Social connectivity in America: Changes in adult friendship network size from 2002 to 2007. *American Behavioral Scientist, 53*(8), 1148–1169. https://doi.org/10.1177/0002764209356247

Wilson, W. J. (1987). *The truly disadvantaged: The inner city, the underclass, and public policy*. University of Chicago Press.

14
Friendships in the Time of COVID-19

Mahzad Hojjat, Anne Moyer, Sydney Brake, Brady D. Nelson,
Lauren L. Richmond, Jessica L. Schleider, and Bonita London

Friendships play an important role in our lives (Hojjat & Moyer, 2017). We value our friendships for a variety of reasons, including companionship, affection, alliance, and self-validation (Sullivan, 1953). But perhaps one of the most important functions of friendship is providing social support during difficult times, when we face stressful life events (Bolger & Eckenrode, 1991; Holt-Lunstad, 2017). The emergence of the COVID-19 pandemic in 2020 was a worldwide emergency on a significant scale, with reverberations at the personal, familial, communal, and societal levels. During the early phase of the pandemic (March 1, 2020–December 31, 2020; Sutin et al., 2022), many relied on friends for comfort and support. At the same time, restrictions on social contact strained friendships. The later stages of the pandemic (January 1, 2021–February 16, 2022; Sutin et al., 2022) were also characterized by uncertainty, fear, and stark disagreement regarding preventative measures (e.g., vaccination). These views were often colored by contrasting political ideologies, which further weakened friendships. This chapter examines the supporting role of friendships in coping with a significant public health crisis, as well as factors that may have led to the deterioration or dissolution of friendships during this pandemic.

Psychological Impact of the Pandemic

The COVID-19 pandemic caused unprecedented social, emotional, and health consequences (González-Sanguino et al., 2020). As of October 26, 2022, approximately 6,562,281 individuals have died worldwide (World Health Organization, 2022). The first months were especially frightening when people around the globe were warned to shelter in place as health professionals tried to understand the new virus. The mental health effects of this uncertainty and threat were documented in more than 8,000 individuals across 79 countries as early as April, 2020, showing, not surprisingly, elevated levels of anxiety and depression (van Mulukom et al., 2021). The number of days in lockdown and social isolation augmented the effect of feelings of threat on these psychological outcomes; however, this impact was diminished for people who had more frequent contact with friends, family, colleagues, or fellow students. Similarly, in a large Spanish sample assessed in March, 2020, feelings of loneliness predicted elevated levels of anxiety, depression, and PTSD (González-Sanguino et al., 2020). In a U.S. sample assessed in April to May 2020, social isolation also predicted worse depression, anxiety, and stress (Smith et al., 2020). Thus, in addition to the health threat posed by the virus, the very measures taken to mitigate its spread, such as social distancing and stay-at-home orders, likely exacerbated mental health challenges by promoting social isolation and loneliness.

Friendships

In describing the sweeping changes that the COVID-19 pandemic has brought for psychological science, Rosenfeld et al. (2022) noted that "the pandemic is inherently a social phenomenon" that has disrupted "virtually every corner of social life" (p. 2) and this no doubt includes our friendships. In early 2020, a longitudinal study was launched to evaluate the social, cognitive, physical, and psychosocial responses to the COVID-19 pandemic among members of a large Northeastern university community, including students, staff, and faculty (Nelson et al., 2020–2021). Two questions assessed participants' perception of whether the pandemic had led to (1) improvements in their friendships, and (2) increases in conflict or strain in their friendships. One wave of data included responses from May to August 2020, a time when the population had already been in lockdown for some time, milestones such as graduations and holidays had been impacted, and the dialogue about social distancing, masking, and school closures was often the source of heated disagreements. This provided a rare opportunity among the 680 individuals who completed the questions to examine perceptions of changes in friendships and these changes' relationship to well-being during a particularly intense historical period. Although data on participants' demographics were incomplete (N's = 590–602), they were largely female (78.2%), undergraduates (66.4%), and an average age of 24.1 years. With regard to ethnicity, they were largely non-Hispanic (86.8%) and identified their race as White (57.6%), Asian (33.7%), Black/African American (3.7%), multiple (4.1%), American Indian or Alaskan Native (0.3%), or Native Hawaiian or Pacific Islander (0.3%).

Only a small group (17.9%) reported the most toxic ratings, endorsing both no perceived improvements in their friendships and increased conflict and strain with friends, whereas a moderate proportion (22.4%) reported the rosiest ratings, endorsing both improvements in their friendships and no increased conflict or strain with friends. The other configurations, reflecting (1) both positive and negative changes, improved relationships, and increased conflict or strain, and (2) no change, no improvement in relationships, and no increased conflict or strain, were endorsed by 6.3% and 53.4% of participants, respectively. Thus, although the majority reported stability in the quality of their friend relationships, conflict and strain in friendships were reported both with and without improvements in nearly a quarter of cases (24.3%).

In terms of how these changes related to interpersonal and intrapersonal outcomes, there were no main or interactive effects of improvements in friendships or conflicts in friendships on loneliness. Perhaps improvements in friendships were not sufficient to remedy the loneliness due to social isolation, as reported in other studies (Maloy et al., 2022; McKinlay et al., 2022). These findings also indicated a main effect of conflict or strain in friendships on level of depressive symptomatology $F(1, 672) = 247.82, p < .05$. So, conflict or strain with friends affected the small proportion of the sample who indicated that they experienced these conflicts intrapersonally. There did not appear to be a synergy such that improvements in friendships buffered this negative effect of conflicts. It is important to note also that, for the majority, there were no reported changes in friendships, suggesting a resilience for this type of relationship. This concurs with other reports from international samples that found that when people were asked to what extent their friendships had become better or worse during the pandemic on a seven-point scale, on average, they scored about in the midrange (Ayers et al., 2022; Li et al., 2022). Overall, the results of this study mirror multiple studies indicating both resiliency and strain of friendships under the heavy toll of the pandemic (Branquinho et al., 2020; Elmer et al., 2020; Killgore et al., 2020; McKinlay et al., 2022; Northfield & Johnston, 2022). In the following sections, we discuss in more detail how friendships were impacted in both positive and negative ways during the pandemic. The chapter will conclude with lessons learned and future directions.

Friendship: A Positive Force

Although there has been little research specifically on the impact of COVID-19 on friendships (Bevan et al., 2022; Espinoza & Hernandez, 2022), the limited literature suggests that friends were essential in supporting each other as they coped with adverse effects of social isolation and anxiety (Juvonen et al., 2021; Killgore et al., 2020; Maloy et al., 2022). Researchers have characterized friendships as a form of self-care along with healthy eating, exercise, engaging in a hobby, and relaxation/meditation. In a sample of U.S. adults assessed in the spring of 2020, spending time with a supportive person and talking to a friend or family member online were engaged in more frequently than these other self-care behaviors (Disabato et al., 2022). Negative affect predicted increases in spending time with a supportive person on the following day, indicating that such contacts were likely used as a coping tool. In another study with a sample of 1,004 U.S. adults from 50 states (ages 18–35) during lockdown, social support from family, friends, and a special caring loved one were each independently associated with greater resilience (Killgore et al., 2020). Northfield and Johnston (2021) explored post-traumatic growth (PTG) during the pandemic along five dimensions: relating to others, new possibilities, personal strength, spiritual enhancement, and appreciation for life. American adults (N = 296) between the ages of 18–78 (M age = 39.7) completed online surveys in August of 2020. The findings indicated a significant relationship between PTG and perceived support from family (b = .14) and to a larger extent, friends (b = .23). In a study with 993 ethnically diverse U.S. adolescents (M age = 16.09), Espinoza and Hernandez (2022) concluded that a combination of support from and communication with friends was an important mechanism that may have helped adolescents to manage pandemic-related challenges.

A number of studies conducted outside the United States also demonstrated the supporting role of friendships. In one study with a sample of 589 older Hungarians (Lábadi et al., 2022), aged 60–83, perceived social support from friends predicted more adaptive coping (i.e., positive refocusing), which resulted in lower depression and anxiety. In another study with younger participants (Branquinho et al., 2020), 617 Portuguese individuals (*M* age = 19.1) responded to online surveys during spring of 2020. Although they acknowledged the loss of contact with friends as a painful negative outcome of the pandemic, consistent with other research (Espinoza & Hernandez, 2022), they also stated that a silver lining was that the experience made them realize how much they valued their relationships and their support, and it even strengthened their friendships. Regular communication with friends and family through video calling was the top way to cope with the isolation and stress of the situation for these young individuals.

Support Via Digital Connection With Friends

Electronic communication made it possible for individuals to maintain contact with friends and other loved ones during COVID-related stay-at-home orders. In a study of American adults of all ages, participants reported greater than typical reliance on, and satisfaction with, video calls during isolation, even though individuals (especially younger people) used texting and connecting via social media the most (Juvonen et al., 2021). In older Americans ≥75 years old ($N = 155$, M age = 81.0), Wu et al. (2022) found that although overall social interaction time decreased due to COVID-19 restrictions, the lost in-person time was partially compensated for by increased communication with friends. Further, writing to friends (via text/email/letter) showed promise for improving low mood in older women. An increase of 1 hour of writing to friends per week was associated with a 23% decrease in the likelihood of experiencing low mood (Wu al., 2022) for older Americans. Nevertheless, using survey data from a national sample of U.S. participants ($N = 2,925$), Nguyen and colleagues (2021) found that during the early phase of the pandemic, those with existing social and digital privilege were better able to maintain or increase their digital communication with friends and family than those who were disadvantaged. The advantaged group included people with higher income and education, those with more Internet skills, and younger people (Nguyen et al., 2021).

Given the importance of socialization with peers for young people (Branquinho et al., 2020; McKinlay et al., 2022) and their skill in using digital communication (Juvonen et al., 2022; Nguyen et al., 2021), it is not surprising that staying in touch with friends via electronic means was found to be critical for this age group. In a study with Australian adolescents (aged 12–18 years old), the majority reported increased use of technology to connect with friends and family, and this connectivity was associated with lower levels of loneliness and a greater sense of well-being (Li et al., 2022). van Mulukom et al. (2021) reported that engaging in frequent communication with close friends and others through a variety of sources (e.g., messages, calls, and video chats) was related to reduced feelings of social isolation. Findings of a panel study with four data collection waves in a sample of young American adults (M age = 26.87) suggested that social closeness among friends remained stable during the pandemic, especially among those who increased their mediated communication, including phone calls, text conversations, text-based messaging via email or social media (e.g., Facebook Messenger), and video-based messaging (e.g., Snapchat) with friends (Bond, 2021).

Mode of Communication

Research suggests that individuals may have used different communication modes to fulfill different needs during the pandemic. For instance, in one study with an American sample, researchers (Choi & Choung, 2021) found that interpersonal forms of communication (e.g., phone calling, video chatting, and texting), which are characterized by a high level of intimacy, were preferred for social connection and associated with decreased loneliness and enhanced satisfaction with life. On the other hand, masspersonal media channels (i.e., Facebook, Instagram, Twitter), considered to be more casual and less intimate due to their public nature, were more frequently used for entertainment and information seeking, and were associated with increased loneliness and decreased life satisfaction (Choi & Choung, 2021). Other studies have also demonstrated that at the height of the pandemic, more intimate forms of digital communication were commonly used to replace face-to-face communication (e.g., Branquinho et al., 2020; Juvonen et al., 2021). In a study of undergraduate students' social networks in Switzerland (Elmer et al., 2020), participants reported that they interacted with the members of their social network (friends) primarily through text messaging, voice, and video calls, and to a lesser degree, social media.

Satisfaction With Communication

In addition to the form of communication, satisfaction with communication with friends has also been shown to be associated with increased well-being during the pandemic, especially for those who live alone (Juvonen et al., 2021). In a large study (N = 1,557) with an ethnically diverse American sample, Juvonen et al. (2022) reported that a greater number of friends and greater satisfaction with electronic communication with friends were related to lower social and generalized anxiety as well as depressive symptoms, over and above prior social-emotional well-being and other relevant factors. They concluded that more satisfying communications were most likely related to greater mutual self-disclosure and intimate conversations with close friends. Accordingly, the findings also suggested that loneliness was lessened by more contact with higher quality friends (Juvonen et al., 2022).

Support From Close Friends

In a normal day, individuals interact with about 11–16 "weak ties" or casual friends/acquaintances, from baristas to classmates to coworkers (Sandstrom & Whillians, 2020). These casual relationships have their place in our lives and contribute to our social and emotional well-being (Sandstrom & Dunn, 2014; Storr et al., 2021). During the early phase of the pandemic, casual contacts (e.g., commercial friendships, acquaintances), which depend primarily on frequent in-person contact to be sustained, were significantly disrupted (Kulcar et al., 2022; Sandstrom & Whillans, 2020; Storr et al., 2021). In the study of Swiss undergraduates' social networks during the early phase of the pandemic (Elmer et al., 2020), although friendship networks remained relatively stable, weaker one-dimensional ties (e.g., classmate) were less likely to survive than stronger ties with more overlapping relational dimensions (e.g., someone who is both one's classmate and dormmate). Research suggests that, at least during the early stage of the pandemic, when personal face-to-face contact was reduced to near zero, individuals were more likely to reach out to close versus casual friends (i.e., strong vs. weak ties; Elmer et al., 2020; Storr et al., 2021).

Our connections with close friends with whom we have a strong bond (e.g., long-term or childhood friends) are established over time and do not depend as heavily on frequent or daily physical contact. We turn to such close and trusted friends in times of stress and trauma (Sandstrom & Whillians, 2020). Individuals tend to expect and receive greater maintenance behaviors, which includes supportiveness, positivity, openness, and interaction, from their close friendships (Oswald, 2017). Indeed, research has suggested that individuals reached out to close friends rather than distant friends or casual acquaintances for support during COVID-19 (Juvonen et al., 2022; Kulcar et al., 2022). In a qualitative study of young adults, Maloy et al. (2022) found that individuals were more willing to commit time and energy to highly valued friends who reciprocated their efforts for support. In a large-scale study (Ye et al., 2022) conducted with 1,032 young Chinese college students (M age = 19.50), the quality of friendship played an important role in perceived stress and satisfaction in life during the early phase of the pandemic. The results showed that for those with high- versus low-quality friendships, perceived stress declined significantly as access to information about the pandemic increased. The findings suggest that high-quality friends may have assisted individuals by making sense of information as well as by providing emotional support that could buffer the impact of perceived stress (Ye et al., 2022).

Negative Impact on Friendship: Early Phase

Although friendships, especially emotionally close ones, provided some protection against loneliness, anxiety, and depression in many instances (Juvonen et al., 2022), social distancing restrictions during the early phase of the pandemic limited the ability of friends to continue with typical interactions, making them feel disconnected from friends (Li et al., 2022). This led to a general sense of decline in many existing friendships and prevented formation of new friendships, thus amplifying the feelings of isolation and loneliness (Kulcar et al., 2022). In a large-scale longitudinal study (Philpot et al., 2021), 1996 Americans of all ages (M age = 60) completed the National Institutes of Health Adult Social Relationship Scales to assess various aspects of social relationships, including friendships from a time prior to the pandemic (February 2018) to when social distancing directives were in place (May 2020). Researchers found that individuals experienced increased emotional and instrumental support, but also loneliness, as well as decreased feelings of friendship during the early phase of the pandemic (Philpot et al., 2021).

Age
Research suggests that the pandemic may have impacted friendships differently across demographics, personality, and settings. There is ample evidence that the pandemic had a disproportionally negative impact on young individuals (Juvonen et al., 2021, 2022). McKinlay and colleagues (2022) stated that young people "experienced the greatest decline in mental health in the first wave of COVID-19, in comparison to people in other age ranges" (p. 1). Many studies have corroborated this statement. A global survey (Varma et al., 2021) of 1,653 participants from 63 countries (M age = 43) found that younger people were more vulnerable to stress, anxiety,

and depression during the COVID-19 pandemic. Another large study (Ayers et al., 2022) conducted in continental Europe ($N = 634$, M age = 29.61) during the summer of 2020 found that younger people reported elevated feelings of loneliness and isolation. Moreover, stress, isolation, and guilt were associated with greater COVID-related social risk-taking (e.g., making and visiting new friends in person) for this age group. Research suggests that adolescents have been especially susceptible. In their study of Australian adolescents, Li et al. (2022) found that three-quarters of the sample experienced a decline in mental health (including higher than normative levels of sleep disturbance and health anxiety) since the beginning of the pandemic, with notable negative consequences for learning, friendships, and family relationships. In a U.S.-based study (Rogers et al., 2021), 470 adolescents of diverse backgrounds (M age 15.24) completed surveys before (October 2019) and during (April 2020) the pandemic. In spite of the ability to connect with friends electronically, adolescents reported a lack of emotional connection with and a perceived decrease in overall support from friends. The perceived social (worsening of friendship dynamics) and emotional (increased negative affect and decreased positive affect) changes were related to elevated depressive and anxiety symptoms, as well as loneliness in April 2020, even after controlling for prior mental health problems (Rogers et al., 2022).

A recent study suggests that the impact of the pandemic on young individuals may extend as far as changes in personality. Sutin and colleagues (2022) conducted longitudinal assessments of personality from the Understanding America Study ($N = 7,109$; 18,623 assessments). They measured changes in personality from before to during the pandemic. Amazingly, in these young adults (<30 years old), there were increases in neuroticism and a decline in agreeableness and conscientiousness. Researchers concluded that "if these changes are enduring, this evidence suggests population-wide stressful events can slightly bend the trajectory of personality, especially in younger adults" (Sutin et al., 2022, p.1). To put these findings in perspective, even after accounting for normative age-related changes, the reported change during the relatively short time of the pandemic approximated the degree of change usually observed over a decade (Sutin et al., 2022).

Several reasons for the vulnerability of the younger individuals have been suggested by various scholars. First, young individuals thrive on companionship of friends and peers. Friendships present important sources of affection, intimacy, and social support during adolescence and young adulthood (Espinoza & Hernandez, 2022). Not being able to have regular in-person contact with friends would certainly undermine young people's emotional well-being and leave them feeling lonely and unsupported (Rogers et al., 2021). Second, adolescence and young adulthood are especially sensitive life stages as individuals experience a number of important life transitions that signify entrance into adulthood (Arnett, 2000). Disruption to these transitions, such as being deprived of attending prom or graduation, can lead to anxiety, uncertainty, and feeling that one has missed out on important moments of life (McKinlay et al., 2022). Third, the closure of educational institutions decreased access to resources associated with such settings, for instance, mental health services at universities, free lunch programs at schools, and especially peer support from fellow students or educators (McKinlay et al., 2022). Finally, it is likely that those from marginalized groups (for instance, LGBTQ youth) were even more strongly affected by the loss of such resources due to their circumstances (Fish et al., 2020; Juvonen et al., 2022; McKinlay et al., 2022).

Setting

Friendships are formed in different settings and thus may be impacted by different processes. In a study on social bonds and friendships in organizations, Jo and colleagues (2021) surveyed MBA students in the Southwestern United States before and after the onset of the pandemic. They specifically looked at the impact on both friendships and "advice ties"—informal social connections that provide instrumental resources to facilitate task performance within organizations. Such ties are also often personally meaningful and strengthen social bonds among peers in organizations although they are not as strong as friendships. Researchers found that COVID-19 reduced the maintenance of advice ties, with emotional exhaustion worsening this effect (Jo et al., 2021). Further, COVID-19 reduced the maintenance of friendship ties. One possible reason was that emotional support opportunities were decreased due to social distancing. Further, worries over job uncertainty may have led to competitive tensions that eroded the friendship network (Jo et al., 2021). In the longitudinal study of college students' social networks and mental health before and during the COVID-19 crisis in Switzerland (Elmer et al., 2020), researchers found a reduction in co-studying networks such that more students were studying alone. Results also pointed to isolation in social networks and lack of emotional support being associated with negative mental health outcomes, which had worsened compared with measures before the crisis.

Another finding of importance in this study is that female students, who were in the minority in this sample, appeared to have worse mental health consequences even after relevant factors were controlled (Elmer et al., 2020). These results are consistent with those from other studies (González-Sanguino et al., 2020; Juvonen et al., 2022) demonstrating that women were more likely to be negatively impacted and at higher risk of experiencing negative mental health consequences during the pandemic. For instance, Philpot et al. (2021) found that women experienced more loneliness compared with men. Further, according to a survey by the Pew Research Center (2020), more women than men (37% vs. 32%) reported that child care responsibilities were very/somewhat difficult for them during this time.

In addition, researchers have cautioned that in educational settings, some students (e.g., international students, racial and sexual minorities) might be at higher risk of social isolation and developing mental health problems during emergencies such as the COVID-19 crisis. In particular, Elmer and colleagues (2020) point out that the most vulnerable students were those who lived by themselves, had less direct contact with close family members and friends, perceived less social support, and had a weaker integration in the social networks of students. Similarly, Juvonen et al. (2021) identified three vulnerable groups during the pandemic: younger individuals, those with prior mental health issues, and people who lived alone. It is essential that university administrators provide at-risk students with needed resources such as "digital forms of study groups, peer group sessions, mentoring, and psychological counseling" during such public health crises in the future (Elmer et al., 2020, p. 19).

Negative Impact on Friendship: Later Phase

Political partisanship is another important factor that has continued to impact friendships from the beginning of the pandemic. In the United States, the extreme polarized views about political issues and public policies preceded the pandemic (Williams & Medlock, 2017). However, debates surrounding how to best manage the worldwide public health emergency moved the political disputes to yet another level. Different political parties perceived the danger of the pandemic differently and advocated for conflicting approaches to manage the COVID-19 crisis (Pew Research Center, 2020). Several studies (Kassas & Nayga, 2021; Kreps & Kriner, 2021) suggested that Republicans and Republican-leaning independents perceived COVID-19 to be less severe, often likening it to the flu, and were hesitant to get vaccinated or wear a mask, citing such safety regulations as impingements on their personal freedoms. Democrats or Democrat-leaning independents, on the other hand, perceived the virus to be quite dangerous, were more likely to get vaccinated, and demanded more strict preventative measures (social distancing, masking, vaccination) to prevent the spread of the virus (Kreps & Kriner, 2021). Research suggests that not only do liberals and conservatives give priority to different moral concerns, but they also tend to exaggerate each other's stereotypical moral values (Graham et al., 2012), which in the current political climate could further sow conflict.

Conflict Over Covid-19 Preventative Strategies
In the later stages of the pandemic beginning in spring 2021, with the implementation of widespread vaccination, social isolation advisories gradually relaxed. At this point, many individuals felt comfortable spending time with their friends in person. Yet, many others faced difficult choices as disagreements over COVID-19 mitigation strategies continued and heated up because many strongly opposed vaccination and masking. At this juncture, the focus of friendship strains changed. Whereas during the early phase, the lack of contact weakened friendships (Kulcar et al., 2022; Philpot et al., 2021), at this later stage, friendship strains centered around whether one should get together with friends with differing views and practices regarding vaccination or masking (Brake & Hojjat, 2022). Several news outlets published articles that reflected this tension on a large scale, featuring stories of individuals who were hesitant to meet unvaccinated friends in person or even decided to end the friendship for that reason (Kale, 2021). As illustrated below, a number of surveys document the conflict among friends and family members about COVID-19 measures.

The results of the South Dakota COVID-19 Family Impact Survey (Wiltse, 2021) revealed deep divisions between friends and family members over COVID-related issues. Participants were 573 registered voters who answered questions about the impact of the COVID-19 pandemic on their daily lives. The results showed that about two-thirds (65%) of participants experienced disagreements either with friends only (13%), family members only (12%), or both (39%) about topics related to COVID-19 prevention strategies (e.g., vaccines, face masks, and social distancing). Importantly, 37% of those who mentioned disagreements with friends stopped interacting with one or more of them as a consequence. Participants reported that the conflict made them feel a range of negative emotions including stress and anger and led to an overall deteriorated sense of emotional and psychological well-being. In a recent *New York Times*/Siena College survey (Homans & McFadden, 2022) of 792 registered voters nationwide in October of 2022, almost 1 in 5 respondents (19%) reported that political disagreements had damaged their friendships or family relationships. Several suggested that Facebook was an "aggravating factor," as this was a public space where relationships and politics mingled.

Conflict Over Politics

Although academic research on this topic is sparse, one recent study (Brake & Hojjat, 2022) explored friendship conflict in participants from the Northeastern United States. Online data were collected from 217 volunteers comprised of 75 men (34.6%), 130 women (59.9%), and 12 others (5.5%). The mean age was 33.8 (SD = 15.2). Respondents self-identified as White (72.4%), Asian (3.2%), Latinx (4.1%), Black (3.2%), and others (17%). Participants responded to a battery of survey questions regarding a recent conflict with a friend, including the outcome of the conflict, and also their closeness with the friend before and after the conflict.

The findings indicated that the majority of participants, almost 80%, have had a disagreement with a friend about political or pandemic-related issues in recent months. A top topic of conflict was whether one should get vaccinated. In over half of cases, participants reported that the friendship worsened or was dissolved after the disagreement. About half of participants judged the conflict as moderately to very serious. Although age and gender, or closeness of the friendship, were not associated with less desirable conflict outcomes, perceived seriousness of conflict was $r = .41, p < .001$. Interestingly, participants who scored higher on an assertive style of conflict resolution, which relies on collaborative problem-solving, experienced a more negative outcome in their friendship conflict. The findings indicated that a problem-solving or fact-finding approach was not the most effective way to approach such disagreements with friends. Future research is needed to explore what conflict resolution styles would be more conducive to helping friends manage their disagreements over political issues and maintain their friendships in the current tense post-pandemic phase.

Overall, the findings regarding friendship conflict during the later phase of the pandemic mirror those related to the overall political divisions that we have witnessed in American society in recent years. Unfortunately, disagreements surrounding the safety procedures associated with the COVID-19 pandemic have provided further fuel for the larger societal divisions, and as a result friendships have been seriously strained. The findings demonstrate that friendships, which are usually an important source of support and companionship, are not immune from deep societal divisions.

Summary and Conclusion

The COVID-19 pandemic devastated the world by taking millions of lives and wreaking havoc on our physical, psychological, and emotional well-being. During the early stage of the pandemic there was a steep rise in anxiety, fear, and sadness as individuals hopelessly witnessed the spread of a new deadly virus worldwide, for which there was no cure or vaccine. The preventative measures of lockdown and social isolation only added to the sense of loneliness and depression as routine in-person contacts were disrupted. Research points to both resiliency and strain of friendships during this crucial time.

As it became untenable to meet in person, individuals reached out to their friends electronically to seek and provide social support. Individuals were also more likely to connect with close versus casual friends. Indeed, communicating with a supportive friend or family member online was used more frequently than the other self-care behaviors, and greater satisfaction with electronic communication with friends was related to reduced anxiety as well as lower depressive symptoms. Further, various modes of communication were chosen for different purposes with different consequences (Choi & Choung, 2021). More intimate interpersonal forms of digital communication (e.g., video chatting, phone calling, texting) were preferred for connecting socially with friends, perhaps due to being more analogous to face-to-face contact, and found to be associated with decreased loneliness and increased life satisfaction. Yet, "masspersonal" forms of digital communication (i.e., Facebook, Instagram, Twitter) were used mostly for entertainment and information seeking and associated with increased loneliness and decreased life satisfaction (Choi & Choung, 2021). There was also a positive side reflected in some of the research, suggesting that the social isolation, painful as it was, made some realize how much they appreciated their friends and even led to the strengthening of friendships (Branquinho et al., 2020) for some, and to an overall sense of post-traumatic growth for others (Northfield & Johnston, 2021).

Although support from friends provided some protection against stress, anxiety, and loneliness during the early stage of the pandemic for many, others felt that the lack of contact with friends weakened or ended their relationships (Li et al., 2022; Philpot et al., 2021). For example, in larger settings (universities, organizations) both casual social relationships (i.e., advice ties) and friendships suffered as individuals felt the impact of social isolation and lack of emotional support brought on by social distancing restrictions. Electronic communication provided some relief but ultimately proved to be an imperfect substitute for in-person contact (Kulcar et al., 2022; Storr et al., 2021). Importantly, certain groups of individuals were reported to be more vulnerable and suffer from more adverse impacts of the pandemic during the isolation phase.

In particular, global research suggests that young people were more susceptible to stress, anxiety, and depression, as they were deprived of close contact with peers, a support lifeline for this age group. Longitudinal research (Sutin et al., 2022) has even indicated an increase in neuroticism and decline in agreeableness and conscientiousness among younger individuals from before to during the pandemic. College students and others who were isolated from close contact with friends and family, and had weaker integration in their social network, were at the highest risk of developing mental health problems (Elmer et al., 2020). Finally, women and those from marginalized groups (e.g., sexual and racial minorities) were reported to feel lonelier and experience more adverse mental health outcomes in many instances. It is essential that government officials and university administrators provide at-risk individuals with necessary resources, should we face another severe public health crisis such as this one, in the future.

During the later phase of the pandemic, political partisanship played a significant role in dividing friends. The pandemic intensified the existing societal divisions to an extreme level. Liberals and conservatives clashed over the best approaches to mitigate the pandemic, leading to intense disagreements in or even breakup of friendships across the United States. In spite of paucity of research, one recent study (Brake & Hojjat, 2022) found that the top topic of friendship conflict was vaccination. Moreover, one of the most important factors associated with the deterioration of the friendship after a conflict was its perceived seriousness. More research is needed to explore cognitions and emotions associated with judgments of seriousness of such conflicts and why individuals feel that such disagreements provide adequate causes for dissolution of their friendships. The role of social media and misinformation in deepening the conflict also warrants further investigation. Finally, it is essential to conduct more research on exactly how friendships, among our most important relationships, might recover their equilibrium and be repaired as the hardship and turmoil of the early 2020s recede into the past.

References

Arnett, J. J. (2000). Emerging adulthood: A theory of development from the late teens through the twenties. *American Psychologist, 55,* 469–480. https://doi.org/10.1037//0003-066X.55.5.469

Ayers, J. D., Guevara Beltrán, D., Van Horn, A., Cronk, L., Todd, P. M., & Aktipis, A. (2022). Younger people and people with higher subjective SES experienced more negative effects of the pandemic on their friendships. *Personality and Individual Differences, 185,* Article 111246. https://doi.org/10.1016/j.paid.2021.111246

Bevan, J. L., Murphy, M. K., Lannutti, P. J., Slatcher, R. B., & Balzarini, R. N. (2022). A descriptive literature review of early research on COVID-19 and close relationships. *Journal of Social and Personal Relationships.* Advance online publication. https://doi.org/10.1177/02654075221115387

Bolger, N., & Eckenrode, J. (1991). Social relationships, personality, and anxiety during a major stressful event. *Journal of Personality and Social Psychology, 61*(3), 440–449. https://doi.org/10.1037/0022-3514.61.3.440

Bond, B. J. (2021). Social and parasocial relationships during COVID-19 social distancing. *Journal of Social and Personal Relationship, 38*(8), 2308–2329.

Brake, S., & Hojjat, M. (2022, July 28–August 2). *Friendship conflict in times of COVID.* Virtual International Association of Relationship Research (IARR) conference [Poster presentation].

Branquinho, C., Kelly, C., Arevalo, L., Santos, A., & Gasper de Matos, M. (2020). "Hey, we also have something to say": A qualitative study of Portuguese adolescents' and young people's experiences under COVID-19. *Journal of Community Psychology, 48*(8), 2740–2752. https://doi.org/10.1002/jcop.22453

Choi, M., & Choung, H. (2021). Mediated communication matters during the COVID-19 pandemic: The use of interpersonal and masspersonal media and psychological well-being. *Journal of Social and Personal Relationships, 38*(8), 2397–2418. https://doi.org/10.1177/02654075211029378

Disabato, D. J., Aurora, P., Sidney, P. G., Taber, J. M., Thompson, C. A., & Coifman, K. G. (2022). Self-care behaviors and affect during the early stages of the COVID-19 pandemic. *Health Psychology: Official Journal of the Division of Health Psychology, American Psychological Association, 41*(11), 833–842. https://doi.org/10.1037/hea0001239

Elmer, T., Mepham, K., & Stadtfeld, C. (2020). Students under lockdown: Comparisons of students' social networks and mental health before and during the COVID-19 crisis in Switzerland. *PLoS ONE*, *15*(7), e0236337. https://doi.org/10.1371/journal.pone.0236337

Espinoza, G., & Hernandez, H. L. (2022). Adolescent loneliness, stress, and depressive symptoms during the COVID-19 pandemic: The protective role of friends. *Infant & Child Development*, *31*(3), 1–13. https://doi.org/10.1002/icd.2305

Fish, J. N., McInroy, L. B., Paceley, M. S., Williams, N. D., Henderson, S., Levine, D. S., & Edsall, R. N. (2020). "I'm kinda stuck at home with unsupportive parents right now": LGBTQ youths' experiences with COVID-19 and the importance of online support. *Journal of Adolescent Health*, *67*(3), 450–452. https://doi.org/10.1016/j.jadohealth.2020.06.002

González-Sanguino, C., Ausín, B., Castellanos, M. Á., Saiz, J., López-Gómez, A., Ugidos, C., & Muñoz, M. (2020). Mental health consequences during the initial stage of the 2020 coronavirus pandemic (COVID-19) in Spain. *Brain, Behavior, and Immunity*, *87*, 172–176. https://doi.org/10.1016/j.bbi.2020.05.040

Graham, J., Nosek, B. A., & Haidt, J. (2012). The moral stereotypes of liberals and conservatives: Exaggeration of differences across the political spectrum. *PLoS ONE*, *7*(12), e50092. doi:10.1371/journal.pone.0050092

Hojjat, M., & Moyer, A. (Eds.). (2017). *The psychology of friendship*. Oxford University Press. https://oxford.universitypressscholarship.com/view/10.1093/acprof:oso/9780190222024.001.0001/acprof-9780190222024

Holt-Lunstad, J. (2017). Friendship and health. In M. Hojjat & A. Moyer (Eds.), *The psychology of friendship* (pp. 233–248). Oxford University Press.

Homans, C., & McFadden, A. (2022, October 18). Today's politics divide parties, and friends and families, too. *The New York Times*. https://www.nytimes.com/2022/10/18/us/politics/political-division-friends-family

Jo, J. K., Harrison, D. A., & Gray, S. M. (2021). The ties that cope? Reshaping social connections in response to pandemic distress. *Journal of Applied Psychology*, *106*(9), 1267–1282. https://doi.org/10.1037/apl0000955

Juvonen, J., Lessard, L. M., Kline, N. G., & Graham, S. (2022). Young adult adaptability to the social challenges of the COVID-19 pandemic: The protective role of friendships. *Journal of Youth & Adolescence*, *51*(3), 585–597. https://doi.org/10.1007/s10964-022-01573-w

Juvonen, J., Schacter, H. L., & Lessard, L. M. (2021). Connecting electronically with friends to cope with isolation during COVID-19 pandemic. *Journal of Social and Personal Relationships*, *38*(6), 1782–1799. https://doi.org/10.1177/0265407521998459

Kale, S. (2021, Feb. 13). "I don't want friends who put others at risk": Has lockdown wrecked friendships? *The Guardian Newspaper*. https://www.theguardian.com/world/2021/feb/13/i-dont-want-friends-who-put-others-at-risk-has-lockdown-wrecked-friendships

Kassas, B., & Nayga, R. M. (2021). Promoting higher social distancing and stay-at-home decisions during COVID-19: The underlying conflict between public health and the economy. *Safety Science*, *140*, Article 105300. http://doi.org/10.1016/j.ssci.2021.105300

Killgore, W., Taylor, E. C., Cloonan, S. A., & Dailey, N. S. (2020). Psychological resilience during the COVID-19 lockdown. *Psychiatry Research*, *291*, Article 113216. https://doi.org/10.1016/j.psychres.2020.113216

Kreps, S. E., & Kriner, D. L. (2021). Factors influencing Covid-19 vaccine acceptance across subgroups in the United States: Evidence from a conjoint experiment. *Vaccine*, *39*, 3250–3258. https://doi.org/10.1016/j.vaccine.2021.04.044

Kulcar, V., Bork-Hüffer, T., & Schneider, A-M. (2022). Getting through the crisis together: Do friendships contribute to university students' resilience during the COVID-19 pandemic? *Frontiers in Psychology, 13*, Article 880646. https://doi.org/10.3389/fpsyg.2022.880646

Lábadi, B., Arató, N., Budai, T., Inhóf, O., Stecina, D. T., Sík, A., & Zsidó, A. N. (2022). Psychological well-being and coping strategies of elderly people during the COVID-19 pandemic in Hungary. *Aging & Mental Health, 26*(3), 570–577. https://doi.org/10.1080/13607863.2021.1902469

Li, S. H., Beames, J. R., Newby, J. M., Maston, K., Christensen, H., & Werner-Seidler, A. (2022). The impact of COVID-19 on the lives and mental health of Australian adolescents. *European Child & Adolescent Psychiatry, 31*(9), 1465–1477. https://doi.org/10.1007/s00787-021-01790-x

Maloy, A., Main, A., Murphy, C., Coleman, L., Dodd, R., Lynch, J., Larkin, D., & Flowers, P. (2022). "I think friendship over this lockdown like saved my life"—Student experiences of maintaining friendships during COVID-19 lockdown: An interpretative phenomenological study. *Frontiers in Psychology, 13*, Article 861192. doi: 10.3389/fpsyg.2022.861192

McKinlay, A. R., May, T., Dawes, J., Fancourt, D., & Burton, A. (2022). "You're just there, alone in your room with your thoughts": A qualitative study about the psychosocial impact of the COVID-19 pandemic among young people living in the UK. *BMJ Open, 12*, 2, e053676. doi:10.1136/bmjopen-2021-053676

Nelson, B., Richmond, L., Schleider, J., & London, B. (2020–2021). [Unpublished raw data from Stony Brook University COVID-19 Longitudinal Study]. Stony Brook University.

Nguyen, M. H., Hargittai, E., & Marler, W. (2021). Digital inequality in communication during a time of physical distancing: The case of COVID-19. *Computers in Human Behavior, 120*(5), Article106717. https://doi.org/10.1016/j.chb.2021.106717

Northfield, E-L., & Johnston, K. L. (2022). "I get by with a little help from my friends": Posttraumatic growth in the COVID-19 pandemic. *Traumatology, 28*(1), 195–201. https://doi.org/10.1037/trm0000321

Oswald, D. L. (217). Maintaining long-lasting friendships. In M. Hojjat & A. Moyer (Eds.), *The psychology of friendship* (pp. 267–282). Oxford University Press.

Pew Research Center. (2020). Most Americans say coronavirus outbreak has impacted their lives. https://www.pewresearch.org/social-trends/2020/03/30/most-americans-say-coronavirus-outbreak-has-impacted-their-lives/

Philpot, L. M., Ramar, P., Roellinger, D. L., Barry, B. A., Sharma, P., & Ebbert, J. O. (2021). Changes in social relationships during an initial "stay-at-home" phase of the COVID-19 pandemic: A longitudinal survey study in the U.S. *Social Science & Medicine, 274*, Article 113779. https://doi.org/10.1016/j.socscimed.2021.113779

Rogers, A., Ha, T., & Ockey, S. (2021). Adolescents' perceived socio-emotional impact of COVID-19 and implications for mental health: Results from a U.S.-based mixed-methods study. *The Journal of Adolescent Health: Official Publication of the Society for Adolescent Medicine, 68*(1), 43–52. https://doi.org/10.1016/j.jadohealth.2020.09.039

Rosenfeld, D. L., Balcetis, E., Bastian, B., Berkman, E. T., Bosson, J. K., Brannon, T. N., Burrow, A. L., Cameron, C. D., Chen, S., Cook, J. E., Crandall, C., Davidai, S., Dhont, K., Eastwick, P. W., Gaither, S. E., Gangestad, S. W., Gilovich, T., Gray, K., Haines, E. L., . . . Tomiyama, A. J. (2022). Psychological science in the wake of COVID-19: Social, methodological, and metascientific considerations. *Perspectives on Psychological*

Science: A Journal of the Association for Psychological Science, 17(2), 311–333. https://doi.org/10.1177/1745691621999374

van Mulukom, V., Muzzulini, B., Rutjens, B. T., van Lissa, C. J., & Farias, M. (2021). The psychological impact of threat and lockdowns during the COVID-19 pandemic: Exacerbating factors and mitigating actions. *Translational Behavioral Medicine*, 11(7), 1318–1329. https://doi.org/10.1093/tbm/ibab072

Sandstrom, G. M., & Dunn, E. W. (2014). Social interactions and well-being: The surprising power of weak ties. *Personality & Social Psychology Bulletin*, 40(7), 910–922. https://doi.org/10.1177/0146167214529799

Sandstrom, G. M., & Whillans, A. (2020, April 22). Why you miss those casual friends so much. *Harvard Business Review*. https://hbr.org/2020/04/why-you-miss-those-casual-friends-so-much

Storr, V. H., Behr, R. K., & Romero, M. R. (September 6, 2021). Commercial friendships during a pandemic. *Review of Austrian Economics*. https://doi.org/10.1007/s11138-021-00556-7

Sullivan, H. S. (1953). *The interpersonal theory of psychiatry*. Norton. https://doi:10.1037/h0050700

Sutin, A. R., Stephan, Y., Luchetti, M., Aschwanden, D., Lee, J. H., Sesker, A. A., & Terracciano, A. (2022). Differential personality changes earlier and later in the coronavirus pandemic in a longitudinal sample of adults in the United States. *PLoS ONE*, 17(9), e0274542. https://doi.org/10.1371/journal.pone.0274542

Varma, P., Junge, M., Meaklim, H., & Jackson, M. L. (2021). Younger people are more vulnerable to stress, anxiety, and depression during COVID-19 pandemic: A global cross-sectional survey. *Progress in Neuro-Psychopharmacology and Biological Psychiatry*, 109, Article 110236. https://doi.org/10.1016/j.pnpbp.2020.110236

Williams, D. R., & Medlock, M. M. (2017). Health effects of dramatic societal events: Ramifications of the recent presidential election. *The New England Journal of Medicine*, 376, 2295–2299. https://10.1056/NEJMms1702111

Wiltse, D. (2021, September 17). *Disagreements over COVID-19 prevention measures strain relationships with friends and family* [Press release]. South Dakota State University. https://www.sdstate.edu/news/2021/09/disagreements-over-covid-19-prevention-measures-strain-relationships-friends-and-family

World Health Organization. (2022). WHO health emergency dashboard, Covid-19 homepage. https://covid19.who.int/

Wu, C. Y., Mattek, N., Wild, K., Miller, L. M., Kaye, J. A., Silbert, L. C., & Dodge, H. H. (2022). Can changes in social contact (frequency and mode) mitigate low mood before and during the COVID-19 pandemic? The I-CONECT project. *Journal of the American Geriatrics Society*, 70(3), 669–676. https://doi.org/10.1111/jgs.17607

Ye, B., Hu, J., Xiao, G., Zhang, Y., Liu, M., Wang, X., Yang, Q., & Xia, F. (2022). Access to epidemic information and life satisfaction under the period of COVID-19: The mediating role of perceived stress and the moderating role of friendship quality. *Applied Research in Quality of Life*, 17(3), 1227–1245. https://doi.org/10.1007/s11482-021-09957-z

15
Diverse Friendships
Formation, Maintenance, and Benefits

J. Nicole Shelton, Kate M. Turetsky, Yeji Park, and Lindsey Eikenburg

Friendships are an essential part of everyday life. Friends are the people with whom we exert effort to maintain contact, form an emotional connection, and share our lives (Dunbar, 2018). Friendships are often constrained by homophily, meaning that people make friends with those who are similar to themselves on dimensions such as race, religion, and politics, as well as behavior and personality, giving weight to the adage "Birds of a feather flock together" (McPherson et al., 2001). Overall, cross-group friendships are less prevalent, reciprocated, and stable than same-group friendships (Jugert et al., 2013; Vaquera & Kao, 2008).

Because cross-group friendships are relatively less common, the rich body of literature on friendships, and close relationships more generally, typically reflects relational processes in same-group friendships. In contrast, the development and maintenance of cross-group friendships has been under-studied. Indeed, a recent review of articles published in top relationship science journals from 2014 to 2018 found that only 3% of articles reported including couples in cross-race relationships, and only 10% included samples that were primarily nonwhite, low-income, and/or sexual or gender minorities (Williamson et al., 2022). This is unfortunate because the intimate connection associated with cross-group friendships has benefits for intergroup relations (Davies et al., 2011). In this chapter, we synthesize recent research on cross-group friendships.

Our review is divided into three parts. First, we review factors that contribute to the initial stage of friendship formation, with a focus on how ecological- and individual-level characteristics influence friendship formation. Second, we discuss psychological processes that facilitate the maintenance of cross-group friendships. Third, given that close-relationships researchers have identified a plethora of benefits associated with friendships in general (see Chapter 14 of this volume), we review the benefits of cross-group friendships specifically, focusing primarily on intergroup benefits. Across these three parts, we apply the processes that close-relationships researchers have identified as integral to friendships in general to understand cross-group friendships specifically. We argue that, although some of these processes function similarly in cross-group friendships, others do not because of the unique aspects of intergroup relations.

Given that the focus of most cross-group friendship has been on race/ethnicity, our review draws primarily from that literature. To the extent possible, we include research across other identities. We acknowledge, however, that some processes for cross-group friendships may differ as a function of the specific group identity. Moreover, we focus primarily on psychological research, drawing on insights from sociology and political science when possible, although this is not an exhaustive review.

Friendship Formation

Much research has been conducted within the close-relationships field to understand what draws people to one another. However, this research has largely focused on partners who are of similar backgrounds. We build upon this literature to consider the factors that shape cross-group friendship formation. We organize the research around ecological and individual-level factors that contribute to the development of cross-group friendships, specifically: (1) the *ecological factors* that allow opportunities for exposure, interaction, and ultimately friendship between out-group members, and (2) the *individual beliefs* that influence the likelihood of forming friendships with out-group members, given opportunities to do so.

Ecological Opportunities for Cross-Group Friendship Formation

To form close relationships, people need the opportunity to meet and interact with others. This contact allows people to determine whether there is mutual attraction in becoming closer. The larger a person's network of interaction partners, the greater the probability that they will form a friendship with some people in the network—and the more hours people spend together, the more likely they are to become close friends (Hall, 2019).

Likewise, intergroup contact is a precursor to cross-group friendship. The more people interact with out-group members, the more likely they are to develop cross-group friendships over time. For example, the more cross-race interactions White and Black students had before and during college, the more cross-race friendships they had at the end of their first year of college (Schofield et al., 2010). Once cross-group friendships are formed, sustained cross-group interaction within these friendships can also predict the development of additional cross-group friendships later on; for example, the more cross-race friends people have in high school, the more cross-race friends they have in college, although the effects vary by racial group (Fischer, 2008; Stearns et al., 2009).

Close-relationships research has demonstrated that opportunities for interaction with others are largely shaped by *proximity* (Festinger et al., 1950; Newcomb, 1956). Proximity is the idea that people are more likely to encounter those who are physically or functionally nearby, and thus more likely to interact and develop relationships with these nearby individuals. Although proximity shapes opportunities for interaction and friendship formation in both same-group and cross-group contexts, unique factors underlie the role of proximity in cross-group friendship formation. In this section, we discuss the role of physical, functional, and social proximity in cross-group friendship development.

Physical Proximity

When asked to list close friends, people are more likely to list others who are physically nearby, including those who live closer within an apartment complex (Newcomb, 1956) or who sit closer within a class (Rohrer et al., 2021). This pattern is driven both by opportunity for interaction, as people are more likely to come into contact with those who are physically close, and by the mere exposure effect, as repeated exposure to the same individual increases familiarity and liking (Bornstein, 1989). This familiarity and liking can lay the foundations for an intimate relationship by increasing the chances of meaningful interaction: People not only prefer others to whom they have been exposed to a greater degree, but they also are more willing to disclose personal information to them, increasing closeness (Brockner & Swap, 1976). Thus, physical proximity to a person creates the opportunity for a possible friendship to develop.

There are two unique considerations related to physical proximity in cross-group contexts. The first is that, whereas people are likely to be physically proximate to other members of their own social groups, persistent segregation along racial, economic, political, and religious lines decreases physical proximity to out-group members (Enos, 2017). If people do not live, work, or go to school near members of out-groups, opportunities for cross-group exposure and interaction are limited. The lack of physical proximity among members of different social groups is thus a barrier to the formation of cross-group friendships, but not to same-group friendships.

The second is that physical proximity has more mixed effects on friendship formation in cross-group (vs. same-group) contexts. On the one hand, physical proximity of out-group members can drive the development of cross-group friendships in a similar manner as in same-group contexts. Living in a neighborhood with more cross-race peers (Sigelman et al., 1996; Vanhoutte & Hooghe, 2012), attending a more diverse high school (Sigelman et al., 1996) or college (Fischer, 2008; Kim et al., 2015), having a cross-race roommate (Mark & Harris, 2012; Stearns et al., 2009), and being in ethnically diverse classes (Bohman & Miklikowska, 2021) have all been associated with greater levels of cross-race friendship. Additionally, longitudinal work shows that the diversity of one's environment increases cross-group friendships over time; for example, students in diverse schools and classrooms are more likely to have cross-group friendships years after leaving that space (Bohman & Miklikowska, 2021). These findings suggest that physical proximity—and the resulting opportunities for exposure and interaction—facilitates cross-group friendship formation, consistent with close-relationships findings on proximity in general.

On the other hand, the effect of physical proximity of out-group members has its limits. Physical proximity may be more likely to increase friendship between same-group individuals than cross-group individuals (Munniksma et al., 2016; Rohrer et al., 2021). For example, although assigned classroom seating for Hungarian students increased the likelihood of students selecting the person seated next to them as their "best friend" over time, this pattern was stronger for same-gender compared with different-gender students, and seating Roma and non-Roma students next to each other did not reliably increase the chance of cross-group friendship. Other studies indicate that students in racially balanced classrooms are still more than twice as likely to choose a same-race peer than a cross-race peer as their best friend (Hallinan, 1982), students are more likely to have same-race friends than what would be predicted by the racial composition of the school (Joyner & Kao, 2000; Quillian & Campbell, 2003), and people are more likely to socialize with same-race others even in public spaces that are racially diverse (e.g., bars and nightclubs; May, 2014). Still other results suggest that increasing diversity may, in some instances, be associated with a *decreased* likelihood of cross-group friendships: Moody (2001) found a positive correlation between school racial diversity and friendship segregation, such that greater heterogeneity was associated with a greater tendency to have same-race friends.

In sum, although increasing physical proximity between out-groups *can* foster cross-group friendships, it does not always. The link between physical proximity and friendship formation is more complex in cross-group than in same-group contexts. This explains why increasing diversity alone, whether in schools, workplaces, or neighborhoods, will not necessarily lead to more cross-group friendships.

Functional Proximity
Close-relationships research has long demonstrated that it is not only *physical* proximity that drives opportunity for interaction and friendship formation, but also *functional* proximity (Festinger et al., 1950). In other words, it is not only the physical distance between two individuals that shapes their likelihood of developing a relationship, but also features of the environment that make interaction between individuals more likely. Classic research on functional proximity has illustrated that those who live near stairways in apartment buildings are more likely to become friends with people on other floors despite their physical separation, because the configuration of the building facilitates their interaction (Festinger et al., 1950).

Functional proximity is an important driver of cross-group interaction. Even when members of different social groups are physically close, they may remain functionally distant, reducing the likelihood of cross-group interaction. For example, highways, train lines, school district boundaries, and other barriers often divide neighborhoods in cities in which people of different racial/ethnic or economic groups live physically close to one another (Noonan, 2005; Roberto & Hwang, 2017). In fact, functional barriers to prevent intergroup mingling may sometimes be *more* common in diverse environments with close physical proximity between groups due to Whites' racial anxieties. An examination of every tennis and golf facility in the United States revealed that the more racially diverse the surrounding community, the more likely these historically White facilities were to have guest policies, fees, dress codes, and other restrictive barriers in place (Anicich et al., 2021). Additionally, even as more White families move into diverse urban neighborhoods, schools remain segregated, as White parents frequently choose not to send their children to local public schools (Candipan, 2019). Despite physical proximity between out-groups in these settings, such barriers—whether physical, embedded in policy, or created through behavior—reduce functional proximity and thus limit opportunities for groups to interact and become friends.

In contrast, actions taken to encourage meaningful interaction between out-groups that occupy the same space, but might not otherwise interact, can facilitate cross-group relationships. A classic example is the jigsaw classroom (Aronson & Bridgeman, 1979), in which a diverse group of students engage in cooperative learning activities that require meaningful interaction between groups on equal footing. In addition, online dating platforms, which increase functional proximity by presenting people with opportunities to meet with potential partners nearby whose paths might not have otherwise crossed, have resulted in more interracial and interreligious relationships (Thomas, 2020). These effects may be small due to individual beliefs and preferences that limit interest in cross-group relationships (as discussed later in this chapter), but they illustrate the importance of functional, not just physical, proximity.

Social Proximity

People's relationships do not exist in a vacuum; rather, they are embedded in a larger social network. Social networks introduce another type of proximity that influences the likelihood of friendship formation: *social proximity*. Social proximity reflects the idea that people are more likely to interact and form friendships with people to whom they are more closely socially connected than with people to whom they are more distantly connected. In particular, people are much more likely to develop friendships with friends of friends (a phenomenon called triadic closure; Granovetter, 1973) than with people with a greater degree of separation.

Social proximity is particularly important in cross-group friendships. Triadic closure greatly exacerbates homophily in friendship networks

(Asikainen et al., 2020). Even a slight tendency of people to form same-group friendships is magnified by the tendency to develop friendships with friends of friends, propelling the entire network toward segregation. For example, if a White student's friends are predominately White, and each of those friends' friends are also predominately White, the student's network will become substantially more White over time due to triadic closure.

Friends of friends can also influence cross-group friendship development by informing attitudes and beliefs about out-group members. Learning that in-group members have out-group friends improves attitudes toward the out-group (Zhou et al., 2019). In turn, these improved attitudes prompted by the social proximity of out-group members may translate into cross-group friendships. For example, people who know that in-group members have out-group friends indicate both that they would like to have and actually have more out-group friends (Gomez et al., 2018; Schofield et al., 2010).

Lastly, given unique concerns regarding social rejection in intergroup contexts, people may also attend to a potential cross-group friend's existing friendships as a cue for whether that person is receptive to friendship formation across group lines. For example, White people report greater interest in befriending a Black person when that person is presented with a White friend than with a Black friend (Shapiro et al., 2010). Black people believe they would be perceived more positively and be accepted by a White person who has a racially diverse friendship network compared with a homogeneously White friendship network (Wout et al., 2010), which has implications for Blacks' willingness to befriend out-group members (Wout et al., 2014). In other words, cross-group friendship development is influenced not just by the social proximity of out-group members in one's existing network, but also by the social proximity of in-group members in an out-group member's network.

Taken together, increased physical, functional, and social proximity to out-group members increases the opportunity to have friendships across group lines. However, these friendships do not always develop. As Khmelkov and Hallinan (1999) argue, proximity is a "necessary but not sufficient" condition for cross-group friendship formation. In some cases, despite proximity to out-group members, people still prefer same-group friends, highlighting the role of individual factors in cross-group friendship formation. We next turn to these individual-level factors.

Individual Beliefs Influencing Cross-Group Friendship Formation

In addition to ecological opportunities to develop friendships, people's individual characteristics also shape friendship formation. Beliefs, personalities, worldviews, and perceptions of similarity in these characteristics are all related to the quantity and quality of relationships (Doroszuki et al., 2019). Although these individual characteristics are related to both same- and cross-group friendships, certain characteristics uniquely impact cross-group relationships. In this section, we describe how intergroup beliefs, personality, and (perceived) similarity shape cross-group friendships.

Intergroup Beliefs

People's beliefs about out-groups play a role in their willingness to form cross-group friendships. Prejudice is negatively associated with perceptions that out-group individuals are even compatible as friends (McGlothlin et al., 2005). Both cross-sectional and longitudinal studies show that prejudice has an adverse effect on actual cross-group friendships as well. For example, college students' racial bias as freshmen negatively predicts their number of cross-race friendships as sophomores and juniors (Levin et al., 2003). Likewise, European students' negative attitudes about ethnic outgroups are associated with a lower quantity and poorer quality of cross-group friendships over time (Binder et al., 2009). Prejudiced majority group members have fewer cross-group friendships in part because they tend to avoid in-group friends who have out-group friends (Stark, 2015). Importantly, no matter how many opportunities someone has in their environment to interact with out-group members, if they have negative attitudes toward the out-group or a preference for their in-group, they are unlikely to form cross-group relationships.

In addition to beliefs about a specific group, intergroup beliefs more generally are precursors for cross-group friendship development. Valuing diversity, for example, is positively associated with having a diverse friendship network. People who report positive beliefs about diversity are likely to have friends of different racial, religious, and sexual orientation groups (Bahns, 2019; Bahns et al., 2015). Perceptions of potential cross-group friends' intergroup beliefs are also influential; the more people believe out-group members value diversity, the more likely they are to be interested in developing and to actually develop cross-group friendships (Rivas-Drake et al.,

2019; Tropp & Bianchi, 2006). Lastly, color-blind ideology is also positively related to cross-group friendships. For example, the more ethnic minorities minimize racism (Gonlin & Campbell, 2017) and religious minorities prefer adopting the dominant culture's views (Zagefka et al., 2016), the more cross-group friends they have. Much of this work is correlational, so one must be careful to make claims about the direction of the relationship. Nonetheless, taken together, these findings suggest that intergroup beliefs are related to cross-group friendship patterns.

Personality
A small but growing body of research suggests that people's tendency to develop cross-group friendships is influenced not only by specific intergroup beliefs, but also by more general personality characteristics. In particular, openness to experience (Jackson & Poulsen, 2005), openness to others (Antonoplis & John, 2022), motivation for self-expansion (Paolini et al., 2016), open-minded thinking (Park et al., 2023), and receptiveness to opposing views (Reschke et al., 2022) have predicted interest in and/or actual development of cross-group friendships. Although this area of research is still developing and mostly correlational thus far, this work may suggest that some underlying construct related to interest in encountering different perspectives, expanding one's worldview, and learning from disagreement may contribute to individuals' tendency to form cross-group friendships.

Perceived Similarity
The close-relationships literature suggests that people prefer to be with others who they believe have similar beliefs as they do (McPherson et al., 2001), and that this perceived similarity is associated with greater relationship quality over and above actual similarity (Montoya et al., 2008). In intergroup contexts, however, the relationship between perceived similarity and friendship may not be as straightforward. In general, people do not expect to have similar beliefs as out-group members, but when they learn they are more similar than expected, it increases their liking for the out-group member (Chen & Kenrick, 2002). Similarly, when people perceive themselves as more similar to out-group members than expected, they have more positive expectations about cross-group interactions and feel less anxious in anticipation of the interaction (West et al., 2014), both of which facilitate friendships. Together, these results suggest that overriding people's default expectations that they will be dissimilar to out-group members increases cross-group

friendship attraction. However, in some circumstances, perceived intergroup *dis*similarity can also increase cross-group friendship attraction. According to social identity theory, people like to feel their groups are distinct, and believing their in-group is too similar to the out-group decreases liking for the out-group (Leonardelli et al., 2010). Consistent with this idea, a study of East Asian–South Asian dyads found that participants instructed to write about differences (vs. similarity) between these two groups expressed greater interest in initiating friendships with their interaction partner (Danyluck & Page-Gould, 2018). Overall, perceived similarity generally predicts friendship development, but the effects of perceived similarity in cross-group friendships are context dependent.

Friendship Maintenance

Once a friendship is formed, people must work to maintain it. In this section, we examine behaviors known to impact close-relationships maintenance in the context of understanding what makes cross-group friendships persist. Admittedly, research has not always been clear as to when these behaviors contribute to the formation or maintenance of relationships. They are likely to play a role in both areas.

Pro-Relationship Behaviors

People engage in a range of pro-relationship behaviors to promote relationship maintenance. For example, disclosing intimate details about oneself and, more importantly, having one's partner be responsive to that self-disclosure are important for increasing intimacy and relationship maintenance (Reis & Shaver, 1988). Moreover, helping, complimenting, and providing security enhances relationship maintenance.

Similar behaviors help maintain cross-group friendships, although people tend to engage in these behaviors less often, which may explain why these friendships are less stable. For example, Blacks and Whites disclose personal and race-related information less often and are less responsive to cross-group friends' disclosures, but partner responsiveness is the mechanism for the relationship between self-disclosure and intimacy for both same-race and cross-race friendships (Chen & Nakazawa, 2009; Sanchez et al., 2022;

Shelton et al., 2010). Moreover, for Black–White friendships, communal motivation (attending to the needs of relationship partners) and communal security (confidence in partners' motivation to attend to one's needs) enhance relationship satisfaction and prosocial behaviors, such as giving compliments, helping the partner, and self-disclosure (Lemay & Ryan, 2021). Overall, similar to same-group friendship, pro-relationship behaviors help maintain cross-group friendships, but cross-group friends engage in these behaviors less often.

Shared Activities

More time spent engaging in shared activities together, often in informal social contexts, is associated with closer friendships (Hall, 2019). Engaging in activities not only fosters interdependence, which is beneficial for the relationship, but also self-expansion, as people come to include the other in their own self-identity, taking on their partner's likes, hobbies, and traits.

Engaging in shared activities may be less likely to occur in cross-group friendships. Various studies report that cross-race friends engage in fewer shared activities than same-race friends (Kao & Joyner, 2004), negatively predicting cross-race friendship retention (Ruda & Herda, 2010). Additionally, cross-group friends may engage in less intimate shared activities. For example, cross-race (vs. same-race) adolescent friends are less likely to visit one another's home, although visiting a friend's home is positively associated with friendship stability (Kao & Joyner, 2004; Lessard et al., 2019). Spending time at home allows for more intimate connections, allowing friends to engage in activities and self-disclose more than might be permitted in formal settings such as schools and workplaces. Thus, the fact that these types of intimate shared activities are less likely to occur in cross-group friendships could be part of the reason that these friendships are less likely to be maintained than same-group friendships.

Benefits of Cross-Group Friendships

Friendships shape many life outcomes. High-quality friendships are associated with health benefits (Holt-Lunstad et al., 2017) and cognitive and educational benefits (Wentzel et al., 2018).

These types of individual benefits also exist for cross-group friendships (Lessard & Juvonen; 2019; Mendoza-Denton & Page-Gould, 2008), but relatively little is known about whether and how they differ from those of same-group friendships. Instead, the focus has been on intergroup benefits, which we review below.

Attitudes

Cross-group friendships embody the essential characteristics posited for improving intergroup attitudes: intimate contact, equal status, and cooperation between partners (Pettigrew, 1998). As a result, perhaps it is no surprise that the most-studied topic in the cross-group friendship literature is its impact on prejudice reduction. A meta-analysis of 135 experimental and longitudinal studies showed that cross-group friendships are associated with more positive intergroup attitudes (Davies et al., 2011). This relationship exists across various types of cross-group contexts and for members of both majority and marginalized groups, but studies involving racial/ethnic groups yield smaller effect sizes than friendships across nationality, sexual orientation, and religious affiliation (Davies et al., 2011). Similarly, a meta-analysis of 115 studies revealed that knowing or perceiving that an in-group friend has an out-group friend is related to positive out-group attitudes, independent of one's own out-group friendships (Zhou et al, 2019). Numerous factors have been identified as mechanisms for these effects, including increased knowledge about the out-group, empathy, and perspective taking and decreased intergroup anxiety, all of which in turn reduce prejudice.

Although cross-group friendships benefit intergroup attitudes for majority and minority groups, their association with other group-relevant outcomes varies across groups. For example, for Whites, having a greater percentage of racial minority friends is associated with an *increased* awareness of racial injustice and involvement in collective action to help minorities (Carter et al., 2018). For racial minorities, however, having a greater percentage of White friends is associated with a *decreased* awareness of racial injustice and involvement in collective action to help minorities (Carter et al., 2018). Similar to intergroup contact (Saguy, 2018), cross-group friendships may allow members of minority groups to see more similarities between them and their majority friends, which can be good for intergroup attitudes but also diminishes their beliefs that majority group members can be biased, undermining the desire for social justice.

Social Support

Cross-group friendships buffer people from a range of negative outcomes associated with intergroup relations. For example, cross-group friends protect people who expect to be rejected in cross-group interactions from stress (Page-Gould, 2012) and low levels of belonging and dissatisfaction in college (Mendoza-Denton & Page-Gould, 2008). Similarly, people who have cross-group friendships experience lower physiological stress reactivity in novel intergroup interactions (Page-Gould et al., 2008). Moreover, cross-group friendships provide social support when faced with cross-group conflict. Whereas people who experience intergroup conflict are less likely to initiate interracial interactions the next day, people with high-quality cross-group friendships demonstrate no change in initiating contact after intergroup conflict (Page-Gould, 2012).

Future Directions

There are many outstanding topics to explore about cross-group friendship. First, more insight into how to effectively facilitate cross-group friendships is needed. Given that the friendships yield important benefits for intergroup relations, we need to know how to facilitate them in the real world. In particular, more work should consider how ecological factors and individual dispositions may interact to yield divergent effects in cross-group friendship formation. Second, compared with the antecedents and consequences of cross-group friendships, there is considerably less research on the maintenance of cross-group friendships. More research on the specific factors that contribute to the maintenance of cross-group friendships would be fruitful, especially given that cross-group friendships often dissolve more quickly than same-group friendships. Third, as most of the literature on cross-group friendships focuses on interracial friendships, more effort is needed to understand cross-group friendships across other identities, including but not limited to political beliefs, socioeconomic status, culture, and sexual orientations. Future work should also consider how these different identities interact with each other in cross-group friendship formation and maintenance. Finally, more research is needed on the benefits and costs of cross-group friendships beyond prejudice reduction. Furthering our understanding in these areas might be beneficial not only for intergroup relations but also for our understanding of close relationships in general.

References

Anicich, E. M., Jachimowicz, J. M., Osborne, M. R., & Phillips, L. T. (2021). Structuring local environments to avoid racial diversity: Anxiety drives Whites' geographical and institutional self-segregation preferences. *Journal of Experimental Social Psychology*, *95*, 104–117. https://doi.org/10.31234/osf.io/yzpr2

Antonoplis, S., & John, O. P. (2022). Who has different-race friends, and does it depend on context? Openness (to other), but not agreeableness, predicts lower racial homophily in friendship networks. *Journal of Personality and Social Psychology*, *122*(5), 894–919. https://doi.org/10.1037/pspp0000413

Aronson, E., & Bridgeman, D. (1979). Jigsaw groups and the desegregated classroom: In pursuit of common goals. *Personality and Social Psychology Bulletin*, *5*(4), 438–446. https://doi.org/10.1177/014616727900500405

Asikainen, A., Iñiguez, G., Ureña-Carrión, J., Kaski, K., & Kivelä, M. (2020). Cumulative effects of triadic closure and homophily in social networks. *Science Advances*, *6*(19), eaax7310. https://doi.org/10.1126/sciadv.aax7310

Bahns, A. J. (2019). Preference, opportunity, and choice. A multilevel analysis of diverse friendship formation. *Group Processes & Intergroup Relations*, *22*(2), 233–252. https://doi.org/10.1177/1368430217725390

Bahns, A. J., Springer, L. S., & The, C. (2015). Fostering diverse friendships: The role of beliefs about the value of diversity. *Group Processes & Intergroup Relations*, *18*(4), 475–488. https://doi.org/10.1177/1368430214566893

Binder, J., Zagefka, H., Brown, R., Funke, F., Kessler, T., Mummendey, A., Maquil, A., Demoulin, S., & Leyens, J. P. (2009). Does contact reduce prejudice or does prejudice reduce contact? A longitudinal test of the contact hypothesis among majority and minority groups in three European countries. *Journal of Personality & Social Psychology*, *96*(4), 843–856. https://doi.org/10.1037/a0013470

Bohman, A., & Miklikowska, M. (2021). Does classroom diversity improve intergroup relations? Short- and long-term effects of classroom diversity for cross-ethnic friendships and anti-immigrant attitudes in adolescence. *Group Processes & Intergroup Relations*, *24*(8), 1372–1390. https://doi.org/10.1177/1368430220941592

Bornstein, R. F. (1989). Exposure and affect: Overview and meta-analysis of research, 1968–1987. *Psychological Bulletin*, *106*(2), 265–289. https://doi.org/10.1037/0033-2909.106.2.265

Brockner, J., & Swap, W. C. (1976). Effects of repeated exposure and attitudinal similarity on self-disclosure and interpersonal attraction. *Journal of Personality and Social Psychology*, *33*(5), 531–540. https://doi.org/10.1037/0022-3514.33.5.531

Candipan, J. (2019). Neighbourhood change and the neighbourhood-school gap. *Urban Studies*, *56*(15), 3308–3333. https://doi.org/10.1177/0042098018819075

Carter, E. R., Brady, S. T., Murdock-Perriera, L. A., Gilbertson, M. K., Ablorh, T., & Murphy, M. C. (2018). The racial composition of students' friendship networks predicts perceptions of injustice and involvement in collective action. *Journal of Theoretical Social Psychology*, 3(1), 49–61. https://doi.org/10.1002/jts5.27

Chen, F. F., & Kenrick, D. T. (2002). Repulsion or attraction? Group membership and assumed attitude similarity. *Journal of Personality and Social Psychology*, 83(1), 111–125. https://doi.org/10.1037/0022-3514.83.1.111

Chen, Y. W., & Nakazawa, M. (2009). Influences of culture on self-disclosure as relationally situated in intercultural and interracial friendships from a social penetration perspective. *Journal of Intercultural Communication Research*, 38(2), 77–98. https://doi.org/10.1080/17475750903395408

Danyluck, C., & Page-Gould, E. (2018). Intergroup dissimilarity predicts physiological synchrony and affiliation in intergroup interaction. *Journal of Experimental Social Psychology*, 74, 111–120. https://doi.org/10.1016/j.jesp.2017.08.001

Davies, K., Tropp, L. R., Aron, A., Pettigrew, T. F., & Wright, S. C. (2011). Cross-group friendships and intergroup attitudes: A meta-analytic review. *Personality and Social Psychology Review*, 15(4), 332–351. https://doi.org/10.1177/1088868311411103

Doroszuki, M., Kupis, M., & Czarna, A. Z. (2019). Personality and friendships. In V. Zeigler-Hill, & T. K. Shackelford (Eds.), *Encyclopedia of personality and individual difference* (pp. 1–9). Springer Nature Switzerland. https://doi.org/10.1007/978-3-319-24612-3_712

Dunbar, R. I. M. (2018). The anatomy of friendship. *Trends in Cognitive Science*, 22(1), 32–51. https://doi.org/10.1016/j.tics.2017.10.004

Enos, R. D. (2017). *The space between us: Social geography and politics*. Cambridge University Press. https://doi.org/10.1017/9781108354943

Festinger, L., Schachter, S., & Back, K. (1950). *Social pressures in informal groups; a study of human factors in housing*. Harper. https://doi.org/10.2307/3348388

Fischer, M. J. (2008). Does campus diversity promote friendship diversity? A look at interracial friendships in college. *Social Science Quarterly*, 89(3), 631–655. https://doi.org/10.1111/j.1540-6237.2008.00552.x

Gomez, A., Tropp, L. R., Vazquez, A., Voci, A., & Hewstone, M. (2018). Depersonalized extended contact and injunctive norms about cross-group friendship impact intergroup orientations. *Journal of Experimental Social Psychology*, 76, 356–370. https://doi.org/10.1016/j.jesp.2018.02.010

Gonlin, V., & Campbell, M. E. (2017). Is blindness contagious? Examining racial attitudes among people of color with close interracial relationships. *Sociological Perspectives*, 60(5), 937–955. https://doi.org/10.1177/0731121417719698

Granovetter, M. S. (1973). The strength of weak ties. *American Journal of Sociology*, 78(6), 1360–1380. https://doi.org/10.1086/225469

Hall, J. A. (2019). How many hours does it take to make a friend? *Journal of Social and Personal Relationships*, 36(4), 1278–1296. https://doi.org/10.1177/0265407518761225

Hallinan, M. T. (1982). Classroom racial composition and children's friendships. *Social Forces*, 61(1), 56–72. https://doi.org/10.2307/2578074

Holt-Lunstad, J. (2017). Friendships and health. In M. Hojjat & A. Moyer (Eds.), *The psychology of friendship* (pp. 233–248). Oxford University Press. https://doi.org/10.1093/acprof:oso/9780190222024.003.0014

Jackson, J. W., & Poulsen, J. R. (2005). Contact experiences mediate the relationship between five-factor model personality traits and ethnic prejudice. *Journal of Applied Social Psychology, 35*(4), 667–685. https://doi.org/10.1111/j.1559-1816.2005.tb02140.x

Joyner, K., & Kao, G. (2000). School racial composition and adolescent racial homophily. *Social Science Quarterly, 81*(3), 810–825.

Jugert, P., Noack, P., & Rutland, A. (2013). Children's cross-ethnic friendships: Why are they less stable than same-ethnic friendships? *European Journal of Developmental Psychology, 10*(6), 649–662. https://doi.org/10.1080/17405629.2012.734136

Kao, G., & Joyner, K. (2004). Do race and ethnicity matter among friends? Activities among interracial, interethnic, and intraethnic adolescent friends. *The Sociological Quarterly, 45*(3), 557–573. https://doi.org/10.1111/j.1533-8525.2004.tb02303.x

Khmelkov, V. T., & Hallinan, M. T. (1999). Organizational effects on race relations in schools. *Journal of Social Issues, 55*(4), 627–645. https://doi.org/10.1111/0022-4537.00139

Kim, Y. K., Park, J. J., Koo, K. K. (2015). Testing self-segregation: Multiple-group structural modeling of college students' interracial friendship by race. *Research in Higher Education, 56*(1), 57–77. https://doi.org/10.1007/s11162-014-9337-8

Lemay, E. P., & Ryan, J. E. (2021). Common ingroup identity, perceived similarity, and communal interracial relationships. *Personality and Social Psychology Bulletin, 47*(6), 985–1003. https://doi.org/10.1177/0146167220953984

Leonardelli, G. J., Pickett, C. L., & Brewer, M. B. (2010). Optimal distinctiveness theory: A framework for social identity, social cognition, and intergroup relations. In M. P. Zanna & J. M. Olson (Eds.), *Advances in experimental social psychology* (Vol. 43, pp. 63–113). Academic Press. https://doi.org/10.1016/S0065-2601(10)43002-6

Lessard, L. M., & Juvonen, J. (2019). Cross-class friendship and academic achievement in middle school. *Developmental Psychology, 55*(8), 1666–1679. https://doi.org/10.1037/dev0000755

Lessard, L. M., Kogachi, K., & Juvonen, J. (2019). Quality and stability of cross-ethnic friendships: Effects of classroom diversity and out-of-school contact. *Journal of Youth and Adolescence, 48*(3), 554–566. https://doi.org/10.1007/s10964-018-0964-9

Levin, S., van Laar, C., & Sidanius, J. (2003). The effects of ingroup and outgroup friendships on ethnic attitudes in college: A longitudinal study. *Group Processes & Intergroup Relations, 6*(1), 76–92. https://doi.org/10.1177/1368430203006001013

Mark, N. P., & Harris, D. R. (2012). Roommate's race and the racial composition of white college students' ego networks. *Social Science Research, 41*, 331–342. https://doi.org/10.1016/j.ssresearch.2011.11.012

May, R. (2014). *Urban nightlife: Entertaining race, class, and culture in public space*. Rutgers University Press. https://doi.org/10.1111/cico.12111

McGlothlin, H., Killen, M., & Edmonds, C. (2005). European-American children's intergroup attitudes about peer relationships. *British Journal of Developmental Psychology, 23*(2), 227–249. https://doi.org/10.1348/026151005x26101

McPherson, M., Smith-Lovin, L., & Cook, J. M. (2001). Birds of a feather: Homophily in social networks. *Annual Review of Sociology, 27*, 415–444. https://doi.org/10.1146/annurev.soc.27.1.415

Mendoza-Denton, R., & Page-Gould, E. (2008). Can cross-group friendships influence minority students' well-being at historically White universities? *Psychological Science, 19*(9), 933–939. https://doi.org/10.1111/j.1467-9280.2008.02179.x

Montoya, R. M., Horton, R. D., & Kirchner, J. (2008). Is actual similarity necessary for attraction? A meta-analysis of actual and perceived similarity. *Journal of Social and Personal Relationships, 25*(6), 889–922. https//doi.org/10.1177/0265407508096700

Moody, J. (2001). Race, school integration, and friendship segregation in America. *American Journal of Sociology, 107*(3), 679–716. https://doi.org/10.1086/338954

Munniksma, A., Scheepers, P., Stark, T. H., & Tolsma, J. (2016). The impact of adolescents' classroom and neighborhood ethnic diversity on same- and cross-ethnic friendships within classrooms. *Journal of Research on Adolescence, 27*(1), 20–33. https://doi.org/10.1111/jora.12248

Newcomb, T. M. (1956). The prediction of interpersonal attraction. *American Psychologist, 11*(11), 575–586. https://doi.org/10.1037/h0046141

Noonan, D. S. (2005). Neighbours, barriers and urban environments: Are things different on the other side of the tracks? *Urban Studies, 42*(10), 1817–1835. https://doi.org/10.1080/00420980500231720

Page-Gould, E. (2012). To whom can I turn? Maintenance of positive intergroup relations in the face of intergroup conflict. *Social Psychological and Personality Science, 3*(4), 462–470. https://doi.org/10.1177/1948550611426937

Page-Gould, E., Mendoza-Denton, R., & Tropp, L. R. (2008). With a little help from my cross- group friend: Reducing anxiety in intergroup contexts through cross-group friendship. *Journal of Personality and Social Psychology, 95*(5), 1080–1094. https://doi.org/10.1037/0022-3514.95.5.1080

Paolini, S., Wright, S. C., Dys-Steenbergen, O., & Favara, I. (2016). Self-expansion and intergroup contact: Expectancies and motives to self-expand lead to greater interest in outgroup contact and more positive intergroup relations. *Journal of Social Issues, 72*(3), 450–447. https://doi.org/10.1111/josi.12176

Park, Y., Turetsky, K. M., Duckworth, A. L., & Tsukayama, E. (2023). *Open-mindedness predicts racial and political diversity of real-world friendship networks* [Manuscript in preparation]. Psychology Department/Princeton University.

Pettigrew, T. F. (1998). Intergroup contact theory. *Annual Review of Psychology, 49*, 65–85. https://doi.org/10.1146/annurev.psych.49.1.65

Quillian, L., & Campbell, M. E. (2003). Beyond black and white: The present and future of multiracial friendship segregation. *American Sociological Review, 68*(4), 540–566. https://doi.org/10.2307/1519738

Reis, H. T., & Shaver, P. (1988). Intimacy as an interpersonal process. In S. W. Duck (Ed.), Handbook of personal relationships (pp. 367–389). Wiley.

Reschke, B. P., Minson, J., Bowles, H. R., de Vaan, M., & Srivastava, S. B. (2022). *Mutual receptiveness to opposing views bridges ideological divides in network formation* [Manuscript in revision]. Brigham Young University—Marriot School.

Rivas-Drake, D., Saleem, M., Schaefer, D. R., Medina, M., & Jagers, R. (2019). Intergroup contact attitudes across peer networks in school: Selection, influence, and implications for cross-group friendships. *Child Development, 90*(6), 1898–1916. https://doi.org/10.1111/cdev.13061

Roberto, E., & Hwang, J. (2017). *Barriers to integration: Physical boundaries and the spatial structure of residential segregation.* https://arxiv.org/abs/1509.02574

Rohrer, J. M., Keller, T., & Elwart, F. (2021). Proximity can induce diverse friendships: A large randomized classroom experiment. *PLoS ONE, 16*(8), 1–15. https://doi.org/10.1371/journal.pone.0255097

Rude, J., & Herda, D. (2010). Best friends forever? Race and the stability of adolescent friendships. *Social Forces, 89*(2), 585–607. https://doi.org/10.1353/sof.2010.0059

Saguy, T. (2018). Downside of intergroup Harmony? When reconciliation might backfire and what to do. *Policy Insights From the Behavioral and Brain Sciences, 5*(1), 75–81. https://doi.org/10.1177/2372732217747085

Sanchez, K. L., Kalkstein, D. A., & Walton, G. M. (2022). A threatening opportunity: The prospect of conversations about race-related experiences between Black and White friends. *Journal of Personality and Social Psychology, 122*(5), 853–872. https://doi.org/10.1037/pspi0000369

Schofield, J. W., Hausmann, L. R. M., Ye, F., & Woods, R. L. (2010). Intergroup friendships on campus: Predicting close and casual friendships between White and African American first-year college students. *Group Processes & Intergroup Relations, 13*(5), 585–602. https://doi.org/10.1177/1368430210362437

Shapiro, J. R., Baldwin, M., Williams, A. M., & Trawalter, S. (2010). The company you keep: Fear of rejection in intergroup interaction. *Journal of Experimental Social Psychology, 47*(1), 221–227. https://doi.org/10.1016/j.jesp.2010.10.006

Shelton, J. N., Trail, T. E., West, T. V., & Bergsieker, H. B. (2010). From strangers to friends: The interpersonal process model of intimacy in developing interracial friendships. *Journal of Social and Personal Relationships, 27*(1), 71–90. https://doi.org/10.1177/0265407509346422

Sigelman, L., Bledsoe, T., Welch, S., & Combs, M. W. (1996). Making contact? Black-white social interaction in an urban setting. *American Journal of Sociology, 101*(5), 1306–1332. https://doi.org/10.1086/230824

Stark, T. H. (2015). Understanding the selection bias: Social network processes and the effect of prejudice on the avoidance of outgroup friends. *Social Psychology Quarterly, 78*(2), 127–150. https://doi.org/10.1177/0190272514565252

Stearns, E., Buchmann, C., & Bonneau, K. (2009). Interracial friendships in the transition to college: Do birds of a feather flock together once they leave the nest? *Sociology of Education, 82*(2), 173–195. https://doi.org/10.1177/003804070908200204

Thomas, R. J. (2020). Online exogamy reconsidered: Estimating the internet's effects on racial, educational, religious, political and age assortative mating. *Social Forces, 98*(3), 1257–1286. https://doi.org/10.1093/sf/soz060

Tropp, L. R., & Bianchi, R. A. (2006). Valuing diversity and interest in intergroup contact. *Journal of Social Issues, 62*(3), 533–551. https://doi.org/10.1111/j.1540-4560.2006.00472.x

Vanhoutte, B., & Hooghe, M. (2012). Do diverse geographical contexts lead to diverse friendship networks? A multilevel analysis of Belgian survey data. *International Journal of Intercultural Relations, 36*(3), 343–352. https://doi.org/10.1016/j.ijintrel.2011.09.003

Vaquera, E., & Kao, G. (2008). Do you like me as much as I like you? Friendship reciprocity and its effects on school outcomes among adolescents. *Social Science Research, 37*(1), 55–72. https://doi.org/10.1016/j.ssresearch.2006.11.002

Wentzel, K., Jablansky, S., & Scalise, N. R. (2018). Do friendships afford academic benefits? A meta-analytic study. *Educational Psychology Review, 30*, 1241–1267. https://doi.org/10.1007/s10648-018-9447-5

West, T. V., Magee, J. C., Gordon, S. H., & Gullett, L. (2014). A little similarity goes a long way: The effects of peripheral but self-revealing similarities on improving and sustaining interracial relationships. *Journal of Personality and Social Psychology, 107*(1), 81–100. https://doi.org/10.1037/a0036556

Williamson, H. C., Bornstein, J. X., Cantu, V., Ciftci, O., Farnish, K. A., & Schouweiler, M. T. (2022). How diverse are the samples used to study intimate relationships? A systematic review. *Journal of Social and Personal Relationships*, *39*(4), 1087–1109. https://doi.org/10.1177/02654075211053849

Wout, D. A., Murphy, M. C., & Barnett, S. (2014). When having Black friends isn't enough: How threat cues undermine safety cues in friendship formation. *Social Psychological and Personality Science*, *5*(7), 844–851. https://doi.org/10.1177/1948550614535820

Wout, D. A., Murphy, M. C., & Steele, C. M. (2010). When your friends matter: The effect of White students' racial friendship networks on meta-perceptions and perceived identity contingencies. *Journal of Experimental Social Psychology*, *46*(6), 1035–1041. https://doi.org/10.1016/j.jesp.2010.06.003

Zagefka, H., Mohamed, A., Mursi, G., & Lay, S. (2016). Antecedents of intra/intergroup friendships and stress levels among ethnic and religious minority members. *International Journal of Psychology*, *51*(6), 403–411. https://doi.org/10.1002/ijop.12201

Zhou, S., Page-Gould, E., Aron, A., Moyer, A., & Hewstone, M. (2019). The extended contact hypothesis: A meta-analysis on 20 years of research. *Personality and Social Psychology Review*, *23*(2), 132–160. https://doi.org/10.1177/1088868318762647

PART V
FAMILIES IN THE 21ST CENTURY

16
Adoption and Relationships in the 21st Century

Ellen E. Pinderhughes, Seungmi M. Lee, and Madeline C. Smith

Adoptive families in the 21st century are quite diverse, starting with three distinct pathways—private domestic infant adoption, domestic foster care to adoption, and intercountry/transnational adoption—although adoptions share dependency on third parties (i.e., lawyers, judges, adoption professionals). Adoptive families vary in parent and child characteristics: the matches of those characteristics have changed dramatically since 1940. Today, LGBTQ parents adopt at higher rates than straight parents: 21% of LGBTQ parents, but 2.9% of straight parents, are raising adoptees (Taylor, 2020). Adoptive parents' socioeconomic status varies dramatically: intercountry adoptive parents are middle-to-upper income and more educated than domestic private adoptive parents, who have higher income and education than foster-to-adoptive parents (Vandivere et al., 2009). Reflecting a notable shift in adoptions (see Herman, 2008; Matthews et al., 2021), 51% of adoptees in the United States are children of color with White parents (Zill, 2017). Transracial adoptions (TRAs; child and parent do not share ethnic/racial backgrounds) vary by adoption pathway: transnational adoptions involve more White parents (92%) and children of color (84%) than private domestic placements (71% of parents are White; 21% are children of color), and foster-to-adopt placements (63% of parents are White; 28% are children of color) (Vandivere et al., 2009).

These and other developments have reshaped our understanding of adoption, its practices, and lifelong experience. Space limitations constrain in-depth discussion of various adoption issues that can promote comprehensive understanding of adoption's complexities. We refer readers elsewhere for such converging depth (Herman, 2008; Pinderhughes &

Ellen E. Pinderhughes, Seungmi M. Lee, and Madeline C. Smith, *Adoption and Relationships in the 21st Century* In: *Modern Relationships*. Edited by: Mahzad Hojjat and Anne Moyer, Oxford University Press. © Oxford University Press 2024. DOI: 10.1093/oso/9780197655504.003.0016

Brodzinsky, 2019; Wrobel et al., 2020). Here, we focus on key processes in adoptees' lives. We discuss common issues and processes—adoptees' identity development, adoption socialization and communication, navigating relationships with birth families, and parenting as an adult adoptee. Because the majority of adoptions are transracial, we include ethnic-racial socialization. We then discuss two less common issues—adopting children with disabilities and adoptive parenting in LGBTQ families. One critical 21st-century issue centers on the lens through which we consider adoption, including choice of terminology. Adoption does not culminate in the legalization of a child's and family's union but is a lifelong process. Thus, because adoptees navigate developmental tasks from infancy through adulthood, we use the terms "child adoptee," "adolescent adoptee," or "adult adoptee." We also refer to adoptees, adoptive families, and birth families as adoptive kinship network members, to acknowledge the psychological and increasingly common physical connection between birth and adoptive families (Grotevant, 2020).

A critical lesson of the past 30 years is the role of context in human development (Bronfenbrenner & Morris, 2006). Contextual influences on adoption and adoptive families' experiences include school, community, policies, and laws. We forefront social media and the Internet as 21st-century influences that have dramatically reshaped adoption processes.

Common Issues Facing Adoptive Families

Aside from universal tasks all families face (e.g., supporting children's development and forming family identity), adoptive families navigate differences between biological and adoptive family life (Kirk, 1964). Researchers study these processes through different approaches. Developmental and clinical psychologists and social workers have centered on adoption socialization (developing relationships and promoting identity within the adoptive family) (Pinderhughes & Brodzinsky, 2019) and ethnic-racial socialization (supporting the ethnic-racial identity development of adoptees of color; Pinderhughes et al., 2021). Researchers also have examined adoption openness (Brodzinsky, 2005), which includes communicative openness (how openly families discuss adoption and adoptees' stories) and structural openness (contact with birth families). Family communication scholars center on how families navigate discourse within the family (internal boundary management) and with others outside the family (external boundary management; e.g., Galvin, 2006). Each approach captures pieces of the complex puzzle that is adoption, including adoptees' outcomes.

Adoptive Identity

Adoptive identity, one of various identity dimensions, comprises three components—individual, family, and community. Adoptees face constructing what it means to be an adoptee, an adoptive family member, and community member, given social attitudes about kinship (Grotevant et al., 2000). Adoptive identity formation is influenced by adoptees' evolving cognitive and emotional capabilities and how families address adoption. Throughout development, adoptees face multiple identity-related tasks; in infancy, adoptees face forming an attachment to adoptive parents; as toddlers and preschoolers, adoptees begin to learn about oneself, one's adoptive family, and one's birth family through constructed narratives. With new cognitive skills in middle childhood, adoptees are able to consider multiple realities regarding their adoption story—notably that in order to be adopted, they had to be "given up." Adoptees gain more nuanced understandings of their family's situation in adolescence. With these latter identity changes, emotional and self-esteem challenges sometimes emerge. Across development, family-based experiences—adoptive family activities and interactions, and for some adoptees, connections with birth families—and extrafamilial experiences—peer interactions in neighborhoods and schools, as well as larger societal messages—evolve as major influences on identity. Balancing multiple identities and learning how they interrelate with one another (e.g., intersecting identities) are a critical task. For example, intercountry transracial adoptees may face navigating identities as an adoptee, a member of their racial/ethnic group, a member of their birth cultural group, and a member of the adoptive family's community (Grotevant et al., 2000). Lee (2003) powerfully discusses the paradox that transracial adoptees experience. Certain identities may be linked to groups with more societally imbued power and privilege (e.g., Whites; being upper income; being a U.S. citizen), whereas other identities may be linked to groups whom society devalues (e.g., adoptees, Blacks, Latinx, LGBTQ individuals). For more information about adoptees' developmental identity-related tasks, see Pinderhughes and Brodzinsky (2019). Next, we discuss some of these influences.

Conversations About Adoption

Adoption Socialization

Pinderhughes and Brodzinsky (2019) describe adoption socialization (AS) as the process of adoptive families communicating about adoption, facilitating relationships within the adoptive family, and promoting adoptees' identity formation. AS also entails providing a shared fate by acknowledging family differences from biological families (Kirk, 1964; Tuan & Shiao, 2011), and managing family ties that outsiders challenge (Galvin, 2006). AS processes can depend on adoptees' developmental and unique family contexts, pathways to adoption, and adoptive family types. For example, as adoptees' identities become more complex, parents can include more nuanced themes in their messages with their children about their adoption. In school, children have greater opportunities to interact with peers, who vary in awareness of adoption's complexities. Adoptive families, then, face the challenge of helping adoptees navigate differences with peers and in school (Suter et al., 2011).

Adoptive families can provide AS by constructing the adoption and birth story for their children. Through this process, adoptive parents affirm adoptees, create familiarity with children's adoption history, and minimize adoptees' birth history fantasies (Harrigan, 2010). Family adoption narratives help children make meaning of their experiences and create a family identity (Kellas, 2005). When families form these narratives together, adoptees can navigate and manage the feelings of loss of and uncertainty about their birth family and heritage (Colaner & Kranstuber, 2010). However, despite good intentions, some narratives may highlight adoptees' differences, leaving them feeling too different from the family. Parents also engage in AS by confronting adoption stigma experienced by families and adoptees, especially in public (Docan-Morgan, 2010). Extant research indicates that, from approximately ages 5–7, adoptees begin to understand that adoption is often stigmatized; their understanding of adoption stigma and bias become more sophisticated during adolescence (Brodzinsky et al., 1986; Pinderhughes & Brodzinsky, 2019).

Building on Sue et al.'s microaggression framework (2007), Baden (2016) theorized adoption microaggressions, which target all adoptive kinship network members. Adoption microaggressions devalue and invalidate adoptees' experiences (e.g., bad seed adoptee), adoptive parents (e.g., altruistic rescuers), and birth parents (e.g., phantom birth parents). We recently reported on parents' messages to their children in response to specific adoption microaggression situations (i.e., *Lucky—Child is lucky to be adopted*; *Destiny—It was meant to be*; *Shameful Birth Parents—Birth parents are poor/drug addicted/young parents*; *Search—Parents are worried the child wants to search for birth parents*; S. Lee et al., 2022). We found that adoptive parents prepared their children for adoption biases in various ways. Many educated their children about the flaws of microaggression messages, whereas some validated children's feelings about invalidating messages. Notably, few parents offered concrete strategies to manage these situations. Thus, further education and research is necessary to support parents.

Boundary Management

Lacking biological ties and, often, shared ethnic-racial background, adoptive families face challenges in developing a shared family identity (Galvin, 2003). Galvin (2006) postulated that, like other families lacking biological ties, adoptive families must depend on discourse to maintain their lifelong family bond. Adoption microaggressions violate family boundaries (Docan-Morgan, 2010), challenging the legitimacy of family bonds. How parents navigate external boundary management and internal boundary management are critical for adoptive families in constructing and maintaining a family identity. Parents engage in internal boundary management by communicating their authentic family bond, including acknowledging differences between adoptee and parents and the adoptive family's differences from biological families (Kirk, 1964; Tuan & Shiao, 2011). When adoptive families acknowledge visible differences, children can reconcile and integrate these differences and, at times, clashing identities (adoptive, racial, family) into their personal identities (Colaner et al., 2018). Parents manage external boundaries violated by adoption microaggressions by educating others or challenging others' assumptions (Docan-Morgan, 2010). Our work suggests that parents may simultaneously engage in internal and external boundary management as they address microaggressions and explicitly teach their children how to manage external boundaries (S. Lee et al., 2022).

Communicative Openness

Adoption-related tasks and challenges may unfold differently depending on the level of communicative openness within the family (Brodzinsky, 2006), which is related to adoptees' adjustment, sense of self, and understanding of their adoption in relation to adoptive and birth families (Grotevant et al., 2017). Open communication about adoption includes parents telling honest stories about the placement and their adoption decision, sharing what they know about the birth family, and discussing a future birth family search and reunion (Grotevant & Von Korff, 2011; Harrigan, 2010). Open communication also incorporates adoptive and biological families' roles in adoptees' lives (Pinderhughes & Brodzinsky, 2019).

Ethnic-Racial Socialization

To support children's identity development, parents raising children of color are tasked with providing ethnic-racial socialization (ERS), which includes four processes (see Hughes et al., 2006, for discussion); we discuss two: cultural socialization (CS) and preparation for bias (PfB). In addition to CS and PfB, TRA families also face providing family heritage socialization—exposure to the family's culture of origin (Pinderhughes et al., 2021), and bicultural socialization—helping children balance identity linked to their own culture and their new country (Benet-Martínez & Haritatos, 2005).

CS exposes children to their ethnic and/or racial heritage and history by promoting cultural traditions and activities (see Zhang & Pinderhughes, 2019, for examples of CS in TRA families). Certain parenting characteristics of TRA parents—beliefs about the value of CS, attitudes about cultural differences, motivation for providing CS—contribute to the depth of CS (Zhang & Pinderhughes, 2019). Adoptees who receive CS feel more connected to their heritage and have fewer behavior problems (e.g., Johnston et al., 2007; Manzi et al., 2014). Through PfB, parents help children become aware of racial/ethnic bias and prepare them to cope with or respond to discrimination (Hughes et al., 2006). Parental engagement in PfB was linked to higher self-esteem and less depression among TRA children (Mohanty & Newhill, 2011). Parents provide CS earlier and more frequently from childhood through adolescence than PfB (Johnston et al., 2007). Both practices change and evolve throughout adoptees' development. Providing PfB may be more challenging for White parents who do not share the racial experiences of their TRA children and who may avoid or limit uncomfortable conversations about racial discrimination (Pinderhughes & Brodzinsky, 2019). TRA children may perceive these parents as less supportive, possibly leading to a sense of isolation, an unhealthy view of ethnic-racial identity, and negative psychological outcomes (Tuan & Shiao, 2011).

ERS does not occur in a vacuum; contextual factors (e.g., neighborhood), family social position (e.g., income, child's ethnicity), parents' racial awareness, and parents' self-efficacy may contribute to ERS (Pinderhughes et al., 2021). Moreover, Pinderhughes et al. (2021) frame ERS as a system of transacting processes among parent, adoptee, and the family that considers children's age and developmental functioning, as well as contextual influences (e.g., the family's daily lives, community or school diversity, adoptees' experiences outside the family, and events in the world). Three key components comprise ERS: parent's role (e.g., parents' acknowledgment of racial or cultural differences), ERS processes (e.g., family involvement in activities), and children's outcomes (e.g., identity, emotional adjustment). This framework offers a dynamic view of the complexities inherent in ERS among TRA families and provides directions for future research, practice, and policy.

Navigating Relations With Birth Parents Across Development

Structural Openness

Structural openness refers to the degree of contact between adoptive and birth families (Brodzinsky, 2006); openness ranges from no contact (e.g., closed adoptions), to ongoing contact (e.g., open adoptions; Grotevant, 2020). Direct contact can vary from exchange of letters, emails, photos, etc., to in-person contact. Indirect contact involves a third person, or adoption agency, to facilitate the exchange of information in a non-identifying way. Historically, adoptions were closed: adoption practitioners advised adoptive families that no contact with birth parents was in everyone's interest (Herman, 2008). However, since the 1970s, adoption practice has shifted toward greater openness. Openness often starts with the adoptive placement between birth and adoptive families. In fact, a distinct 21st-century development is birth parents' central role in choosing their child's adoptive parents (Adoption Network, n.d.). With the Internet, having contact with birth families is easier than maintaining a closed adoption (Whitesel & Howard, 2013). As Grotevant (2020) extensively discusses, ongoing contact provides opportunities for a "reality-based understanding" of both families' lives

(p. 268), which can help all adoptive kinship network members. Openness also can shift over time, allowing for receipt of new information and/or adjustments in relationships. Generally, when adoptive kinship network members are satisfied with their openness arrangements, adjustment is positive (Grotevant, 2020).

Contact between birth and adoptive families can have different implications among foster-to-adoptions. When foster children are adopted, usually following termination of parental rights, whether contact is in the adoptee's best interest may be in question. Longitudinal research in the United Kingdom has documented that when there is minimal conflict, and birth and adoptive parents recognize the child's connection to each family, ongoing contact can be positive for adoptees (Neil, 2019). However, this process can be quite challenging and birth parents may need support (Neil, 2019).

Structural openness generally is not possible with intercountry placements, which typically are only made when the country of origin "verifies" that the adoptee has no biological family available, as stipulated by the Hague Convention on Protection of Children and Co-operation in Respect of Intercountry Adoption (n.d.). In fact, some adoptive parents choose this pathway in order to avoid the birth family (Pinderhughes et al., 2013). Adoptive parents can regret that decision when their adoptees express interest in knowing their birth family. Intercountry adoptive parents also may have to navigate learning—well after placement—that the adoptee did, in fact, have a birth family, and some type of illegal activity—trafficking, bribery, or kidnapping may have occurred (Steenrod, 2021). Reports of these illegal activities prompt questioning and soul-searching among some parents (Marn & Tan, 2015); as a result, some choose to search for birth parents (Groves, 2009).

Search and Reunion
Search and reunion in closed adoptions involve two critical steps, which reflect normative curiosity about one's origins (Müller & Perry, 2001). First, one searches for identifying information about missing family members; birth parents or adoptees might search, as might adoptive parents with or on behalf of the adoptee. For some searchers, getting information is sufficient. Others need to take the second step to physically search and have a reunion. Searches and reunions can involve ambiguities and complex emotions for all, notably for birth parents (March, 2015). The adoption-related experiences

that adoptive kinship network members have may shape how they navigate search and reunion complexities. Intercountry adoptions between countries with different culturally grounded values about the meaning of adoption can be quite challenging. Roby and Matsumura (2002) documented how adoptive families returning to the Marshall Islands had to navigate birth parents' assumptions in that communal culture that their children would return to them in adulthood. The Western notion of permanent termination of parental rights had no place in that culture. For more on adoption search, see Herman (2008) and Matthews et al. (2021).

Adult Adoptees: Overall Adjustment and Parenting Issues

As adoption is a lifelong process, understanding long-term outcomes of adult adoptees is critical. Extant research has focused on their adjustment, close relationships, and parenting. In a recent meta-analysis of 18 studies, adult adoptees tended to have more problems than non-adoptees with anger, social adjustment, and criminally related behaviors (Corral et al., 2021). Having skills in close relationships with peers or partners was linked to positive adjustment (Cashen & Grotevant, 2020). Adult adoptees report needs for key supports regarding contact with birth family, ethnic identity and birth culture, and general functioning (Sánchez-Sandoval et al., 2020). Evidence-based interventions are critically needed.

The nascent literature on adult adoptees as parents suggests important areas for longitudinal inquiry. The transition to parenthood creates opportunities for adoptees to reassess adoption socialization and childhood experiences (e.g., Greco et al., 2015). Adoptees with birth family contact or prior foster care may reassess experiences with birth families (Neil, 2021). While raising their children, adult transracial adoptees may reconsider childhood ethnic-racial socialization (Zhou et al., 2021).

Unique Issues Facing Certain Adoptive Families

Adoption of Children With Disabilities

Many adoptive families formed through foster care and intercountry adoption face challenges of supporting children who have a disability (i.e., special need) or developmental delay at placement. Unrealistic and unmet expectations can be highly stressful for parents, especially if they feel unable to meet their adoptee's needs (Moyer & Goldberg, 2017). Parents are particularly vulnerable when they learn of additional disabilities after placement, which was notably the case among intercountry adoptions (Pinderhughes et al., 2013). Adoptees leaving foster families or institutions may have histories of trauma, which can negatively impact all areas of development, including neurological, physiological, language, social-emotional, and academic functioning; yet, with appropriate supports, some adoptees can substantially catch up, showing great resilience (see Miller & Pinderhughes, in press, for review). Some disabilities have predictable manifestations (i.e., physical disabilities and developmental delays), whereas others are more unpredictable (i.e., emotional and behavioral problems). Adoptive parents who can reliably anticipate their adoptee's functioning have more placement satisfaction and are better able to provide support; families also experience less stress, increasing the placement's success (Glidden, 1991; Rosenthal, 1993). In contrast, parents who cannot reliably anticipate their child's functioning are less likely to have their needs for post-placement services met (Hill & Moore, 2015) and are at greater risk for adoption breakdown, whether disruption (placement termination before adoption legalization) or dissolution (placement termination after legalization). For more on adoption breakdown, see Palacios (2020).

LGBTQ Parents

For many lesbian, gay, bisexual, transgender, and queer (LGBTQ) individuals, adoption is the pathway of choice; however, they face significant institutional and attitudinal barriers in their parenthood pathway (Farr & Vázquez, 2020). Most research includes primarily lesbian and gay parents; thus, this discussion centers on LG families. LG-headed adoptive families tend to live in diverse communities and provide adoptees with experiences that promote connection with birth families, along with adoption socialization, and ethnic-racial socialization (Farr & Vázquez, 2020). In fact, given the homophobia that LG parents have faced, they are more likely to help their children address racial and adoption bias (Goldberg & Smith, 2016). Moreover, LG-headed families normalize diversity in sexual orientation, and LG parents are highly satisfied with their marital/partner relationship, as well as with how child care is shared. In sum, LG adoptive families tend to function well in the major areas of parenting and relationships.

Twenty-First Century Realities in Adoption

Adoption in the Context of Larger Systems

A critical 21st-century issue centers on the different perspectives on whose interest adoption serves. Some scholars broadened the focus to the larger systems and contexts that operate to produce adoptions (Homans et al., 2018; McKee, 2018). Consequently, the historic notion of adoption as serving the interests of children or birth parents who cannot care for their children is disrupted and replaced with a perspective that centers processes of power, privilege, and oppression in adoption practice. Birth parents are viewed as casualties of a process that takes children from struggling families with limited resources (notably intercountry adoptions) and places them in families with greater resources. These issues are briefly summarized in Matthews et al. (2021). A countervailing perspective argues that appropriate international protections and guidelines can ensure adoption is a critical life-altering resource for children who have experienced early adversities and/or have no options for parenting within their birth family network (Palacios et al., 2019).

Birth Family Contact and Reunion and Identity

Advancing technology, a globally connected world, and frequent exposure to popular media constitute other 21st-century challenges, impacting processes of adoption across the life span in ways that bring benefits and risks (Whitesel & Howard, 2013). First, as recommended now by some adoption agencies, prospective adoptive parents may find that they have to "market" themselves through social media to appeal directly to birth parents, with videos that tell their stories. Ongoing contact in adoption may be facilitated by email and social media that support private communication. Previous restrictions on access to birth families' information are being dismantled through easy access to social network platforms that provide public, yet personal, information about others (Haralambie, 2013; Samuels, 2018). Thus, kinship network members in less open placements can surreptitiously "follow" other members for updates about their lives. The Internet provides the potential for immediate reunification between adoptees and their birth families (Samuels, 2018; Whitesel & Howard, 2013): Social media platforms such as Facebook and Instagram have made it easy to search, message, and contact birth relatives. There is no longer need for a mediator to gain access to knowledge about birth families (Haralambie, 2013). There are various implications for adoptive kinship network members. Some adoptive families may assist an adoptee's search for birth family, which may limit the isolation that an adoptee searching alone might experience (Samuels, 2018). On the other hand, an adoptee who contacts the birth family without a mediator may risk reopening unresolved emotions and trauma if rejected by their birth family (Samuels, 2018). Birth parents who agreed to a confidential adoption may not be prepared to be contacted by adoptees, especially through social media. Medical technology advances have enhanced search opportunities within the adoption community (H. Lee et al., 2021). Customer-based genetic testing kits such as 23andMe and ancestry.com enable adoptees to find birth relatives online (K. Lee, 2021; Marcoux, 2021). However, how adoptees navigate these life and identity changing opportunities should be further explored. Social media platforms also enable adoptees to construct their adoption narrative, thus negotiating, resisting, and reframing public perceptions of adoption, which often overlook adoption's complexities (Suh, 2021). The Internet will continue to shape and redefine all adoption processes across the life span.

Adoption-Related Services

Despite the documented challenges that adoptive parents face, finding effective services has historically been difficult. Medical care has been more broadly available than mental health support. The mental health needs that adoptive kinship network members have are complex and varied. However, two broad themes are common—the need for service providers who understand the complexities of adoption and can work through an adoption lens to support members of the triad and the need for those who can bring a trauma-informed approach to their work. Neither approach is sufficient alone. A critical 21st-century reality is the development of evidence-informed training that incorporates an adoption lens and a trauma-informed approach (Riley & Singer, 2020) to promote adoption-competent clinical practice (Atkinson, 2020). These new developments offer promise that adoptive kinship network members can find effective supports that will enable them to successfully navigate adoption-related issues and challenges and to thrive. However heartening these developments are, Riley and Singer (2020) call for expansion of evidence-informed adoption competency training programs into multiple settings (higher ed curricula, in-service and continuing education) so that the varied needs of adoptive kinship network members are met.

Conclusion

The complexities in adoption warrant acknowledgment and understanding by the broader public. The complexities take different shape depending on whose lens we use to understand adoption. When taking an individual, relational, and familial lens, we understand that the universal issues of identity formation, parenting, communication, and socialization are significantly more complex among adoptive families. When we consider the traumatic early experiences of many adoptees, we understand the compensatory power of adoption to promote healthier development. When focused on the larger systemic and structural forces that promote and maintain domestic and intercountry adoption, we understand that processes of power, privilege, and oppression are part of the reality of adoption. These processes shape experiences of all adoptive kinship network members, even if indirectly. Birth parents are especially vulnerable. When we focus on adoptees who use social media to call attention to their realities and engage in identity exploration, we more deeply appreciate how adoption reverberates throughout development. When we consider current contexts—notably the Internet—that have fundamentally altered all adoption processes, we must consider how our own lens on adoption is shaped by what we see and access. Broadening our lenses on adoption can promote deeper appreciation of the complexities that adoptive kinship network members face, which the authors hope leads to greater advocacy and less adoption stigma.

References

Adoption Network. (n.d.). *7 considerations for birth mothers when choosing adoptive parents*. https://adoptionnetwork.com/birth-mothers/adoptive-families/choosing-a-family/considerations-when-choosing-adoptive-parents/

Atkinson, A. J. (2020). Adoption competent clinical practice. In G. M. Wrobel, E. Helder, & E. Marr (Eds.), *The Routledge handbook of adoption* (pp. 435–448). Routledge, Taylor & Francis Group.

Baden, A. L. (2016). "Do you know your *real* parents?" and other adoption microaggressions. *Adoption Quarterly, 19*(1), 1–25. https://doi.org/10.1080/10926755.2015.1026012

Benet-Martínez, V., & Haritatos, J. (2005). Bicultural Identity Integration (BII): Components and psychosocial antecedents. *Journal of Personality, 73*(4), 1015–1050. https://doi.org/10.1111/j.1467-6494.2005.00337.x

Brodzinsky, D. (2005). Reconceptualizing openness in adoption: Implications for theory, research, and practice. In J. Palacios & D. Brodzinsky (Eds.), *Psychological issues in adoption: Research and practice* (pp. 145–166). Praeger.

Brodzinsky, D. (2006). Family structural openness and communication openness as predictors in the adjustment of adopted children. *Adoption Quarterly, 9*(4), 1–18. https://doi.org/10.1300/J145v09n04_01

Brodzinsky, D., Schechter, M., Braff, A. M., & Brodzinsky, A. B. (1986). Children's knowledge of adoption: Developmental changes and implications for adjustment. In R. D. Ashmore & D. Brodzinsky (Eds.), *Thinking about the family: Views of parents and children* (pp. 205–232). Lawrence Erlbaum Associates.

Bronfenbrenner, U., & Morris, P. A. (2006). The bioecological model of human development. In *Handbook of child psychology: Theoretical models of human development* (Vol. 1, 6th ed., pp. 793–828). John Wiley & Sons Inc.

Cashen, K. K., & Grotevant, H. D. (2020). Relational competence in emerging adult adoptees: Conceptualizing competence in close relationships. *Journal of Adult Development, 27*(2), 83–94. https://doi.org/10.1007/s10804-019-09328-x

Colaner, C. W., Horstman, H. K., & Rittenour, C. E. (2018). Negotiating adoptive and birth shared family identity: A social identity complexity approach. *Western Journal of Communication, 82*(4), 393–415. https://doi.org/10.1080/10570314.2017.1384564

Colaner, C. W., & Kranstuber, H. (2010). "Forever kind of wondering": Communicatively managing uncertainty in adoptive families. *Journal of Family Communication, 10*(4), 236–255. https://doi.org/10.1080/15267431003682435

Corral, S., Herrero, M., Martín, N., Gordejuela, A., & Herrero-Fernández, D. (2021). Psychological adjustment in adult adoptees: A meta-analysis. *Psicothema, 33*(4), 527–535. https://doi.org/10.7334/psicothema2021.98

Docan-Morgan, S. (2010). Korean adoptees' retrospective reports of intrusive interactions: Exploring boundary management in adoptive families. *Journal of Family Communication, 10*(3), 137–157. https://doi.org/10.1080/15267431003699603

Farr, R. H., & Vázquez, C. P. (2020). Adoptive families headed by LGBTQ parents. In G. M. Wrobel, E. Helder, & E. Marr (Eds.), *The Routledge handbook on adoption* (pp. 164–175.). Routledge, Taylor & Francis Group.

Galvin, K. (2003). International and transracial adoption: A communication research agenda. *Journal of Family Communication, 3*(4), 237–253. https://doi.org/10.1207/S15327698JFC0304_5

Galvin, K. M. (2006). Diversity's impact on defining the family: Discourse-dependence and identity. In Lynn H. Turner & Richard West (Eds.), *The family communication sourcebook* (pp. 3–20). SAGE Publications, Inc. https://doi.org/10.4135/9781452233024.n1

Glidden, L. M. (1991). Adopted children with developmental disabilities: Post-placement family functioning. *Children and Youth Services Review, 13*(5), 363–377. https://doi.org/10.1016/0190-7409(91)90026-E

Goldberg, A. E., & Smith, J. Z. (2016). Predictors of race, adoption, and sexual orientation related socialization of adoptive parents of young children. *Journal of Family Psychology, 30*(3), 397–408. https://doi.org/10.1037/fam0000149

Greco, O., Rosnati, R., & Ferrari, L. (2015). Adult adoptees as partners and parents: The joint task of revisiting the adoption history. *Adoption Quarterly, 18*(1), 25–44. https://doi.org/10.1080/10926755.2014.895468

Grotevant, H. D. (2020). Open adoption. In G. M. Wrobel, E. Helder, & E. Marr (Eds.), *Routledge handbook of adoption* (pp. 311–330). Routledge, Taylor & Francis Group.

Grotevant, H. D., Dunbar, N., Kohler, J. K., & Esau, A. M. L. (2000). Adoptive identity: How contexts within and beyond the family shape developmental pathways. *Family Relations, 49*(4), 379–387. https://doi.org/10.1111/j.1741-3729.2000.00379.x

Grotevant, H. D., Lo, A. Y. H., Fiorenzo, L., & Dunbar, N. D. (2017). Adoptive identity and adjustment from adolescence to emerging adulthood: A person-centered approach. *Developmental Psychology, 53*(11), 2195–2204. https://doi.org/10.1037/dev0000352

Grotevant, H. D., & Von Korff, L. (2011). Adoptive identity. In S. J. Schwartz, K. Luyckx, & V. L. Vignoles (Eds.), *Handbook of identity theory and research* (pp. 585–601). Springer New York. http://link.springer.com/10.1007/978-1-4419-7988-9_24

Groves, M. (2009, Nov. 11). Painful questions for adoptive parents. *Los Angeles Times*. https://www.latimes.com/archives/la-xpm-2009-nov-11-me-china-adopt11-story.html

Hague Convention on Protection of Children and Co-operation in Respect of Intercountry Adoption. (n.d.). https://www.hcch.net/en/instruments/conventions/full-text/?cid=69

Haralambie, A. M. (2013). Use of social media in post-adoption search and reunion. *Capital University Law Review, 41*(2), 177–236.

Harrigan, M. M. (2010). Exploring the narrative process: An analysis of the adoption stories mothers tell their internationally adopted children. *Journal of Family Communication, 10*(1), 24–39. https://doi.org/10.1080/15267430903385875

Herman, E. (2008). *Kinship by design: A history of adoption in the modern United States.* The University of Chicago Press.

Hill, K., & Moore, F. (2015). The postadoption needs of adoptive parents of children with disabilities. *Journal of Family Social Work, 18*(3), 164–182. https://doi.org/10.1080/10522158.2015.1022846

Homans, M., Phelan, P., Ellerby, J. M., Walker, E., Balcom, K., Myers, K., Nelson, K. P., Briggs, L., Callahan, C., Peñta, R., Wesseling, E., Perreau, B., Curzon, L., Leighton, K., & Yngvesson, B. (2018). Critical adoption studies: Conversation in progress. *Adoption & Culture, 6*(1), 1–49. https://doi.org/10.1353/ado.2018.0015

Hughes, D., Rodriguez, J., Smith, E. P., Johnson, D. J., Stevenson, H. C., & Spicer, P. (2006). Parents' ethnic-racial socialization practices: A review of research and directions for future study. *Developmental Psychology, 42*(5), 747–770. https://doi.org/10.1037/0012-1649.42.5.747

Johnston, K., Swim, J., Saltsman, B., Deater-Deckard, K., & Petrill, S. (2007). Mother's racial, ethnic, and cultural socialization of transracially adopted Asian children. *Family Relations, 56*(4), 13. https://doi.org/10.1111/j.1741-3729.2007.00468.x

Kellas, J. K. (2005). Family ties: Communicating identity through jointly told family stories. [This paper is based on the author's dissertation study and was presented on the Top Four Panel of the Family Communication Division at the National Communication Association Convention, November 2003, Miami, FL.] *Communication Monographs, 72*(4), 365–389. https://doi.org/10.1080/03637750500322453

Kirk, H. D. (1964). *Shared fate*. Free Press. https://www.amazon.com/Shared-Fate-H-D-Kirk/dp/002917340X

Lee, H., Vogel, R. I., LeRoy, B., & Zierhut, H. A. (2021). Adult adoptees and their use of direct-to-consumer genetic testing: Searching for family, searching for health. *Journal of Genetic Counseling, 30*(1), 144–157. https://doi.org/10.1002/jgc4.1304

Lee, K. (2021, November 27). Finding family: A reporter shares her personal story of adoption and reunion. *PBS NewsHour*. https://www.pbs.org/newshour/show/finding-family-a-reporter-shares-her-personal-story-of-adoption-and-reunion

Lee, R. M. (2003). The transracial adoption paradox: History, research, and counseling implications of cultural socialization. *The Counseling Psychologist, 31*(6), 711–744. https://doi.org/10.1177/0011000003258087

Lee, S., Liu, J., Kimura, A. M., Zhang, X., Kupa, J., Jurca, A., Boland, K., & Pinderhughes, E. E. (2022). Adoptive parents navigating adoption microaggressions through discourse dependency and preparation for bias lenses. *Journal of Family Communication, 22*(3), 208–229. https://doi.org/10.1080/15267431.2022.2097237

Manzi, C., Ferrari, L., Rosnati, R., & Benet-Martinez, V. (2014). Bicultural identity integration of transracial adolescent adoptees: Antecedents and outcomes. *Journal of Cross-Cultural Psychology, 45*(6), 888–904. https://doi.org/10.1177/0022022114530495

March, K. (2015). Finding my place: Birth mothers manage the boundary ambiguity of adoption reunion contact. *Qualitative Sociology Review, 11*(3), 106–122.

Marcoux, H. (2021, October 20). 3 Chinese cousins were adopted by different families in the US. They found each other decades later with 23andMe. *Insider*. https://www.insider.com/found-documentary-chinese-cousins-dna-testing-2021-10

Marn, T. M., & Tan, T. X. (2015). Adoptive parents' suspicion and coping with the possibility of child abduction for international adoption in China. *The Family Journal, 23*(4), 407–416. https://doi.org/10.1177/1066480715601114

Matthews, J. A. K., Pinderhughes, E. E., & Pott, M. L. (2021). Adoptive parenting is more complex than evolutionary theory would predict: Evidence from historical and contemporary perspectives. In V. A. Weekes-Shackelford & T. K. Shackelford (Eds.), *The Oxford handbook of evolutionary psychology and parenting* (1st ed., pp. 375–410). Oxford University Press. https://doi.org/10.1093/oxfordhb/9780190674687.001.0001

McKee, K. (2018). Adoption as a reproductive justice issue. *Adoption & Culture, 6*(1), 74. https://doi.org/10.26818/adoptionculture.6.1.0074

Miller, L. C., & Pinderhughes, E. E. (in press). Adoption and foster care. In M. H. Bornstein & P. E. Shah (Eds.), *Pediatric psychology and developmental-behavioral pediatrics: Clinical applications of developmental science*. American Psychological Association.

Mohanty, J., & Newhill, C. E. (2011). Asian adolescent and young adult adoptees' psychological well-being: Examining the mediating role of marginality. *Children and Youth Services Review, 33*(7), 1189–1195. https://doi.org/10.1016/j.childyouth.2011.02.016

Moyer, A. M., & Goldberg, A. E. (2017). "We were not planning on this, but...": Adoptive parents' reactions and adaptations to unmet expectations. *Child & Family Social Work, 22*, 12–21. https://doi.org/10.1111/cfs.12219

Müller, U., & Perry, B. (2001). Adopted persons' search for and contact with their birth parents II. *Adoption Quarterly, 4*(3), 39–62. https://doi.org/10.1300/J145v04n03_03

Neil, E. (2019). *Planning and supporting birth family contact when children are adopted from care*. Rudd Adoption Research Program Publication Series. https://www.umass.edu/ruddchair/sites/default/files/rudd.neil.pdf

Neil, E. (2021, July 8). *Studying adoptive families beyond childhood: What do we know about adoptive families when adoptees become parents?* [Keynote speech]. International Conference on Adoption Research 7, Milan, Italy.

Palacios, J. (2020). Adoption instability, adoption breakdown. In G. M. Wrobel, E. Helder, & E. Marr (Eds.), *The Routledge handbook of adoption* (pp. 417–432). Routledge, Taylor & Francis Group.

Palacios, J., Rolock, N., Selwyn, J., & Barbosa-Ducharme, M. (2019). Adoption breakdown: Concept, research, and implications. *Research on Social Work Practice, 29*(2), 130–142. https://doi.org/10.1177/1049731518783852

Pinderhughes, E. E., & Brodzinsky, D. M. (2019). Parenting in adoptive families. In M. H. Bornstein (Ed.), *Handbook of parenting: Vol. 1: Children and parenting* (3rd ed., pp. 322–367). Routledge.

Pinderhughes, E. E., Matthews, J. A. K., Deoudes, G., & Pertman, A. (2013). *A changing world: shaping best practices through understanding of the new realities of intercountry adoption*. https://www.adoptioninstitute.org/wp-content/uploads/2013/12/2013_10_AChangingWorld.pdf

Pinderhughes, E. E., Matthews, J. A. K., Zhang, X., & Scott, J. C. (2021). Unpacking complexities in ethnic–racial socialization in transracial adoptive families: A process-oriented transactional system. *Development and Psychopathology, 33*(2), 493–505. https://doi.org/10.1017/S0954579420001741

Riley, D., & Singer, E. (2020). Training for adoption competency curriculum. In Gretchen Miller Wrobel, Emily Helder, & Elisha Marr (Eds.), *The Routledge handbook of adoption* (pp. 449–463). Routledge, Taylor & Francis Group.

Roby, J. L., & Matsumura, S. (2002). If I give you my child, aren't we family? A study of birthmothers participating in Marshall Islands-U.S. adoptions. *Adoption Quarterly, 5*(4), 7–31. https://doi.org/10.1300/J145v05n04_02

Rosenthal, J. A. (1993). Outcomes of adoption of children with special needs. *The Future of Children, 3*(1), 77–88. https://doi.org/10.2307/1602403

Samuels, J. (2018). Adoption in the digital age. In J. Samuels (Ed.), *Adoption in the digital age: Opportunities and challenges for the 21st century* (pp. 29–50). Springer International Publishing. https://doi.org/10.1007/978-3-319-70413-5_2

Sánchez-Sandoval, Y., Jiménez-Luque, N., Melero, S., Luque, V., & Verdugo, L. (2020). Support needs and post-adoption resources for adopted adults: A systematic review. *The British Journal of Social Work, 50*(6), 1775–1795. https://doi.org/10.1093/bjsw/bcz109

Steenrod, S. A. (2021). The legacy of exploitation in intercountry adoptions from Ethiopia: "We were under the impression that her birth parents had died." *Adoption Quarterly*. Advance online publication. https://doi.org/10.1080/10926755.2021.1884157

Sue, D. W., Capodilupo, C. M., Torino, G. C., Bucceri, J. M., Holder, A. M. B., Nadal, K. L., & Esquilin, M. (2007). Racial microaggressions in everyday life: Implications for clinical practice. *American Psychologist, 62*(4), 271–286. http://dx.doi.org/10.1037/0003-066X.62.4.271

Suh, E. K. (2021). Adoptees SPEAK: A multimodal critical discourse analysis of adult Korean adopted persons' adoption narratives on Instagram. *Critical Inquiry in Language Studies, 18*(1), 65–84. https://doi.org/10.1080/15427587.2020.1796486

Suter, E. A., Reyes, K. L., & Ballard, R. L. (2011). Parental management of adoptive identities during challenging encounters: Adoptive parents as "protectors" and "educators." *Journal of Social and Personal Relationships, 28*(2), 242–261. https://doi.org/10.1177/0265407510384419

Taylor, D. (2020). *Same-sex couples are more likely to adopt or foster children*. United States Census Bureau. https://www.census.gov/library/stories/2020/09/fifteen-percent-of-same-sex-couples-have-children-in-their-household.html#:~:text=Same%2Dsex%20couples%20were%20also,Fertility%20and%20Family%20Statistics%20Branch.

Tuan, M., & Shiao, J. L. (2011). *Choosing ethnicity, negotiating race: Korean adoptees in America*. Russell Sage Foundation.

Vandivere, S., Malm, K., & Radel, L. (2009). *Adoption USA. A chartbook based on the 2007 National Survey of Adoptive Parents*. U.S. Department of Health and Human Services. https://aspe.hhs.gov/report/adoption-usa-chartbook-based-2007-national-survey-adoptive-parents

Whitesel, A., & Howard, J. A. (2013). *Untangling the web II: A research-based roadmap for reform*. Donaldson Adoption Institute. https://www.adoptioninstitute.org/wp-content/uploads/2013/12/2013_12_UntanglingtheWeb2.pdf

Wrobel, G. M., Helder, E., & Marr, E. (2020). *The Routledge handbook of adoption*. Routledge.

Zhang, X., & Pinderhughes, E. E. (2019). Depth in cultural socialization in families with children adopted from China. *Family Process, 58*(1), 114–128. https://doi.org/10.1111/famp.12355

Zhou, X., Kim, J., Lee, H., & Lee, R. M. (2021). Korean adoptees as parents: Intergenerationality of ethnic, racial, and adoption socialization. *Family Relations, 70*(2), 637–652. https://doi.org/10.1111/fare.12439

Zill, N. (2017). *The changing face of adoption in the United States*. Institute for Family Studies. https://ifstudies.org/blog/the-changing-face-of-adoption-in-the-united-states

17

Communication and Resilience in Stepfamilies

Talking Close Relationships With Parents, Siblings, and Family Members Into Being

Dawn O. Braithwaite and Bailey M. Oliver-Blackburn

Stepfamilies appear in nearly every culture, with a higher incidence in Western societies in both formal and informal structures (Stewart & Limb, 2020). Stepfamilies form after remarriage or re-partnering and include one or more children from a previous marriage or relationship (Ganong & Coleman, 2017). One-third of all weddings in the United States involve a stepfamily (Carlson, 2020), with 42% of adults reporting at least one step-relationship (Pew, 2015). Scholars estimate 45% of stepchildren live with a parent and cohabiting partner (Eickmeyer, 2017), with a slightly higher incidence of cohabiting stepfamilies for minoritized children.

As stepfamily numbers increase, researchers seek to better understand how stepfamily interactions, roles, and expectations are impacted within restructured family systems (Braithwaite et al., 2022; Ganong & Coleman, 2017; Papernow, 2013). One trend in stepfamily research across multiple disciplines has been a "deficit approach," wherein stepfamilies are compared with first-marriage or "intact" families and found to fall short of these family systems (Amato, 2010; Ganong & Coleman, 2017). Certainly, seeking to understand challenges of stepfamily life is not unreasonable, as many stepfamilies experience a lack of role clarity within the stepfamily household and boundary ambiguity with those outside the household (e.g., Afifi, 2003; Papernow, 2013, 2018; Stewart, 2005). Stepfamily roles and expectations are often unclear as stepparents, parents, stepchildren, and siblings lack cultural models for how to "do" or "be" a stepfamily, finding themselves caught in the middle and experiencing loyalty challenges (Afifi & Schrodt, 2003; Braithwaite et al., 2008; Ganong & Coleman, 2017).

Dawn O. Braithwaite and Bailey M. Oliver-Blackburn, *Communication and Resilience in Stepfamilies* In: *Modern Relationships*. Edited by: Mahzad Hojjat and Anne Moyer, Oxford University Press. © Oxford University Press 2024. DOI: 10.1093/oso/9780197655504.003.0017

As scholars focus on stepfamily challenges, they can easily neglect opportunities to understand thriving stepfamilies. A few scholars have turned their focus towards how stepfamilies can adapt and develop positive and resilient relationships (e.g., Ganong et al., 1999, 2021a; Golish, 2003; King et al., 2014), and this is the direction we have taken in our recent research (Braithwaite et al., 2018a; Oliver-Blackburn et al., 2022; Waldron et al., 2018, 2022). One way to help scholars and practitioners understand stepfamily strengths is to focus on the important role that communication plays in positive stepfamilies (Afifi, 2003; Braithwaite et al., 2022; Pace et al., 2015; Schrodt, 2006a).

In this chapter, we center on ways stepfamilies communicate to foster resilient relationships among stepfamily members. To follow, we consider how stepfamilies interact and co-create their new family form by organizing the literature into Buzzanell's (2010, 2018) typology of five resilient family processes.

Talking Stepfamilies Into (and Out of) Being

We greatly value the diverse perspectives and important contributions of multidisciplinary stepfamily researchers and practitioners. As communication scholars, we center our work within a constitutive lens on stepfamily experiences, meaning that we move beyond looking at sending and receiving messages and instead focus on communication patterns and processes by which identities are socially constructed and reflected in and through interaction (e.g., Baxter, 2004, 2014; Braithwaite et al., 2018b, Braithwaite & Suter, 2022; Burr, 2015; Foster & Bochner, 2008; Galvin, 2006, 2014; Ganong et al., 2018). Leeds-Hurwitz (2006) described this perspective on communication as an engagement of social practices that "uses talk to make things happen: by naming things, we give them substance" (p. 230), enlightening how family identities are co-created via interaction. As Foster and Bochner (2008) argued, "to root one's work in social construction is to plant one's feet squarely in the world of interactive communication" (p. 86).

A constitutive vantage point on family interaction, development, and enactment is a perfect fit for understanding both the strengths and challenges of stepfamily life, centering on what family communication scholar Kathleen Galvin (2006, 2014) conceptualized as "discourse dependent families." Discourse-dependent families, such as single-parent families,

LGBTQIA+ families, multiethnic/multiracial families, adoptive families, and stepfamilies, often lack cultural models that can help them negotiate family boundaries, expectations, and roles, leaving them "especially reliant on interaction to create, legitimize, and alter their family form" (Braithwaite & Suter, 2022, p. 536). As Galvin (2006) highlighted, discourse-dependent families are reliant on interactional labor to create, validate, and live out their relationships, acting as family (Pylyser et al., 2018) and talking family into being (Baxter, 2014). Galvin (2006) described a variety of communication strategies that discourse-dependent families use with those external to the family unit (labeling, explaining, legitimizing, defending) and those within the family (naming, discussing, narrating, ritualizing) to accomplish these goals. A perspective on discourse-dependent families helps scholars underscore the socially-constructed nature of stepfamilies, what Ganong et al. (2018) referred to as "kin construction" (p. 1728). We can envision how, as discourse-dependent families, stepfamily members may use different strategies to help understand, explain, and legitimize their family system inside the stepfamily household and with/for those outside the family, including extended family members.

Stepfamily Interaction and Resilience

In this chapter, we organize our understanding of stepfamily experiences within the frames of communication and resilience (Buzzanell, 2010, 2018), to better understand stepfamily strengths and opportunities. As scholars and stepfamily members ourselves, we have long reflected on stepfamily resilience. Communication scholar Patrice Buzzanell (2010) explained that human resilience is not just about bouncing back following adversity; rather, it is "constituted in and through communicative processes that enhance people's abilities to create new normalcies . . . drawing upon discursive and material resources" (p. 9). Focusing on stepfamilies as co-created in communication, stepfamily members interact and transform a collection of individuals into a new family system. Adopting a communication focus to understand stepfamily life is particularly important as, among the complex set of structural and social influences of risk and resilience in stepfamilies, "communication is central to all stepfamily relationships and is linked to almost every aspect of a stepfamily member's psychosocial adjustment" (Gosselin & David, 2007, p. 49). Buzzanell (2018) developed the communication theory of resilience to understand and explain how resilience is activated following trigger events. In the case of stepfamilies, this would follow family disruption and relational change: relational dissolution, divorce, or the death of a partner/parent as an impetus to form new relationships. Buzzanell (2018) stressed that "once activated by disruption, there are several processes that can promote adaptive-transformational possibilities" (p. 100).

Buzzanell conceptualized the communication theory of resilience around five interrelated processes that families engage in as they interact, transform, and co-create a new state. Following Buzzanell's (2018) conceptualization, we consider how stepfamilies interact and co-create their new family system via: (a) crafting normalcy, (b) foregrounding productive action while backgrounding negative feelings, (c) affirming identity anchors, (d) maintaining and using communication networks, and (e) putting alternative logics to work.

Resilience and Interaction Processes in Stepfamilies

Crafting Normalcy

The first resilience process is *crafting normalcy*, by which relational parties engage language in ways that actively frame their stories and build new ways of relating following change. Stepfamily scholars explain how stepfamilies develop and function in ways that are both similar and different from families of origin, primarily focusing on negotiating stepfamily difficulties and challenges. Focusing on stepfamily challenges is not without merit, as stepfamilies do form following the loss of a family of origin and change, if not upheaval, in the family system. For parents and stepparents, this process dovetails the positive aspects of falling in love and starting a new relationship. On the other hand, for children especially, the involuntary nature of stepfamily membership often compounds the lack of "traditional markers of kinship, [and] stepchildren and stepparents generally cannot easily discern how to relate to each other and how to think about themselves in these relationships" (Ganong et al., 2018, p. 1717).

While stepfamily membership is most often involuntary for stepchildren, they do possess agency in deciding whether stepparents and others will be included in their conception of family. At the same time the stepfamily is developing, other family members are also experiencing change and loss. For example, members of the extended family (e.g., grandparents) and former partners/co-parents may struggle with issues such as loyalty conflicts, ambiguity over roles (especially the stepparent), discrepant conflict styles, and challenges establishing and navigating boundaries (e.g., Coleman et al., 2005; Golish, 2003).

Examining the new normal and how stepfamilies can develop positively, stepfamily researchers and clinicians have sought to identify developmental pathways for stepfamilies. The earliest attempts were chronological stage models (e.g., Papernow, 2008), which grew into more nuanced models such as Papernow's (2013) seven-stage stepfamily cycle model and Ganong and colleagues' (2011) six patterns of stepfamily development reflected in stepchildren's experiences (accepting as a parent, liking from the start, accepting with ambivalence, changing trajectory, rejecting, and coexisting). One limitation of stage models is that they do not account for family variability and can oversimplify the process (Baxter et al., 1999; Braithwaite et al., 2018a). To that end, Schrodt (2006a, 2006b, 2006c) created and tested five stepfamily types. For example, Schrodt (2006c) found that stepchildren from stepfamilies he labeled "bonded" and "functional" were more likely to demonstrate greater communicative competence and reduced mental health symptoms compared with those from stepfamilies that were ambivalent, evasive, and conflictual.

Another research approach is to identify multiple developmental pathways stepfamilies follow by examining relational turning points (critical events resulting in relational change) and developing different stepfamily trajectories (e.g., Baxter et al., 1999). A focus on turning points helps avoid thinking about resilience as springing from singular trigger events and enlightens stepfamily paths over the years (Amato, 2010). For example, Baxter and colleagues (1999) focused on the first four years of stepfamily development while others have focused on the full trajectory/lifespan of a stepfamily (e.g., Braithwaite et al., 2018a, Graham, 1997; Oliver-Blackburn et al., 2022). Baxter et al. (1999) interviewed parents, stepparents, and stepchildren about the first four years of their stepfamily life (often considered the "make or break period") and identified 15 turning point types. Most frequent were (a) changes in household configuration, (b) conflict and disagreement, and (c) holidays/special events (rituals). From these turning points, Baxter et al. (1999) identified five stepfamily developmental trajectories, which highlight the importance of understanding that there is more than one way of developing the new normal. Oliver (2019) studied turning points among half-siblings within stepfamilies to understand different relational maintenance behaviors that characterized their stepfamily experience, concluding the importance of communicating positivity through prosocial behaviors. Nuru and Wang (2014) called specific attention to turning point types in cohabiting stepfamilies.

Our research team focused on understanding multiple pathways in stepfamilies that stepchildren (Braithwaite et al., 2018a) and stepparents (Oliver-Blackburn et al., 2022) perceived as overall positive. Interviewing stepchildren aged 25+ we found (a) prosocial actions, (b) quality time, and (c) conflict and disagreements to be the most frequent turning points (Braithwaite et al., 2018a). For stepparents, the most frequent turning points in overall positive relationships with stepchildren were (a) changes in household configuration, (b) communicating support, and (c) role change from stepparent to parent or friend/peer (Oliver-Blackburn et al., 2022). Stepparents often enacted a friend or peer role and adopted a more traditional parenting role only when they perceived stepchildren wanted or needed it. Thus, stepparents often diverged from advice to enact a purely affinity-seeking based friendship role (e.g., Ganong & Coleman, 2017; Ganong & Coleman, 2019; Speer & Trees, 2007) or what some stepfamily trainers describe as taking a "Nacho Kids" (not your kids) approach (Murray, 2022). A "nacho kids, nacho problem" mindset strikes us as overly prescriptive and simplistic and is not represented in our findings of multiple pathways and stepparent roles.

Finally, we have also considered whether the search for a functional new normal is aided by intentional approaches such as forgiveness. We found that many adult stepchildren navigated forgiveness both explicitly and implicitly and cultivated relational resilience over time (Waldron et al., 2018). Communicating forgiveness, spending quality time, and stepparents being attuned to when a stepchild needs a friend versus parent are ways stepfamilies can communicate and craft their new normal.

Foregrounding Productive Action While Backgrounding Negative Feelings

The second resilience process is *foregrounding productive action while backgrounding negative feelings*. This calls for individuals to focus on the positive and remain hopeful, while acknowledging that hardships exist, and retain the right to any negative feelings (Buzzanell, 2010). Buzzanell argued backgrounding negative feelings and focusing on the positive "is not repression nor is it putting on a happy face" (2010, p. 9). Rather, it is acknowledging that anger, or other negative emotions, are legitimate but ultimately prove to be counterproductive to more meaningful goals.

Given the challenges with restructuring into a stepfamily, conflict was found to be common and normative in stepfamilies (e.g., Baxter et al., 1999; Coleman et al., 2005). Even in positive stepfamily relationships, stepchildren acknowledged conflict, especially early on in the stepfamily around common adolescence-focused subjects such as curfew and parenting style (Braithwaite et al., 2018a). It is important for stepfamily researchers and practitioners to be mindful that *all* families experience some levels of conflict, especially in adolescence, and to not attribute all conflicts to the stepfamily structure. Stepparents also recalled conflict episodes, although less often than stepchildren. Stepparents instead highlighted conflict over shared resources and disciplinary actions (Oliver-Blackburn et al., 2022). Coleman et al. (2005) studied sources of stepfamily conflict and their corresponding conflict management strategies, such as parents and stepparents presenting a united front, compromising on rules, and engaging in direct talk about conflicts, all of which highlight the central role of communication in enacting functional conflict management.

For both stepchildren and stepparents in overall positive stepfamilies, conflict is often associated with a reduction in the positivity of their relationships, but only modestly or for a short amount of time (Braithwaite et al., 2018a; Oliver-Blackburn et al., 2022). Focusing on resilience-building strategies that foreground productive interaction and surmount negative feelings dovetails with findings that conflict is avoided or mitigated by stepparents who interact and engage in a variety of relationship-building strategies. For example, stepparents build closer and more satisfying relationships by avoiding a problem focus, spending quality time together, offering emotional support, communicating acceptance, and practicing openness (Braithwaite et al., 2018a; Ganong et al., 2021b). All of these behaviors render conflict less negatively impactful.

Another conflict-influencing aspect of stepfamily life is the multitude of changes to the household/family composition over time, including marriages, births, or family members moving in or out of the family residence. For example, in our research a stepdaughter described the negative cumulative effect of many life changes, such as her parent and stepparent cohabiting, noting, "I wasn't ready for that shock and you just arrive there, plus in a different town, in a different school, and you are start[ing] school yourself... all of this at once" (Braithwaite et al, 2001, p. 236). Even in positive stepfamilies, the impact of change presented a challenge for stepchildren, particularly in the early days of the new family (e.g., Braithwaite et al., 2018a; Coleman et al., 2013).

During these pivotal turning points in stepfamily development, our advice is that it would benefit stepfamily members, especially parents and stepparents (and perhaps co-parents), to anticipate and engage in communication designed to mitigate changes and potential negative emotions, such as grieving the "old family" (Braithwaite et al., 1998) while simultaneously focusing on how new changes could be beneficial moving forward. For example, one in six children in the United States live with a half sibling, or siblings who share only one biological parent/parent of origin (United States Census Bureau, 2014). Children in these stepfamilies may be apprehensive about a new sibling or fearful their residential parent's attention will be shared with another (Ganong et al., 2018). However, in our recent study of positive stepfamilies, stepparents believed the birth of a half-sibling positively contributed to their relationship with a stepchild and helped the stepfamily feel more unified (Oliver-Blackburn et al., 2022). Stepfamily members who foreground and communicate family change as positive appear to help negate potential negative feelings and help foster resilience.

Affirming Identity Anchors

The third resilience process is *affirming identity anchors*, which involves talking resilient stepfamilies into being. Buzzanell (2010) noted the need to have expansive and flexible identity anchors, which she defined as "a relatively enduring cluster of identity discourses upon which individuals and their familial, collegial, and/or community members rely on when explaining who they are for themselves and in relation to each other" (p. 4). For example, companies experiencing organizational hardship may seek to encourage resilience by reminding employees of their shared mission statement or their brand. Similarly, families may use descriptors such as "we bend and don't break" to communicate resilience during a difficult time. Stepfamily members can demonstrate communicative competence in the use of mantras, metaphors, and terms of address to communicate who they are, what they are capable of, and/or the significance their new family holds in their lives.

The lack of cultural models for discourse-dependent stepfamilies (Galvin, 2006, 2014) may leave members uncertain over identity-related issues. One important set of communicative choices for stepfamilies involves negotiating address terms, which range from formal ("my father's wife"), familiar ("Tereasa"), or familial ("mother," "daughter"). Choosing and adapting address terms is important, as they can signify either solidarity or separateness within a stepfamily (Koenig Kellas et al., 2008).

Address terms are also important to half-siblings as some researchers argue they are less likely to show social support and affection toward one another due to sharing less genetic or legal relatedness (Mikkelson et al., 2011). However, researchers have also demonstrated that one unique way half-siblings show each other affection is by avoiding the term "half." Rather, referencing a half-sibling as simply "brother" or "sister" within and external to the stepfamily confirms the importance of that relationship to the sibling (Oliver, 2019). Anecdotally, we have heard this point stressed within our research, especially by African American children living in blended households.

It is important to remember that address terms and other identity anchors will continue to develop over the years/trajectory of the stepfamily, both within the stepfamily unit itself and in communication with extended family (e.g., grandparents, nonresidential parents), reflecting how well these relationships are accommodated (DiVerniero, 2013). How stepfamily members negotiate, implement, and enact address terms and other identity anchors can help foster or hinder resilience.

Maintaining and Using Communication Networks

The fourth resilience process is *maintaining and using communication networks*, which ranges from engaging in person to mediated communication. Buzzanell (2018) argued that resilience grows from disruption, which involves assessing the situation, maximizing relationships that are strong, and "reconfiguring networks and using different means of connection as [individuals] enact resilience processes" (p. 102). Adapting old or finding new communication practices or networks can help stepfamily members enact the other four resilience processes.

Over years of interviews with stepfamily members, we have seen members labor to adapt or create new and functional ways to interact. For example, some stepfamilies developed a practice of calling family meetings to navigate conflicts or make decisions together (Braithwaite et al., 2001). Interestingly, family meetings were a new practice developed in the stepfamily era. In other cases, adults reported using email or audio recordings to chronicle agreements made or broken. In a diary study we undertook of interaction between adults in different stepfamily households (what we called "parent teams"), conflict was kept to a minimum when co-parents could keep the focus of communication on the children rather than on their own expectations or relationship (Braithwaite et al., 2003). Communicating via text, email, or other technologies is one way for co-parents to function in more businesslike ways, tamping down emotional expressions that may negatively impact the interaction or goal achievement.

Messages on social media can also provide clues about relationship status. For example, stepfamily members may alter their address terms, such as referring to "my stepfather" on social media but as "Frank" face to face. Interestingly, we searched for studies focused specifically on social media in stepfamilies and have not found any of those to date. We can imagine social media use to have both advantages and drawbacks for stepfamilies, in particular with nonresidential parents. When we interviewed young adult stepchildren about their nonresidential parent, while they desired to maintain these relationships, many found mediated contacts with a nonresidential parent disruptive. For example, they described how a nonresidential parent might call or text at inopportune times, disrupting daily life. Children also feared doing the same when they contacted their nonresidential parent (Braithwaite & Baxter, 2006).

We also envision relational threats when family members learn about life in the other household via social media. For example, we interviewed a father who became enraged when he saw photos of the stepfather sitting on his preteen daughter's bed to say goodnight. This father was embarrassed to report he initiated a fistfight on the front lawn with the stepfather. Clearly, anything that increases feelings of divided loyalties and being caught in the middle (Afifi, 2003; Afifi & Schrodt, 2003; Amato & Afifi, 2006) is a threat to resilience. However, calling family meetings or choosing particular mediums of communication for cross-residence communication may prove useful to stepfamilies.

Putting Alternative Logics to Work

The fifth and final resilience process is *putting alternative logics to work*, which centers on communication practices that can lead to resilient relationships via engaging in reframing. Buzzanell (2010) argued that individuals create alternative logics in order to make sense of a difficult or uncertain situation. Buzzanell pointed out that this form of sense-making is particularly needed if a stressor or hardship cannot be remedied by typical patterns or routines. Instead, stepfamilies may need to develop a new way of handling a problem, including reframing previous identity anchors or calling upon available systems or communication networks in new or novel ways (Buzzanell, 2018).

Members of resilient stepfamilies understand that conflict is likely and are therefore less afraid of it. Instead, they often find ways to embrace conflict as a way to learn about the roles and expectations of their new family, and, as Coleman et al. (2005) stressed, "conflict was often the catalyst for positive family changes, particularly when it led to thoughtful discussions and compromise" (p. 71). Resilient stepfamilies allow their interpretation of conflict to change over time, reframing conflict as needed and in ways beneficial to developing their bonds. While stepparents identify conflicts with a stepchild, they also articulate the role of conflict management in problem-solving and reconciliation (Coleman et al., 2013; Oliver-Blackburn et al., 2022). This includes negotiating communication rules that had not been previously discussed, which holds positive implications for the entire family system (Oliver-Blackburn et al., 2022). In the best of circumstances, successfully negotiating conflict can contribute to resilient and positive relationships over time.

Communicating forgiveness is another way stepfamilies engage in reframing through reconciliation and problem-solving after conflict. Communicating forgiveness not only aids in crafting normalcy but also allows stepfamily members to heal family connections and show acceptance and compassion for family members, and it can be evidence of relational growth (Waldron et al., 2018). Oftentimes though, forgiveness is only communicated after some time has passed or once a stepchild has matured and can reflect on a previous conflict in a new, more enlightening way (Braithwaite et al., 2018a). The passage of time can allow stepfamily members to reframe a conflict and see it in more affirmative ways. Stepchildren who described stepparents ending conflict with an apology noted this communicative act served as meaningful evidence of the relationship's resilience and the family's ability to endure the hard times or embrace and reframe conflict as beneficial to their stepfamily relationships (Braithwaite et al., 2018a).

Reframing is not only significant to stepfamily conflict, but to stepfamily roles as well. Stepparents historically have been instructed to mostly serve as a friend to their stepchildren, particularly early on in their family's development, as taking on the role of disciplinarian too early can negatively impact the parent–child bond. However, recent researchers show that stepchildren expect and desire their stepparents to serve in a multitude of roles throughout their relationship, including that of a friend, nurturer, protector, mentor, casual acquaintance, or even an ambivalent figure (Ganong et al., 2021b). Resilient stepparents can reframe their role throughout the trajectory of the relationship, using subtle communication cues from their stepchild to know when to adjust (Oliver-Blackburn et al., 2022). Unclear stepparent roles are often seen as a challenge to stepfamily development and functioning, yet resilient stepparents use this lack of "normative expectations in a positive way, creating roles that work for them without concerns about meeting societal expectations about parental roles and responsibilities" (Ganong et al., 2021a, p. 939).

Conclusions

In this chapter, we reflected on social processes that can function positively in stepfamilies and help them foster resilience. We organized our understanding alongside Buzzanell's (2010) five resiliency processes and centered our view of stepfamilies as created and enacted in interaction, negotiating internal and external boundaries experienced by discourse-dependent families (e.g., Braithwaite et al., 2022; Galvin 2006). It is important to note that resilience processes are a mix of individual, dyadic, and whole family systems relating and overlapping sense-making processes (Braithwaite et al., 2018a; Coleman et al., 2013). We believe that research methods that assist scholars in examining stepfamily interaction and experience over time are pivotal to understanding how resilience processes develop and are sustained

(Zautra, 2009). Understanding stepfamilies as discourse-dependent and centering attention on how their roles, expectations, and boundaries are negotiated in interaction is central knowledge about how these families are talked into (and out of) being (Buzzanell, 2010). Finally, in considering stepfamily resilience, we agree with Coleman et al. (2013), who stressed the need for research and clinical interventions to focus on family strengths and normalizing stepfamily experiences, explaining that "applying resilience to stepfamilies means focusing on family strengths and acknowledging diverse ways for families to accomplish goals and tasks" (p. 97).

As we consider interaction and the developmental trajectories of stepfamilies, we seek to better understand some of the significant events that influence and reflect shared experiences and developing positive relationships. While we appreciate those events in which stepfamily development and resilience turn, we are also struck by the importance of everyday talk in stepfamilies (Schrodt et al., 2007). While everyday talk might seem mundane, it is especially important for stepchildren and stepparents, as engaging in prosocial interactions and spending quality time together permeate positive stepfamilies. For example, one stepdaughter told us,

> I really wanted to paint my room red when I was like 16. . . . [My stepfather is] the only parent that's ever been like, "I just want to make you happy." It's a little thing like him going out at 11 at night to go get me Twinkies if I wanted a Twinkie. Just little things like that. He's extremely thoughtful and he's never judged me. Like, not once. . . . I remember my real dad and my stepmom were like, "No you can't paint a room. If you want to do this, you have to do it at your mom's." Dan was like, "It's just a wall." And he told me I would "probably hate it in like a year, but we can always repaint it." (Braithwaite et al., 2018a, p. 98)

This rich example also helps us frame the importance of stepparents communicating warmth, engaging in openness, seeking affinity, providing support, and negotiating clear boundaries (e.g., Ganong et al., 1999; Golish, 2003). We have been struck by efforts that might seem simple on their face but help stepfamilies, stepparents especially, work toward functional and positive relationships. Both communicating emotional support and developing trust (Kinniburgh-White et al., 2010) in the stepchild–stepparent dyad can, in the best of circumstances, permeate the larger stepfamily system and continue to grow resilience and functional stepfamilies over the years.

References

Afifi, T. D. (2003). "Feeling caught" in stepfamilies: Managing boundary turbulence through appropriate communication privacy rules. *Journal of Social and Personal Relationships, 20*(6), 729–755. https://doi.org/10.1177/0265407503206002

Afifi, T. D., & Schrodt, P. (2003). "Feeling caught" as a mediator of adolescents' and young adults' avoidance and satisfaction with their parents in divorced and non-divorced households. *Communication Monographs, 70*(2), 142–173. https://doi.org/10.1080/0363775032000133791

Amato, P. R. (2010). Research on divorce: Continuing trends and new developments. *Journal of Marriage and Family, 72,* 650–666. https://doi.org/10.1111/j.1741-3737.2010.00723.x

Amato, P. R., & Afifi, T. D. (2006). Feeling caught between parents: Adult children's relations with parents and subjective well-being. *Journal of Marriage and Family, 68*(1), 222–235. https://doi.org/10.1111/j.1741-3737.2006.00243.x

Baxter, L. A. (2004). Relationships as dialogues. *Personal Relationships, 11,* 1–22. https://doi.org/10.1111/j.1475-6811.2004.00068.x

Baxter, L. A. (2014). Theorizing the communicative construction of "family": The three R's. In L. A. Baxter (Ed.), *Remaking "family" communicatively* (pp. 33–50). Peter Lang.

Baxter, L. A., Braithwaite, D. O., & Nicholson, J. H. (1999). Turning points in the development of blended families. *Journal of Social and Personal Relationships, 16*(3), 291–313. https://doi.org/10.1177%2F0265407599163002

Braithwaite, D. O., & Baxter, L. A. (2006). "You're my parent but you're not": Dialectical tensions in stepchildren's perceptions about communicating with the nonresidential parent. *Journal of Applied Communication Research, 34,* 30–48. https://doi.org/10.1080/00909880500420200

Braithwaite, D. O., Baxter, L. A., & Harper, A. M. (1998). The role of rituals in the management of the dialectical tension of "old" and "new" in blended families. *Communication Studies, 49*(2), 101–120. https://doi.org/10.1207/S15327698JFC0304_3

Braithwaite, D. O., Foster, E. A., & Bergen, K. M. (2018b). Social construction theory: Communication co-creating families. In D. O. Braithwaite, E. A. Suter, & K. Floyd (Eds.), *Engaging theories in family communication: Multiple perspectives* (2nd ed., pp. 267–278). Routledge.

Braithwaite, D. O., McBride, M. C., & Schrodt, P. (2003). Parent teams and the everyday interactions of co-parenting children in stepfamilies. *Communication Reports, 16,* 93–111. https://doi.org/10.1080/08934210309384493

Braithwaite, D. O., Olson, L., Golish, T., Soukup, C., & Turman, P. (2001). "Becoming a family": Developmental processes represented in blended family discourse. *Journal of Applied Communication Research, 29,* 221–247. https://doi.org/10.1080/00909880128112

Braithwaite, D. O., Schrodt, P., & Oliver-Blackburn, B. M. (2022). Stepfamilies as developed and enacted in communication. In A. Vangelisti (Ed.), *Handbook of family communication* (3rd ed., pp. 143–157). Routledge.

Braithwaite, D. O., & Suter, E. A. (2022). Family communication. In K. Adamsons, A. Few-Demo, C. Proulx, & K. Roy (Eds.), *Sourcebook of family theories and methodologies: A dynamic approach* (pp. 531–548). Springer.

Braithwaite, D. O., Toller, P., Daas, K., Durham, W., & Jones, A. (2008). Centered but not caught in the middle: Stepchildren's perceptions of dialectical contradictions in the communication of co-parents. *Journal of Applied Communication Research, 36*(1), 33–55. https://doi.org/10.1080/00909880701799337

Braithwaite, D. O., Waldron, V. R., Allen, J., Oliver, B., Bergquist, G., Storck, K., Marsh, J., Swords, N., & Tschampl-Diesing, C. (2018a). "Feeling warmth and close to her": Communication and resilience reflected in turning points in positive adult stepchild–stepparent relationships. *Journal of Family Communication, 18*(2), 92–109. https://doi.org/10.1080/15267431.2017.1415902

Burr, V. (2015). *Social constructionism* (3rd ed.). Routledge.

Buzzanell, P. M. (2010). Resilience: Talking, resisting, and imagining new normalcies into being. *Journal of Communication, 60*(1), 1–14. https://doi.org/10.1111/j.1460-2466.2009.01469.x

Buzzanell, P. M. (2018). Communication theory of resilience: Enacting adaptive-transformative processes when families experience loss and disruption. In D. O. Braithwaite & P. Schrodt (Eds.), *Engaging theories in family communication* (2nd ed., pp. 98–109). Routledge.

Carlson, L. (2020). *Stepfamilies in first marriages.* Family profiles, FP-20-28. National Center for Family & Marriage Research. https://doi.org/10.25035/ncfmr/fp-20-28

Coleman, M., Fine, M. A., Ganong, L. H., Downs, K., & Pauk, N. (2005). When you're not the Brady Bunch: Identifying perceived conflicts and resolution strategies in stepfamilies. *Personal Relationships, 8*(1), 55–73. https://doi.org/10.1111/j.1475-6811.2001.tb00028.x

Coleman, M., Ganong, L., & Russell, L. T. (2013). Resilience in stepfamilies. In D. Beckvar (Ed.), *Handbook of family resilience* (pp. 85–103). Springer.

DiVerniero, R. D. (2013). Children of divorce and their nonresidential parent's family: Examining perceptions of communication accommodation. *Journal of Family Communication, 13*(4), 301–320. https://doi.org/10.1080/15267431.2013.823429

Eickmeyer, K. J. (2017). *American children's family structures: Stepparent families.* Family profile, National Center for Family & Marriage Research. https://www.bgsu.edu/content/dam/BGSU/college-of-arts-and-sciences/NCFMR/documents/FP/eickmeyer-stepparent-families-fp-17-16.pdf

Foster, E., & Bochner, A. (2008). Social constructionist perspectives in communication research. In J. Gubrium & J. Holstein (Eds.), *Handbook of constructionist research* (pp. 85–106). Guilford.

Galvin, K. (2006). Diversity's impact on defining the family: Discourse-dependence and identity. In L. H. Turner & R. West (Eds.), *The family communication sourcebook* (pp. 3–19). SAGE.

Galvin, K. M. (2014). Blood, law, and discourse: Constructing and managing family identity. In L. A. Baxter (Ed.), *Remaking "family" communicatively* (pp. 17–32). Peter Lang.

Ganong, L. H., & Coleman, M. (2017). *Stepfamily relationships: Development, dynamics, and interventions* (2nd ed.). Springer.

Ganong, L. H., & Coleman, M. (2019). Resilience processes in postdivorce families and stepfamilies. *NCFR Report* (FF81). https://www.ncfr.org/ncfr-report/fall-2019

Ganong, L. H., Coleman, M., Chapman, A., & Jamison, T. (2018). Stepchildren claiming stepparents. *Journal of Family Issues, 39*(6), 1712–1736. https://doi.org/10.1177/0192513X17725878

Ganong, L. H., Coleman, M., Fine, M., & Martin, P. (1999). Stepparents' affinity-seeking and affinity-maintaining strategies with stepchildren. *Journal of Family Issues, 20*(3), 299–327. https://doi.org/10.1177%2F019251399020003001

Ganong, L. H., Coleman, M., & Jamison, T. (2011). Patterns of stepchild-stepparent relationship development. *Journal of Marriage and Family, 73*(2), 396–413. https://doi.org/10.1111/j.1741-3737.2010.00814.x

Ganong, L., Coleman, M., Sanner, C., & Berkley, S. (2021a). Summary and synthesus if research on what works in stepfamily childrearing. *Family Relations, 71*(3), 935–952. https://doi.org/10.1111/fare.12634

Ganong, L., Coleman, M., Sanner, C., & Berkley, S. (2021b). Effective stepparenting: Empirical evidence of what works. *Family Relations, 71*(3), 884–899. https://doi.org/10.1111/fare.12624

Golish, T. D. (2003). Stepfamily communication strengths: Understanding the ties that bind. *Human Communication Research, 29*(1), 41–80. https://doi.org/10.1093/hcr/29.1.41

Gosselin, J., & David, H. (2007). Risk and resilience factors linked with the psychosocial adjustment of adolescents, stepparents, and biological parents. *Journal of Divorce and Remarriage, 48*, 29–53. https://doi.org/10.1300/J087v48n01_02

Graham, E. E. (1997). Turning points and commitment in post-divorce relationships. *Communication Monographs, 64*(4), 351–367. https://doi.org/10.1080/03637759709376428

King, V., Thorsen, K. L., & Amato, P. R. (2014). Factors associated with positive relationships between stepfathers and adolescent stepchildren. *Social Science Research, 47*, 16–29. https://doi.org/10.1016/j.ssresearch.2014.03.010

Kinniburgh-White, R., Cartwright, C., & Seymour, F. (2010). Young adults' narratives of relational development with stepfathers. *Journal of Social and Personal Relationships, 27*(7), 890–907. https://doi.org/10.1177/0265407510376252

Koenig Kellas, J., LeClair-Underberg, C., & Normand, E. L. (2008). Stepfamily address terms: "Sometimes they mean something and sometimes they don't." *Journal of Family Communication, 8*(4), 238–263. https://doi.org/10.1080/15267430802397153

Leeds-Hurwitz, W. (2006). Social theories: Social constructionism and symbolic interactionism. In D. O. Braithwaite & L. A. Baxter (Eds.), *Engaging theories in family communication: Multiple perspectives* (pp. 229–242). SAGE.

Mikkelson, A. C., Floyd, K., & Pauley, P. M. (2011). Differential solicitude of social support in different types of adult sibling relationships. *Journal of Family Communication, 11*(4), 220–236. https://doi.org/10.1080/15267431.2011.554749

Murray, S. H. (2022, April 19). The stepparent's dilemma. *The Atlantic*. https://www.theatlantic.com/family/archive/2022/04/stepparenting-kids-advice-nacho-disengage/629600/

Nuru, A. K, & Wang, T. R. (2014). "She was stomping on everything that we used to think of as a family": Communication and turning points in cohabiting (step)families. *Journal of Divorce and Remarriage, 55*(2), 145–163. https://doi.org/10.1080/10502556.2013.871957

Oliver, B. M. (2019, November 13–17). *Blended family resilience: Communication practices in positive adult half sibling relationships* [Paper presentation]. National Communication Association Conference, Baltimore, MD, United States.

Oliver-Blackburn, B. M., Braithwaite, D. O., Waldron, V., Hall, R., Hackenburg, L., & Worman, B. (2022). Protector and friend: Turning points and discursive constructions of the stepparent role. *Family Relations, 71*, 1–22. https://doi.org/10.1111/fare.12642

Pace, G. T., Shafer, K., Jensen, T. M., & Larson, J. H. (2015). Stepparenting issues and relationship quality: The role of clear communication. *Journal of Social Work, 15*(1), 24–44. https://doi.org/10.1177/1468017313504508

Papernow, P. L. (2008). A clinician's view of "stepfamily architecture": Strategies for meeting the challenges. In J. Pryor (Ed.), *The international handbook of stepfamilies: Policy and practice in legal, research, and clinical environments* (pp. 423–454). Wiley.

Papernow, P. L. (2013). *Surviving and thriving in stepfamily relationships: What works and what doesn't*. Routledge.

Papernow, P. L. (2018). Clinical guidelines for working with stepfamilies: What family, couple, individual, and child therapists need to know. *Family Process, 57*(1), 25–51. https://doi.org/10.1111/famp.12321

Pew Research Center. (2015). The American family today. https://www.pewsocialtrends.org/2015/12/17/1-the-american-family-today

Pylyser, C. B., Buysse, A., & Loeys, T. (2018). Stepfamilies doing family: A meta-ethnography. *Family Process, 57*(2), 496–509. https://doi.org/10.1111/famp.12293

Schrodt, P. (2006a). The Stepparent Relationship Index: Development, validation, and associations with stepchildren's perceptions of stepparent communication competence and closeness. *Personal Relationships, 13*(2), 167–182. https://doi.org/10.1111/j.1475-6811.2006.00111.x

Schrodt, P. (2006b). Development and validation of the Stepfamily Life Index. *Journal of Social and Personal Relationships, 23*(3), 427–444. https://doi.org/10.1177%2F0265407506064210

Schrodt, P. (2006c). A typological examination of communication competence and mental health in stepchildren. *Communication Monographs, 73*(3), 309. https://doi.org/10.1080/03637750600873728

Schrodt, P., Braithwaite, D. O., Soliz, J., Tye-Williams, S., Miller, A., Normand, E. L., & Harrigan, M. M. (2007). An examination of everyday talk in stepfamily systems. *Western Journal of Communication, 71*(3), 216–234. https://doi.org/10.1080/10570310701510077

Speer, R. B., & Trees, A. R. (2007). The push and pull of stepfamily life: The contribution of stepchildren's autonomy and connection-seeking behaviors to role development in stepfamilies. *Communication Studies, 58*(4), 377–394. https://doi.org/10.1080/10510970701648590

Stewart, S. D. (2005). Boundary ambiguity in stepfamilies. *Journal of Family Issues, 26*(7), 1002–1029. https://doi.org/10.1177/0192513X04273591

Stewart, S. D. & Limb, G. L. (Eds.) (2020). *Multicultural stepfamilies*. Cognella.

United States Census Bureau. (2014). *Survey of income and program participation (SIPP)*. https://www.census.gov/programs-surveys/sipp.html

Waldron, V. R., Braithwaite, D. O., Oliver, B. M., Kloeber, D. N., & Marsh, J. (2018). Discourses of forgiveness and resilience in stepchild–stepparent relationships. *Journal of Applied Communication Research, 46*(5), 561–582. https://doi.org/10.1080/00909882.2018.1530447

Waldron, V., Braithwaite, D. O., Oliver-Blackburn, B. M., & Avalos, B. (2022). Paths to positivity: Relational trajectories and interaction in positive stepparent-stepchild dyads. *Journal of Family Communication, 22*(1), 33–54. https://doi.org/10.1080/15267431.2021.1999243

Zautra, A. J. (2009). Resilience: One part recovery, two parts sustainability. *Journal of Personality, 77*, 1935–1943. https://doi.org/10.1111/j.1467-6494.2009.00605.x

18

Technology-Assisted Parenthood and Modern Families in the 21st Century

Sofia Gameiro

Medically assisted reproduction (MAR) refers to reproduction brought about through various interventions, procedures, surgeries, and technologies to treat different forms of fertility impairment and infertility. These include ovulation induction, ovarian stimulation, ovulation triggering, all Assisted Reproduction Technologies (ART) procedures, uterine transplantation and intra-uterine, intracervical, and intravaginal insemination with semen of husband/partner or donor. (Zegers-Hochschild et al., 2017; p. 1796)

A worldwide large increase in the use of MAR to have children has been observed during the last decades. For instance, a recent study showed that the proportion of MAR births in Australia increased from 5.1% in 2009 to 6.7% in 2017, representing a 30% increase over the decade (Choi et al., 2022). In the United States, 2% of children are conceived with MAR (Hamilton et al., 2019). The use of MAR to have children has allowed for the proliferation of new forms of families, generally denominated modern families, as they fall outside the normative heterosexual family. In 2018, 6.4% of fertility treatments used in the United Kingdom were by women in same-sex relationships, 3.2% by single patients, and 0.04% by surrogates (Human Fertilisation and Embryology Authority, 2020). New reproductive techniques continue to emerge, introducing new forms of complexity into family building. For instance, one of the latest innovations is shared motherhood, whereby one woman's egg is used to create an embryo with donated sperm and the other woman undergoes the pregnancy. This means one mother has a genetic connection to the child and the other a gestational

Sofia Gameiro, *Technology-Assisted Parenthood and Modern Families in the 21st Century* In: *Modern Relationships*. Edited by: Mahzad Hojjat and Anne Moyer, Oxford University Press. © Oxford University Press 2024.
DOI: 10.1093/oso/9780197655504.003.0018

one. Polyparenting, in which more than two adults act as parental figures to a child is also an emergent reality facilitated by the use of MAR (Simon, 2013). This is in addition to what now have become mainstream routes to have children, such as surrogacy or donor insemination.

While reproductive technologies have been allowing minority groups to exercise their reproductive rights, these are now at stake with the recent ruling to overturn *Roe v. Wade*. Defining personhood from the time of fertilization opens the door to restricting any embryo manipulation in the IVF laboratory. In practice, this may mean several groups may be prevented from using IVF to conceive, for instance, patients wanting to preserve their fertility prior to oncological treatment, people needing third-party reproduction to conceive, LGBTQ+ people wanting to have children, or people carrying genetically transmissible health conditions. It is therefore timely to reflect on how MAR has enabled diverse groups of people to have children and how children born within these modern families develop.

Historically, concerns for the welfare of the children created with MAR started to be raised in 1978, when *in vitro fertilization* (IVF) was introduced. During the 1980s, attention was called to the implications of using MAR for family building, in particular how the parent–child relationship would be affected (Mahlstedt & Greenfield, 1989). As technologies and knowledge evolved, so did the specific concerns mentioned, but broadly they fell into four areas: MAR can impact parents and parenting, the lack of a genetic link can impact parenting and parent–child relationships, the implications of nontraditional families and family complexity are unknown, and secrecy about conception can impact family communication. An aspect that is less explored is the implications of not being able to have children with MAR. In this chapter, we will review theory and evidence related to these five topics.

Can Infertility and Assisted Reproduction Impact Parents and Parenting?

As the number of people using MAR to have children increased and innovative technologies such as IVF were introduced, the field was called upon to discuss the consequences of using MAR for the newly formed families, including the children born through these procedures. It was initially suggested that the stress of infertility and MAR could create dysfunctional patterns of parenting that would ultimately impact the children. While initially, attention focused on identifying those who were particularly vulnerable, for instance those who had overt psychopathology, to preclude them from receiving treatment and thus safeguard the welfare of the unborn child (Seibel & Levin, 1987), it soon became clear that infertility and its treatments posed challenges for everyone using them and these needed to be better understood.

Initial theorizing about potential negative consequences of using MAR focused on how realizing a long-sustained wish for children with such novel (and yet unknown) technologies could create heightened anxiety about the viability of the pregnancy and health of the fetus, as well as unrealistic expectations about the realities of parenting (van Balen, 1998). Theoretically framed by attachment theory and models of the determinants of parenting (Belsky, 1984), the reasoning was that these experiences could adversely affect parenting, for instance via diminished maternal confidence, or hypervigilant and overprotective parenting, which would create difficulties in parent–child attachment and ultimately negatively impact child development. These concerns were reinforced by qualitative research suggesting that pregnancy and parenting were experienced in a more psychologically complex way after MAR than after spontaneous conception (e.g., Sandelowski et al., 1990). To address these concerns, since the early 1990s, multiple cohort studies examined couples who had genetically related children, both during pregnancy and the early postpartum period (usually 1–2 years after childbirth). The research aimed to compare couples who conceived with MAR (usually IVF or intracytoplasmic sperm injection, ICSI) with those conceiving spontaneously on their psychosocial functioning, operationalized in terms of their mental health and well-being, quality of the partnership, and social adjustment, as well as the quality of the parent–infant relationship and associated child outcomes.

Although evidence is still emerging, knowledge gathered so far has been reassuring about the use of MAR to conceive. First, it revealed that the population of people using MAR to conceive differed from the general population in that they did not tend to present typical risk factors for maladjustment during the transition to parenthood, such as being young, un-partnered, of low socioeconomic status, and experiencing marital conflict (Hammarberg et al., 2008). On the contrary, these parents-to-be tended to be financially "well-off" and to come from favorable sociocultural backgrounds. Their engagement with protracted fertility treatment reflected high commitment toward their parenting project, and the experience of treatment was shown to further strengthen their partnership (Schmidt et al., 2005). They also tended to be older by the time they achieved parenthood, and, although older age makes pregnancy and parenting more physically demanding (Boivin et al., 2009), it also translates into higher resilience and more "mature" parenting (Camberis et al., 2016).

Consistently, the evidence from this strand of research showed that couples who conceive with MAR do not report more mental health problems or lower well-being, partnership satisfaction, and self-esteem during the transition to parenthood. Indeed, anxiety and depression rates tend to be similar to rates of those who conceive spontaneously (Hammarberg et al., 2008). Nonetheless, the evidence also showed that these mothers and fathers were more likely to report more anxiety related to the health of the pregnancy and the fetus and lower maternal self-efficacy, in particular if they had experienced prolonged treatment failure or high infertility-related stress when trying to conceive, or when treatment resulted in multiple pregnancies (Gameiro et al., 2010; Gibson et al., 2000; Hjelmstedt et al., 2009; McMahon et al., 1999). This heightened anxiety about pregnancy seemed to reflect a realistic appraisal of personal health circumstances, as IVF was associated with a higher incidence of perinatal complications such as preterm birth (Bergh et al., 1999), which was mostly the consequence of multiple pregnancies rather than the IVF technique itself. Indeed, when safety concerns led to a normative shift from multiple to single embryo transfer in the early 2000s, these adverse outcomes were resolved.

Parenting during the early postpartum was shown to be mostly similar in couples who conceived with MAR and spontaneously. Some differences were observed, however. For instance, detailed observational studies showed MAR infants exhibit more difficult behaviors than spontaneously conceived infants (Gibson et al., 1998). Paradoxically, other studies also revealed that parents conceiving with MAR express higher enjoyment of parenthood and parental investment in their children (Gameiro et al., 2011; Golombok, 2002). Some authors speculated about the direction of this relationship, suggesting MAR parents may be more tolerant of problematic infant behavior (Repokari et al., 2006).

Follow-up studies suggest that whatever differences are observed during early parenthood are likely to vanish with time. Indeed, multiple studies failed to identify differences in parenting and adolescent socioemotional development between families created with MAR, spontaneously, and with adoption (Colpin & Bossaert, 2008; Golombok et al., 2009). Furthermore, by the time they reach adulthood, people conceived with MAR report no distress about their mode of conception (Golombok et al., 2009).

Overall, this research showed that the method of conception is not a risk factor for parental maladjustment, poor parenting, or developmental problems in children. Consistently, contemporary healthcare delivery focuses on reassuring parents-to-be and providing tailored support to those who may present with specific vulnerabilities (Gameiro et al., 2015).

Can the Lack of Genetic Link Impact Parenting and Parent–Child Relationships?

With the introduction of gamete donation, a layer of complexity was added, due to the lack of genetic link between parent(s) and children. Based on observations made in early adoption studies, where adopted children exhibited significant adjustment difficulties, concerns were expressed that a lack of genetic link between parents and children conceived with gamete donation could impact parenting and parent–children relationships. Based on attachment theory, the representations parents create of their child affect the way they parent (George & Solomon, 1996), and if these were negatively framed due to the lack of a genetic link, then parenting could be suboptimal. The specific concerns raised were that those parents who were not genetically related to the child could be distant or even hostile toward them or could feel less entitled to parent. This issue became even more relevant later on, when removal of donor anonymity became the norm across countries. In the United Kingdom, gamete donation then started operating under identity-release donation, meaning that the donor is unknown to parents (i.e., recipients), but any resultant children may access identifying donor information when they reach 18.

Research shows the first concern, that is, that parents without a genetic link with the child would be distant, to be unwarranted. Longitudinal studies from Golombok and colleagues (e.g., Golombok et al., 2004, 2006) with families formed by egg and sperm donation assessed multiple times from infancy to adolescence showed well-functioning parent–child relationships, in some instances even better than the control group of families formed without MAR. The children also showed good psychological adjustment. Meanwhile, it became clear that adjustment difficulties reported in adoption studies are related to adoption-specific factors, the most relevant being the adversity that children experience pre-adoption.

To better disentangle the impact of using gamete donation from the experience of undergoing MAR, more recent studies focused on comparing families who used MAR with and without donation. A recent qualitative study based on individual interviews with 85 women who had children via identity release egg donation showed that these mothers have specific concerns that result from the lack of the genetic link with their child; for instance, they worry that the baby may not feel like their own. However, the study also showed that there is variability in the importance that mothers attribute to the genetic link and that worries regarding connectedness with the baby tend to disappear after the birth. In this study, women reported using a variety of cognitive strategies to "make the child theirs"; for instance they highlighted the importance of pregnancy and the influence of mothering in shaping their relationship with the child. Results also indicated that most participants felt secure and confident as mothers. However, when mothers experienced difficulties with their child, they tended to attribute these to the lack of the genetic link (Imrie et al., 2020). Other studies by the same team revealed some worse outcomes in parental mental health, parenting confidence, and parent–infant interaction in families who used identity release egg donation than in families with no gamete donation, but these differences disappeared when twin conceptions and maternal age were controlled for (Imrie, Jadva, Fishel, et al., 2019; Imrie, Jadva, & Golombok, 2019).

More recently, to enable both mothers in lesbian families to have a biological connection with the child, lesbian couples began to have children through shared biological parenting. In these families, one woman's egg is used to create an embryo with donated sperm and the other woman undergoes pregnancy. Research on these families is emergent and therefore knowledge is limited; however, the few qualitative studies published indicate that the desire to ensure biological connections with the child and the social and legal implications of these connections are important motivations to use the technique (Shaw et al., 2022). Consistently, these mothers report less jealousy around parenting than lesbian mothers using traditional egg donation due to perceptions of more equal ties to the child (Pelka, 2009).

Overall, this strand of research suggests that perceptions about the relevance of having a genetic link with one's child can shape experiences of parenting but not necessarily the quality of the parenting.

What Are the Implications of Establishing Complex Nontraditional Families?

Technological developments in MAR and gamete donation have allowed for the proliferation of nontraditional forms of families such as single parents and LGBT families, as well as complex families where a child can have more than two parents, as is the case with surrogacy (e.g., two biological and one gestational) and polyparenting. Given the nontraditional elements of these families, a need for scrutiny emerged, based on arguments that the implications for children were unknown.

One issue raised was related to the lack of a male role model in lesbian and single-mother families. During the 1980s and 1990s, studies with lesbian couples who did donor insemination indicated that the children they parented developed as well as children with heterosexual parents (e.g., Brewaeys et al., 1997). In the United States, the National Lesbian Family Study has been following lesbian families and their offspring for over 25 years, now on its sixth assessment wave with a 92% retention rate. Findings from this study are that children in lesbian families report the same or fewer psychological problems than children from population samples when they are 10, 17, and 25 years old (e.g., Gartrell et al., 2018).

Multi-methods and multi-informant studies with single mothers by choice also show that their children are well adjusted and have equally good relationships with their mothers as donor-conceived children in two-parent families up until they are nine years old (Golombok et al., 2016). Although these findings differ from other studies with single mothers where children had a higher risk of experiencing cognitive, social, and emotional problems, the risk seems to be mainly related to economic hardship, parental conflict (for instance, in divorced families), and parental mental health problems (McLanahan & Sandefur, 2009). These risk factors do not usually apply to single women who use MAR to have children, as they tend to have favorable social and financial contexts, as well as highly planned pregnancies.

Focusing on gay families, concerns were raised that it was not common for fathers to be primary caregivers. In addition, children from gay couples have to be conceived with the help of a surrogate mother who provides the eggs and gestation, and this technology can bring additional challenges. Therefore, research focused on ascertaining if gay fathers were competent at parenting and if children born via surrogacy in these families developed well. Golombok and colleagues (2018) addressed these questions by comparing gay families created with surrogacy with lesbian families created via sperm donation. All children were between three and nine years old. Results indicated that gay fathers had equally positive relationships with their children as lesbian mothers. Gay fathers reported their children had lower levels of emotional problems, suggesting gay parents were either less sensitive in identifying these problems or more effective in parenting than lesbian mothers. A more recent multi-methods study examined father–child relationships, parenting quality, and child psychological adjustment in single-gay-father surrogacy families, single-heterosexual-father surrogacy families, gay two-father surrogacy families, and heterosexual two-parent IVF families. The only differences found were when children were between 3 and 10 years old and indicated greater parenting stress for single parents, regardless of sexual orientation (Carone et al., 2020).

Similarly, positive results were found in studies from the Golombok team following heterosexual families created with surrogacy. Indeed, these parents showed greater warmth toward and enjoyment in their babies when they were one and two years old than heterosexual families created with donor insemination, mothers were more affective and interactive when children were three, and similar parent–child relationships were observed when children were seven. At this age, children in surrogacy families reported more psychological problems than children in traditional heterosexual families, but by the time they were 10 and 14 years of age no differences in adjustment were observed (e.g., Golombok et al., 2011).

In a later study, individual semi-structured interviews with the then-adolescent offspring in these families showed that most felt positive or indifferent about their surrogacy or donor conception, most were interested in their surrogate or donor, and most of those who were in contact with their surrogate or donor expressed positive feelings toward them (Zadeh et al., 2018).

Overall, these results indicate that family structure and method of conception have little importance for how children develop. Indeed, the number of parents, their gender, sexual orientation, and genetic and gestational connection to their children do not determine the quality of the parenting they offer them. However, parenting happens in context, and different studies showed that nontraditional families and their children are more likely to be subjected to stigma than traditional families. In the National Lesbian Family Study, 41% of adolescent offspring (aged 17) of lesbian families reported experiencing homophobic stigmatization. This experience was associated with lower self-confidence and more problem behavior. Fortunately, this and other studies have shown there are factors that can counteract this negative impact of stigma, specifically, having frequent contact with other offspring of same-sex parents, schools that teach tolerance, and good family relationships (Bos & Gartrell, 2010; Bos & Van Balen, 2008).

In sum, despite multiple concerns raised, the evidence collected so far overwhelmingly indicates that children who are born into nontraditional families develop well.

Can Secrecy About Conception Impact Family Communication and Child Development?

Another worry was that secrecy surrounding how children were conceived could be detrimental. Specific arguments were that secrets disrupt family harmony, that secrets distance those who know them from those who do not know them, and that children become aware of secrecy and taboos within the family and this can make them confused, anxious, or even develop psychopathological symptoms (Daniels & Taylor, 1993). In the United Kingdom, anonymous gamete donation was prohibited in 2005 due to an increasing acceptance that donor-conceived people often wish to know their origins. This means that when donor-conceived people reach 18, they can request disclosure of their donor's identity. Therefore, parents are encouraged to tell their child they were conceived using donated eggs or sperm at a young age. Direct-to-consumer DNA testing sites allow people to locate other people who are genetically related to them. These have been increasingly used by donor-conceived individuals to locate their donors and/or siblings (Crawshaw, 2018). While these novel legislation and technologies render anonymous donor conception unfeasible, the reality is that many parents are still reluctant to disclose gamete donation (and the lack of a genetic link) to their children, in particular, those in heterosexual two-parent families.

One study conducted in the United States found that only 43% of parents who intended to disclose donation to their child did as they initially intended. The study, conducted when the children were on average 13 years old, showed that main reasons for disclosure were the child's right to know, the desire to be open and honest, and the notion that family secrets are harmful. Those who delayed disclosure, but still intended to do it, justified their delay by not finding the "right time" and being uncertain about when and how to do it (Applegarth et al., 2016). Another study, run in the United Kingdom with 101 families conceived with gamete donation and surrogacy, showed that only 27.8% and 40.6% of parents who used donated sperm and eggs, respectively, had disclosed this to their children by the time they were seven years old. By contrast 95.2% and 75.0% of parents who used genetic and gestational surrogacy, respectively, had disclosed. Reasons to disclose were similar to those listed above. Reasons not to disclose were no perceived need to do so, to protect the child, that it was a personal matter and, in some cases, to protect the partner (Readings et al., 2011). Stigma and social disapproval can also contribute to nondisclosure (Wyverkens et al., 2015).

Research focusing on the process of disclosure indicates this happens in different ways for different groups, different ages of disclosure, and according to the gender of parent and child. Research also suggests disclosure during preschool years seems better than later on. Indeed, children told at an early age react with curiosity or disinterest. Furthermore, waiting beyond 8 years of age seems to lead to further delay, and late disclosure seems harder for parents (Applegarth et al., 2016; Mac Dougall et al., 2007). Finally, there is evidence that people who find out about their donor conception later in life can feel shocked and betrayed (Jadva et al., 2009). It is important to note, though, that disclosure is a process that unfolds over time and therefore this differentiation can mask complexity. Parents who disclose do not regret it and many experience relief (Mac Dougall et al., 2007). However, follow-up studies revealed no overall differences in psychological well-being and quality of family relationships between families in which parents disclosed and those who did not (Widbom et al., 2022).

Overall, there is some indication that disclosure is a challenging process for parents and that the way it happens can affect perceptions of family relationships. However, it does not seem to have long-lasting impacts on the well-being and quality of parent–child relationships. Moving forward, the more is known about disclosure from the perspective of those who experience it, the better families can be supported in this process.

What Are the Implications of Not Transitioning to Parenthood After (Unsuccessful) MAR?

The delays in starting to try to have children are causing more and more people to have to use MAR to conceive. However, around 4 out of all 10 individual patients or couples who start MAR do not achieve a live birth (McLernon et al., 2016). In the United Kingdom and other European countries, around 1 in 5 women reach 45 without a child, and only 3% of these are childless by choice (Präg et al., 2017). Many have argued that childless families are a modern type of 21st-century family, but one that is often overlooked (Dykstra & Hagestad, 2007). Some authors have used the expression "transition to non-parenthood" to describe the transition from an anticipated status of potential parenthood to the unwanted status of non-parenthood (Matthews & Matthews, 1986). This expression is particularly relevant for those who use MAR, given their strong desire for children and commitment to undergo multiple treatment cycles to achieve it, despite treatment being protracted, physically and emotionally demanding, and disruptive of personal and professional routines (Gameiro et al., 2013).

Considering the above, it is important to also reflect on the implications of undergoing unsuccessful MAR treatment. Identity theories suggest people will experience adjustment difficulties during this transition because it represents the loss of a central life goal, and adjustment will be harder for those who hold parenthood as very central to their life and identity, or who lack alternative identities or goals (Thoits, 1992). According to the dual process model of grief, adjustment will depend on peoples' ability to process the loss of parenthood and its implications, for instance, the impact it may have on the partnership (Stroebe & Schut, 1999). Self-regulation theories also hypothesize that, from the moment parenthood becomes unachievable, those individuals who are able to disengage from it and pursue other meaningful life goals (e.g., career, focus on the partnership) adjust better (Heckhausen et al., 2001).

Meta-synthesis of quantitative studies investigating psychosocial adjustment after unsuccessful MAR have confirmed that this life event is associated with moderate to large impairments in people's mental health and well-being (Gameiro & Finnigan, 2017). Research seems to indicate that it is the longing for a child, more than one's actual parental status, that correlates with adjustment difficulties (Gameiro et al., 2014). Considering people take time to let go of their desire for children—specifically, 44% of individuals still desire to have (more) children 3–5 years after ending treatment, 25% 10 years after, and 6% 11–17 years after (Gameiro et al., 2016; Verhaak et al., 2007; Wischmann et al., 2012)—it is not surprising that former patients report taking on average two years to adjust to this transition (Daniluk, 2001). Furthermore, synthesis of qualitative research studies indicates people engage in meaning making as a way to solve the cognitive dissonance between their previous goal of having children and the new meanings the loss triggers (e.g., by trying to find positives in the loss), try to develop tolerance to the suffering caused by the unfulfilled desire for a child and to learn to live with it, and pursue alternative life goals (or even just hobbies), in order to distract themselves from the pain and find self-fulfillment (Gameiro & Finnigan, 2017).

Overall, the evidence indicates that unsuccessful MAR is a highly stressful life event that triggers a significant grief and loss process, whose successful resolution requires a complex process of identity and life goal restructuring. Although 9 in 10 people eventually adjust and develop a new sense of balance in life, the pain never fully disappears.

Critical Appraisal of the Literature

Most of the research reviewed is based on self-reports from parents and their children or people who did not manage to have children with MAR. Many studies had small samples, and these can be biased to include people from favorable backgrounds who are committed to showing their family is functional. Studies also tended to have a higher proportion of female than male participation, which is common in reproductive research. However, some studies relied on multiple methods and informants, and overall results were consistent. Of note is that these more reliable studies did not tend to show better performance in MAR families. Finally, many of these studies were conducted by a small number of researchers integrated in an even smaller number of research teams.

Conclusion

This literature review indicates that the psychosocial development and well-being of children is not dependent on the method through which they are conceived or the genetic link they have with their parents. Important factors are instead the well-being of the parents, the quality of the family relationships that are formed, and the social context in which family life unfolds. Gamete donation can create challenges for families, as different patterns of genetic connections can lead to curiosity and the establishment of new relationships and stigmatization is likely to happen, in particular toward same-sex families. In this context protective factors are strong family relationships, contact with other children from same-sex parents, supportive schools, communities, and legislation. Those families who do not manage to have children with MAR face a significant life challenge to come to terms with it and to reconstruct new fulfilling and hopeful lives. Overall, the evidence points to the importance of ensuring MAR is kept legal (although regulated), accessible, and affordable for all people who want to exercise their reproductive rights.

References

Applegarth, L. D., Kaufman, N. L., Josephs-Sohan, M., Christos, P. J., & Rosenwaks, Z. (2016). Parental disclosure to offspring created with oocyte donation: Intentions versus reality. *Human Reproduction, 31*(8), 1809–1815. https://doi.org/10.1093/humrep/dew125

Belsky, J. (1984). The determinants of parenting: A process model. *Child Development, 55,* 83–96. https://doi.org/10.2307/1129836

Bergh, T., Ericson, A., Hillensjo, T., Nygren, K., & Wennerholm, U. (1999). Deliveries and children born after IVF treatment in Sweden 1982-95—A complete cohort study. *Lancet, 354,* 1579–1585.

Boivin, J., Rice, F., Dale, H., Allyson, L., van den Bree, M., & Thapar, A. (2009). Associations between maternal older age, family environment and parent and child wellbeing in families using assisted reproductive techniques to conceive. *Social Science & Medicine, 68*(11), 1948–1955. https://doi.org/10.1016/j.socscimed.2009.02.036

Bos, H., & Gartrell, N. (2010). Adolescents of the USA National Longitudinal Lesbian Family Study: Can family characteristics counteract the negative effects of stigmatization? *Family Process, 49*(4), 559–572. https://doi.org/10.1111/j.1545-5300.2010.01340.x

Bos, H. M., & Van Balen, F. (2008). Children in planned lesbian families: Stigmatisation, psychological adjustment and protective factors. *Culture, Health & Sexuality, 10*(3), 221–236. https://doi.org/10.1080/13691050701601702

Brewaeys, A., Ponjaert, I., Van Hall, E. V., & Golombok, S. (1997). Donor insemination: child development and family functioning in lesbian mother families. *Human Reproduction, 12*(6), 1349–1359. https://doi.org/10.1093/humrep/12.6.1349

Camberis, A. L., McMahon, C. A., Gibson, F. L., & Boivin, J. (2016). Maternal age, psychological maturity, parenting cognitions, and mother–infant interaction. *Infancy, 21*(4), 396–422. https://doi.org/10.1111/infa.12116

Carone, N., Baiocco, R., Lingiardi, V., & Barone, L. (2020). Gay and heterosexual single father families created by surrogacy: Father–child relationships, parenting quality, and children's psychological adjustment. *Sexuality Research and Social Policy, 17*(4), 711–728. https://doi.org/10.1007/s13178-019-00428-7

Choi, S. K., Venetis, C., Ledger, W., Havard, A., Harris, K., Norman, R. J., Jorm, L. R., & Chambers, G. M. (2022). Population-wide contribution of medically assisted reproductive technologies to overall births in Australia: Temporal trends and parental characteristics. *Human Reproduction, 37*(5), 1047–1058. https://doi.org/10.1093/humrep/deac032

Colpin, H., & Bossaert, G. (2008). Adolescents conceived by IVF: Parenting and psychosocial adjustment. *Human Reproduction*, *23*(12), 2724–2730. https://doi.org/10.1093/humrep/den297

Crawshaw, M. (2018). Direct-to-consumer DNA testing: the fallout for individuals and their families unexpectedly learning of their donor conception origins. *Human Fertility*, *21*(4), 225–228. https://doi.org/10.1080/14647273.2017.1339127

Daniels, K. R., & Taylor, K. (1993). Secrecy and openness in donor insemination. *Politics and the Life Sciences*, *12*(2), 155–170. https://doi.org/10.1017/S0730938400023984

Daniluk, J. C. (2001). Reconstructing their lives: A longitudinal, qualitative analyses of the transition to biological childlessness for infertile couples. *Journal of Counselling and Development*, *79*(4), 439–449. https://doi.org/10.1002/j.1556-6676.2001.tb01991.x

Dykstra, P. A., & Hagestad, G. O. (2007). Roads less taken: Developing a nuanced view of older adults without children. *Journal of Family Issues*, *28*(10), 1275–1310. https://doi.org/10.1177/0192513X07303822

Gameiro, S., Boivin, J., Dancet, E., de Klerk, C., Emery, M., Lewis-Jones, C., Thorn, P., Van den Broeck, U., Venetis, C., Verhaak, C. M., Wischmann, T., & Vermeulen, N. (2015). ESHRE guideline: Routine psychosocial care in infertility and medically assisted reproduction—A guide for fertility staff. *Human Reproduction*, *30*(11), 2476–2485. https://doi.org/10.1093/humrep/dev177

Gameiro, S., Canavarro, M. C., Boivin, J., Moura-Ramos, M., Soares, I., & Santos, T. A. (2011). Parental investment in couples who conceived spontaneously or with assisted reproductive techniques. *Human Reproduction*, *26*(5), 1128–1137. https://doi.org/10.1093/humrep/der031

Gameiro, S., & Finnigan, A. (2017). Long-term adjustment to unmet parenthood goals following ART: A systematic review and meta-analysis. *Human Reproduction Update*, *23*(3), 322–337. https://doi.org/10.1093/humupd/dmx001

Gameiro, S., Moura-Ramos, M., Canavarro, M. C., & Soares, A. (2010). Psychosocial adjustment during the transition to parenthood of Portuguese couples who conceived spontaneously or through Assisted Reproductive Technologies. *Research in Nursing and Health*, *33*, 207–220. https://doi.org/10.1002/nur.20377

Gameiro, S., van den Belt-Dusebout, A. W., Bleiker, E., Braat, D., van Leeuwen, F. E., & Verhaak, C. M. (2014). Do children make you happier? Sustained child-wish and mental health in women 11–17 years after fertility treatment. *Human Reproduction*, *29*(10), 2238–2246. https://doi.org/10.1093/humrep/deu178

Gameiro, S., van den Belt-Dusebout, A. W., Smeenk, J., Braat, D., van Leeuwen, F. E., & Verhaak, C. M. (2016). Women's adjustment trajectories during IVF and impact on mental health 11–17 years later. *Human Reproduction*, *31*(8), 1788–1798. https://doi.org/10.1093/humrep/dew131

Gameiro, S., Verhaak, C. M., Kremer, J. A. M., & Boivin, J. (2013). Why we should talk about compliance with Assisted Reproductive Technologies (ART): A systematic review and meta-analysis of ART compliance rates. *Human Reproduction Update*, *19*(2), 124–135. https://doi.org/10.1093/humupd/dms045

Gartrell, N., Bos, H., & Koh, A. (2018). National longitudinal lesbian family study—Mental health of adult offspring. https://doi.org/10.1056/NEJMc1804810

George, C., & Solomon, J. (1996). Representational models of relationships: Links between caregiving and attachment. *Infant Mental Health Journal*, *17*(3), 198–216. https://doi.org/10.1002/(SICI)1097-0355(199623)17:3<198::AID-IMHJ2>3.0.CO;2-L

Gibson, F. L., Ungerer, J. A., Leslie, G. I., Saunders, D. M., & Tennant, C. C. (1998). Development, behaviour and temperament: A prospective study of infants conceived through in-vitro fertilization. *Human Reproduction*, *13*(6), 1727–1732. https://doi.org/10.1093/humrep/13.6.1727

Gibson, F. L., Ungerer, J., Tennant, C., & Saunders, D. (2000). Parental adjustment and attitudes to parenting after in vitro fertilization. *Fertility and Sterility*, *73*, 565–574. https://doi.org/10.1016/S0015-0282(99)00583-X

Golombok, S. (2002). The European study of assisted reproduction families: The transition to adolescence. *Human Reproduction*, *17*, 830–840. https://doi.org/10.1093/humrep/17.3.830

Golombok, S., Blake, L., Slutsky, J., Raffanello, E., Roman, G. D., & Ehrhardt, A. (2018). Parenting and the adjustment of children born to gay fathers through surrogacy. *Child Development*, *89*(4), 1223–1233. https://doi.org/10.1111/cdev.12728

Golombok, S., Lycett, E., MacCallum, F., Jadva, V., Murray, C., Rust, J., Abdalla, H., Jenkins, J., & Margara, R. (2004). Parenting infants conceived by gamete donation. *Journal of Family Psychology*, *18*(3), 443. https://doi.org/10.1037/0893-3200.18.3.443

Golombok, S., MacCallum, F., Murray, C., Lycett, E., & Jadva, V. (2006). Surrogacy families: Parental functioning, parent–child relationships and children's psychological development at age 2. *Journal of Child Psychology and Psychiatry*, *47*(2), 213–222. https://doi.org/10.1111/j.1469-7610.2005.01453.x

Golombok, S., Owen, L., Blake, L., Murray, C., & Jadva, V. (2009). Parent–child relationships and the psychological well-being of 18-year-old adolescents conceived by in vitro fertilisation. *Human Fertility*, *12*(2), 63–72. https://doi.org/10.1080/14647270902725513

Golombok, S., Readings, J., Blake, L., Casey, P., Marks, A., & Jadva, V. (2011). Families created through surrogacy: Mother–child relationships and children's psychological adjustment at age 7. *Developmental psychology*, *47*(6), 1579. https://doi.org/10.1037/a0025292

Golombok, S., Zadeh, S., Imrie, S., Smith, V., & Freeman, T. (2016). Single mothers by choice: Mother–child relationships and children's psychological adjustment. *Journal of Family Psychology*, *30*(4), 409. https://doi.org/10.1037/fam0000188

Hamilton, B. E., Martin, J. A., Osterman, M. J., & Rossen, L. M. (2019). Births: Provisional data for 2018. https://stacks.cdc.gov/view/cdc/78430

Hammarberg, K., Fisher, J. R., & Wynter, K. H. (2008). Psychological and social aspects of pregnancy, childbirth and early parenting after assisted conception: A systematic review. *Human Reproduction Update*, *14*, 395–414. https://doi.org/10.1093/humupd/dmn030

Heckhausen, J., Wrosh, C., & Fleeson, W. (2001). Developmental regulation before and after a developmental deadline: The sample case of "biological clock" for childbearing. *Psychology and Aging*, *16*(3), 400–413. https://doi.org/10.1037/0882-7974.16.3.400

Hjelmstedt, A., Widström, A., Wramsby, H., & Collins, A. (2009). Patterns of emotional responses to pregnancy, experience of pregnancy and attitudes to parenthood among IVF couples: A longitudinal study. *Journal of Psychosomatic Obstetrics and Gynaecology*, *24*, 153–162. https://doi.org/10.3109/01674820309039669

Human Fertilisation and Embryology Authority. (2020). *Family formations in fertility treatment 2018*. HFEA.

Imrie, S., Jadva, V., Fishel, S., & Golombok, S. (2019). Families created by egg donation: Parent–child relationship quality in infancy. *Child Development*, *90*(4), 1333–1349. https://doi.org/10.1111/cdev.13124

Imrie, S., Jadva, V., & Golombok, S. (2019). Psychological well-being of identity-release egg donation parents with infants. *Human Reproduction, 34*(11), 2219–2227. https://doi.org/10.1093/humrep/dez201

Imrie, S., Jadva, V., & Golombok, S. (2020). "Making the child mine": Mothers' thoughts and feelings about the mother–infant relationship in egg donation families. *Journal of Family Psychology, 34*(4), 469. https://doi.org/10.1037/fam0000619

Jadva, V., Freeman, T., Kramer, W., & Golombok, S. (2009). The experiences of adolescents and adults conceived by sperm donation: Comparisons by age of disclosure and family type. *Human Reproduction, 24*(8), 1909–1919. https://doi.org/10.1093/humrep/dep110

Mac Dougall, K., Becker, G., Scheib, J. E., & Nachtigall, R. D. (2007). Strategies for disclosure: How parents approach telling their children that they were conceived with donor gametes. *Fertility and Sterility, 87*(3), 524–533. https://doi.org/10.1016/j.fertnstert.2006.07.1514

Mahlstedt, P., & Greenfield, D. (1989). Assisted reproductive technology with donor gametes: The need for patient preparation. *Fertility and Sterility, 52*, 908–914. https://doi.org/10.1016/s0015-0282(16)53150-1

Matthews, R., & Matthews, A. M. (1986). Infertility and involuntary childlessness: The transition to nonparenthood. *Journal of Marriage and the Family, 48*(3), 641–649. https://doi.org/10.2307/352050

McLanahan, S., & Sandefur, G. D. (2009). *Growing up with a single parent: What hurts, what helps.* Harvard University Press.

McLernon, D. J., Maheshwari, A., Lee, A. J., & Bhattacharya, S. (2016). Cumulative live birth rates after one or more complete cycles of IVF: A population-based study of linked cycle data from 178,898 women. *Human Reproduction, 31*(3), 572–581. https://doi.org/10.1093/humrep/dev336

McMahon, C., Ungerer, J., Tennant, C., & Saunders, D. (1999). "Don't count your chickens": A reproductive study of the experience of pregnancy after IVF conception. *Journal of Reproductive and Infant Psychology, 17*, 345–356. https://doi.org/10.1080/02646839908404600

Pelka, S. (2009). Sharing motherhood: Maternal jealousy among lesbian co-mothers. *Journal of homosexuality, 56*(2), 195–217. https://doi.org/10.1080/00918360802623164

Präg, P., Sobotka, T., Lappalainen, E., Miettinen, A., Rotkirch, A., Tarács, J., Donno, A., Tanturri, M. L., & Mills, M. (2017). *Childlessness and assisted reproduction in Europe.* Families and Societies Working Paper Series.

Readings, J., Blake, L., Casey, P., Jadva, V., & Golombok, S. (2011). Secrecy, disclosure and everything in-between: Decisions of parents of children conceived by donor insemination, egg donation and surrogacy. *Reproductive Biomedicine Online, 22*(5), 485–495. https://doi.org/10.1016/j.rbmo.2011.01.014

Repokari, L., Punamäki, R. L., Poikkeus, P., Tiitinen, A., Vilska, S., Unkila-Kallio, L., Sinkkonen, J., Almqvist, F., & Tulppala, M. (2006). Ante- and perinatal factors and child characteristics predicting parenting experience among formerly infertile couples during the child's first year: A controlled study. *Journal of Family psychology, 20*(4), 670–679. https://doi.org/10.1037/0893-3200.20.4.670

Sandelowski, M., Harris, B. G., & Holditch-Davis, D. (1990). Pregnant moments: The process of conception in infertile couples. *Research in Nursing & Health, 13*(5), 273–282. https://doi.org/10.1002/nur.4770130503

Schmidt, L., Holstein, B., Christensen, U., & Boivin, J. (2005). Does infertility cause marital benefit? An epidemiological study of 2250 women and men in infertility treatment. *Patient Education and Counselling, 59*, 244–251. https://doi.org/10.1016/j.pec.2005.07.015

Seibel, M. M., & Levin, S. (1987). A new era in reproductive technologies: The emotional stages of in vitro fertilization. Journal of in Vitro and Embryo Transfer, *4*, 135–140. https://doi.org/10.1007/BF01555459

Shaw, K., McConnachie, A., Bower-Brown, S., Jadva, V., Ahuja, K., Macklon, N., & Golombok, S. (2022). P-501 Sharing motherhood: Same-sex female couples' reasons for choosing shared biological motherhood. *Human Reproduction, 37*(Suppl. 1), Article deac107.464.

Simon, R. A. (2013). Polyparenting: The psychological impact of having multiple parents in a child's life. *Family Advocate., 36*, 35.

Stroebe, M., & Schut, H. (1999). The dual process model of coping with bereavement: Rationale and description. *Death Studies, 23*(3), 197–224. https://doi.org/10.1080/074811899201046

Thoits, P. A. (1992). Identity structures and psychological well-being: Gender and marital status comparisons. *Social Psychology Quarterly, 55*(3), 236–256. https://doi.org/10.2307/2786794

van Balen, F. (1998). Development of IVF children. *Developmental Review, 18*, 30–46. https://doi.org/10.1006/drev.1997.0446

Verhaak, C. M., Smeenk, J. M., Nahuis, M. J., Kremer, J. A. M., & Braat, D. D. (2007). Long-term psychological adjustment to IVF/ICSI treatment in women. *Human Reproduction, 22*(1), 305–308. https://doi.org/10.1093/humrep/del355

Widbom, A., Sydsjö, G., & Lampic, C. (2022). Psychological adjustment in disclosing and non-disclosing heterosexual-couple families following conception with oocytes or sperm from identity-release donors. *Reproductive Biomedicine Online, 45*(5), 1046–1053. https://doi.org/10.1016/j.rbmo.2022.06.011

Wischmann, T., Korge, K., Scherg, H., Strowitzki, T., & Verres, R. (2012). A 10-year follow up study of psychosocial factors affecting couples after infertility treatment. *Human Reproduction, 27*(11), 3226–3232. https://doi.org/10.1093/humrep/des293

Wyverkens, E., Van Parys, H., & Buysse, A. (2015). Experiences of family relationships among donor-conceived families: Ameta-ethnography. *Qualitative Health Research, 25*(9), 1223–1240. https://doi.org/10.1177/1049732314554096

Zadeh, S., Ilioi, E., Jadva, V., & Golombok, S. (2018). The perspectives of adolescents conceived using surrogacy, egg or sperm donation. *Human Reproduction, 33*(6), 1099–1106. https://doi.org/10.1093/humrep/dey088

Zegers-Hochschild, F., Adamson, G. D., Dyer, S., Racowsky, C., De Mouzon, J., Sokol, R., Rienzi, L., Sunde, A., Schmidt, L., & Cooke, I. D. (2017). The international glossary on infertility and fertility care, 2017. *Human Reproduction, 32*(9), 1786–1801. https://doi.org/10.1093/humrep/dex234

PART VI
CURRENT TRENDS IN HEALTH AND CLOSE RELATIONSHIPS IN THE 21ST CENTURY

19
Relationships and Health

Anne Moyer, K. Olivia Mock, and Rose Martillotti

> Health is the greatest gift, contentment the greatest wealth, faithfulness the best relationship.
>
> —Buddha

The blessing of good physical health is indeed the foundation of a high quality of life. Romantic, familial, and friendly ties can support humans by uplifting them in their successes and bolstering them in their challenges, translating to emotions, beliefs, physiological reactions, and behaviors conducive to physical well-being, reducing morbidity and even mortality. It is also possible for a lack of social ties to be deleterious to physical health or for relationships to have toxic influences or promote health-damaging behaviors. This chapter highlights research examining the connection between our social relationships and our physical well-being, focusing on major findings that have accumulated over the approximately 40 years of this formal line of inquiry, including newer work that has examined the mechanisms underlying this connection, and contemporary topics in this area growing out of our current social context.

Aspects of Relationships Related to Various Types of Health Outcomes

Our social connections are multifaceted and can be described in terms of a number of types of relationships (e.g., spouse, parent, friend), as well as functions, perceptions, and behaviors. A helpful organizing framework developed by Holt-Lunstad (2018) divides the multiple components of social connections into those that are related to their structure, function, and quality. Structural aspects are often assessed quantitatively, such as the number of friends in one's network, or fairly objectively, such as whether someone lives alone. Functional aspects of social connections involve the instrumental aspects, or perceived instrumental aspects, of relationships, such as whether one feels lonely or not. The quality of our social connections involves a subjective assessment of their positivity or negativity, such as whether someone feels socially excluded by one's friends. Other useful taxonomies have further broken down elements of these three components, such as social support, which can be further delineated as received support and perceived support, and also in terms of its function as informational, emotional, or instrumental (House et al., 1985).

Similarly multifaceted are the measures of health that have been assessed in research investigating the impact of social relationships on physical wellbeing. These have included objective outcomes, such as mortality, disease incidence, and progression, and subjective outcomes, such as symptom presence and intensity, or global ratings of physical health status.

Effects of the Structure, Function, and Quality of Social Connections on Health and Illness

In a landmark study, Berkman and Syme (1979) found evidence of social isolation's predictive link to all-cause mortality. Findings were among men and women in a random sample of 4,725 residents of Alameda County, California, who were followed from 1965 to 1974. This effect held after multiple potential confounding factors were controlled for. The assessment of social and community ties was a weighted combination of scores, called the Social Network Index (SNI), capturing involvement in different types of relationships: marriage; level of contact with friends and relatives; church membership; and involvement in other types of groups. Importantly, deficits in one type of relationship seemed to be offset by others, such that "only in the presence of mounting social disconnection, when individuals failed to have links in several different spheres of interaction that mortality rates rose sharply" (Berkman & Syme, 1979, p. 96).

This study spurred further inquiry into the effects of social isolation, some of which produced varied results for men versus women, by race, or geographic locale (House et al., 1988). To provide evidence from a more nationally representative (U.S.) sample, data from 16,849 adults responding to the

National Health and Nutrition Examination Survey collected between 1988 and 1994 were examined (Pantell et al., 2013). SNI scores were associated with mortality at levels that were similar to, or higher than, the effects of other important risk factors such as smoking or high blood pressure. A later meta-analysis of the accumulated literature on this topic estimated that social isolation was associated with a 29% increase in mortality (Holt-Lunstad et al., 2015).

Of course, the nature of social connections has changed with the ubiquity of social media, leading some to assert that new methodology is necessary to account for the "new, consuming, and almost inseparable ways in which we interact through technology" and the ways in which these same technologies can promote isolation and sedentary behaviors (Aiello, 2017, p. 1090). This juxtaposition of benefits and drawbacks was illustrated in a study that examined the effects of both online and real social network interaction on measures of well-being, including self-reported mental and physical health, life satisfaction, and body mass index (BMI; Shakya & Christakis, 2017). Using actual Facebook utilization data and self-reported information about one's real-life social network, Facebook use was predictive of worse well-being whereas real-world interactions were predictive of superior well-being. The authors controlled for the likelihood that those who were initially more isolated were prone to use Facebook more often, mitigating this as an explanation. This study reflected the new methodology referred to above by considering rich aspects of social engagement: Facebook involvement included not only respondents' number of friends on the site, but the number of times that they had "liked" a post, the number of links that they had clicked on, and the number of times they had posted something; the real-world assessments involved naming up to four friends with whom respondents discussed important matters and up to four friends with whom they spent time, as well as their level of closeness to these friends and their frequency of in-person, face-to-face interaction. Future research on social media use can benefit from these types of creative questions and nuanced assessments.

Whereas social integration is thought to have a main effect on well-being by virtue of providing positive psychological states and health-promoting physiological responses, social support is thought to promote well-being by buffering stressful experiences by promoting effective coping strategies and fostering less threatening interpretations of adverse events (Cohen, 2004). A compelling example of evidence in support of this notion comes from study of Swedish men over 50 who were followed over seven years

(Rosengren et al., 1993). The number of stressful life events, such as being forced to move or having serious financial trouble, assessed in the year before baseline was associated with later mortality, but this was not the case for those who had higher emotional support. Although subsequent reviews have found this relationship to be somewhat less clear cut and more complex (Smith et al., 1994), the stress-buffering hypothesis continues to guide research for various types of diseases and interventions.

Our earliest relationships, with our caregivers and families, have the potential to shape our physical health in infancy, childhood, and beyond. Whereas supportive parenting and a warm family environment are related to positive health behaviors and less chronic illness in later life, negative parenting and family conflict can result in health difficulties, deficiencies in growth, obesity, poor management of chronic conditions such as diabetes, and later cardiac or serious illness (Tobin et al., 2013). Our intimate relationships, particularly our long-term romantic partnerships, also loom large in influencing our emotions, physiological reactions, and behaviors related to health. Better marital quality showed associations with superior subjective indices of physical health ($r = .14$, $k = 67$) and objective health endpoints ($r = .15$, $k = 17$) in a meta-analysis of cross-sectional and longitudinal studies (Robles et al., 2014). Theoretically, the "strength and strain" model of marital quality's effects on health proposes that, in addition to negative processes (i.e., conflict) that can compromise health, positive relationship processes (i.e., intimacy and capitalization) are relevant to protecting health, and also that individual differences, such as attachment style, moderate this relationship (Slatcher & Selcuk, 2017). Perceptions of a partner's responsiveness are thought to reduce negativity and increase positivity. In a longitudinal investigation, change in perceptions of partners' responsiveness over 10 years predicted negative affect in response to stressors at 10 years and mortality 10 years later, controlling for important demographic, health, and psychosocial covariates (Stanton et al., 2019).

Mechanisms for Relationships' Effects on Health

Berkman and Syme (1979) noted that their social network index was related to multiple causes of death and suggested that there might be multiple pathways from social isolation to illness. One potential pathway is health practices, because health-relevant behaviors (i.e., eating, smoking, exercise, sleep) and adherence to medical care have a social component. For example, social isolation and loneliness may influence poor health due to poor sleep, and social support may influence good health due to better sleep (National Academies of Sciences & Medicine, 2020). One compelling analysis showed the dynamic way in which smoking cessation spread in a large social network of 12,067 individuals followed for 32 years (Christakis & Fowler, 2008). People quit smoking in clusters, such that when one person quit, their spouse's likelihood of quitting was 67%; for friends and siblings these likelihoods were 36% and 24%, respectively. Longitudinal analyses allowed examination of potential causal explanations, which favored the conclusion that the phenomenon was driven by people's social contacts exerting an influence rather than both parties being affected by external factors (such as smoking cessation campaigns or cigarette taxes). This so-called social control of health behaviors, either through indirect feelings of responsibility to others or direct requests from them, is considered an important determinant of health, among other social factors, such as social support and companionship, particularly in close relationships (Sarason & Sarason, 2001). In a meta-analysis of 122 studies, medical adherence was shown to be most strongly related to practical support, but also to emotional support, general social support, family cohesiveness, less family conflict, being married, and living with someone (DiMatteo, 2004).

However, Berkman and Syme (1979) also noted that health practices only explained some of the connection between social isolation and mortality and pointed to psychological and physiological responses that relate to depression, suicide and risky behavior, or resistance to disease as other potential explanatory factors. In the years since, the focus on psychological and physiological mechanisms has intensified. Social support has been linked to reduced cardiovascular reactivity, lower ambulatory blood pressure, reduced secretion of the stress hormone cortisol, immune function, and inflammation (Uchino, 2006). An emerging social neuroscience model postulates that, as a social species for which aspects of sociality contributed to survival and reproduction, our brains, genes, and hormonal profiles evolved along with our social behaviors and are sensitive to social threats; thus, the brain and central nervous system may mediate the effects of social factors on health (S. Cacioppo et al., 2014). In support of this model, using functional magnetic resonance imaging (fMRI) of the brain, individual differences in loneliness were shown to relate to different neural responses to social stimuli, suggesting that for lonelier individuals pleasant depictions were less rewarding and attention was drawn toward unpleasant depictions (J. T. Cacioppo et al., 2009). Similarly, the field of social genomics has led to intriguing discoveries regarding the ways in which social conditions and our subjective interpretation of them can influence the expression of our genes and our susceptibility to disease (Slavich & Cole, 2013). In this framework, formerly adaptive neurobiological activation of genes is thought to increase inflammation and inhibit antiviral genes in response to social or physical threat in ways that were suited to humans' prior historical conditions when such threats were related to wounds or bacterial infection. These same responses can be maladaptive in today's context where social threats may be more related to socially mediated viral infections. Moreover, repeated, merely imagined social threat can lead to chronic activation of proinflammatory genes, promoting inflammation-related conditions such as cardiovascular disease, depression, metabolic syndrome, neurodegenerative disorders, and certain cancers. Supporting this explanatory framework, using DNA microarray analyses, genome-wide transcription was shown to be impaired for anti-inflammatory genes and over-expressed for pro-inflammatory genes in people who were high versus low in loneliness (Cole et al., 2007). Similarly, data from postmortem brain tissue (dorsolateral prefrontal cortex) of donors who completed psychosocial assessments of loneliness five years prior to death revealed that the up- and downregulation of genes associated with higher levels of loneliness were preferentially involved for those associated with Alzheimer's disease, psychiatric disorders, immune function, and cancer (Canli et al., 2018).

Contemporary Themes in Relationships and Health

Sociocultural, economic, and contextual factors have fundamentally changed whether or at what life phase we form relationships, with whom we form relationships, and the structure of those relationships. We turn to just a few examples here related to the inclusion of nonhuman animals in our lives, the trend of staying single, and new living arrangements.

Companion Animals and Health

It may seem misguided to consider the ways in which "relationships" with nonhuman animals can be beneficial to health, as interactions with companion and other animals are necessarily constrained by their capabilities, meaning that humans must necessarily use some degree of projection and anthropomorphism in their understanding of social connections with them. However, McConnell and colleagues point out that such connections are worthy of psychological study, not only because there is some degree of projection inherent in relationships with other humans, too, but because key focuses of social psychology such as expectations, theory of mind, and integrating others into one's sense of self are part of our relationships with animals (McConnell et al., 2017). Others have noted that "the unambivalent nature of the exchange of affection between people and animals differs from exchanges with close family members and other relatives" and have seen this as a reason for studying these relationships (Friedmann et al., 1980, p. 310). Increasingly pets are considered to be part of the family in U.S. households, endorsed by 95% in 2015, up from 88% in 2007 (The Harris Poll, 2015).

Intriguing early studies dating back more than 40 years and a subsequent recent meta-analysis showed that pet ownership, particularly dog ownership, was related to survival following myocardial infarction (Friedmann et al., 1980; Friedmann & Thomas, 1995; Kramer et al., 2019). The American Heart Association even states that dog ownership may be reasonable in reducing cardiovascular disease risk (but cautions that acquiring a dog should not be undertaken primarily for this purpose; Kazi, 2019). Companion animals can provide psychosocial support in situations where human companionship is unavailable, such as for those living alone (Mubanga et al., 2019). Pets have also been shown to serve as a source of social support that ameliorates the stress of social rejection (McConnell et al., 2011). Dogs in particular can provide an opportunity for physical activity, which is generally health promoting but also particularly important to rehabilitation following cardiovascular events (Mubanga et al., 2019).

Despite the fact that pets can provide pleasure, some findings have been mixed. For instance, in a community sample, although pet owners reported that they exercised more and were more physically fit, they did not have any advantage in terms of self-reported physical symptoms (McConnell et al., 2011). Other reviewers have attested that "the empirical studies of the effects of pets on human health and well-being are a mishmash of conflicting results" (Herzog, 2011, p. 237). This inconsistency in human–animal interaction research is explained by variations in the methodologies used; variability in the human and animal participants studied; small and heterogeneous samples; the fact that, for research topics that are considered "hot," negative findings may languish in obscurity; and even the pro-pet personal beliefs of investigators who are drawn to study human–animal interactions (Herzog, 2011; Rodriguez et al., 2020). Other authors have pointed to weak research designs and failure to control for other influences (Chur-Hansen et al., 2010). In the predominantly naturalistic studies of those who own versus those who do not own pets, it is important to note that pet owners differ in terms of important demographic and contextual variables, such as being female, White/non-Hispanic, having less education, having a higher likelihood of being employed, living in a family with children and in a rural area, having higher levels of moderate physical activity (in dog owners), having higher levels of depression, and likelihood of having an anxiety disorder (Mueller et al., 2021). It appears that it is important to attend to nuance in terms of the functions that companion animals are serving.

Indeed, when the extent to which people anthropomorphized their dogs was taken into account, it was found that owners with low levels of social support took more medications and visited doctors more but had no difference in self-rated physical health (Duvall Antonacopoulos & Pychyl, 2010). It was presumed that humanizing their dogs more was an insufficient way for owners to alleviate their lack of social connection. Another study suggested that the function that a connection with one's dog provides matters, such that those who reported that their dog fulfilled more social functions (related to belongingness, self-esteem, meaningful existence, and control) reported less stress and superior psychological outcomes in terms of less depression, less loneliness, greater self-esteem, greater happiness, but not more physical illness symptoms and fitness (McConnell et al., 2011). In addition, dogs with particular personality traits (less fearful, more active, less aggressive) fulfilled these functions better. Similarly, in a recent large-scale prospective study of 336,313 Swedish individuals suffering a myocardial infarction or an ischemic stroke, which controlled for a number of relevant covariates, dog owners had a lower risk of death over 12 years, and this effect was especially pronounced among those who lived alone relative to those who lived with a partner or a child—however; this effect differed by breed of dog (Mubanga et al., 2019). This difference, specifically that hounds and retrievers had a protective effect, whereas "companion and toy" breeds did not, could be explained by differences in the energy level and need for walks of the dogs and by some degree of self-selection, but the finding that mixed-breed dogs did not show the protective effect that purebred dogs did is something that remains unexplained (Herzog, 2019).

The New Singlehood and Health

With the many benefits connected to strong social support, especially with respect to one's health, it would seem as though more people would want to seek long-term romantic relationships. However, people are increasingly choosing to stay single longer—or indefinitely (see Chapter 4). There are many factors that can be attributed to a desire for singlehood. These include the idea that there is an increase in the chance of finding a better mate in the future due to increases in resources, social status, education, and so forth, and that some individuals may lack characteristics conducive to attracting a mate (Apostolou, 2017). Reasons for staying single can also differ based on an individual's gender and personality. Men have reported wanting to remain single because they do not want to commit to a long-term relationship, and women report reluctance to get hurt and concern about their desirability (Apostolou & Esposito, 2020). For people who scored high on Machiavellianism (manipulativeness, emotional coldness), and psychopathy (antisocial behavior, low empathy), a desire for freedom of choice and difficulties with relationships were noted as reasons for staying single (Burtăverde & Ene, 2021).

Never-married (single) people have higher suicide rates, elevated all-cause mortality, and overall worse health compared with married individuals and are more likely to have worse economic support, have less social support, and engage in risky behaviors (Roelfs et al., 2011). A meta-analysis indicated that individuals who were single had a 30% increased risk of mortality and that these risks have been rising over the past few decades (Roelfs et al., 2011). Similar to other aspects of health, single individuals tend to have higher levels of stress and worse mental health. In particular, singles report higher levels of stress associated with social commitments, loneliness, and finances, reflecting the fact that those who are married have tangible resources in coping with stress such as higher income and fewer tax burdens as well as the companionship provided by cohabitation with a partner (Ta et al., 2017). Importantly, those who choose to remain single (voluntarily single) should be distinguished from those who are actively seeking a romantic relationship but fail to do so (involuntarily single). Although the results of one study demonstrated that there were no differences between voluntarily and involuntarily single individuals when it came to mental well-being, involuntarily single adults had a higher rate of romantic loneliness (Adamczyk, 2017). As more people continue to remain single, it is important to understand the reasons and impact that it has on one's health.

The Rise of the "Roommate Household" and Health

As mentioned earlier, there has been an increasing deviation away from the common household foundation: a married couple. Roommates are now common past college dorms, accompany us into the "real world," and follow us to into retirement age. Studies published by the Pew Research Center reported that 20% of households in 2019 are "shared," 3% more than in 2007 (Fry, 2019). A shared household is one with at least one adult that is not the household head, partner of the household head, or an 18-to-24-year-old student (Fry, 2018). Economic factors, including student debt and the economic crisis in the mid-2000s, have led many young adults to search for roommates to rent an apartment with after graduation or face moving back in with their parents.

Given the increased prevalence in shared households and the number of stay-at-home orders due to the COVID-19 pandemic, it is worth exploring what benefits or detriments there are to this type of habitation. These relationships can influence frequency of risky health behaviors in particular. One of the most commonly assessed behaviors is alcohol consumption.

Longitudinal studies of college students have indicated that roommate drinking behaviors are associated with a person's own alcohol consumption (Eisenberg et al., 2014; Guo et al., 2015; Smith et al., 2019). Although in Guo et al.'s study, a person had to already have a history of drinking to be influenced by their roommate's drinking behavior; it is interesting to note that friendship between roommates augmented this peer effect. Smith et al. (2019) reported that a roommate's self-reported drinking informed an individual's alcohol use, but that same effect was not found across residence halls. These studies indicate that a roommate may have a larger impact on behavior than peers in general and that the quality of the relationship has a mitigating effect. A significant limitation of these studies is the use of college students living on campus, so we must be cautious when generalizing these results, but there is evidence that having roommates beyond college is a risk factor for binge drinking. People who live with roommates as opposed to living with parents or a spouse between the ages of 18 and 25 are significantly more likely to binge-drink (Leech et al., 2020).

Approximately 17% of 25-to-64-year-olds are current cigarette smokers (Centers for Disease Control and Prevention, 2019), and exposure to smoking is associated with partaking later on in life (National Center for Chronic Disease Prevention and Health Promotion, U.S. Office on Smoking and Health, 2012). It is important to note that exposure to a negative health behavior is not limited to influencing that one behavior in another person (Holahan et al., 2015). An analysis of cross-sectional data revealed that having a housemate who was a smoker was associated with lower reports of health commitment, which were in turn associated with physical inactivity, even when controlling for the participant's own smoking status. Potential explanations for this may be due to behavior modeling, peer pressure, or low social support from the roommate for health behaviors.

Given the research findings presented, it might be tempting to assume that despite financial benefits, having roommates is harmful to physical health. However, the existing literature is skewed to look at the negatives. A review by Clark et al. (2018) highlights this issue and emphasizes the need for further research to assess positive health behaviors and explore mediating effects of social support provided by roommate households. In fact, segregating living situations by alone, with relatives, and with nonrelatives may not be a useful distinction, as the concepts of family, friends, and roommates have become blurred (Roseneil & Budgeon, 2004). An article published in *The Atlantic* (Volpe, 2018) provided an illustrative and optimistic look at why young adults are choosing to have roommates for non-financial reasons; sometimes "it's just nice to have someone to come home to." In fact, the increased rates of roommate households are not limited to just young adults; baby boomers are also joining this demographic, as documented in the *Washington Post* (Youn, 2022). As boomers age, they retire, spouses pass away, and their health declines, all of which makes having a roommate financially and socially beneficial.

There are several potential directions for research in this area due to the dearth of studies specifically designed to examine roommate living situations (Clark et al., 2018). The number of roommates, gender, sex, sexual orientation, romantic/sexual relationships (within or outside the roommate group), quality of individual relationships between roommates, and overall dynamic are all factors that can be explored in future research. Friction in any of these domains may lead to increased stress, which, as this chapter has shown, negatively affects physical health, while a positive household dynamic may be an excellent source of social support.

Conclusion

In this chapter, we have discussed how different aspects of our social lives influence our physical health through several different avenues. Overall, strong positive social connections act as a protective factor against morbidity and mortality. This finding can be observed in our behavior and on the biological level. Poor social connection, whether it is weak or fraught, can have a significant deleterious effect on health outcomes by promoting inflammation and enabling damaging lifestyle choices. These results have far-reaching implications for people's health given changing trends in how we interact with each other and what relationships we form. As rates of long-term singledom rise, it is worth exploring how this may impact morbidity and mortality rates and if pet ownership and shared households could act as buffers to associated negative health outcomes. As the context in which relationships occur continues to shift there will certainly be meaningful impacts on health. Examples include ideological polarization, legal rulings limiting access to abortion, and instability due to the effects of climate change, which may threaten well-being, whereas policies that support families, increases in equity, and cultural trends toward tolerance and understanding are examples of developments that will likely support it.

References

Adamczyk, K. (2017). Voluntary and involuntary singlehood and young adults' mental health: An investigation of mediating role of romantic loneliness. *Current Psychology*, 36, 888–904. https://doi.org/10.1007/s12144-016-9478-3

Aiello, A. E. (2017). Invited commentary: Evolution of social networks, health, and the role of epidemiology. *American Journal of Epidemiology*, 185, 1089–1092. https://doi.org/10.1093/aje/kwx076

Apostolou, M. (2017). Why people stay single: An evolutionary perspective. *Personality and Individual Differences*, 111, 263–271. https://doi.org/10.1016/j.paid.2017.02.034

Apostolou, M., O., J., & Esposito, G. (2020). Singles' reasons for being single: Empirical evidence from an evolutionary perspective. *Frontiers in Psychology*, 11, Article 746. https://doi.org/10.3389/fpsyg.2020.00746

Berkman, L. F., & Syme, S. L. (1979). Social networks, host resistance, and mortality: A nine-year follow-up study of Alameda County residents. *American Journal of Epidemiology*, 109, 186–204. https://doi.org/10.1093/oxfordjournals.aje.a112674

Burtăverde, V., & Ene, C. (2021). Individuals high on the Dark Triad traits choose to stay single if they are low on sociosexuality. *Personality and Individual Differences*, 177, Article 110843. https://doi.org/10.1016/j.paid.2021.110843

Cacioppo, J. T., Norris, C. J., Decety, J., Monteleone, G., & Nusbaum, H. (2009). In the eye of the beholder: Individual differences in perceived social isolation predict regional brain activation to social stimuli. *Journal of Cognitive Neuroscience, 21*, 83–92. https://doi.org/10.1162/jocn.2009.21007

Cacioppo, S., Capitanio, J. P., & Cacioppo, J. T. (2014). Toward a neurology of loneliness. *Psychological Bulletin, 140*, 1464–1504. https://doi.org/10.1037/a0037618

Canli, T., Yu, L., Yu, X., Zhao, H., Fleischman, D., Wilson, R. S., De Jager, P. L., & Bennett, D. A. (2018). Loneliness 5 years ante-mortem is associated with disease-related differential gene expression in postmortem dorsolateral prefrontal cortex. *Translational Psychiatry, 8*, Article 2. https://doi.org/10.1038/s41398-017-0086-2

Centers for Disease Control and Prevention. (2019). *Current cigarette smoking among adults in the United States*. Centers for Disease Control and Prevention. https://www.cdc.gov/tobacco/data_statistics/fact_sheets/adult_data/cig_smoking/index.htm

Christakis, N. A., & Fowler, J. H. (2008). The collective dynamics of smoking in a large social network. *The New England Journal of Medicine, 358*, 2249–2258. https://doi.org/10.1056/NEJMsa0706154

Chur-Hansen, A., Stern, C., & Winefield, H. (2010). Gaps in the evidence about companion animals and human health: Some suggestions for progress. *International Journal of Evidence-Based Healthcare, 8*, 140–146. https://doi.org/10.1111/j.1744-1609.2010.00176.x

Clark, V., Tuffin, K., Bowker, N., & Frewin, K. (2018). A fine balance: A review of shared housing among young adults. *Social and Personality Psychology Compass, 12*(10), e12415. https://doi.org/10.1111/spc3.12415

Cohen, S. (2004). Social relationships and health. *American Psychologist, 59*, 676–684. https://doi.org/10.1037/0003-066X.59.8.676

Cole, S. W., Hawkley, L. C., Arevalo, J. M., Sung, C. Y., Rose, R. M., & Cacioppo, J. T. (2007). Social regulation of gene expression in human leukocytes. *Genome Biology, 8*, Article R189. https://doi.org/10.1186/gb-2007-8-9-r189

DiMatteo, M. R. (2004). Social support and patient adherence to medical treatment: A meta-analysis. *Health Psychology, 23*, 207–218. https://doi.org/10.1037/0278-6133.23.2.207

Duvall Antonacopoulos, N. M., & Pychyl, T. A. (2010). The possible role of companion-animal anthropomorphism and social support in the physical and psychological health of dog guardians. *Society & Animals: Journal of Human-Animal Studies, 18*, 379–395. https://doi.org/10.1163/156853010X524334

Eisenberg, D., Golberstein, E., & Whitlock, J. L. (2014). Peer effects on risky behaviors: New evidence from college roommate assignments. *Journal of Health Economics, 33*, 126–138. https://doi.org/10.1016/j.jhealeco.2013.11.006

Friedmann, E., Katcher, A. H., Lynch, J. J., & Thomas, S. A. (1980). Animal companions and one-year survival of patients after discharge from a coronary care unit. *Public Health Reports (1974–2023), 95*, 307–312.

Friedmann, E., & Thomas, S. A. (1995). Pet ownership, social support, and one-year survival after acute myocardial infarction in the Cardiac Arrhythmia Suppression Trial (CAST). *The American Journal of Cardiology, 76*, 1213–1217. https://doi.org/10.1016/s0002-9149(99)80343-9

Fry, R. (2018). *More adults now share their living space, driven in part by parents living with their adult children*. Pew Research Center. http://pewrsr.ch/2E2mdcF

Fry, R. (2019). *The number of people in the average U.S. household is going up for the first time in over 160 years*. Pew Research Center. https://pewrsr.ch/2mEhnMa

Guo, G., Li, Y., Owen, C., Wang, H., & Duncan, G. J. (2015). A natural experiment of peer influences on youth alcohol use. *Social Science Research, 52*, 193–207. https://doi.org/10.1016/j.ssresearch.2015.01.002

The Harris Poll. (2015, July 16). *More than ever, pets are members of the family*. https://www.prnewswire.com/news-releases/more-than-ever-pets-are-members-of-the-family-300114501.html

Herzog, H. (2011). The impact of pets on human health and psychological well-being: Fact, fiction, or hypothesis? *Current Directions in Psychological Science, 20*, 236–239. https://doi.org/10.1177/0963721411415220

Herzog, H. (2019, October 31). Do purebreds (but not mutts) reduce dog owner death rates? *Psychology Today*. https://www.psychologytoday.com/us/blog/animals-and-us/201910/do-purebreds-not-mutts-reduce-dog-owner-death-rates

Holahan, C. K., Holahan, C. J., & Li, X. (2015). Living with a smoker and physical inactivity: An unexplored health behavior pathway. *American Journal of Health Promotion, 30*(1), 19–21. https://doi.org/10.4278/ajhp.130820-ARB-434

Holt-Lunstad, J. (2018). Why social relationships are important for physical health: A systems approach to understanding and modifying risk and protection. *Annual Review of Psychology, 69*, 437–458. https://doi.org/10.1146/annurev-psych-122216-011902

Holt-Lunstad, J., Smith, T. B., Baker, M., Harris, T., & Stephenson, D. (2015). Loneliness and social isolation as risk factors for mortality: A meta-analytic review. *Perspectives on Psychological Science, 10*, 227–237. https://doi.org/10.1177/1745691614568352

House, J. S., Kahn, R. L., McLeod, J. D., & Williams, D. (1985). Measures and concepts of social support. In S. Cohen & S. L. Syme (Eds.), *Social support and health* (pp. 83–108). Academic Press. http://proxy.library.stonybrook.edu/login?url=https://search.ebscohost.com/login.aspx?direct=true&db=psyh&AN=1985-97489-005&site=ehost-live

House, J. S., Landis, K. R., & Umberson, D. (1988). Social relationships and health. *Science (New York, N.Y.), 241*, 540–545. https://doi.org/10.1126/science.3399889

Kazi, D. S. (2019). Who is rescuing whom? Circulation: *Cardiovascular Quality and Outcomes, 12*, e005887. https://doi.org/10.1161/CIRCOUTCOMES.119.005887

Kramer, C. K., Mehmood, S., & Suen, R. S. (2019). Dog ownership and survival: A systematic review and meta-analysis. *Circulation. Cardiovascular Quality and Outcomes, 12*, e005554. https://doi.org/10.1161/CIRCOUTCOMES.119.005554

Leech, T. G., Jacobs, S., & Watson, D. (2020). Factors associated with binge drinking during the transition into adulthood: Exploring associations within two distinct young adult age ranges. *Substance Abuse: Research and Treatment, 14*, Article 1178221820951781. https://doi.org/10.1177/1178221820951781

McConnell, A. R., Brown, C. M., Shoda, T. M., Stayton, L. E., & Martin, C. E. (2011). Friends with benefits: On the positive consequences of pet ownership. *Journal of Personality and Social Psychology, 101*, 1239–1252. https://doi.org/10.1037/a0024506

McConnell, A. R., Lloyd, E. P., & Buchanan, T. M. (2017). Animals as friends: Social psychological implications of human-pet relationships. In M. Hojjat & A. Moyer (Eds.), *The psychology of friendship*. (pp. 157–174). Oxford University Press. http://proxy.library.stonybrook.edu/login?url=https://search.ebscohost.com/login.aspx?direct=true&db=psyh&AN=2016-59521-010&site=ehost-live

Mubanga, M., Byberg, L., Egenvall, A., Ingelsson, E., & Fall, T. (2019). Dog ownership and survival after a major cardiovascular event: A register-based prospective study. *Circulation. Cardiovascular Quality and Outcomes*, *12*, e005342. https://doi.org/10.1161/CIRCOUTCOMES.118.005342

Mueller, M. K., King, E. K., Callina, K., Dowling-Guyer, S., & McCobb, E. (2021). Demographic and contextual factors as moderators of the relationship between pet ownership and health. *Health Psychology and Behavioral Medicine*, *9*, 701–723. https://doi.org/10.1080/21642850.2021.1963254

National Academies of Sciences, Engineering & Medicine. (2020). *Social isolation and loneliness in older adults: Opportunities for the health care system*. The National Academies Press. https://doi.org/10.17226/25663

National Center for Chronic Disease Prevention and Health Promotion (US) Office on Smoking and Health. (2012). *Preventing tobacco use among youth and young adults: A report of the surgeon general*. National Center for Chronic Disease Prevention and Health Promotion (US) Office on Smoking and Health. https://www.ncbi.nlm.nih.gov/books/NBK99237/

Pantell, M., Rehkopf, D., Jutte, D., Syme, L. S., Balmes, J., & Adler, N. (2013). Social isolation: A predictor of mortality comparable to traditional clinical risk factors. *American Journal of Public Health*, *103*(11), 2056–2062.

Robles, T. F., Slatcher, R. B., Trombello, J. M., & McGinn, M. M. (2014). Marital quality and health: A meta-analytic review. *Psychological Bulletin*, *140*, 140–187. https://doi.org/10.1037/a0031859

Rodriguez, K. E., Herzog, H., & Gee, N. R. (2020). Variability in human-animal interaction research. *Frontiers in Veterinary Science*, *7*, Article 619600. https://doi.org/10.3389/fvets.2020.619600

Roelfs, D. J., Shor, E., Kalish, R., & Yogev, T. (2011). The rising relative risk of mortality for singles: Meta-analysis and meta-regression. *American Journal of Epidemiology*, *174*(4), 379–389. https://doi.org/10.1093/aje/kwr111

Roseneil, S., & Budgeon, S. (2004). Cultures of intimacy and care beyond "the family": Personal life and social change in the early 21st century. *Current Sociology*, *52*, 135–159. https://doi.org/10.1177/0011392104041798

Rosengren, A., Orth-Gomér, K., Wedel, H., & Wilhelmsen, L. (1993). Stressful life events, social support, and mortality in men born in 1933. *British Medical Journal*, *307*(6912), 1102–1105. https://doi.org/10.1136/bmj.307.6912.1102

Sarason, B. R., & Sarason, I. G. (2001). Ongoing aspects of relationships and health outcomes: Social support, social control, companionship, and relationship meaning. In J. Harvey & A. Wenzel (Eds.), *Close romantic relationships: Maintenance and enhancement* (pp. 277–298). Lawrence Erlbaum Associates Publishers; APA PsycInfo. http://proxy.library.stonybrook.edu/login?url=https://search.ebscohost.com/login.aspx?direct=true&db=psyh&AN=2001-01654-014&site=ehost-live

Shakya, H. B., & Christakis, N. A. (2017). Association of Facebook use with compromised well-being: A longitudinal study. *American Journal of Epidemiology*, *185*, 203–211. https://doi.org/10.1093/aje/kww189

Slatcher, R. B., & Selcuk, E. (2017). A social psychological perspective on the links between close relationships and health. *Current Directions in Psychological Science*, *26*, 16–21. https://doi.org/10.1177/0963721416667444

Slavich, G. M., & Cole, S. W. (2013). The emerging field of human social genomics. *Clinical Psychological Science, 1*, 331–348. https://doi.org/10.1177/2167702613478594

Smith, C. E., Fernengel, K., Holcroft, C., & Gerald, K. (1994). Meta-analysis of the associations between social support and health outcomes. *Annals of Behavioral Medicine, 16*, 352–362. APA PsycInfo.

Smith, R. L., Salvatore, J. E., Aliev, F., Neale, Z., Barr, P., Spit for Science Working Group, & Dick, D. M. (2019). Genes, roommates, and residence halls: A multidimensional study of the role of peer drinking on college students' alcohol use. *Alcoholism: Clinical and Experimental Research, 43*, 1254–1262. https://doi.org/10.1111/acer.14037

Stanton, S. C. E., Selcuk, E., Farrell, A. K., Slatcher, R. B., & Ong, A. D. (2019). Perceived partner responsiveness, daily negative affect reactivity, and all-cause mortality: A 20-year longitudinal study. *Psychosomatic Medicine, 81*, 7–15. https://doi.org/10.1097/PSY.0000000000000618

Ta, V. P., Gesselman, A. N., Perry, B. L., Fisher, H. E., & Garcia, J. R. (2017). Stress of singlehood: Marital status, domain-specific stress, and anxiety in a national U.S. sample. *Journal of Social and Clinical Psychology, 36*, 461–485. https://doi.org/10.1521/jscp.2017.36.6.461

Tobin, E. T., Slatcher, R. B., & Robles, T. F. (2013). Family relationships and physical health: Biological processes and mechanisms. In M. L. Newman & N. A. Roberts (Eds.), *Health and social relationships: The good, the bad, and the complicated* (pp. 145–165). American Psychological Association. https://doi.org/10.1037/14036-007

Uchino, B. N. (2006). Social support and health: A review of physiological processes potentially underlying links to disease outcomes. *Journal of Behavioral Medicine, 29*, 377–387. https://doi.org/10.1007/s10865-006-9056-5

Volpe, A. (2018, August 13). The strange, unique intimacy of the roommate relationship. *The Atlantic*. https://www.theatlantic.com/family/archive/2018/08/the-strange-unique-intimacy-of-the-roommate-relationship/567296/

Youn, S. (2022, February 25). The new Golden Girls: Baby boomers are moving in together to save money. *The Washington Post*. https://www.washingtonpost.com/business/2022/02/25/baby-boomers-move-in-retirement/

20
Close Relationships and Mental Health

Charlotte R. Esplin, S. Gabe Hatch, and Scott R. Braithwaite

Romantic Relationships and Mental Health

The greatest thing you'll ever learn is just to love and be loved in return.—Nat King Cole

Why Do Relationships Matter?

During the heyday of behaviorism in psychology, it was very much out of fashion to think love and connection mattered. John Watson did not just take a dim view of these things; he specifically told parents that they should not be affectionate with their children. He suggested that tenderness would spoil them by making them needy for approval. Instead, he advised,

> let your behavior always be objective and kindly firm. Never hug and kiss them, never let them sit in your lap. If you must, kiss them once on the forehead when [you] say good night. Shake hands with them in the morning. Give them a pat on the head if they have made an extraordinarily good job of a difficult task. (pp. 81–82; Watson & Watson, 1928)

Harry Harlow was skeptical of these prevailing attitudes. He had begun to sense that these views were motivated not by evidence, but by a desire to discard inconvenient parts of human nature so the discipline could seem more scientific.

In his program of research, Harry Harlow examined his hunch that love and affection mattered. He used rhesus monkeys in experiments examining whether infants responded to their mothers only because they satisfied basic needs. He (in)famously removed infant monkeys from their real mothers and created wire "monkeys" to test his questions. Some inanimate surrogates provided food to their "children," but nothing else. They were made only of wire and could not offer a feeling of comfort or safety. He also provided cloth "mothers" that were soft and potentially comforting. During moments of stress, the monkeys did not run to the wire mother; instead, they ran to the cloth monkey, who gave them a sense of safety and security. Something about the warmth this mother provided went beyond tangible needs. Harlow began to surmise that the need for safety and security is more primary than the practical need for calories (Blum, 2002).

Similar outcomes have been observed among humans. After the fall of communism in Romania, the consequences of the toppled regime came to light. Orphanages became overrun with children without sufficient staff or resources (Nelson, 2014). As a result, the children were found "stacked on the shelves of a cart like loaves of bread." (ABC News, 2006). The children in these orphanages had been given calories but not love or connection. Deprived of what comes naturally to most parents, the neglected children exhibited poor impulse control, emotional dysregulation, and difficulty forming relationships. Things got better when the orphaned children were placed in families who provided the kind of care they had not yet experienced. An essential task in recovery was whether they could make a secure attachment to others. In other words, being able to pull out of the sterile environment of disconnection and feel safe enough to develop a sense of belonging was a critical mechanism explaining recovery.

All of this highlights the bedrock importance of attachment and connection. It is not merely an enjoyable part of life; it is fundamental to our mental health. When we feel that we belong, we are free to grow in other areas of life. When the need to belong is thwarted, other higher order tasks feel irrelevant and bereft of meaning—even our will to live is diminished (Van Orden, et al., 2010). Few things foster more safety than the deep, lasting connection of a healthy, stable, loving marriage or committed relationship.

How Do Romantic Relationships Matter?

Romantic relationships play a central role in our experience of life. Fundamental human motives are deep-seated needs that all humans share. People have proposed many different primary human motives, but the need for intimate relationships is included on every list (Aunger et al., 2021). Meta-analytic studies show that the quality of romantic relationships has the highest overall correlation with happiness and life satisfaction (Heller et al., 2004). Healthy relationships are associated with happiness, but the corollary is also true—unhealthy relationships are associated with misery and psychopathology. But how does this association operate—how do relationships help or hurt? Or is it the case that psychopathology and unhappiness are the causal agents and relationship quality the consequence? In this chapter, we briefly review existing research on the broad theories of how these effects operate, such as selection and experience but then illuminate the mediating pathways by which relationships and mental health are associated with one another.

Research examining why relationships are associated with better mental health can be framed as supporting theories of selection, experience, or both. Selection refers to the conclusion that mentally healthy individuals are more likely to "select" into enduring marriages (Braithwaite & Holt-Lunstad, 2017). In this view, the same enduring assets that promote mental health also promote a lasting marriage, and the same enduring vulnerabilities that contribute to poorer mental health also contribute to a lower likelihood of lasting marriage. For example, it is unlikely that someone with a psychotic disorder that requires periodic inpatient hospitalization is as likely to marry and remain married as someone without that condition.

In contrast, the experience hypothesis suggests that the experience of being in a healthy relationship is intrinsically beneficial to mental health because marriage contributes to a sense of meaning, provides social support, and fulfills fundamental human needs for intimacy and belonging (Braithwaite & Holt-Lunstad, 2017). According to Baumeister and Leary, the need to belong is met when two things co-occur: frequent interaction and persistent caring (1995). Having frequent contact seems obvious enough, but what does it mean that there must be persistent caring? These authors state that there needs to be a relationship that is (1) stable, (2) has an emotional bond, and (3) will continue into the future. Few relationships, if any, could meet these conditions better than marriage, where couples commit to a lifetime of intense emotional connection.

Rigid one-directional models are rarely accurate, so the consensus view—that both selection and experience matter—is likely the "truest" of these perspectives. More mentally healthy individuals select into enduring marriages, but marriage also influences mental health and well-being in a dynamic, interdependent way as illustrated in Figure 1 (Braithwaite & Holt-Lunstead, 2017).

The questions that need to be more fully explored are of when relationships matter and by what mechanisms these effects operate. Consistent with Karney and Bradbury's vulnerability stress adaptation model (VSA Model; 1995), we propose that existing vulnerabilities (e.g., personality and mental health issues) operate via adaptive and maladaptive processes (interpersonal dynamics such as communication), and that these variables further interact with life stressors and relationship stress in a dynamic way that creates positive or negative feedback loops. If this is true, both interpersonal and intrapersonal strategies play an essential role in promoting romantic relationship quality and mental health. Moreover, improving interventions for relationship quality are likely a viable way to improve mental health.

When Do Romantic Relationships Matter?

Mental Health is not monolithic. Different disorders, behavioral patterns, and traits are likely to have a differential link with relationship quality. In this section, we explore when relationships matter. That is, are specific diagnoses more strongly associated with relationship problems? And how do specific enduring vulnerabilities relate to poor relationship outcomes? Many factors play a role in the association between mental health and romantic relationships, like the nature of the mental health problem, each partner's underlying personality traits, and what mental health services are available to the couple. We will first examine clusters of psychiatric diagnoses and then move to broader, normal-range personality traits.

Internalizing Disorders

Some of the most commonly occurring mental disorders are depressive and anxious disorders, with 12-month prevalence estimates around approximately 7%–14% (Hasin et al., 2018). Multiple studies show that close relationships play a role in the onset, course, and treatment of anxiety and depressive disorders (Priest, 2013; Whisman, 2007). Generally, men and women who are free from anxiety disorders purport much higher rates of marital quality (Pankiewicz et al., 2012). Regarding onset, relationship distress is associated with a diagnosis of generalized anxiety disorder (GAD; $B = 0.93$), posttraumatic stress disorder (PTSD; $B = 0.83$), and major depressive disorder (MDD; $B = 0.52$; Whisman, 2007). To illustrate, imagine someone experiencing frequent, intense arguments with their partner that culminate in threats of divorce while simultaneously experiencing low mood, chronic worries, and sleep problems. Still, based on these studies alone, it is unclear whether the psychiatric symptoms occur before the marital distress or whether marital distress occurs before the psychiatric symptoms.

Longitudinal studies examining relationship quality and psychiatric diagnoses confirm the same association but provide more information about temporality. In a nationally representative sample of 4,796 couples, low levels of marital quality at baseline predicted a diagnosis of an anxiety disorder two years later (Overbeek et al., 2006). The same has been found for depressive disorders, where marital dissatisfaction predicts subsequent depressive symptoms (Clavarino et al., 2011; Du Rocher Schudlich et al., 2011). For example, marital discord and depressive symptomatology were significantly associated cross-sectionally at baseline ($r = -.36$, $p < .05$) and longitudinally at an 8–12 week follow-up ($r = -.46$, $p < .01$; Christian-Herman et al., 2001). Thus, there is evidence that in some studies, low relationship quality temporally precedes internalizing symptoms. On the other hand, a meta-analysis demonstrated a robust bidirectional relationship between depressive symptoms and lowered levels of marital quality (Goldfarb & Trudel, 2019). Most likely, both influence one another in a dynamic way.

The association between internalizing disorders and low relationship quality holds in both adolescence and adulthood, and across varying sexual orientations and racial identities. Youth who identify as a sexual minority are typically at risk for internalizing disorders (Marshal et al., 2011). However, Whitton et al. (2018) found that when young gay/lesbian participants or young Black participants were in a relationship, their internalizing symptoms decreased over time (Whitton, et al., 2018). These findings suggest that being in a relationship serves as a protective factor among youths of diverse sexual orientations and ethnicities, whereas the opposite can be true if a relationship is tumultuous: in adulthood, experiencing divorce or separation predicted increased depressive symptoms at later time periods (Simon, 2002). Indeed, these longitudinal studies provide evidence for the experience hypothesis—the belief that relationship problems come first, with anxiety/depression coming later (perhaps as a result), or that when a relationship is flourishing, mental health problems decrease. As we move to more persistent and severe mental illnesses, we find more evidence for the opposite—that mental health problems precede relationship problems.

Externalizing Disorders

Externalizing disorders include symptoms like inattention, hyperactivity, disruption, behavioral problems, and even criminal activity. Greater levels of externalizing symptoms have been linked to higher levels of sexual activity, particularly casual sex (Grello et al., 2003), but what bearing do these symptoms have on romantic relationships? Vergunst et al. (2021) used ratings of 2,960 10-to-12-year-olds on scales of inattention, hyperactivity, aggression, opposition, anxiety, and prosociality to explore whether externalizing symptoms were linked to relationships in adulthood. Inattention, aggression, and opposition were linked to a greater likelihood of separating from a partner between the ages of 18 and 35, while on the other hand, prosocial behaviors were linked to being in a stable relationship (Vergunst et al., 2021). Therefore, we can see that children who had higher levels of externalizing behaviors likely had more trouble in their relationships, perhaps a part of why they separated from their partners.

A particularly dangerous externalizing disorder, antisocial personality disorder (ASPD), is associated with lower levels of empathy, callousness, coldness, and a superficial charm (American Psychiatric Association, 2013). Overall, individuals with ASPD traits tend to have distressing and less satisfactory relationships (Woodward, et al., 2002). Those with ASPD have been found to have fewer positive behaviors in the relationship, like confiding in their partner, and be more likely to lie, cheat, beat their partner, and separate from them as well as have serious "behavioral problems" like engaging in excessive drinking, undergoing multiple arrests, and generally being cruel to their partner (Bell, 2009; Robins, 1966). Marriages that include individuals with ASPD have been found to be impaired, unstable, shorter in duration, and less likely to produce children (Brem et al., 2018; Robins, 1966). Clearly, mental health problems that manifest either through internalizing or externalizing symptoms seem to affect romantic relationships.

Psychosis and Personality Disorders

Given the intractable nature of these conditions, researchers have also examined other severe and persistent mental illnesses and how they relate to romantic relationships. Psychotic and personality disorders (PD) occur less commonly than anxiety and depression, but they have a lasting negative influence on quality of life (Grant et al., 2004). Individuals with a personality disorder have tumultuous relationships due to the problematic interpersonal features of these conditions, such as distrust, lack of empathy, and emotional dysregulation (American Psychiatric Association, 2013). By definition, personality disorders include stable and enduring behavior patterns, meaning they are more likely to persist regardless of treatment. Given this, personality-disordered individuals tend to have rocky and unstable romantic relationships.

Regarding studies of personality pathology and psychotic disorders, longitudinal studies have shown that adolescents diagnosed with PD report more relationship distress and elevated levels of partner conflict in emerging adulthood (Chen et al., 2004). Among those with psychotic disorders, dating and intimate relationships can be difficult due to social and sexual functioning problems. Although these are common problems, providers feel less competence in addressing them and often focus only on the central features of psychosis (Cloutier at al., 2021; Östman & Björkman, 2013). Because of these kinds of interpersonal issues, the social spheres of individuals with a psychotic disorder tend to be small and usually consist only of family members (Jakubowska et al., 2019).

Yet relationships still matter for those with these conditions. A meta-analysis found that psychotic individuals who were married reported a higher quality of life than those who were not married (Cloutier et al., 2021). However, in these studies, few psychotic individuals were married, and those who were married reported less marital and sexual satisfaction than non-psychotic counterparts (Cloutier et al., 2021). Given the intractable nature of these disorders and the lack of evidence for effective treatments, these conditions seem more consistent with the selection hypothesis. That is, people with these disorders are less likely to select into and sustain enduring marriages, although there is some evidence that those who do manage to marry report experiencing greater well-being to the extent they can sustain a satisfying relationship.

Personality Traits and Romantic Relationships

Each human has a personality of some kind, regardless of whether it enters the realm of a clinical personality disorder or not. You have probably seen personality tests on the Internet that tell you what type/color/animal you would be or you should marry. Unfortunately, many of these tests are not scientifically sound and typically have little to no reliability or validity (Hook et al., 2021). But some normal-range personality models—namely, the Big Five—have remarkable empirical support, including predictive accuracy for important life outcomes such as mortality, divorce, and occupational attainment, as strong as socioeconomic status or IQ (McAdams, 1997; Perkmen et al., 2018).

All people fall somewhere along the spectrum of the Big Five personality traits: neuroticism, extraversion, openness to experience, agreeableness, and conscientiousness (Costa & McCrae, 1992). The most consistent Big Five trait associated with poor relationship outcomes is neuroticism (Mousavi, 2017). Behaviorally, high neuroticism can manifest as being impulsive, highly strung, worrying a lot, and being prone to feelings of insecurity, jealousy, and tension (McCrae & Costa, 1987). In a relationship, this could translate into behaviors like checking a partner's phone, constant reassurance seeking, arguing, and perceiving slights from one's partner even when they did not intend them. Further, neuroticism has been recognized as a risk factor for anxiety and depression, so it may contribute to poorer mental health at the extremes.

A large body of research has linked higher levels of neuroticism with lower levels of relationship satisfaction (Braithwaite et al., 2016; Fisher & McNulty, 2008; Karney & Bradbury, 1997). Two meta-analyses have shown an aggregated effect size for the relationship between neuroticism and relationship satisfaction, one (Sayehmiri et al., 2020) with an effect size of $r = -.44$ (95% confidence interval [CI] [−.27, −.60]) and another (Malouff et al., 2010) with a more modest effect size of $r = -.22$ (95% CI [−.26, −.19]). Several other studies have outlined a very similar relationship, which shows that as neuroticism increases, relationship satisfaction decreases (Braithwaite et al., 2016; Fisher & McNulty, 2008; Karney & Bradbury, 1997). This same relationship holds regardless of where the sample was recruited from (e.g., China, the United States, Sweden, India, and others), how long they had been in a relationship with one another, the age of the participants, or whether the data collected were cross-sectional or longitudinal (Cao et al., 2017; Russell & McNulty, 2011). Despite having such a strong foundation for their relationship, little is known about the actual behaviors that occur on a day-to-day basis that connect neuroticism to lower levels of relationship satisfaction. As a fairly stable personality trait, it would be difficult to "take someone's neuroticism away" in order to improve their relationship. However, if we can work on the behaviors to which neuroticism gives rise, or work on the relationship itself, perhaps we would see reduced levels of relationship distress, despite not having lowered actual levels of neuroticism.

But how does neuroticism operate to actually decrease relationship satisfaction? Both interpersonal and intrapersonal models of neuroticism offer explanations for the ways in which neuroticism might operate to hurt a relationship. Interpersonal dynamics within a relationship relate to behaviors that are exchanged *between* the couple. Examples of this could be the way they argue with one another, the tone they use when they speak to each other, whether they surprise each other with gifts and dates, or their sexual relationship, among many other possibilities. Interpersonal models are rooted in the observable phenomena, or most specifically, the interactions that take place between the partners (Schaffhuser et al., 2014); as such, partners determine whether they are satisfied by their relationship based on their communication with their partner (Gottman, 1990).

On the other hand, intrapersonal dynamics relate to the emotions, feelings, and interpretations *within* a partner (Whitton & Kuryluk, 2012). Essentially, it is the preexisting traits and tendencies that a partner already has, which they bring into the relationship with them, that color the way an individual perceives everything (Karney & Bradbury, 1997; Whitton & Kuryluk, 2012). Examples of this could be how high the individual is in neuroticism, the way one partner interprets their partner's ambiguous text, and whether one partner gives their significant other the benefit of the doubt when they are let down. People with a neurotic intrapersonal style will be more likely to perceive something negatively and in turn feel more negative emotions toward a relationship (Watson & Clark, 1984).

Most likely, neuroticism operates through elements of both interpersonal and intrapersonal mechanisms, leading to lower levels of relationship satisfaction. The theory of dynamic interactionism posits that there is an ongoing transaction between the person and the environment, meaning that someone's interpersonal or intrapersonal style will shape their experience, interpretation, and reaction to the environment (Schaffhuser et al., 2014). With that in mind, the individual's interpersonal/intrapersonal style will shape their environment, and the environment will in turn shape the individual's interpersonal/intrapersonal style. As an environment can shape a person's interpersonal/intrapersonal style, couples therapy can be a useful intervention to increase satisfaction within a relationship. Attending couples therapy could be part of an "environment" that can change one or both partner's communication techniques, interpretation style, and even levels of depression or anxiety. In this way, interventions can target both relationship satisfaction and the mental health of those within the relationship, which, as shown earlier, are largely intertwined with one another.

How Can We Make Our Romantic Relationships Better?

Couple and relationship interventions are reliable ways to improve relationship well-being and ameliorate relationship distress. Two of the most recognized treatment options in the literature for intervening with relationship distress include couples therapy and relationship education. A recently published meta-analysis across 40 independently collected samples and more than 2,000 couples indicated that, compared with a waitlist control, those who attended couples therapy saw large effects on relationship satisfaction (Hedge's $g = 0.91$), medium-sized impacts on self-reported and observed communication (Hedge's $g = 0.57$–0.76), and small impacts on emotional intimacy (Hedge's $g = 0.39$; Roddy et al., 2020).

However, couples therapy has received less funding in recent years as federal funding initiatives have changed. In response, many relationship interventionists have transitioned to disseminating relationship education either online or in groups. These programs have traditionally reported smaller effect sizes than couples therapy, have been more educational than therapy, and less tailored. Yet these programs have been easier to disseminate, have resulted in larger samples with more sophisticated designs, and have been shown to produce reliable gains in relationship functioning. For example, in one meta-analysis of relationship education investigating 86 reports with more than 500 effect sizes, the authors concluded that experimental studies investigating relationship education had small-sized effects on relationship quality (Cohen's $d = 0.36$) and medium-sized effects on communication conflict (Cohen's $d = 0.44$; Hawkins et al., 2008).

Couple interventions seek to capitalize on changing both intrapersonal and interpersonal dynamics between the couple to improve the relationship. For instance, within the behavioral therapy framework, intrapersonal dynamics can be changed through unified detachment (i.e., a therapist-driven mindfulness exercise for the couple; Doss & Hatch, 2022). This introspection encourages both dyad members to be aware of their particular behavior patterns that lead to relationship distress. This process then may translate into fewer arguments and less distress. Equally, rule-governed behavior techniques (e.g., speaker-listener technique, XYZ statements, or "time-out") typically employed in behavioral couples therapies seek to modify the relationship dynamic by altering how couples communicate with one another, blatantly and explicitly changing the interpersonal dynamic (Braithwaite & Fincham, 2007). The benefits and impacts of couple interventions are well understood. This has led some relationship interventionists to see whether these effects can "spill over" into other key areas to impact individual well-being including mental health and stress (Doss & Hatch, 2022).

Couples Therapy for Mental Health Outcomes

During the 1990s, many were dissatisfied with the pharmacological and psychological treatments for depression (Jacobson et al., 1991). Indeed, pharmacological treatments during the time only produced temporary effects, and early evidence from cognitive-behavioral therapy suggested it may have prophylactic effects (Jacobson et al., 1991). Research showed that interpersonal problems predict poorer treatment adherence and dropout in groups designed to combat depressive symptoms (McEvoy et al., 2014). These considerations led some to adopt a relational approach to treating depression with the justification that involving a partner in treatment may increase treatment adherence and support.

These interventions have been summarized as belonging to one of three groups: partner-assisted interventions, disorder-specific interventions, and couples therapy (Whisman & Baucom, 2012). Partner-assisted interventions focus on leveraging partner support for individuals seeking to change their behavior whereas disorder-specific interventions create fundamental changes in the couple's relationship that are focal client's disorder through psychoeducation and behavior change. Both couple interventions place individual psychopathology as the primary treatment concern. Thus, these interventions are individually focused, and evidence suggests they are effective treatment options for obsessive compulsive disorder, agoraphobia, and depression. Couples therapy, however, assumes the presence of relationship distress, and treating any underlying psychopathology can only be accomplished by attending to this stressor. These interventions are relationally focused but reduce psychopathology by alleviating a source of chronic stress (i.e., relationship distress; e.g., Emanuels-Zuurveen & Emmelkamp, 1996; Jacobson et al., 1991).

Relationship Education for Mental Health Outcomes

Even when relationship interventions are at their weakest, they still produce effects on relationship well-being and key mental health correlates. For instance, two of the most evidence-based relationship education programs to date include OurRelationship and ePREP. OurRelationship is a web-based adaptation of integrative behavioral couple therapy (Doss & Hatch, 2022), whereas ePREP is a web-based adaptation of the Prevention and Relationship Enhancement Program (Braithwaite & Fincham, 2007). Both are significantly shorter and less tailored than a typical course of couples therapy. When the OurRelationship program was delivered to individuals instead of couples, small (but non-significant) improvements were noted in relationship well-being (Cohen's d = 0.09–0.26) when compared with the waitlist control condition (Nowlan et al., 2017). Similar-sized improvements were noted in key areas of mental health functioning including reductions in depressive (Cohen's d = −0.05) and anxious (Cohen's d = −0.23) symptoms when compared with a waitlist control condition (Braithwaite & Fincham, 2009). Like OurRelationship, compared with a control group, when ePREP was delivered to individuals instead of couples, those in the ePREP condition saw small-sized improvements in relationship well-being (Hedge's = 0.39) but large-sized reductions in depressive (Hedge's g = 1.28) and anxious symptoms (Hedge's g = 1.00) over follow-up (Braithwaite & Fincham, 2009). Thus, improving relationship functioning impacts relationship well-being and other key areas of mental health functioning.

Regardless of whether the couples break up, participating in web-based relationship education can have meaningful impacts on individual and relationship functioning. When comparing couples who broke up in a waitlist control condition with couples who received either the OurRelationship or ePREP programs, those in the waitlist condition saw increases in psychological distress leading up to the breakup whereas those who received OurRelationship or ePREP saw decreases in their psychological distress leading up to the breakup (Hatch et al., 2021). This suggests that these programs buffer couples against well-founded pre-breakup increases in stress (Amato, 2010; Booth & Amato, 1991). Further, some have documented that regardless of whether a relationship ends after completing ePREP, the benefits are still maintained and presumably carry over into the next relationship (Braithwaite & Fincham, 2009). Even when delivered during stressful life events such as relationship dissolution, relationship education has demonstrated the power to improve individual functioning and carry over the relationship and individual gains afforded by the programming into future relationships.

Conclusion

In their classic review on the need to belong, Baumeister and Leary note,

> Not all relationships are interchangeable, of course. Close relationships based on romantic love may offer a variety of satisfactions that are not easily obtained through non-romantic, nonsexual friendships. . . . There are certain kinds of relationships that cannot effectively be replaced with other kinds of relationships. (1995, p. 517)

As this chapter highlights, there is something unique and powerful about the commitment and permanence of marriage and other intensely committed romantic relationships. There is a reason that movies, books, and music make love and relationships a central focus. When this central relationship in one's life is not going well, individuals must devote lots of resources to improving it, dealing with it, or ending it. But at its best, marriage makes life rich, rewarding, and abundant. There is no question that certain enduring traits can make our ability to attain and maintain a happy marriage easier. But if we can get there, a healthy marriage makes many other things about life easier and better. When our need to belong has been met and we feel safe and satisfied in that domain, we become free to grow in other areas of life.

References

Amato, P. R. (2010). Research on divorce: Continuing trends and new developments. *Journal of Marriage and Family, 72*(3), 650–666. https://doi.org/10.1111/j.1741-3737.2010.00723.x

ABC News. (2006, January 5). Inhumane conditions for Romania's lost generation. *ABC News*. https://abcnews.go.com/2020/story?id=124078&page=1)

American Psychiatric Association. (2013). *Diagnostic and statistical manual of mental disorders (DSM-5®)*. American Psychiatric Pub.

Aunger, R., Foster, D., & Curtis, V. (2021). Psychometric analysis of a postulated set of evolved human motives. *Frontiers in Psychology, 12*, Article 680229. https://doi.org/10.3389/fpsyg.2021.680229

Baumeister, R. F., & Leary, M. R. (1995). The need to belong: Desire for interpersonal attachments as a fundamental human motivation. *Psychological Bulletin, 117*(3), 497–529. https://doi.org/10.1037/0033-2909.117.3.497

Bell, M. C. (2009). *Antisocial personality disorder and romantic relationship functioning in an epidemiologically-based sample*. (Doctoral dissertation, University of Maryland, Baltimore).

Blum, D. (2002). *Love at Goon Park: Harry Harlow and the science of affection*. Merloyd Lawrence Books.

Booth, A., & Amato, P. (1991). Divorce and psychological stress. *Journal of Health and Social Behavior, 32*(4), 396–407. https://doi.org/10.2307/2137106

Braithwaite, S. R., & Fincham, F. D. (2007). ePREP: Computer based prevention of relationship dysfunction, depression and anxiety. *Journal of Social and Clinical Psychology, 26*(5), 609–622. https://doi.org/10.1521/jscp.2007.26.5.609

Braithwaite, S. R., & Fincham, F. D. (2009). A randomized clinical trial of a computer based preventive intervention: Replication and extension of ePREP. *Journal of Family Psychology, 23*(1), 32–38. https://doi.org/10.1037/a0014061

Braithwaite, S., & Holt-Lunstad, J. (2017). Romantic relationships and mental health. *Current Opinion in Psychology, 13*, 120–125. https://doi.org/10.1016/j.copsyc.2016.04.001

Braithwaite, S. R., Mitchell, C. M., Selby E. A., & Fincham, F. D. (2016). Trait forgiveness and enduring vulnerabilities: Neuroticism and catastrophizing influence relationship satisfaction via less forgiveness. *Personality and Individual Differences, 94*, 237–246. https://doi.org/10.1016/j.paid.2015.12.045

Brem, M. J., Florimbio, A. R., Elmquist, J., Shorey, R. C., & Stuart, G. L. (2018). Antisocial traits, distress tolerance, and alcohol problems as predictors of intimate partner violence in men arrested for domestic violence. *Psychology of Violence, 8*(1), 132. https://doi.org/10.1037/vio0000088

Cao, H., Zhou, N., Fang, X., & Fine, M. (2017). Marital well-being and depression in Chinese marriage: Going beyond satisfaction and ruling out critical confounders. *Journal of Family Psychology, 31*(6), 775. https://doi.org/10.1037/fam0000312

Chen, H., Cohen, P., Johnson, J. G., Kasen, S., Sneed, J. R., & Crawford, T. N. (2004). Adolescent personality disorders and conflict with romantic partners during the transition to adulthood. *Journal of Personality Disorders, 18*(6), 507–525. https://doi.org/10.1521/pedi.18.6.507.54794

Christian-Herman, J. L., O'Leary, K. D., & Avery-Leaf, S. (2001). The impact of severe negative events in marriage on depression. *Journal of Social and Clinical Psychology, 20*(1), 24–40. https://doi.org/10.1521/jscp.20.1.24.22250

Clavarino, A., Hayatbakhsh, M. R., Williams, G. M., Bor, W., O'Callaghan, M., & Najman, J. M. (2011). Depression following marital problems: Different impacts on mothers and their children? A 21-year prospective study. *Social Psychiatry and Psychiatric Epidemiology, 46*(9), 833–841. https://doi.org/10.1007/s00127-010-0253-8

Cloutier, B., Francoeur, A., Samson, C., Ghostine, A., & Lecomte, T. (2021). Romantic relationships, sexuality, and psychotic disorders: A systematic review of recent findings. *Psychiatric Rehabilitation Journal*, *44*(1), 22. https://doi.org/10.1037/prj0000409

Costa Jr., P. T., & McCrae, R. R. (1992). Four ways five factors are basic. *Personality and Individual Differences*, *13*(6), 653–665. https://doi.org/10.1016/0191-8869(92)90236-I

Du Rocher Schudlich, T. D., Papp, L. M., & Cummings, E. M. (2011). Relations between spouses' depressive symptoms and marital conflict: A longitudinal investigation of the role of conflict resolution styles. *Journal of Family Psychology*, *25*(4), 531. https://doi.org/10.1037/a0024216

Doss, B. D., & Hatch, S. G. (2022). Harnessing technology to provide online couple interventions. *Current Opinion in Psychology*, *43*, 114–118. https://doi.org/10.1016/j.copsyc.2021.06.014

Emanuels-Zuurveen, L., & Emmelkamp, P. M. (1996). Individual behavioural–cognitive therapy v. marital therapy for depression in maritally distressed couples. *The British Journal of Psychiatry*, *169*(2), 181–188. https://doi.org/10.1192/bjp.169.2.181

Fisher, T. D., & McNulty, J. K. (2008). Neuroticism and marital satisfaction: The mediating role played by the sexual relationship. *Journal of Family Psychology*, *22*(1), 112. https://doi.org/10.1037/0893-3200.22.1.112

Gottman, J. M. (1990). How marriages change. *Depression and Aggression in Family Interaction*, *75*, 101.

Goldfarb, M. R., & Trudel, G. (2019). Marital quality and depression: A review. *Marriage & Family Review*, *55*(8), 737–763. https://doi.org/10.1080/01494929.2019.1610136

Grant, B. F., Hasin, D. S., Stinson, F. S., Dawson, D. A., Chou, S. P., Ruan, W. J., & Pickering, R. P. (2004). Prevalence, correlates, and disability of personality disorders in the United States: Results from the national epidemiologic survey on alcohol and related conditions. *The Journal of Clinical Psychiatry*, *65*(7), 948–958. http://dx.doi.org/10.4088/JCP.v65n0711

Grello, C. M., Welsh, D. P., Harper, M. S., & Dickson, J. W. (2003). Dating and sexual relationship trajectories and adolescent functioning. *Adolescent & Family Health*, *3*(3), 103–112.

Hasin, D. S., Sarvet, A. L., Meyers, J. L., Saha, T. D., Ruan, W. J., Stohl, M., & Grant, B. F. (2018). Epidemiology of adult DSM-5 major depressive disorder and its specifiers in the United States. *JAMA Psychiatry*, *75*(4), 336–346. https://doi.org10.1001/jamapsychiatry.2017.4602

Hatch, S. G., Le, Y., & Doss, B. D. (2021). Make up or break up? Charting the well-being of low-income help-seeking couples through the breakup process. *Journal of Family Psychology*, *35*(8), 1107–1116. https://doi.org/10.1037/fam0000859

Hawkins, A. J., Blanchard, V. L., Baldwin, S. A., & Fawcett, E. B. (2008). Does marriage and relationship education work? A meta-analytic study. *Journal of Consulting and Clinical Psychology*, *76*(5), 723–734. https://doi.org/10.1037/a0012584

Heller, D., Watson, D., & Ilies, R. (2004). The role of person versus situation in life satisfaction: A critical examination. *Psychological Bulletin*, *130*(4), 574–600. https://doi.org/10.1037/0033-2909.130.4.574

Hook, J. N., Hall, T. W., Davis, D. E., Van Tongeren, D. R., & Conner, M. (2021). The Enneagram: A systematic review of the literature and directions for future research. *Journal of Clinical Psychology*, *77*(4), 865–883. https://doi.org/10.1002/jclp.23097

Jacobson, N. S., Dobson, K., Fruzzetti, A. E., Schmaling, K. B., & Salusky, S. (1991). Marital therapy as a treatment for depression. *Journal of Consulting and Clinical Psychology*, *59*(4), 547–557. https://doi.org/10.1037/0022-006X.59.4.547

Jakubowska, A., Kaselionyte, J., Priebe, S., & Giacco, D. (2019). Internet use for social interaction by people with psychosis: A systematic review. *Cyberpsychology, Behavior, and Social Networking*, *22*(5), 336–343. http://dx.doi.org/10.1089/cyber.2018.0554

Karney, B. R., & Bradbury, T. N. (1995). The longitudinal course of marital quality and stability: A review of theory, methods, and research. *Psychological Bulletin*, *118*(1), 3–34. https://doi.org/10.1037/0033-2909.118.1.3

Karney, B. R., & Bradbury, T. N. (1997). Neuroticism, marital interaction, and the trajectory of marital satisfaction. *Journal of Personality and Social Psychology*, *72*(5), 1075–1092. https://doi.org/10.1037/0022-3514.72.5.1075

Malouff, J. M., Thorsteinsson, E. B., Schutte, N. S., Bhullar, N., & Rooke, S. E. (2010). The five-factor model of personality and relationship satisfaction of intimate partners: A meta-analysis. *Journal of Research in Personality*, *44*(1), 124–127. https://doi.org/10.1016/j.jrp.2009.09.004

Marshal, M. P., Dietz, L. J., Friedman, M. S., Stall, R., Smith, H. A., McGinley, J., . . . & Brent, D. A. (2011). Suicidality and depression disparities between sexual minority and heterosexual youth: A meta-analytic review. *Journal of Adolescent Health*, *49*(2), 115–123. https://doi.org/10.1016/j.jadohealth.2011.02.005

McAdams, D. P. (1997). A conceptual history of personality psychology. In R. E. Hogan, J. A Johnson, & Stephen R. Briggs (Eds.), *Handbook of Personality Psychology* (pp. 3–39). Academic Press.

McCrae, R. R., & Costa, P. T. (1987). Validation of the five-factor model of personality across instruments and observers. *Journal of Personality and Social Psychology*, *52*(1), 81–90. https://doi.org/10.1037/0022-3514.52.1.81

McEvoy, P. M., Burgess, M. M., & Nathan, P. (2014). The relationship between interpersonal problems, therapeutic alliance, and outcomes following group and individual cognitive behaviour therapy. *Journal of Affective Disorders*, *157*, 25–32. https://doi.og/10.1016/j.jad.2013.12.038

Mousavi, R. (2017). Relationship between Big Five personality factors neuroticism, extraversion, agreeableness, openness, loyalty and marital adjustment. *NeuroQuantology*, *15*(4), 63–68. https://doi.org/10.14704/nq.2017.15.4.1154

Nelson, C. A. (2014). *Romania's abandoned children*. Harvard University Press.

Nowlan, K. M., Roddy, M. K., & Doss, B. D. (2017). The online OurRelationship program for relationally distressed individuals: A pilot randomized controlled trial. *Couple and Family Psychology: Research and Practice*, *6*(3), 189–204. https://doi.org/10.1037/cfp0000080

Östman, M., & Björkman, A. C. (2013). Schizophrenia and relationships: The effect of mental illness on sexuality. *Clinical Schizophrenia & Related Psychoses*, *7*, 20–24. http://dx.doi.org/10.3371/CSRP.OSBJ.012513

Overbeek, G., Vollebergh, W., de Graaf, R., Scholte, R., de Kemp, R., & Engels, R. (2006). Longitudinal associations of marital quality and marital dissolution with the incidence of DSM-III-R disorders. *Journal of Family Psychology*, *20*(2), 284–291. https://doi.org/10.1037/0893-3200.20.2.284

Pankiewicz, P., Majkowicz, M., & Krzykowski, G. (2012). Anxiety disorders in intimate partners and the quality of their relationship. *Journal of Affective Disorders*, *140*(2), 176–180. https://doi.org/10.1016/j.jad.2012.02.005

Perkmen, S., Toy, S., Caracuel, A., & Shelley, M. (2018). Cross-cultural search for Big Five: Development of a scale to compare personality traits of pre-service elementary school teachers in Turkey and Spain. *Asia Pacific Education Review, 19*(4), 459–468. http://dx.doi.org/10.1007/s12564-018-9549-2

Priest, J. B. (2013). Anxiety disorders and the quality of relationships with friends, relatives, and romantic partners. *Journal of Clinical Psychology, 69*(1), 78–88. https://doi.org/10.1002/jclp.21925

Robins, L. N. (1966). *Deviant children grown up: A sociological and psychiatric study of sociopathic personality.* Oxford: Williams & Wilkins.

Roddy, M. K., Walsh, L. M., Rothman, K., Hatch, S. G., & Doss, B. D. (2020). Meta-analysis of couple therapy: Effects across outcomes, designs, timeframes, and other moderators. *Journal of Consulting and Clinical Psychology, 88*(7), 583–596. https://doi.org/10.1037/ccp0000514

Russell, V. M., & McNulty, J. K. (2011). Frequent sex protects intimates from the negative implications of their neuroticism. *Social Psychological and Personality Science, 2*(2), 220–227. https://doi.org/10.1177/1948550610387162

Sayehmiri, K., Kareem, K. I., Abdi, K., Dalvand, S., & Gheshlagh, R. G. (2020). The relationship between personality traits and marital satisfaction: A systematic review and meta-analysis. *BMC Psychology, 8*(1), 15. http://dx.doi.org/10.1186/s40359-020-0383-z

Schaffhuser, K., Wagner, J., Lüdtke, O., & Allemand, M. (2014). Dyadic longitudinal interplay between personality and relationship satisfaction: A focus on neuroticism and self-esteem. *Journal of Research in Personality, 53*, 124–133. https://doi.org/10.1016/j.jrp.2014.08.007

Simon, R. W. (2002). Revisiting the relationships among gender, marital status, and mental health. *American Journal of Sociology, 107*(4), 1065–1096. http://dx.doi.org/10.1086/339225

Van Orden, K. A., Witte, T. K., Cukrowicz, K. C., Braithwaite, S. R., Selby, E. A., & Joiner Jr., T. E. (2010). The interpersonal theory of suicide. *Psychological Review, 117*(2), 575. https://doi.org/10.1037/a0018697

Vergunst, F., Zheng, Y., Domond, P., Vitaro, F., Tremblay, R. E., Nagin, D., Park, J, & Côté, S. M. (2021). Behavior in childhood is associated with romantic partnering patterns in adulthood. *Journal of Child Psychology and Psychiatry, 62*(7), 842–852. https://doi.org/10.1111/jcpp.13329

Watson, D., & Clark, L. A. (1984). Negative affectivity: The disposition to experience aversive emotional states. *Psychological Bulletin, 96*(3), 465–490. https://doi.org/10.1037/0033-2909.96.3.465

Watson, J. B. & Watson, R. R. (1928). *Psychological care of the infant and child.* New York: Norton.

Whisman, M. A. (2007). Marital distress and DSM-IV psychiatric disorders in a population-based national survey. *Journal of Abnormal Psychology, 116*(3), 638–643. https://doi.org/10.1037/0021-843X.116.3.638

Whisman, M. A., & Baucom, D. H. (2012). Intimate relationships and psychopathology. *Clinical Child and Family psychology Review, 15*(1), 4–13. https://doi.org/10.1007/s10567-011-0107-2

Whitton, S. W., Dyar, C., Newcomb, M. E., & Mustanski, B. (2018). Romantic involvement: A protective factor for psychological health in racially-diverse young sexual minorities. *Journal of Abnormal Psychology, 127*(3), 265–275. https://doi.org/10.1037/abn0000332

Whitton, S. W., & Kuryluk, A. D. (2012). Relationship satisfaction and depressive symptoms in emerging adults: Cross-sectional associations and moderating effects of relationship characteristics. *Journal of Family Psychology, 26*(2), 226. https://doi.org/10.1037/a0027267

Woodward, L., Fergusson, D., & Horwood, L. (2002). Romantic relationships of young people with childhood and adolescent onset antisocial behavior problems. *Journal of Abnormal Child Psychology, 30*(3), 231–243. https://doi.org/10.1023/A:1015150728887

Conclusion

Arthur Aron

This volume focuses on how our close relationships have changed in the 21st century. Since around 2000, there have been substantial developments across all kinds of close relationships, arising largely due to the advances in technology and to the continued and, indeed it seems, accelerated easing of longstanding tight and restrictive cultural norms. In this conclusion, I will briefly review each chapter's key contributions to understanding the changes we are seeing, just what specifically is changing, and their causes and effects. These chapters primarily review what is known about how things have changed, plus new things learned from research not done until after 2000, and suggestions for future directions, all covering diverse aspects of romantic/marital relationships, friendships, and family, as well as how relationships across the spectrum affect physical and mental health. I should also say that if you haven't read Elaine Hatfield and Dick Rapson's Foreword, I'd recommend reading it first. It gives a great brief history of how scientific research on relationships got to this point and is a very enjoyable and moving read.

Turning to Claudia Brumbaugh and Jaclyn Doherty's Chapter 1 on ideal partner characteristics, a detailed, engaging review of the literature comparing more recent to pre-2000 findings, it indicates primarily that likely evolutionary-based preferences (e.g., appearance, status, perceived similarities) have largely remained unchanged. However, some things have clearly changed. For example, due to the effects of women having more economic equality, women who are better off overall are needing to focus on men's income (although still somewhat) less and thus are freed up to care more about men's looks. Plus, focusing just on the more recent research, they found some interesting clear patterns, such as new findings showing more evidence for dark traits, even among men seeking women partners, and the general role of humor in finding a partner attractive (with some exceptions of course), plus including work on same-sex attractions.

In Chapter 2, Kathryn Coduto considers the role of online dating, an obviously strong example of how new technology developments are affecting relationship formations: making finding potential partners much less limited by the social environment and much less demanding and providing many more alternatives and more initial information about them. Another major change is that potential partners can have initial online interactions before actually having to meet in person. However, those initial online interactions, even across multiple online methods (including "secret tests"), although increasing one's confidence, can still mislead us in some ways as to what we will find in person. Online searches are used for finding both long-term and short-term relationships, indeed, sometimes just for sex, and sometimes just for friendship. Another interesting advantage of online initial interactions, compared to in-person ones, is that they give us more chances to edit what we want to say and to pause and reflect on what the other has said before responding. On the other hand, meeting online can lead to over-idealizations (both ways) that undermine relationships when individuals try to develop the relationship in person.

In Chapter 3, Sharon Sassler focusses on cohabitation versus marriage. In her substantial and thorough (and easy to follow) review of the quantitative and qualitative research (primarily in the United States), she finds considerable increases in cohabitation. For example, about a quarter of Americans will never marry, with considerably more acceptance of cohabitation—a clear example of the lessening of rigid social norms. Overall, cohabitation both prior to marriage and replacing marriage seem to be increasingly common, especially among younger individuals. Although most young adults still believe they will marry at some point, the number who think marriage is not a good idea seems to be increasing. In addition to age, there is also variation in acceptance/preference for cohabitation by ethnicity—with minorities approving of it less (possibly due to more conservative attitudes). At the same time, the less educated (and more economically poor) are more likely to cohabit (and to do so at an earlier age and relationship stage). And, among young people especially, cohabitation often develops into a long-term relationship, some of whom go on to marry, though many do not.

In Chapter 4, Elyakim Kislev focuses on singlehood, for which most of the existing research has been conducted since 2000. It begins with a discussion of the difficulty of defining singlehood (both for researchers and for the general public), in particular, in distinguishing between voluntary and involuntary singlehood, and explores some of the key issues. Notably, there appear to be at least three categories of chosen singlehood: wanting freedom, practical barriers (like professional issues), and not trusting relationships (attachment insecurity). And, of course, the chapter discusses the stigma associated with singlehood (especially for women) and notes that this stigma seems to be in the process of becoming less strong—another key example of the effect of the loosening of rigid social norms. Kislev also discusses the impact of singlehood—interestingly, while marriage is often associated with great happiness, if those who are single actively seek other close relationships (as they often do), today they can be even happier than married people on the average.

In Chapter 5, Dan Perlman and Rowland Miller focus on our expectations (and how they are and are not being met for marital quality in modern times). First, they consider the substantial body of long-term research now available that shows strong average declines in martial satisfaction over the years of marriage. Specifically, they explore some new ideas and changes that have happened relatively recently (such as increasing expectations, noting Finkel's [2019] work on the increasingly common all-or-nothing marriage norm), and lots of recent research supporting ideas that have been around awhile, but providing new angles on them. They also lay out work in this current domain that gives us important directions for fostering a marriage, such as trying to cultivate a "growth" mindset for marriage (that relationship success requires effort), seeing our partner as positively as one realistically can, doing fun/novel things together, savoring the positive, and not having too high expectations!

In Chapter 6, Grace Wetzel and Diana Sanchez consider the roles of equity and gender in heterosexual marriage, and how modern developments may have affected this. Overall, their literature review finds that there has been some increase in gender equity (another example of some easing of rigid social norms); however, it is far from being reached fully. Inequity still remains substantial across domains, including household labor, childcare, expected financial contributions, and sexual interest (with all such inequity increasing during the COVID pandemic). They do, however, note that inequity is doing a bit better (though still there) in cohabiting versus married couples. Nevertheless, the cultural stereotypes of how each gender should behave do remain to a considerable extent and have substantial influence on married life—not just in how they divide work, but in what they believe is appropriate (e.g., men doing child raising is more common, but still stigmatized). Indeed, same-sex relationships report more equality in these aspects, and greater satisfaction overall, suggesting that equity can be achieved in a relationship. Indeed, even within heterosexual couples, when the work is shared more equally, the women report greater martial happiness.

In Chapter 7, Rhonda Balzarini, Karen Blair, and Marissa Walter carefully and extensively review the research on the recent increase in consensually non-monogamous relationships, as well as other kinds of nontraditional relationships, including same-sex and interracial. Indeed, these nontraditional relationships, which are more common in modern times, are clearly resulting from some easing of rigid social norms. However, as the authors document, there remains considerable stigmatization that those in nontraditional relationships face, which can have diverse negative effects on their relationships and general well-being.

In Chapter 8, Stan Gaines focuses specifically on intergroup marriages including interracial, inter-religious, and cross-nationality (with an interesting consideration of the situation in diverse cultures). These kinds of marriages have increased in recent years (once again largely resulting from easing of traditional norms), but stigmatization of individuals (especially in the context of ethnicity) remains considerable. Indeed, when one partner is of a stigmatized race, it can strongly affect a marriage—the partner of stigmatized race the most, although both can experience it. He also illustrates that the ways this is dealt with, and its effects can be understood more deeply by taking into account standard relationships theories.

In Chapter 9, Abdullah Salehuddin, Tamara Afifi, and Jade Salmon consider how the role of divorce has changed in modern times, notably focusing on "conscious uncoupling"—how divorcing individuals can work to undermine the traditionally negative outcomes to shape a more positive outcome. They begin by noting that in modern times (in part due to easing of norms, but also to longer life spans—an indirect result of advances in medical technology) divorce is more common, and serial monogamy (multiple marriages and divorces) has also become more common. And all of this suggests that we need to rethink the traditional understanding of marriage and consider more positive ways to separate. Indeed, based on research, they suggest several steps for conscious uncoupling: seeing the situation more positively, finding positives in the new life without the partner; expanding our abilities and opportunities; reflecting on the emotions and trying to dissolve negative feelings; and finally, trying to work out a new understanding with our former partner and finding ways to handle the divisions that occur. They then review considerable work showing how these various steps do appear to be helpful in coping with (and even gaining from) the divorce process (including for children by providing positive co-parenting). They conclude with a substantial discussion of how all this leads to clearly needed further research.

In Chapter 10, Jasna Jovanovic and Jean Williams examine how sexuality has changed in modern times, focusing on emerging adulthood, and considering sex in both casual and committed relationships. Much of this arises of course from the easing of cultural norms, permitting more freedom in our choices about where and how to enjoy sexual relations (including more casual relationships), as well as the gendered aspects of our choices and identity. Although casual sex is quite common, surprisingly, there has actually been a small decrease in reports of casual sex since 2000, in part due to other factors such as a decrease in alcohol use and an increase in engagement in online time. Casual sex involving "hookups" is especially common. And sort-of sex, sexting (something made possible by technology), is increasingly common in emerging adults. At the same time, sex with friends, a non-committed but not entirely casual arrangement, is quite common. Yet, while there may be some change, gender differences remain in how women and men (and same versus cross-gender) are viewed for participating in sex (or even enjoying sex).

In Chapter 11, Karen Blair, Erin Courtice, and Rhea Hoskin focus primarily on how gender identity and orientation have changed over this time, including starting back in the 20th century when traditional religious rules began to be less influential. However, even as negative views of homosexuality have gotten less strong in recent years to some extent, there is a much smaller decline in negative attitudes toward femininity (especially in gay men), which continues to be devalued and controlled. And, of course, AIDS had a terrible influence on increasing antigay sentiment. Yet, overall, there is a positive trend, with, for example, widespread legalization of same-sex marriage (which also seemed to have an effect on easing prejudice!) And, as people are more educated and interactive, there is an increase in being aware of others, and even having friends and family who are LGBTQ+. Yet prejudices do remain and present serious problems.

And what about friendships? The next few chapters specifically address how the role and nature of friendships in people's lives have evolved. In Chapter 12, Kelly Sweeney, Daniel Lee, and Andrew High focus on the impact of the emergence of social media. A key, and very major development, is online friendships, which research shows are typically as close and committed (and long lasting) as those with face-to-face nearby friends. In addition to providing more potential friends and keeping friends who move, social media can provide greater opportunities to just be in regular and frequent touch and for providing support. Of course, social media can also have negatives effects on friendships, such as by being used to keep conflict going or to distract from a person-to-person meeting. Their chapter concludes with suggestions for understanding how and why people should use particular combinations of social media channels.

In Chapter 13, Emily Beauparlant, Mahzad Hojjat, Nicole Melancon, and Laura Machia focus on the variables that increase the prevalence of friendships. The authors discuss that factors related to the changes in social norms, especially individualism (and variables like greater economic independence for women) throughout the world, have led to an increased delay in marriage for some, and the decision not to marry at all or to choose to cohabit with a partner for others. They also note evidence that singles who have more independence and self-fulfillment motives were happier than nonsingles with these views. Of course, the decrease in marriage also leads to more time to have close friends, and the importance of friends in satisfying support needs is increasingly common. Another factor that the authors note in regard to increasing the prevalence and potential depth of friendships is social media, making friends around the world possible. More generally, key relationship theories suggest that how well someone does in being single (and thus being more likely to need friends) depends on having good alternatives to marriage or cohabiting, such as strong friendships.

In Chapter 14, Mahzad Hojjat and her coauthors (including Anne Moyer, her co-editor of this book) explore how friendship is operating in the current age, for which the COVID-19 pandemic provides a deep understanding, particularly of how it operates today during difficult times (both individually and collectively). Two key factors that have changed in modern times have played a big role: social media and the growth of intense political divisions (particularly in the United States). Thoroughly summarizing extensive research (a considerable portion of which is conducted by the chapter's authors), they found that social media (particularly more direct forms of digital connection) overall helped deal with the isolation during the early phase by providing opportunities to retain and strengthen friendships (particularly for young people who rely especially on friends for social support and were isolated from school and such). However, there were also a considerable minority of people for whom these circumstances created conflict with friends and, overall, reduced opportunity to have usual interactions or to create new friendships. In general, electronic communication continued to be largely useful as the pandemic continued, but by the time of the second phase, the political divisions greatly undermined many friendships.

In Chapter 15, Nicole Shelton, Kate Turetsky, Yeji Park, and Lindsey Eikenburg review research on essential aspects of cross-group friendships focusing primarily on research conducted in the 21st century (or the very end of the 20th) and of course note that ethnic diversity in the United States has been substantially increasing. Considering first how such friendships are formed, they note that even if there is some increase in physical proximity (which generally makes friendship more likely), there are obstacles in forming cross-group friendships, and they are much less likely than same-group friendships to emerge as a result of such proximity. On the other hand, compared with those of just physical proximity, cross-group friendships occur more frequently in situations that involve more interaction between same-status individuals, and also where this is a social network such that you are aware that other in-group members have out-group friends (both factors that I would argue have resulted at least in part from the easing of rigid social norms). Cross-group friendships are also more likely for individuals who have positive attitudes toward the out-group, favor diversity, and have certain personality characteristics, or who see the potential partner as similar to themselves in other key ways (again, a factor likely arising from easing of rigid social norms). However, once formed, cross-group friendships are less likely to last because each friend is less comfortable disclosing their personal information related to race and less likely to be responsive to that of their partner's, and they are less likely to share activities, especially close ones. On the other hand, such friendships do have unique benefits—including enhanced attitudes toward the friend's group overall, and a sense of protection from (or supported when it happens) out-group mistreatment received by either friend.

The next three chapters turn to family relations. In Chapter 16, Ellen Pinderhughes, Seungmi Lee, and Madeline Smith focus on adoption. This chapter provides a strong review overall but focuses especially on more recent research and specifically notes at the outset some key recent developments, following from changes in social norms, such as the dramatic increase in adoptions by LGBTQ parents, greater socioeconomic diversity of adopters, and increased cross-ethnic adoptions. Another big change is how it is increasingly common for adopting families to interact with biological parents (and biological parents even having a say in who does the adoption). Another recent change, resulting largely from the Internet (and also from advances in genetic testing), is increased reunions of adoptees with their birth parents. And yet another advance is improved (based on research) clinical training for providing support to adopting families.

In Chapter 17, Dawn Braithwaite and Bailey Oliver-Blackburn focus on the increased prevalence of stepfamilies, and the greatly increased research—nearly all studies cited are since 2000—focusing on understanding stepfamilies and developing means to help make them function optimally. The main thrust of the chapter is summarizing research informing people how to manage these stepfamilies in optimal ways. Lots of newly researched, valuable, good advice is provided, including how to create a sense of normalcy, focusing on the positives, developing identities that indicate resilience, creating and maintaining strong interactions among and across stepfamily members, and learning how to reframe.

In Chapter 18, Sofia Gameiro focuses on recently developed, and greatly increased, use of medically assisted reproduction technologies in the years since 2000, primarily considering how these affect parenting and the parent–child relationship. One key issue is the role of the conception: Individuals using these technologies seem to function well, although they do tend to be more tense regarding the birth process and health of the fetus. But, over time, they tend to show no distress about the conception process. Another issue is having or not having a genetic link—with research suggesting that the lack of one parent having a link can affect how they feel about parenting, but their parenting itself seems not to be affected. Yet another issue is being in a nontraditional family, mainly lesbian and gay couple-headed families, with research suggesting that even though the families face some stigma, their children on the average do as well as those from traditional families. And yet another issue is about whether, how, and when to disclose this to the child. It can be challenging for parents, but the research to date suggests that it does not affect the parent–child relationships or how well the child does. Finally, they address the situation in which it does not lead to parenthood—research suggests that this is hard on the intended parents, especially due to their ongoing desire for a child.

The last two chapters (19 and 20) focus on recent research on how our various relationships affect physical and mental health. In Chapter 19, Anne Moyer, Olivia Mock, and Rose Martillotti focus on what we have learned about the mechanisms through which our relationships affect our health, especially noting recent changes that impact our relationships. Overall, the quality of our relationships is known to play a crucial role in health and longevity. However, recent work finds, as expected, a positive relation with real-world social interactions, but a negative link with Facebook interactions. As for overall underlying processes of the role of relationships in health and longevity in general, one of course is relational support for healthy behaviors; another is being free from relationship difficulties. Focusing specifically on recent relationship trends across multiple types, they consider first the role of pets, finding mixed results, although in some studies, particularly for people with heart conditions and strokes, at least some breeds of dogs do seem to promote health, especially for individuals living alone. More generally, singlehood (as noted in Chapter 4) has increased in recent years, and its overall effects on health (compared with being married) is largely negative, due in part to less support and greater stress, although it is difficult to control for factors that affect who becomes single and why. Finally, they considered the role of having a roommate. The limited research, all focusing on the negatives, tends to support that that there are negative impacts, such as increasing binge drinking, smoking, and less physical activity.

Finally, In Chapter 20, Charlotte Esplin, Gabe Hatch, and Scott Braithwaite consider the role of relationships in mental health. Covering a lot of relatively recent research, they focus on not just overall effects, but sorting out mechanisms and directions of causality (where and which ways relationships affect mental health and vice versa), in the context of a wide range of traits. Indeed, it seems common from the research that most factors operate both ways—mental health problems worsen relationships and problematic relationships worsen mental health. Regarding the effect of mental health on relationships, relationships are negatively influenced by diverse individual factors, notably including personality disorders and neuroticism. Regarding the key issue of what can be done, considerable recent developments provide some valuable advances, suggesting that couple therapy can be very effective, but couple education only moderately so. In sum, they conclude, that although clearly some individual characteristics shape relationship quality, relationship quality can make our life—and health—better, and anything we can do to promote it can make a difference.

Overall, this groundbreaking volume explores and deepens our understanding of why and how close relationships have changed in the 21st century, focusing on and acutely exploring research on diverse relationship types and processes, and including, in many cases, research-based suggestions for how things can be improved, as well as in each case important suggestions for future research directions. As noted throughout this concluding chapter, most of the changes we are seeing are due to the impact of easing of rigid social norms and technology developments.

Also, as I read all this great work, I naturally saw much of it through a lens of the self-expansion model (Aron & Aron, 1986; Aron et al., 2022). Building on other research, the model proposes that there are two fundamental biological motivations: survival and growth (self-expansion). As basic survival needs have become increasingly easily met, this has made it less necessary to have tight restrictions and has opened up opportunities for broad work on technological advances beyond just survival. Thus, it seems to me, that much of what we are seeing arising from this is taking advantage of the increased possibility for self-expansion (although sometimes overdoing it, leading to problems!). This tendency for taking advantage of new possibilities can be seen from the outset of the book, starting with benefits of increased dating opportunities, to the opportunities for forming relationships with others who are more different from oneself, to expanded opportunities for forming legal unions and families.

References

Aron, A., & Aron, E. (1986). *Love and the expansion of self: Understanding attraction and satisfaction*. Hemisphere.

Aron, A., Lewandowski, G., Branand, B., Mashek, D., & Aron, E. (2022). Self-expansion motivation and inclusion of others in self: An updated review. *Journal of Social and Personal Relationships*, 39(12), 3821–3852. https://doi.org/10.1177/02654075221110630

Finkel, E. J. (2019). *The all-or-nothing marriage: How the best marriages work*. Penguin.

Index

For the benefit of digital users, indexed terms that span two pages (e.g., 52–53) may, on occasion, appear on only one of those pages.

Tables and figures are indicated by *t* and *f* following the page number

accommodation, within interethnic marriage, 134
adoptive families, 273, 285
    adoption socialization, 276–77
    adoptive identity, 275
    adult adoptees and parenting, 281
    boundary management, 277
    and children with disabilities, 281–82
    common issues facing, 274–81
    conversations about adoption, 276–77
    ethnic-racial socialization, 278–79
    LGBTQ parents, 282–83
    open communication, 277–78
    perspectives on adoption, 283
    relations with birth parents, 279–81, 283–84
    services for, 284–85
adulthood, sex and sexuality in emerging, 161–62, 168, 171–72
    deconstructing sexuality and heteronormativity, 170–71
    "friends with benefits," 165–66
    hookups, 163–65
    sexting, 167
    sexual agency, and gendered double standard, 168–69
    social media, role of, 166–67
    trends in behavior, 162–66
affect
    and singlehood, 225–26
    and social connections, 330
    and use of support systems, 235, 239–41
affordances, by computer-mediated communication
    balancing across multiple communication channels, 208–12
    complementary hypothesis, 209–10
    maximization hypothesis, 210–11
    minimization hypothesis, 211–12
    of multiple communication channels, 206–8
age
    as feature of potential romantic partners, 11
    and friendships in the time of COVID-19, 239–41
agency, core traits of, 90–91
altruism, as feature of romantic partners, 7–8
animals, companion, 332–34
appearance, as feature of potential romantic partners, 9, 22
Ata, A., 129–30
attitudes
    intergroup attitudes, 126–27
    of therapists toward interreligious marriage, 129–30
    toward cohabitation, 42
    toward cross-group friendships, 262–63
    toward gender-diverse relationships, 187–88
    toward gender identity, 178–84
    toward interracial marriage, 109
    toward marriage, 38
    toward same-sex relationships, 184–87
attraction
    and mate selection, 22–25
    and online profiles, 24–25
attractiveness, defining, 9–12
Australia, interreligious marriage in, 129–30

Baumeister, R. F., 345, 355
Beauparlant, E. T., 219
beauty, as feature of potential romantic partners, 9
behaviors
 in friendships, 260–61
 health behaviors, 337
 offline behaviors and mate selection, 22–25
beliefs, and cross-group friendship formation, 258–60
benefit finding, conscious uncoupling and, 146
benefits of cross-group friendship, 261–63
 improved intergroup attitudes, 262–63
 social support, 263
Berkman, L. F., 328–32
Big Five traits, 146, 349–50
Buzzanell, Patrice, 293–94, 298–99, 301

Caughlin, J. P., 204–6
characteristics, ideal for romantic partners, 3
 among gay men, 13
 among lesbian and bisexual women, 14
 and COVID-19 pathogen prevalence, 14
 and defining attractiveness, 9–12
 and gender norms, 5
 negative characteristics, appeal of, 6–7
 positive features sought, 7–9
 shifts in preference, 5–6
childbearing, and cohabitation *versus* marriage, 47
child care, and gender roles in marriage, 93–94
children, effects of conscious uncoupling on, 148–51
children with disabilities, adoptive families and, 281–82
class dynamics, and marital satisfaction, 94
cohabitation, *versus* marriage
 changing meaning of cohabitation, 46–48
 declining transitions into marriage, 45
 economic barriers to marriage, 48–49
 and educational attainment, 43f, 43–44
 pregnancy and childbearing, 47
 prevalence of cohabitation, 42–45, 43f
 racial and ethnic disparities, 39–40
 and relationship tempo, 44–45
 retreat from marriage, 39–41
 serial cohabitation, 45
 and social class, 44, 48–49
 in the 21st century, 41–45
 trends among young Americans, 38, 41–42, 50
cohousing, and growing singles population, 64–65
collectivism, and conscious uncoupling, 153
commitment
 and interethnic romantic relationships, 127
 investment model of, 224–26, 225t
communality, core traits of, 90–91
communication
 in adoptive families, 277–78
 DNA testing, and family communication, 316
 in stepfamilies, 300–1
communication, in modern friendships, 199–200, 212–13
 affordances, balancing across multiple channels, 208–12
 affordances, complementary combination of, 209–10
 affordances, maximization hypothesis, 210–11
 affordances, minimization hypothesis, 211–12
 affordances of multiple communication channels, 206–8
 bandwidth of communication channels, 207–8
 communicative interdependence perspective, 204–6
 disclosure, levels of, 201
 life transitions, 201
 media multiplexity theory, 202–4
 mixed-media friendships, 200–2
 network association, 207–8
 relational benefits of technology, 202
 relational maintenance, 200–1
 social presence, 208

synchronous *versus* asynchronous channels, 207
text messages *versus* phone calls, affordances of, 207
communicative interdependence perspective, and communication in modern friendships, 204–6
companion animals, health and, 332–34
comparison level, and marital satisfaction, 73–74
computer-mediated communication, modern friendships and, 199–200, 212–13
   affordances, balancing across multiple channels, 208–12
   affordances, complementary combination of, 209–10
   affordances, maximization hypothesis, 210–11
   affordances, minimization hypothesis, 211–12
   affordances of multiple communication channels, 206–8
   bandwidth of communication channels, 207–8
   communicative interdependence perspective, 204–6
   digital connection during COVID-19, 236–38
   disclosure, levels of, 201
   life transitions, 201
   media multiplexity theory, 202–4
   mixed-media friendships, 200–2
   network association, 207–8
   relational benefits of technology, 202
   relational maintenance, 200–1
   social presence, 208
   synchronous *versus* asynchronous channels, 207
   text messages *versus* phone calls, affordances of, 207
conscious uncoupling, 153
   children, effects on, 148–51
   future research directions, 151–53
   interparental conflict and co-parenting, 149–51
   positive outcomes, 147–48
   predictors of, 146–47
   in romantic relationships, 145–48
conscious uncoupling, divorce and, 141
   defining conscious uncoupling, 144–45
   history of, 142–45
   life expectancy, marital expectations and, 142–44
Conscious Uncoupling (Thomas), 144–45
consensual non-monogamy, legal recognition of, 114–17
contentment, pursuit of in marriage, 81–83
co-parenting, conscious uncoupling and, 149–51
courtship, and attracting attention, 22–23
COVID-19, and health as feature of romantic partners, 14
COVID-19, friendships in the time of, 232, 245–47
   age, impact of, 239–41
   closeness of, 238–39
   digital connections, 236–38
   early negative impact on friendship, 239–42
   improvements *versus* strain or tension, 233–35
   later negative impact on friendship, 242–45
   positive impacts of, 235–39
   psychological impact of the pandemic, 232–33
Cox, Catherine, 180
cross-group friendships, 251–52
   benefits of, 261–63
   friendship formation, 252–60
   functional proximity and formation of, 255–56
   future research directions, 263–64
   individual beliefs and formation of, 258–60
   intergroup beliefs, influence of, 258–59
   maintenance of, 260–61
   opportunities to develop, 252–53
   perceived similarities, and formation of, 259–60
   personality, influence of, 259
   physical proximity and formation of, 253–55
   pro-relationship behaviors, 260–61

374　INDEX

cross-group friendships (cont.)
　　shared activities, and maintenance of, 261
　　social proximity and formation of, 256–57
　　culture
　　and conscious uncoupling, 152–53
　　ethnic-racial socialization in adoptive families, 278–79
　　hook-up culture, 163–65

dating
　　market metaphor in, 23–24
　　role of social media in, 166–67
dating, and finding ideal partners, 21, 34–35
　　attraction, 22–25
　　hyperpersonal model, and online dating, 31–33
　　messaging, on dating apps and sites, 30–31
　　modalities, using multiple, 27–28
　　motivations for online dating, 28–31
　　online dating, concerns regarding, 33–34
　　relationship escalation, 25–28
disclosure, levels of in modern friendships, 201
discourse-dependent families, 292–94
discrimination, definition of, 126
disillusionment, and marital satisfaction, 80–81
diverse friendships, 251–52
　　benefits of, 261–63
　　friendship formation, 252–60
　　functional proximity and formation of, 255–56
　　future research directions, 263–64
　　individual beliefs and formation of, 258–60
　　intergroup beliefs, influence of, 258–59
　　maintenance of, 260–61
　　opportunities to develop, 252–53
　　perceived similarities, and formation of, 259–60
　　personality, influence of, 259
　　physical proximity and formation of, 253–55

　　pro-relationship behaviors, 260–61
　　shared activities, and maintenance of, 261
　　social proximity and formation of, 256–57
diversity, historical attitudes toward, 178–84
divorce, conscious uncoupling and, 141, 153
　　children, effects of conscious uncoupling on, 148–51
　　conscious uncoupling in romantic relationships, 145–48
　　defining conscious uncoupling, 144–45
　　future research directions, 151–53
　　history of, 142–45
　　interparental conflict and co-parenting, 149–51
　　life expectancy, marital expectations and, 142–44
　　positive outcomes of conscious uncoupling, 147–48
　　predictors of conscious uncoupling, 146–47
DNA testing, and family communication, 316

educational attainment, and cohabitation, 43–44
emerging adulthood, sex and sexuality in, 161–62, 168, 171–72
　　deconstructing sexuality and heteronormativity, 170–71
　　"friends with benefits," 165–66
　　hookups, 163–65
　　sexting, 167
　　sexual agency, and gendered double standard, 168–69
　　social media, role of, 166–67
　　trends in behavior, 162–66
emotions
　　and communication in stepfamilies, 296–98
　　and conscious uncoupling, 145
　　and impact of COVID-19, 246–47, 336
equity, and gender roles in marriage, 90–91, 100
　　household labor and child care, 91–94

mental labor, 94–95
  same-sex relationships, 99–100
  and sexuality, 97–99
  societal expectations of working fathers, 96
  work and financial contributions, 95–96
ethnic disparities, and cohabitation *versus* marriage, 39–40
ethnicity, and interethnic marriage, 124–26, 136–37
  around the world, 131–33
  dyadic model of, 132–36, 133*f*
  interdependence theory, 129
  intergroup attitudes and behavior, 126–27
  international marriage in Thailand, 130–31
  interreligious marriage in Australia, 129–30
  partnering and partnership, 131
  resource exchange theory, 127–28
  social exchange, 130

face-work, social interactions and, 128–29, 130
families, adoptive, 273, 285
  adoption socialization, 276–77
  adoptive identity, 275
  adult adoptees and parenting, 281
  boundary management, 277
  and children with disabilities, 281–82
  common issues facing, 274–81
  conversations about adoption, 276–77
  ethnic-racial socialization, 278–79
  LGBTQ parents, 282–83
  open communication, 277–78
  perspectives on adoption, 283
  relations with birth parents, 279–81, 283–84
  services for, 284–85
families, complex nontraditional, 314–16
femmephobia, 188–91
financial contributions, and gender roles in marriage, 95–96
financial resources, as feature of potential romantic partners, 11–12
forgiveness, in stepfamilies, 301–2
Fox, J., 207

friendship, new and significant role of, 217, 227
  and changes in relational value system, 217–19
  future research, 226–27
  increasing importance of friendship, 221–22
  and investment model of commitment, 224–26, 225*t*
  need fulfillment and singlehood satisfaction, 222–23
  postponement of marriage, 219–20
  singlehood, increase in, 220–21
friendship formation, and cross-group friendships, 252–60
  ecological opportunities to develop, 252–53
  functional proximity, 255–56
  individual beliefs, influence of, 258–60
  intergroup beliefs, influence of, 258–59
  and perceived similarities, 259–60
  personality, influence of, 259
  physical proximity, 253–55
  social proximity, 256–57
friendship maintenance, and cross-group friendships, 260–61
  pro-relationship behaviors, 260–61
  shared activities, 261
friendships, communication in modern, 199–200, 212–13
  affordances, balancing across multiple channels, 208–12
  affordances, complementary combination of, 209–10
  affordances, maximization hypothesis, 210–11
  affordances, minimization hypothesis, 211–12
  affordances of multiple communication channels, 206–8
  bandwidth of communication channels, 207–8
  communicative interdependence perspective, 204–6
  disclosure, levels of, 201
  life transitions, 201
  media multiplexity theory, 202–4
  mixed-media friendships, 200–2

friendships, communication in modern (*cont.*)
   network association, 207–8
   relational benefits of technology, 202
   relational maintenance, 200–1
   social presence, 208
   synchronous *versus* asynchronous channels, 207
   text messages *versus* phone calls, affordances of, 207
friendships, diverse, 251–52
   benefits of, 261–63
   friendship formation, 252–60
   functional proximity and formation of, 255–56
   future research directions, 263–64
   individual beliefs and formation of, 258–60
   intergroup beliefs, influence of, 258–59
   maintenance of, 260–61
   opportunities to develop, 252–53
   perceived similarities, and formation of, 259–60
   personality, influence of, 259
   physical proximity and formation of, 253–55
   pro-relationship behaviors, 260–61
   shared activities, and maintenance of, 261
   social proximity and formation of, 256–57
friendships, in the time of COVID-19, 232, 245–47
   age, impact of, 239–41
   closeness of, 238–39
   digital connections, 236–38
   early negative impact on friendship, 239–42
   improvements *versus* strain or tension, 233–35
   later negative impact on friendship, 242–45
   positive impacts of, 235–39
   psychological impact of the pandemic, 232–33
friendships, singlehood and, 62–63, 64
   "friends with benefits," 165–66
functional proximity, and formation of cross-group friendships, 255–56
Furlong, M., 129–30

Galvin, Kathleen, 292–93
gender binary, and online dating, 34
gender-diverse relationships, current attitudes toward, 187–88
gender diversity, historical attitudes toward, 178–84
gendered double standard, sexual agency and, 168–69
gender identity, shifting attitudes regarding, 178
   current attitudes toward gender-diverse relationships, 187–88
   current attitudes toward same-sex relationships, 184–87
   and femmephobia, 188–91
   historical attitudes, 178–84
gender norms, in romance, 5
gender roles, and equity in marriage, 90–91, 100
   household labor and child care, 91–94
   mental labor, 94–95
   same-sex relationships, 99–100
   and sexuality, 97–99
   societal expectations of working fathers, 96
   work and financial contributions, 95–96
Germany, homophobia in Nazi era, 182–83
Goffman, E., 125–26, 128–29, 130, 131, 132
Gottman, J. M., 351

Hall, E. D., 206
Harlow, Harry, 343–44
Haythornthwaite, C., 202–4
health, as feature of potential romantic partners, 9–11
health, relationships and, 327, 338
   companion animals, 332–34
   and health outcomes, 327–28
   mechanisms for effects on health, 330–32
   roommate households, 336–37
   and singlehood, 335–36
   social connections, and health and illness, 328–30

and social genomics, 331–32
and social media, 329
See also romantic relationships, and mental health
heroism, as feature of romantic partners, 7–8
heteronormativity, deconstructing, 170–71
Hojjat, M. 218
homophobia, Germany in Nazi era, 182–83
homosexuality
    current attitudes toward, 189–90
    history of attitudes toward, 110–11, 178–84
Hooker, Evelyn, 110–11
hookups, and sex in emerging adulthood, 163–65
household labor, and gender roles in marriage, 91–94
humor, as feature of romantic partners, 8
hyperpersonal model, and online dating, 32–33

idealization, and online dating, 32
identities, dyadic model of within interethnic marriage, 132–36, 133f
income
    and "divorce divide," 93–94
    wage gap between women and men, 12, 95–96
individualism
    and conscious uncoupling, 153
    and friendship, 218–19
    and singlehood, 62
intelligence, as feature of romantic partners, 8
interactionist role theory, 128–29
interdependence theory, and interethnic marriage, 129, 132–36, 133f
interethnic marriage, 124–26, 136–37
    around the world, 131–33
    dyadic model of, 132–36, 133f
    interdependence theory, 129
    intergroup attitudes and behavior, 126–27
    international marriage in Thailand, 130–31
    interracial marriage in Singapore, 127–29
    interreligious marriage in Australia, 129–30
    partnering and partnership, 131
    resource exchange theory, 127–28
    social exchange, 130
interracial marriages, 107–10
intimacy
    and conscious uncoupling, 148
    and "friends with benefits," 165–66
    and modern marital satisfaction, 80
investment model of commitment, 224–26
in vitro fertilization, introduction of, 309

jealousy
    and CNM relationships, 115
    and parent-child relationships in lesbian families, 313
    and personality traits in romantic relationships, 350

Kelley, Harold, 73–74
Kurdek, Lawrence, 111–12

Leary, M. R., 345, 355
lesbian families, and medically assisted reproduction, 313
LGBTQ families and individuals
    gay fathers and medically assisted reproduction, 314–16
    lesbian families and medically assisted reproduction, 313
    lesbian relationships, orgasm in 99–100
    LGBTQ parents, 282–83
    romantic partners, ideal characteristics among gay men, 13
    romantic partners, ideal characteristics among lesbian and bisexual women, 14
life expectancy, marital expectations and, 142–44
life transitions, and communication in modern friendships, 201
loneliness, and relationships' effects on health, 63, 330–32

marginalization, by societal institutions, 126–27
marginalized identities, and online dating, 34

378 INDEX

marital satisfaction
  adverse events and, 78
  beneficial beliefs, 81
  benevolent perceptions, 82
  contentment, pursuit of, 81–83
  counterproductive personal
    beliefs, 76–77
  cultural exemplars, effect of, 75–76
  disillusionment, 80–81
  and disinterest in attractive others, 79
  expectations of, 75
  gender roles and equity, 94
  and idealized partners, 77–78
  interdependence, theory of, 73–74
  interdependent intimacy, costs of, 80
  playfulness and, 82–83
  relational realism, a call for, 83
marriage
  deinstitutionalization of, 218–19
  postponement of, 219–20
marriage, contemporary appearances of,
    107, 117–19
  consensual non-monogamy, 114–17
  defining marriage, 106–7
  interracial marriages, 107–10
  same-sex marriage, 110–14
marriage, equity and gender roles in, 90–
    91, 100
  household labor and child care, 91–94
  mental labor, 94–95
  same-sex relationships, 99–100
  and sexuality, 97–99
  societal expectations of working
    fathers, 96
  work and financial contributions, 95–96
marriage, interethnic, 124–26, 136–37
  around the world, 131–33
  dyadic model of, 132–36, 133f
  interdependence theory, 129
  intergroup attitudes and
    behavior, 126–27
  international marriage in
    Thailand, 130–31
  interreligious marriage in
    Australia, 129–30
  partnering and partnership, 131
  resource exchange theory, 127–28
  social exchange, 130

marriage, *versus* cohabitation
  changing meaning of
    cohabitation, 46–48
  declining transitions into marriage, 45
  economic barriers to marriage, 48–49
  and educational attainment, 43f, 43–44
  pregnancy and childbearing, 47
  prevalence of cohabitation, 42–45, 43f
  racial and ethnic disparities, 39–40
  and relationship tempo, 44–45
  retreat from marriage, 39–41
  serial cohabitation, 45
  and social class, 44, 48–49
  in the 21st century, 41–45
  trends among young Americans, 38,
    41–42, 50
marriage equality movement, 110–14
Masculinity-Femininity (M-F)
    test, 180–81
mate selection, attraction and, 22–25
McEwan, B., 207
media multiplexity theory, and
    communication in modern
    friendships, 202–4
medically assisted reproduction,
    308, 319–20
  concerns expressed, 309
  critically appraising research
    literature, 319
  gay fathers and, 314–16
  impacts on parents and
    parenting, 309–12
  implications of nontraditional
    families, 314–16
  implications of unsuccessful
    attempts, 317–19
  and lack of genetic links, 312–13
  lesbian families and, 313
  and polyparenting, 308–9
  and secrecy regarding
    conception, 316–17
  and shared motherhood, 308–9
mental health, romantic relationships
    and, 355
  couple and relationship
    interventions, 352–53
  couples therapy for mental health
    outcomes, 353–54

externalizing disorders, 348–49
how romantic relationships
    matter, 344–46
and internalizing disorders, 346–47
and interpersonal dynamics, 351–52
and personality traits, 349–52
psychosis and personality
    disorders, 348–49
relationship education and mental
    health outcomes, 354–55
why relationships matter, 343–44
mental labor, and gender roles in
    marriage, 94–95
messaging, on dating apps and sites, 30–31
minority groups, reproductive rights
    of, 309
minority stress model, same-sex marriage
    and, 112–13
Mixed Matches (Owen), 124
mixed-media friendships, 200–2
modern friendships, communication in,
    199–200, 212–13
    affordances, balancing across multiple
        channels, 208–12
    affordances, complementary
        combination of, 209–10
    affordances, maximization
        hypothesis, 210–11
    affordances, minimization
        hypothesis, 211–12
    affordances of multiple communication
        channels, 206–8
    bandwidth of communication
        channels, 207–8
    communicative interdependence
        perspective, 204–6
    disclosure, levels of, 201
    life transitions, 201
    media multiplexity theory, 202–4
    mixed-media friendships, 200–2
    network association, 207–8
    relational benefits of technology, 202
    relational maintenance, 200–1
    social presence, 208
    synchronous *versus* asynchronous
        channels, 207
    text messages *versus* phone calls,
        affordances of, 207

Monitoring the Future (National High
    School Senior Survey), 41
monogamy
    consensual non-monogamy, 115–16
    serial monogamy, 143–44
motherhood, shared, 308–9

National High School Senior Survey, 41
"networked life," and singlehood, 64
neuroticism, and poor relationship
    outcomes, 350

offline behaviors, mate selection and, 22–25
old age, and mate selection, 11
online considerations, mate selection
    and, 22–25
online dating, and finding ideal partners,
    21, 34–35
    attraction, 22–25
    concerns regarding, 33–34
    hyperpersonal model, 31–33
    messaging, on dating apps and
        sites, 30–31
    modalities, using multiple, 27–28
    motivations for online dating, 28–31
    relationship escalation, 25–28
online dating, market metaphor in, 23–24
online profiles, attraction and, 24–25, 32
open relationships, and consensual
    non-monogamy, 115–16
orgasm
    gender roles and, 97–99
    lesbian relationships, 99–100
OurRelationship, 354–55
Owen, June Duncan, 124

parent-child relationships, genetic links
    and, 312–13
parental divorce, and effects of conscious
    uncoupling on children, 148–51
parents
    birth parents, adoptive families and,
        279–81, 283–84
    LGBTQ parents, adoptive families
        and, 282–83
    medically assisted reproduction, 309–12
partners, finding ideal, 21, 34–35
    attraction, 22–25

380 INDEX

partners, finding ideal (*cont.*)
   hyperpersonal model, and online dating, 31–33
   messaging, on dating apps and sites, 30–31
   modalities, using multiple, 27–28
   motivations for online dating, 28–31
   online dating, concerns regarding, 33–34
   relationship escalation, 25–28
partners, ideal characteristics for romantic, 3
   among gay men, 13
   among lesbian and bisexual women, 14
   and COVID-19 pathogen prevalence, 14
   and defining attractiveness, 9–12
   and gender norms, 5
   negative characteristics, appeal of, 6–7
   positive features sought, 7–9
   shifts in preference, 5–6
partnership, in interethnic marriage, 131
personality, and formation of cross-group friendships, 259
personality traits, and romantic relationships, 349–52
phone calls *versus* text messages, affordances of, 207
physical appearance, as feature of potential romantic partners, 9
physical proximity, and formation of cross-group friendships, 253–55
playfulness, and marital satisfaction, 82–83
polyparenting, 308–9
power
   and financial resources, 11–12
   and gender norms in romance, 4–5
pregnancy, and cohabitation *versus* marriage, 47
prejudice, definition of, 126
Prevention and Relationship Enhancement Program (ePrep), 354–55
profiles, online, 24–25, 32
proximity, and formation of cross-group friendships, 253–57
psychology, evolutionary, 34
psychotherapy, and interethnic marriage, 129–30

racial disparities, and cohabitation *versus* marriage, 39–40
racial integration, and interracial marriages, 109
racial stereotypes, and gendered expectations, 91
rejection, in social contexts, 257
relational histories, and marital satisfaction, 73–74
relational maintenance, and communication in modern friendships, 200–1
relational realism, and marital satisfaction, 83
relational value system, changes in, 217–19
relationship education, 354–55
relationship escalation, 25–28
relationships and health, 327, 338
   companion animals, 332–34
   and health outcomes, 327–28
   mechanisms for effects on health, 330–32
   roommate households, 336–37
   and singlehood, 335–36
   social connections, and health and illness, 328–30
   and social genomics, 331–32
   and social media, 329
   See also romantic relationships, and mental health
relationship initiation, and gender norms in romance, 4–5
relationship tempo, and cohabitation, 44–45
religion
   and same-sex relationships, 179
   as tribal stigma, 127, 131
remarriage, stepfamilies and, 291
reproduction, medically assisted, 308, 319–20
   concerns expressed, 309
   critically appraising research literature, 319
   gay fathers and, 314–16
   impacts on parents and parenting, 309–12
   implications of nontraditional families, 314–16

implications of unsuccessful
    attempts, 317–19
and lack of genetic links, 312–13
lesbian families and, 313
and polyparenting, 308–9
reproductive rights of minority
    groups, 309
and secrecy regarding conception, 316–17
and shared motherhood, 308–9
resilience, impacts of conscious
    uncoupling on, 152–53
resource exchange theory, and interethnic
    marriage, 127–28
responsiveness, and effects of relationships
    on health, 330
retirement, roommate households
    and, 336
Roe v. Wade, ruling to overturn, 309
romance, gender norms in, 5
romantic love, mental health outcomes
    and, 355
romantic partners, ideal characteristics
    of, 3
  among gay men, 13
  among lesbian and bisexual women, 14
  and COVID-19 pathogen
    prevalence, 14
  and defining attractiveness, 9–12
  and gender norms, 5
  negative characteristics, appeal of, 6–7
  positive features sought, 7–9
  shifts in preference, 5–6
romantic relationships, and mental
    health, 355
  couple and relationship
    interventions, 352–53
  couples therapy for mental health
    outcomes, 353–54
  externalizing disorders, 348–49
  how romantic relationships
    matter, 344–46
  and internalizing disorders, 346–47
  and interpersonal dynamics, 351–52
  and personality traits, 349–52
  psychosis and personality
    disorders, 348–49
  relationship education and mental
    health outcomes, 354–55
  why relationships matter, 343–44
romantic relationships, conscious
    uncoupling in, 145–48
roommate households, and health and
    illness, 336–37
Rusbult, C., investment model of
    relationship commitment, 111–12

same-sex marriage
  current attitudes toward, 184–85
  history and development of, 110–14
same-sex relationships
  current attitudes toward, 184–87
  and equity in marriage, 99–100
  historical attitudes toward, 178–84
satisfaction, marital
  adverse events and, 78
  beneficial beliefs, 81
  benevolent perceptions, 82
  contentment, pursuit of, 81–83
  counterproductive personal
    beliefs, 76–77
  cultural exemplars, effect of, 75–76
  disillusionment, 80–81
  and disinterest in attractive others, 79
  expectations of, 75
  gender roles and equity, 94
  and idealized partners, 77–78
  interdependence, theory of, 73–74
  interdependent intimacy, costs of, 80
  playfulness and, 82–83
  relational realism, a call for, 83
  satisfaction, in singlehood, 222–23
"second shift," and gender roles in
    marriage, 91–94
selective self-presentation, and online
    dating, 32
self-disclosure, 200–1, 212, 237–38, 260–61
self-esteem, and adoptive identity, 275
self-expansion
  and cross-group friendships, 259
  and need fulfillment, 224
  and shared activities, 261
serial cohabitation, 45
serial monogamy, 143–44
Sex and Personality (Terman &
    Cox), 180
sexting, in emerging adulthood, 167

sexual agency, and gendered double standard, 168–69
sexual diversity, historical attitudes toward, 178–84
sexuality, and gender roles in marriage, 97–99
sexuality, deconstructing, 170–71
sexuality, feminist and queer theoretical perspective on, 161–62, 168, 171–72
   deconstructing sexuality and heteronormativity, 170–71
   "friends with benefits," 165–66
   hookups, 164–65
   sexting, 167
   sexual agency, and gendered double standard, 168–69
   social media, role of, 166–67
   trends in behavior, 162–66
sexual orientation, shifting attitudes regarding, 178
   current attitudes toward gender-diverse relationships, 187–88
   current attitudes toward same-sex relationships, 184–87
   and femmephobia, 188–91
   historical attitudes, 178–84
Sharabi, L. L., 204–6
shared motherhood, 308–9
similarity, as feature of romantic partners, 8–9
Singapore, interracial marriage in, 127–29
singlehood
   and cohousing, 64–65
   consequences of, 60–63
   cultural norms of, 59–60, 65
   definitions of, 55–57
   and friendships, 62–63, 64
   and health and illness, 335–36
   and "networked life," 64
   reasons for, 57–59
   and social support, 61–63
   and technology, 65
   See also friendship, new and significant role of
social class, and cohabitation, 44, 48–49
social connections, and health and illness, 328–30
social exchange, interethnic marriage and, 130
social genomics, 331–32
social information processing theory (SIPT), 31–33
social media
   and communication in stepfamilies, 300–1
   role in sex and sexuality in emerging adulthood, 166–67
   and social connection and isolation, 329
social networks
   during COVID-19, 237
   and increasing importance of friendship, 221–22
social proximity, and formation of cross-group friendships, 256–57
social stability, anticipation of within interethnic marriage, 135
social stigma, interethnic marriage and, 126–27
social support
   cross-group friendship and, 263
   singlehood and, 61–63
societal expectations, of working fathers, 96
societal norms, shared perceptions within interethnic marriage, 132–36
Statham, P., 130–31
status, and gender roles in marriage, 91
stepfamilies, communication and resilience in, 291–92, 302–3
   alternative logics, 301–2
   communicating forgiveness, 301–2
   communication networks, 299–301
   crafting normalcy, 294–96
   developmental pathways, 295–96
   discourse-dependent families, 292–94, 299
   identity anchors, 298–99
   influencing conflict, 297–98, 301–2
   reframing, 302
   stepfamily interaction, 293–94
   stressing productive action *versus* negative feelings, 296–98
stereotyping, definition of, 126
stigma
   consensual non-monogamy and, 115–16

interracial relationships and, 109–10
and nontraditional families, 315–16
Stigma (Goffman), 125–26, 128–29, 130, 131, 132
stress, minority stress model, 112–13
Syme, S. L., 328–32

technology, and communication in modern friendships, 199–200, 212–13
  affordances, balancing across multiple channels, 208–12
  affordances, complementary combination of, 209–10
  affordances, maximization hypothesis, 210–11
  affordances, minimization hypothesis, 211–12
  affordances of multiple communication channels, 206–8
  bandwidth of communication channels, 207–8
  communicative interdependence perspective, 204–6
  digital connection during COVID-19, 236–38
  disclosure, levels of, 201
  life transitions, 201
  media multiplexity theory, 202–4
  mixed-media friendships, 200–2
  network association, 207–8
  relational benefits of technology, 202
  relational maintenance, 200–1
  social presence, 208
  synchronous *versus* asynchronous channels, 207
  text messages *versus* phone calls, affordances of, 207

technology, and growing singles population, 65
Terman, Lewis, 179–84, 188–91
text messages *versus* phone calls, affordances of, 207
Thailand, international marriage in, 130–31
therapy
  conversion therapy, 181
  couples' therapy, 351–54
  and interreligious marriages, 129–30
Thibaut, John, 73–74
Thomas, K. W., 144–45
tribal stigmas, and interethnic marriage, 127

uncoupling, conscious, 141, 153
  children, effects on, 148–51
  defining, 144–45
  future research directions, 151–53
  history of, 142–45
  interparental conflict and co-parenting, 149–51
  life expectancy, marital expectations and, 142–44
  positive outcomes, 147–48
  predictors of, 146–47
  in romantic relationships, 145–48

Velayutham, S., 127–29
violence, intimate partner
  and gender-diverse individuals, 187–88, 191
  and same-sex unions, 113

wage gap, and gender roles in marriage, 95–96
Wise, A., 127–29